SOCIAL LIFE IN GREECE

FROM

HOMER TO MENANDER

MACMILLAN AND CO., Limited
LONDON · BOMBAY · CALCUTTA · MADRAS
MELBOURNE

THE MACMILLAN COMPANY
NEW YORK · BOSTON · CHICAGO
DALLAS   SAN FRANCISCO

THE MACMILLAN CO. OF CANADA, Ltd.
TORONTO

SOCIAL LIFE IN GREECE

FROM

HOMER TO MENANDER

BY

J. P. MAHAFFY

FELLOW ETC. OF TRINITY COLLEGE, DUBLIN; HON. FELLOW OF
QUEEN'S COLLEGE, OXFORD; KNIGHT OF THE ORDER OF THE REDEEMER;
CORRESPONDING MEMBER OF THE ACADEMY OF VIENNA;
AUTHOR OF
'PROLEGOMENA OF ANCIENT HISTORY'; 'KANT'S PHILOSOPHY FOR ENGLISH READERS';
'GREEK LIFE AND THOUGHT, FROM THE AGE OF ALEXANDER TO THE ROMAN
CONQUEST'; 'THE GREEK WORLD UNDER ROMAN SWAY'; 'RAMBLES
AND STUDIES IN GREECE'; 'A HISTORY OF CLASSICAL GREEK
LITERATURE'; 'THE EMPIRE OF THE PTOLEMIES';
EDITOR OF THE PETRIE PAPYRI, ETC.

MACMILLAN AND CO., LIMITED
ST. MARTIN'S STREET, LONDON
1925

PRINTED IN GREAT BRITAIN

WILSONO KING

PIGNUS

AMICITIÆ

PREFACE

TO THE 1898 EDITION.

THIS book had already in the fourth edition assumed its final form, nor was it my intention hereafter to enlarge it, but rather to add companion volumes upon the later portions of old Greek life. Indeed, maturer study has led me to reject some changes which I had introduced in deference to the censure of professional critics, and I added in the fourth edition some considerations concerning the moral standard of Greek politics in Demosthenes' day, which seem to me of much importance, and which have been generally accepted among later Greek historians, though likely to increase the displeasure with which certain scholars regard my estimate of old Greek civilisation. It is too homely for them; it detracts too much from the ideal they have framed for themselves; it asserts the weaker and commoner side of the nation in the face of their unreal speculations. Nor is it true that homely views imply a grudging appreciation of the perfections of Greek literature and art. What they really imply is only this, that the greatest poets and the greatest artists were not the average representatives of the nation at large, and that the social life of the people was not of that extraordinary perfection which the men of books had imagined. I had long felt that the extremely learned often miss the practical infer-

ences which may be drawn from our classics by plain
common sense, and it occured to me to seek the materials
for sketching the Social Life of the Greeks, not in previous commentators, but in the Greek books themselves, which I re-read one by one specially, with particular attention to the social points they contained.
This was the method which led me to draw a picture
of the Greeks from their ancient books corresponding in many points to the Greeks of to-day, nor do I
know of any attempt to dispute the accuracy of my
statements, except some vague assertions put forward
without evidence. On a few details I at first surrendered my own opinion too readily ; but these points
are not worth discussing here. So far as they turn
upon the internal evidence for spuriousness in extant
orations and other documents I have said all that is
necessary in my *History of Greek Classical Literature*, a work which treats of the literary aspects of
the life portrayed in the following pages, and is therefore an important supplement for all those who desire
to get a general view of Greek civilisation in its
various phases. Thus objections have been answered
and a want supplied, so that the present volume may
maintain the favour with which the general public
has honoured it. And now, when I am saying the
last word about it, and in some sense taking leave
of it, I may be excused for dwelling on the circumstances which gave it a peculiar interest, and have
obtained for it a longer life and a better name than
I could have hoped.

The same favour has been extend to my *Rambles*

and Studies in Greece (3rd ed. 1887, Macmillan), which give my impressions of modern life among the successors of the old Hellenes, and in the land which produced so many centuries of splendid civilization. To this study I had appended a chapter on Greek Music and Painting, which was rightly considered to belong to the present volume. I have therefore added it to this edition, to make way for new matter upon mediaeval Greece in future editions of my *Rambles*.

I have since been enabled to complete two new volumes, covering part of the huge gap between classical and modern Greece, and have given in my *Greek Life and Thought from the death of Alexander to the Roman Conquest*, and in *The Greek World under Roman Sway*, the evidence culled from the Greek authors between Menander and Plutarch, as well as some estimate of that literature. These volumes were therefore strictly a sequel to the present one, worked out in the same way from the texts themselves, and will answer the objection that I had paused in the middle of my great subject. There yet remains the appreciation of Greek Life under the Roman Empire ; from the days when Christianity became a social force. I trust I may yet be able to complete this task.

Trinity College, Dublin,
   May, 1898.

TABLE OF CONTENTS.

CHAPTER IV.

The Greeks of the Lyric Age.

CHAPTER V.

The Greeks of the Lyric Age (continued).

CHAPTER VI.

The Greeks of the Attic Age.

CHAPTER X.

Attic Culture.—Certain Trades and Professions.

CHAPTER XI.

Attic Culture.—Entertainments and Conversation.—The Education of Boys.—The Streets in Athens.

CHAPTER XII.

Religious Feeling in the Attic Age.

CHAPTER XIII.

The Business Habits of the Attic Greeks.

CHAPTER XIV.

The Social Aspects of Greek Art.

CHAPTER XV.

Greek Music and Painting.

CHAPTER I.

INTRODUCTION.

AMONG the nations which stand out in the course of history as having done most to promote human knowledge, human art, and human culture, the Greeks are first in the judgment of all competent observers. The hold which Greek literature retains on our modern education is not the mere result of precedent or fashion. Every thinking man who becomes acquainted with the masterpieces of Greek writing, must see plainly that they stand to us in a far closer relation than the other remains of antiquity. They are not mere objects of curiosity to the archæologist, not mere treasure-houses of roots and forms to be sought out by comparative grammarians. They are the writings of men of like culture with ourselves, who argue with the same logic, who reflect with kindred feelings. They have worked out social and moral problems like ourselves; they have expressed them in such language as we should desire to use. In a word, they are thoroughly modern, more modern even than the epochs quite proximate to our own. The disjointed sentences of the Egyptian moralist,

the confused metaphors of the Hebrew prophet, show
that were *they* transplanted into our life, and taught
our language, they would still be completely at a
loss to follow the reasoning of our modern literature.
Ptah-hotep or Ezechiel could not move in modern
society. Aristotle or Menander, on the other hand,
would only need to understand the names invented
for our modern discoveries. In all moral and social
questions they would at once find their way, and
enjoy even our poetry and our fiction. But what is
more striking, even the mediæval baron and the
mediæval saint would feel vastly more out of place
among us than the intelligent Greek. The satire and
scepticism of our modern society, the decay of fixed
belief, the omnipotence of free discussion as shown
by press and platform, the rule of private interest
over patriotism and self-sacrifice—all these features
would be very congenial to the Greek, while they
would shock and perplex the Crusader. Commerce
and speculation, debate and diplomacy, would delight
the clever Athenian. He would recognise the teaching of his nation in poetry, architecture, and painting; and the manifest superiority of the old models
would save him from feeling inferior in the face of
our other progress. Let us invert the whole case,
and the result would be very analogous. If one of
us were transported to Periclean Athens, provided
he were a man of high culture, he would find life and
manners strangely like our own, strangely modern, as
he might term it. The thoughts and feelings of
modern life would be there without the appliances,

and the high standard of general culture would more than counterbalance sundry wants in material comfort. For these reasons Greek social life must be far more interesting to general readers than any other phase of ancient history. Some of the problems which are still agitating our minds were settled by the Greeks, others, if not settled, were at least discussed with a freedom and an acuteness now unattainable. Others, again, were solved in strange violation of our notions of morals and good taste; and when such a people as the Greeks stand opposed to us, even in vital principles, we cannot reject their verdict without weighing their reasons.

The social life of the Greeks has often been handled, especially by German and French authors. But the ponderous minuteness and luxury of citation in the works of the former have obscured the general effect, and leave the ordinary reader with no distinct impression on his mind. The crushing weapon of modern criticism has in Germany shivered classical philology into splinters, and each man is intent on gathering up, and claiming as his own a fragment or two, which he analyses with wearying accuracy. The French essays on Greek life are of an opposite description. They usually aim at brilliancy and *esprit* alone, and gain these qualities at the frequent sacrifice of accuracy and critical research. Their authors are often ready to uphold, for example, a spurious treatise against all critical objections, however sound, provided it affords them a striking *trait* to complete their social picture. In

fact, a sound knowledge of Greek has not yet been
diffused among the French, and so their isolated
Hellenists, brilliant as they are, do not write in an
atmosphere of correcting friends and carping critics.
In spite, therefore, of the abundance of materials at
hand, and the abundance of theories based upon
them, there is still room for attempts to select
salient features, and to bring before the modern
public an accurate picture of Greek life, not in its
trivial details, but in its large and enduring features.
A more than incidental notice of the peculiarities of
food and dress, and of the plan and arrangement of
houses, is but weariness and idle labour. We want
to know how they reasoned, and felt, and loved;
why they laughed and why they wept; how they
taught and what they learned.

But alas! to these questions we can only find full
answers from one city, and from one brief epoch.
Athenian culture under the Athenian democracy
may indeed be regarded as the highest type and
outcome of the Greek mind. But there, and there
only, can we find sufficient materials to discuss the
principal social question in separate essays. The
earlier ages are only known to us through the
scanty remains of epic and lyric poetry, which afford
many hints and suggestions, and in the case of the
simpler epic age even allow us to draw a general
sketch of life and manners; but in the far more
interesting lyric age—the transition from the old to
the new life—they fail us utterly, and allow little
more than scattered reflections often inconsistent,

and scanty inferences always uncertain. The essays therefore on the Greeks of the epic and lyric ages may be regarded as introductory to those in which Athenian life is more amply described. However unsatisfactory, these earlier chapters seem necessary in an historical work, where the later stages cannot be regarded as born in full armour, like the goddess Athene, but as growing insensibly from long sown seed and in long prepared soil.

In connection, more particularly, with such theories as those of Mr. Froude, which endeavour to get rid of the refinements of philosophers and politicians, and to reduce the motives of society to rude violence and successful force—in relation to such theories I cannot but think that the best possible antidote is to study the various phases through which the society and the morals of such a people as the Greeks passed. It will be seen how they began with rude notions, how in the Homeric days the now fashionable theory that 'Might is Right' was practically carried out—of this the present essay will give ample proofs. Even delicacy of feeling and chivalry of sentiment will be very inadequate, if the check of sound laws, based upon pure moral feeling diffused throughout a society, be not ever there to repress and to educate. We may then see, in succeeding ages, this social and moral force contending, and in the end contending successfully, against the disintegrating and barbarising forces opposed to it—the party struggles and social hatreds so prominent in Greece. And so we arrive at the Attic period, in which the free citizen could boast that the state protected him both from violence and injustice, so that men learned to postpone wounded feelings and outraged honour to the majesty of the law, that forbad all violence, even in the vindication of personal injury. And so the refinement of Greek manners culminated in the gentle Menander, who brings his philosophy to aid the dictates of the law, and warns us that controversy and disputes are disagreeable and inconsistent with true comfort, and that a true gentleman would rather lose advantages and even submit to annoyance than ruffle his temper, and agitate himself with either wrangling or retaliation[1]. Unfortunately these developments within single states were not accompanied by similar improvements in their external relations. The Greeks never attained the higher condition of subjecting their public disputes to a system of international law or public arbitration. But we may well excuse it in them, seeing that in our nineteenth century this wise and civilised method of avoiding war is but seldom invoked, and only submitted to with discontent and with grumbling. I think it will farther be shown that

---

[1] See his Γεωργός, frag. 3 (ed. Meineke), ' He is the best man, Gorgias, who knows best how to control himself when injured (ὅστις ἀδικεῖσθαι πλεῖστ' ἐπίστατ' ἐγκρατῶς), for this hot temper and extreme bitterness is clear evidence to all of smallness of mind.' This sentiment, so different from those of Euripides, is repeated in other fragments; see frag. incert. 25, and γνῶμαι 47. The latter passage is almost Christian in tone: ' Prefer to be injured rather than to injure, for (in so doing) you will blame others, and you will escape censure.' If he had not promised us the luxury of blaming others, the sentiment would be thoroughly Christian.

the general public of ancient Greece did not approach so nearly to the enlightenment of its intellectual leaders, as our modern public does. We find, for example, in the ordinary life of Athens, cruelties and barbarities so violently in conflict with the humanity of a Socrates, a Euripides, or a Plato, as to astonish us, and make us doubt our estimate of Attic culture. These harsh contrasts would, I think, exist now among us, but for two great differences in our society—one of them the direct result of Christianity. They are the invention of printing, and the abolition of slavery.

The former has brought the leaders of public opinion into a close contact with the masses, quite unattainable in ancient days. In its modern development, the newspaper press, with all its faults, certainly brings home to the public mind all cases of cruelty and injustice with a promptness impossible even in busy and gossiping Athens, and so the public conscience is not only made sensitive, but has obtained a powerful organ for uttering its immediate censure.

The latter has weaned the dominant classes from that contempt of human rights and human emotions which, even in our own day, is manifest in those who live as masters or rulers over degraded populations. Nothing, for example, is more frequent in our Colonial Official, and still more in his wife, than their impatience of the rights and feelings of the lower classes at home, which they are obliged to respect, after their habit of lording it over inferior races.

I suppose the planters of the slave states in America
would exhibit similar feelings. If these things be
true, it will appear that the points of superiority in
our condition to that of the Greeks were partly due
to an accident in our civilisation—the discovery of
a rapid means of multiplying books, but partly to
a higher and better religion. This latter is of course
the great contrast, and the great advantage which we
have gained. But I confess that when I compare the
religion of Christ with that of Zeus, Apollo, and
Aphrodite, and consider the enormous, the unspeak-
able contrasts, I wonder not at the greatness, but
at the smallness of the advance in public morality
which has been attained. It is accordingly here,
where the difference ought to be greatest, that we are
led to wonder most at the superiority of Greek
genius which, in spite of an immoral and worthless
theology, worked out in its higher manifestations a
morality approaching in many points the best type
of modern Christianity. Socrates and Plato are far
superior to the Jewish moralist, they are far superior
to the average Christian moralist ; it is only in the
matchless teaching of Christ himself that we find them
surpassed. So then the social life of the Greeks is
more than a matter of antiquarian curiosity, it is of
practical value and interest to us all.

CHAPTER II.

THE GREEKS OF THE HOMERIC AGE.

THE great vexed question of the origin and composition of the Homeric poems lies happily beyond
our present scope[1]. To those who desire to study
the social indications in these great epics, it is a
matter of small importance to know whether they
were composed by one poet, by two, or by many;
whether they grew up gradually in a school of
rhapsodists, or whether they sprang complete from
a single genius. Even the ultra-sceptical theory,
which holds that the Iliad and Odyssey, as we have
them, did not acquire their present form till late
in the Attic age,—even this theory, supposing it were
shown not impossible, would little affect us. Two
facts alone we demand, and these will doubtless be
conceded by critics of every description; first, that
whenever or wherever the Homeric poems were
arranged or produced, the great result was accomplished by building with pre-existing materials, by
assimilating or embodying older and shorter lays:
secondly, that whatever may be the exact age of
these older materials, at least this is certain, that
they describe a state of society different from and

[1] My views will be found in *Macmillan's Magazine* for October, 1878,
and February, 1879.

more primitive than that implied in any other relic
of Greek literature.

A qualified exception, as to antiquity, may perhaps
be made in favour of Hesiod, but the social state
described by him, if contemporaneous, yet belongs
to a different part of Greece and to a different rank
in society.   So far then as he is contemporaneous,
we may call in his assistance as affording a contrast,
and possibly as completing the picture left us by
Homer. For the social attitude of Hesiod seems
to differ curiously from that of all the rest of the
earlier Greek poets, except perhaps Hipponax.   It
has hardly been remarked, how intensely aristocratic
was their tone, and how they uniformly addressed
themselves to the powers that be, often in pointed
exclusion of all inferior classes.   The Rhapsodists
addressed kings and princes, and sang at courts.
The Lyric poets addressed either the gods, the tyrants, or those close aristocratic circles that swayed the
Greek cities on the abolition of monarchies.   Even
the Gnomic poets were aristocrats, and spoke their
wisdom to their compeers only. No Greek poet addressed the Demos till it too became the sovereign
Demos, and till the distinction of higher and lower
classes became as it were inverted by the radical
spirit of the times. Apart, then, from the scanty
fragments of popular songs, no voice directly addressed to the lower classes has reached us, save
the plain shrewdness of Hesiod, whose 'Works and
Days' (unlike the Georgics of his Roman imitator,
written in the interests of the rulers) gives us some

evidence of the poor and shady side of Greek life in early days. It is even possible that he describes the Homeric society from a widely diverse point of view[1].

And if it be the same society, there can be little doubt that the genuine Hesiod's picture must be in many respects truer than Homer's. It is almost painful to say anything in the least derogatory to the Iliad or Odyssey, especially when they are almost our only authority for the earliest phase of Greek society. But I am convinced that all the critics, even Grote and the sceptical Germans, have overrated the accuracy of the pictures of life given in these poems. They have been persuaded by the intense reality and the natural simplicity which have made these scenes unapproachable in their charm, and they have thought that such qualities could only coexist with a simple and faithful reproduction of the circumstances actually surrounding the poet's life. But surely this argument, irresistible up to a certain point, has been carried too far. A poet of genius may surely be capable of modifying and colouring, even when he is observing and copying nature. Moreover, he must even endeavour to do so, if he sets himself to describe an ideal state of things, or if he desires to please a rich patron, to whom actual surroundings are in many respects unpleasant. Now these were the very conditions under which the epic poets composed. Their poems

---

[1] Cp. Hom. δ 490. I quote the Books of the Odyssey by small Greek letters, those of the Iliad by capitals, according to a convenient German habit.

were certainly intended for recitation at the courts
of kings and chiefs. They were intended to honour
these chiefs by extolling the deeds and lives of their
ancestors. And so an ideal state must be described—
a state evidently differing only in degree from the
poet's own experience, else the truth and reality of his
picture must have suffered—but yet differing from
it in the greater interference of the gods, in the
larger size and strength of the heroes, and in the
greater valour of their deeds.

These differences are acknowledged by the poets
themselves, but are we sure that they confined themselves to these? Are we sure that they did not accommodate other matters to the wishes or the regrets
of their noble hearers? Thus, for example, the rank
and file of the army are there to be marshalled by
the kings, and to raise the shout of battle, but then
they disappear from the action, and leave the field
perfectly clear for the chiefs to perform their deeds
of valour. There is not, I think, an example in all
the Iliad of the chief falling, or even being wounded,
by an ignoble hand. Such a misfortune was too
shocking to the sensibilities of an aristocratic audience. Amid the cloud of missiles that were flying
on the plains of Troy, amid the crowd of chiefs and
kings that were marshalled on either side, we never
hear how a 'certain man drew a bow at a venture,
and smote a king between the joints of the harness.'
Yet this must surely have occurred in any prolonged
combats such as those about the walls of Troy.

Here, then, is a plain departure from truth, and

even from reasonable probability. It is indeed a
mere omission which does not offend the reader; but
such inaccuracies suggest serious reflections. If the
epic poets ignore the importance of the masses on
the battlefield, is it not likely that they underrate
it in the *agora*? Is it not possible that here, too,
to please their patrons, they describe the glorious
ages of the past as the days when the assembled
people would not question the superior wisdom of
their betters, but merely came together to be taught
and to applaud? I cannot, therefore, as Mr. Grote
does, accept the political condition of things in the
Homeric poems, especially in the Iliad, as a safe
guide to the political life of Greece in the poet's
own day. The figure of Thersites seems drawn
with special spite and venom, as a satire upon the
first critics that rose up among the people, and
questioned the divine right of kings to do wrong.
We may be sure the real Thersites, from whom the
poet drew his picture, was a very different and a
far more serious power in debate, than the mis-
shapen buffoon of the Iliad. But the king who
had been thwarted and exposed by him in the day
would over his evening cups enjoy the poet's tra-
vesty, and long for the good old times, when he
could put down all impertinent criticism by the
stroke of his knotty sceptre. Indeed the Homeric
agora could hardly have existed had it been so idle
a form as the poets represent. As the lower classes
were carefully marshalled on the battlefield from a
full sense of the importance which the poet denies

them, so they were marshalled in the public assembly, where we may be sure their weight told with equal effect, though the poet neglected it for the greater glory of the counselling chiefs. Would that we had fuller sketches from the tamer Hesiod! He, at least, does not sing in the interest of courts and kings, and he moreover gives us a glimpse into the sorrows and severities which encompassed the lower classes while the courts may have revelled in luxury and splendour.

Yet even his wisdom, as we have it, is not without suspicion from a very different cause, for his works have suffered more than most Greek poems from interpolations and additions. Their moral and didactic tone, as well as their fragmentary character, made them at an early period a favourite handbook of education, especially as the moral advices of later Gnomic poets could be foisted in, and taught under the venerable name of the older Hesiod. Though I am not here concerned with critical questions, it were not right to begin a social sketch based upon such evidence, without at once telling the reader the nature and the imperfections of that evidence. More especially when I intend making considerable use of Grote's remarkable chapter on the 'Manners of the Heroic Age,' it is necessary to warn the reader against the too ready faith here shown by a great writer, sometimes imbued with a very sceptical spirit. Other points of difference will disclose themselves in the sequel.

But I cannot pass on without supplementing briefly

a large defect in the attitude of Grote and other English authors on the Homeric age. They lay aside all inquiry into the previous conditions of Greece as impossible and useless. The very civilised life of the Greek and Trojan heroes is assumed as a starting-point, having developed itself, we know not how, from the rude barbarism which Thucydides rightly considers to have been the really primitive state, the veritable *juventus* of Hellenism. Yet surely the wonder of Aristotle is justified, when he expreses himself at a loss to explain how a monarchy such as that of Agamemnon could spring from such conditions.

I cannot but think that the consistent voice of the older Greek legends, coupled with what we know of early Phœnician and Egyptian history, wellnigh solves the difficulty. The remains of the stone age found lately under the lava at Therasia[1], are too remote and isolated to admit of any safe inferences. But the older Semitic histories, the Egyptian inscriptions, and the traditions of the Greeks them-

[1] Cp. *Revue Archéologique*, vol. xvi. pp. 141-7. The islands of Santorin and Therasia in the Ægean Sea are the sides of a gigantic volcano, of which the crater is now a deep sea basin, surrounded by precipitous cliffs, which slope gradually outward to the open sea. Deep under these lava slopes there have been found buried the remains of what the French call an ante-historic Pompeii. Stone implements, some rude gold ornaments, pottery with ornamental patterns, a rude house, and some skeletons have been disinterred. Our oldest Greek authorities on Thera, such as Pindar, make no allusion to its having been a volcano, so that even the tradition of this great irruption had died away in historical Greece. I mention these facts here, as not sufficiently known; to discuss them would be irrelevant.

selves, agree that the Phœnicians certainly, and perhaps the Egyptians, sailed with powerful fleets through the Ægean, and traded at enormous advantage with the rude inhabitants of the coasts and islands, by means of their imposing wealth and culture. They settled also in the Greek waters, partly for commercial and mining purposes, as for example at Thasos,—where Herodotus saw a whole mountain disembowelled by their operations[1],—but partly also from the desire of forming new empires. Just as distinguished Athenians, like Miltiades or Iphicrates, became great princes among the 'butter-eating Thracians,' so we may suspect that the legends of Minos, of Cadmus, and of Danaus indicate sovereignties set up by these civilised foreigners in prehistoric days among the Greeks. They possessed the requisites which Aristotle sought in vain among the chiefs of his own nation, and gained their power by introducing great public benefits to the ruder Greeks, as well as by the splendour of their circumstances, and the superior arms of their followers. The legend of Minos[2] seems to us the echo of the most important of these sovereignties, but the prehistoric ruins at Argos, Mycenæ, and Orchomenus, show that Crete was not the only seat of culture.

Gradually the national spirit was roused against

---

[1] οὖρος μέγα ἀνατετραμμένον ἐν τῇ ζητήσει. vi. 47.

[2] I agree rather with Holm, who considers Minos to represent a purely Phœnician power, than with E. Curtius, who thinks it was an Hellenic, or semi-Hellenic power. All the legends point to Phœnician sources, and to Phœnician mythology, in connection with this king, nor do I see any Greek feature in his rule, so far as we know it.

these foreigners. As the legends tell us of Theseus conquering the Amazon worshippers of Astarte, and refusing his tribute to the servants of Moloch, so I suppose Greek, perhaps at first semi-Greek, chiefs, the offspring of connections between the invaders and the natives, began gradually to dispossess and supplant the Semitic forerunners of Greek culture. But the splendour of their rule was too attractive to be abolished. The native chiefs seem therefore to have succeeded to the power and wealth already centred at Argos, Mycenæ, Crete, Orchomenus, and other such favourable positions. The great Cyclopean ruins are found on the very sites indicated in Homer, as the seats of the greatest monarchs. Accordingly, I conceive Agamemnon, Menelaus, Nestor, and other of the richer chiefs, but especially the Atreidæ, to have rather inherited a power and wealth established originally by the enlightened despotism of Semitic merchant princes, and not gradually acquired by the extension of a local patriarchal sway. The legends are with me, and so is Aristotle, who cannot conceive monarchies arising in Greece gradually, but rather in consequence of some special circumstance, such as some great public benefit conferred by a prominent individual. The splendour of the palaces of Menelaus and of Alcinous, who had their walls covered with a profusion of bright metal, seems to point to a kind of decoration essentially Eastern and not Hellenic. Even in late times, the only old hereditary monarchy in Greece, that of Sparta, retained, in the public mourning for the

C

kings, features so strikingly foreign and Asiatic, that they called for special notice from Herodotus[1]. If therefore Agamemnon inherited his splendour from such predecessors, it will follow that the earliest form of the monarchy was not patriarchal but despotic, and that the Homeric King of men succeeded to a power with great pretensions, but practically limited in all directions by the rise of petty chieftains, more or less independent.

The general tone of the Iliad and Odyssey implies then, not a nascent, but a decaying order of things; subordinate chiefs rebelling against their suzerains; nobles violating the rights of their absent chiefs. The fierce spirit of independence in the Greek already stood opposed to the idea of a monarchy hallowed by precedent and tradition; and it was even then plain to thinking men (like Hesiod) that this profound antagonism could only be solved by such a change in the order of things as would give the majority an interest in maintaining the government. This majority, at first, only included the aristocracy, and so, when the Dorian invasion had dislocated Greece, aristocratical types of government resulted. But with the development of commerce, and with the depression of the nobles by the tyrants

---

[1] vi. 58. 'The custom of the Lacedæmonians upon the death of their kings is the same as that of the barbarians in Asia, for most of the barbarians now practise the same custom when their kings die.' He describes these customs in detail. The public lament over the deceased king, 'affirming that the last king is always the best,' is very like the 'Irish cry' still practised in the mountainous regions of Kerry and Connemara.

who rose up among them, the lower classes awoke to a sense of *their* rights, and so, upon a second dislocation of Greece (the Persian wars) democracies resulted as an equally natural development.

These later stages are beyond my present scope. I wish merely to indicate how the Homeric poems represent to me the close of an epoch—almost a state of decay preceding a newer order of things—and that I, therefore, estimate the society and the morals of the Iliad and Odyssey quite differently from those writers who have compared them with primitive conditions in other nations. Of course primitive features remained, as they do in every nation; but they were combined with vices which betray the decadence of culture, and with virtues rather springing from mature reflection and long experience than from the spontaneous impulse of a generous instinct.

Mr. Grote, Mr. Gladstone, and others, have made the Homeric age more familiar than any other phase of Greek life to English readers. They have accepted the descriptions of the rhapsodists as a literal account of a real contemporaneous society; they have moreover deduced, with exceeding subtlety, all the inferences which can be extracted from the poems in favour of Homeric honour and purity. Every casual utterance is weighted with the deepest possible meaning; every ordinary piece of good-nature attributed to profound and self-denying benevolence. We are told that morals in historic Greece had decayed; that a social state of real refinement and purity had passed away, to make

way for cold calculation and selfish aggrandisement.
How far this picture is real we shall see in the sequel.
But the labours of these ingenious authors have relieved me of the task of minutely describing all the
details of Homeric life. The great masterpieces themselves are accessible to all in the translations which
have of late years poured from the press. I shall,
therefore, confine myself to the features in which the
Homeric Greek was the parent of the historical Greek,
noticing incidentally such contrasts as must naturally
suggest themselves in the inquiry.

The mediæval knights, with whom it is fashionable
to compare the princes of the Iliad and Odyssey, were
wont to sum up the moral perfection which they esteemed under one complex term—a term for which
there is no equivalent in Greek—the term HONOUR.
It may be easily and sufficiently analysed into four
component ideas, those of *courage, truth, compassion,*
and *loyalty.* No man could approach the ideal of
chivalry, or rank himself among gentlemen and men
of honour, who was not ready to contend, when
occasion arose, against any odds, and thus to encounter death rather than yield one inch from
his post. He must feel himself absolutely free from
the stain of a single lie, or even of an equivocation.
He must be ever ready to help the weak and the
distressed, whether they be so by nature, as in the
case of women and children, or by circumstances, as
in the case of men overpowered by numbers. He
must with his heart, and not with mere eye-service,
obey God and the king, or even such other authority

as he voluntarily pledged himself to obey. A knight who violated any of these conditions, even if he escaped detection at the hands of his fellows, felt himself degraded, and untrue to the oath taken before God, and the obligation which he had bound himself to fulfil. This, I conceive, was the ideal of knighthood.

Let us now turn to the Homeric poems to obtain information on these four points, remembering that, as the real knight may have fallen short of the ideal we have just sketched, so doubtless the real Homeric Greeks were considerably worse than the ideal characters depicted by the rhapsodists.

I believe I shall run counter to an old-established belief when I say that the *courage* of the Homeric chiefs—in this types of their historical descendants—was of a second-rate order. It was like the courage of the modern French, dependent upon excitement, and vanishing quickly before depression and delay. No doubt the Greeks were a warlike nation, like the French, fond of glory, and revelling in excitement ; but they did not possess that stubborn valour which was the duty of the mediæval knight, and which is the physical characteristic of the English and German soldier. With the exception of Achilles and of Diomede, all the chiefs in the Iliad are subject to panics, and fly before the enemy. Of course, the flattering bard ascribes these disgraceful scenes to the special interference of the gods, but as he equally attributes special feats of valour to a like interference, we may discount the marvellous element, and regard these men, as we do a French army, to be capable of splendid acts of daring and of courage, but liable to sudden relapse into dismay and craven flight[1]. Even Achilles flies in fear from the pursuit of the river Scamander, but this is rather the dread of an ignoble death, as he himself says, than proper cowardice. Ajax, who approaches nearest of the ordinary men in the poem to our notions of a stubborn soldier—even he is surprised by panic, and makes for the ships.

There are farther indications of the same thing in the Odyssey. When Ulysses hears from Circe (κ 496) what sufferings he has yet to undergo, he tells us himself : 'So she spake, but my spirit was broken within me, and I sat crying on the bed, and I felt no more desire to live and see the light of the sun.' This was natural enough, but very different from the courage, not only of the mediæval knight, but of the modern gentleman.   Still worse, when the hero is telling Achilles among the Shades of the valour of his son Neoptolemus, he says that as the chiefs entered the wooden horse, though they were the best of the Greeks, yet 'the other leaders of the Danai wiped tears from their eyes, and the limbs of each trembled beneath him, but Neoptolemus alone neither grew pale nor wept[2].'

---

[1] The courtly Pindar maintains the Homeric doctrine (*Nem.* ix. 27) when he says : ἐν γὰρ δαιμονίοισι φόβοις φεύγοντι καὶ παῖδες θεῶν—'in panics even sons of the gods run away'—a sentiment which no troubadour would have ventured to utter.

[2] Cp. λ 524 sq.

> ἔνθ' ἄλλοι Δαναῶν ἡγήτορες ἠδὲ μέδοντες
> δάκρυά τ' ὠμόργνυντο τρέμον θ' ὑπὸ γυῖα ἑκάστου

These hints in an ideal description, professing to tell of the highest possible heroism, indicate plainly that the Greeks of the heroic age were no extraordinary heroes, and that they were not superior in the quality of courage to the Greeks of history. In this respect, then, the Achæan chiefs were indeed but the forerunners of their descendants. The same combination of warlike ardour, but of alternating valour, meets us all through Greek history[1]. The Athenians, the brave people who first ventured to look the barbarians in the face, whether at Sardis, or at Marathon, as Herodotus says—these brave Athenians are frequently seized with panics and run for their lives. The same may be said of all the Greeks, except the Spartans, who succeeded in curing their national defect by a very strict and complete discipline. But this discipline controlled all their lives,

κεῖνον δ᾽ οὔποτε πάμπαν ἐγὼν ἴδον ὀφθαλμοῖσιν
οὔτ᾽ ὠχρήσαντα χρόα κάλλιμον οὔτε παρειῶν
δάκρυ᾽ ὁμορξάμενον.

See also κ 198 sq., where the weeping of Ulysses and his men is almost ludicrous. I may as well here cite an historical parallel to show the unity of Greek sentiment at every epoch. At the conclusion of the 21st oration in our remains of Lysias (the ἀπολογία δωροδοκίας) the speaker says, 'whenever I was about to risk my life in the naval battles, I never lamented or wept, or kept talking about my wife and children, and saying how dreadful it would be, if I dying for my country were to leave them orphans and desolate.' Thus the speaker takes special credit to himself as an exception to the general rule.

[1] Thus in a curious passage of Plato's *Gorgias* (Jowett, iii. 94), Callicles, in answer to Socrates, tells us that brave men and cowards are equally pained at the approach of the enemy, and equally pleased at their departure. He does not contemplate that bravery which delights in danger, and seeks it out.

and sacrificed all higher objects to that of making them stand firm in their ranks. I conclude this discipline to have been unnatural and strained, from the fact that no other Greek city, much as they all admired Spartan organisation, ever attempted to imitate it. When we now-a-days see the German armies better disciplined than our own, we forthwith propose to reform ourselves on their model. No such attempt ever occurs in Greek history. This could hardly have been so, but for the reason just assigned. The Spartan training was so oppressive that not even the certainty of victory in battle could induce other Greek politicians to recommend it, or other Greek citizens to adopt it. Thucydides hints at this very plainly, and, in the mouth of Pericles, shows that, even with inferior military training, the real advantages are on the side of wider culture. Aristotle supports the same view in stronger and more explicit terms. I cite these authorities to show how artificial and factitious a thing the Spartan valour was, and how different from the spirit of the Viking, the Baron, and the Yeoman. We know too how even the Spartan valour collapsed as soon as Epaminondas met it with superior tactics, and how little idea there was, either at Leuctra or Sphacteria, of resisting to the death. The Greeks, then, though a very warlike were not a very courageous people, and we may affirm of them, in a lesser degree indeed, what Tacitus says of the Britons: 'In deposcendis periculis eadem audacia, et ubi advenere, in detrectandis eadem formido.'

The reasons of this curious combination are obvious enough, and worth a moment's digression. In the first place, the Greeks, from Homer's day downward, were an exceedingly sensitive people. Evidences of this feature crowd upon us in the Iliad and Odyssey. The delicate tact with which unpleasant subjects are avoided in conversation shows how easily men were hurt by them, and how perfectly the speaker could foretell it by his own feelings. In fact, so keenly alive are the Homeric Greeks to this great principle of politeness, that it seriously interferes with their truthfulness, just as in the present day the Irish peasant, with the same lively imagination and the same sensitiveness, will instinctively avoid disagreeable things, even if true, and 'prophesy smooth things' when he desires especially to please. He is not less reluctant to be the bearer of bad news than the typical messenger in Greek tragedy, who complains, in regular stock phrases, of the hard and ungrateful duty thrust upon him by untoward circumstances.

To this mental sensitiveness there was doubtless joined a corresponding bodily sensitiveness. An acute sense of pain and of pleasure, delicate nerves of taste and touch—these gifts were essential for the artistic products in which the Greeks excelled. We know how important a place was held in historical times by cooks, and how keenly the Greeks enjoyed the more refined pleasures of the table. So we may find Plato's contemporaries disputing in music on the difference of notes almost identical, showing that they appreciated dissonances which we consider unimportant.

I cannot parallel these facts in Homer, except by a
curious case of sensitiveness in smell. When Menelaus
is windbound off the coast of Egypt, and at his wit's
end, a goddess (Eidothea) explains to him how to
catch and interrogate Proteus, and engages to place
him in ambush, which she does by concealing him
with three comrades under fresh sealskins (δ 440 sqq.).
These men were in danger of their lives, and were
engaged on the perilous errand of doing violence to
a marine god. Yet the point which left its mark
most strongly on Menelaus' mind was the bad smell
of the sealskins! 'That would have been a most
dreadful ambush; for a most deadly stench of sea-
bred seals distressed us sore. For who would lie
down beside a sea-monster? But the goddess saved
us, and devised a great boon. She brought and
put very sweet-smelling ambrosia under our nostrils,
and it destroyed (counteracted) the smell of the
seal.'

If we combine with this great delicacy of sensibility
the gloomy and hopeless views which the Homeric
Greeks held concerning a future life, we shall see
good reason for their dread of death. For although
Homer distinctly admits an after life, and even introduces us to it in the Odyssey, he represents the
greatest kings and heroes in weakness and in misery,
without hope or enjoyment, save in hearing the vague
and scanty rumours that reached them from the
world of mortal men. The blessed islands of the
West were indeed even then a home for the dead
(δ 564 sqq.), but they had not yet been opened to

moral worth, as in the days of Pindar[1]. They were reserved for those who, like Menelaus, had the good fortune of being nearly related to the gods by marriage or family connections. From this aristocratic heaven therefore even Agamemnon, Achilles. and Ajax were excluded, and wandered forlorn in the doleful meadow of asphodel.

There will be less controversy as to the low sense of *truth* among Homeric Greeks. At no period did the nation ever attain that high standard which is the great feature in Germanic civilisation. Even the Romans, with all their coarseness, stood higher in this respect. But neither in Iliad nor Odyssey is there, except in phrases, any reprobation of deceit as such. To deceive an enemy is meritorious, to deceive a stranger innocent, to deceive even a friend perfectly unobjectionable, if any object is to be gained. So it is remarked of Menelaus, as it were exceptionally, that he *will* tell the truth, if you press him, for he is very considerate (πεπνυμένος). This was said to Telemachus, who was expecting melancholy news, and in such a case I have already observed that the Greeks would almost certainly avoid the truth. But the really leading characters (except Achilles) in the Odyssey and Iliad do not hesitate at all manner of lying. Ulysses is perpetually inventing, and so is his patroness, Pallas Athene, and she actually mentions this quality of wily deceit as her special ground of love and affection for him (ν 328). Zeus deceives both gods and men, the other gods deceive Zeus; in

---

[1] Cp. *Ol.* ii. 57 sqq., and the famous frag. of his θρῆνος.

fact the whole Homeric society is full of guile and falsehood.

There is indeed as yet a check upon men, which is often ignored in later Greek society. There is still a belief in the gods, and an expectation that if they are called to witness a transaction by means of an oath, that they will punish deceit. This belief, apparently surviving from an earlier and simpler state of society, must have been rudely shaken in Homeric times, when we consider the morality of Olympus in the epic poetry. The poets clearly held that the gods, if they were under no restraint, or fear of punishment from Zeus, were at liberty to deceive as they liked. One safeguard as yet remained, the oath by the Styx, the penalties of violating which are enumerated in Hesiod's *Theogony,* and consist of nine years' transportation, with solitary confinement and hard labour[1]. As for other oaths, the Hymn to Hermes shows that in succeeding generations their solemnity was openly ridiculed. Among the Homeric gods, as well as among the heroes, there were indeed old-fashioned characters who adhered to probity. The character of Apollo is unstained by deceit. So is that of Menelaus. But Apollo fails in defending his favourite against the reckless party politics of Here and Pallas; he gives way in battle before Poseidon ; he is like Menelaus among men, an eminently respectable, but second-rate personage. The experience of Homeric men was aged enough to know that probity secured no man from the troubles

[1] Cp. his *Theog.* 793 sqq.

of life and the reverses of fortune. The gods were often ungrateful and thankless, and so the weight of public opinion inclined decidedly to the belief that honesty was indeed respectable, and of better repute than deceit, but that it was not safe to practise it without the help of superior force[1]. So Achilles was master of the situation, and to him lying was useless to attain ends that might be better attained by force. This subject will naturally recur when we come to compare the Homeric with later Greeks[2].

We pass to the third element in chivalrous honour, a sense of *compassion* for the weak, and an obligation to assist the oppressed. Unfortunately this duty appears to have been delegated to Zeus, whose amours and other amusements often prevented him from attending to his business. How badly he performed it in this respect is plain from the very pathetic passages

---

[1] As similar states of society produce similar philosophies, so we find the very same attitude in Machiavelli's *Principe*, especially in his celebrated 18th chapter, entitled ' In che modo i principi debbiano osservare la fede.' He begins by praising good faith, but observing that history shows great princes to have succeeded by the opposite principle. In fact the prince must be partly a fox, to detect snares, and partly a lion, to terrify the wolves. ' Non puo pertanto un signor prudente nè debbe osservar la fede, quando tale osservanzia gli torni contro, e che sono spente le cagioni che la feciono promettere.' He adds the usual excuse : ' E se gli uomini fossero tutti buoni, questo precetto non saria buono, ma perchè son tristi, e non l' osserverebbono a te, tu ancora non l' hai da osservare a loro.' He goes on to show that the virtues of honour, probity, and good faith must be simulated, or else men will not be deceived, though he observes that men are so silly, or so bound by present necessities, that there is little difficulty in deceiving them. The whole chapter is the most characteristic in a very characteristic treatise.

[2] Cf. below, p. 115.

in which the condition of the decrepit father, the forlorn widow, and the helpless orphan are described.
We must not for a moment imagine that the Homeric
age was wanting in sympathy for children. On the
contrary, Herodotus alone, of later Greek authors,
shows this sympathy as strongly as we find it in the
Iliad. The Homeric similes — and no similes are more
thoroughly realistic and drawn from actual experience
—constantly imply it. 'As a mother drives away the
fly from her child when it lies in sweet sleep.' 'Why
do you weep like an infant girl, who running along by
her mother, begs to be carried, and holding on by
her dress delays the hurrying woman, but looks up
at her with her eyes full of tears in order that she may
be taken up and carried.' Apollo destroys the earth-
works of the Greeks 'very easily, as a child treats the
shingle by the sea-side, who, when he has heaped it up
in his childish sport, in his sport again levels it all with
his hands and feet[1].' These comparisons are evidently
drawn from the same society which suggested the delightful picture (in Z) of Andromache with her nurse
and darling son, coming to bid farewell to Hector as
he was hurrying to the battle. The whole picture—the
child 'fair as a star,' his terror at Hector's helmet and
nodding crest, the strong love of the parents sorrowing
at the very prospect of misfortune for their child;—this
picture, which I dare not abridge, and which is too
long for quotation, shows no ordinary feeling for helpless innocence. But all this sympathy in the poet,
and doubtless in the society which he described, did

[1] Cf. Δ 130; Ο 361; and Π 7.

not save little children from cruelty and from neglect. There is no passage in the two poems, if we except that on the dog Argus, which will bring more tears into hard modern eyes than the lament of Andromache over Hector (X 482 sqq. Lord Derby's transl.),

> ' Now thou beneath the depths of earth art gone,
> Gone to the viewless shades; and me has left
> A widow in thy house, in deepest woe,
> Our child an infant still, thy child and mine.
> Ill-fated parents both! nor thou to him,
> Hector, shalt be a guard, nor he to thee;
> For though he 'scape this tearful war with Greece,
> Yet nought for him remains but ceaseless woe,
> And strangers on his heritage shall seize.
> No young companions own the orphan boy.
> With downcast eyes, and cheeks bedewed with tears,
> His father's friends approaching, pinched with want,
> He hangs upon the skirt of one, of one
> He plucks the cloak; perchance in pity some
> May at their tables let him sip the cup,
> Moisten his lips, but scarce his palate touch:
> While youths with both surviving parents blest
> May drive him from their feast with blows and taunts:
> Begone, thy father sits not at our board!
> Then weeping to his widowed mother's arms
> He flies, that orphan boy, Astyanax,' etc.

It is here the lamentable condition of the orphan that strikes us so forcibly. 'Qui a vu la misère des hommes n'a rien vu, il faut voir la misère des femmes; qui a vu la misère des femmes, n'a rien vu, il faut voir la misère des enfants.' How different, for example, do we find the Irish peasants, with whom I have already compared the Greeks, where the neighbours divide among them without complaint the children left destitute by the death or emigration of the parents, and extend their scanty fare and their wretched homestead to the orphan as to their own children. The Homeric gentleman, of whose refinement and delicate politeness we hear so much, was far removed from such generosity. We feel almost painfully the beauty of the simile, by which the poet pictures the joy of Ulysses, when, after two nights and two days in the deep, he sees land from the summit of the great rocking wave (ϵ 394):

> 'As when a father on the point to die,
> Who for long time in sore disease hath lain,
> By the strong fates tormented heavily
> Till the pulse faileth for exceeding pain,
> Feels the life stirring in his bones again,
> While glad at heart his children smile around;
> He also smiles—the gods have loosed his chain—
> So welcome seemed the land, with forest crowned,
> And he rejoicing swam, and yearned to feel the ground[1].'

And again (θ 523): 'As when a woman weeps falling upon the body of her dear lord, who has fallen before his city, and commanding his people, in defending the town and his children from the pitiless day [of slavery]. She then, seeing him gasping in death, casts her arms about him with shrill cries. But they (the enemy) striking her with spears on the back and shoulders, bring her into slavery, to have sorrow and misery, and her cheeks waste with piteous woe.'

Little, indeed, need be said about the respect for

[1] Worsley's transl.

the rights of women. As is well known, when a town was captured, the noblest and fairest ladies, whether married or not, became the property of the victors as their concubines. But a still more significant fact has not been adequately noted—that such a fate, though felt as a lamentable misfortune, was in no sense a dishonour to the Greek lady, of which she need afterwards be ashamed. In spite of all the courtliness with which ladies are treated in the Homeric poems, in spite of the refinement of their characters and the politeness of their ordinary life, the hard fact remains that they were the property of the stronger, and that they submitted to this fate without being compromised in society. Neither Briseis nor Chryseis seem the least disgraced by their residence in the Greek camp; and still worse, Helen, after living for years with Paris, is then handed over to Deiphobus, and finally taken back by Menelaus without scruple or difficulty. If we weigh carefully her appearance in the Odyssey, we shall see that her regrets are chiefly for the turmoil she has caused, and for the tears and blood wasted upon her recovery; her dignity has suffered no great shock, nor does she avoid (except in words) the eyes of men[1].

These facts show with great clearness how com-

---

[1] Xenophon, in a passage which will hereafter be discussed, announces this principle distinctly. ' If such an accident,' he says, ' happen to a woman without her own fault, *she is not the less honoured among men.*' He would not of course agree with the courtly rhapsodist, in admitting an adulteress to this class, even though she alleged compulsion on the part of Aphrodite.

pletely the law of force prevailed over the weak, and
how the Homeric lady was so constrained by its iron
necessity, that all delicate feeling, however ornamental to the surface of society, vanished in stern
practice. The case of Penelope corroborates this
view. It was hateful to her to marry one of the rude
and ungentlemanly suitors, who thrust their attentions
upon her in her grief. Yet if Ulysses were surely
dead, there was no help, she must pass into their
hands, whether she choose it or not.

Stranger and not less characteristic is the treatment of old age. The king or chief, as soon as his
bodily vigour passed away, was apparently pushed
aside by younger and stronger men. He might either
maintain himself by extraordinary usefulness, like
Nestor, or be supported by his children, if they
chanced to be affectionate and dutiful; but except
in these cases his lot was sad indeed. We hear
Achilles (Λ 492 sq.) lamenting that doubtless in his
absence the neighbouring chiefs are ill-treating the
aged Peleus, and he longs to dye his spear in their
blood. We see Laertes, the father of Ulysses, exiled,
apparently by grief and disgust, to a barren farm in
the country, and spending the close of his life, not in
honour and comfort, but in poverty and hardship.
When these princes, who had sons that might return
any day to avenge them, were treated in such a way,
it is surely no strained inference to say that unprotected old age commanded very little veneration or
respect among the Homeric Greeks. While therefore
we find here, too, much courtliness of manner, and

respectfulness of address toward the aged from their younger relations, the facts indicate that helpless women and children and worn-out men received scanty justice and little consideration. Among friends and neighbours, at peace and in good humour, they were treated with delicacy and refinement, but with the first clash of conflicting interests such considerations vanished. The age was no longer, as I have said, a believing age; the interference of the gods to protect the weak was no longer the object of a simple faith, and Greek chivalry rested on no firmer basis.

I may add, by anticipation, that at no period of Greek history can we find old age commanding that respect and reverence which has been accorded it in modern Europe. We hear, indeed, that at Sparta the strictest regulations were made as to the conduct of young men towards elders, but this seems an exceptional case, like most things at Sparta. There is a hackneyed story of an old man coming into the crowded theatre at Athens, and looking in vain for a seat, till he came near the Spartan embassy, who at once stood up and made room for him. Though the whole theatre applauded this act of courtesy, I am sure they did not habitually imitate it. The lyric and tragic poets, as I shall show by ample quotations in future chapters, were perpetually cursing the miseries of old age, and blessing youth, fair in poverty, fairer still in riches. Probably old Athenian gentlemen were for these reasons like old Frenchmen, who are very prone to prolong their youth by artificial means, and strive to maintain a place among their fellows which they will lose when they are confessedly of the past generation. And so in Greece, as in France, old age may have come to lack that dignity and that importance which it obtains in the British army, on our Governing Boards, and in Chinese society. The comic features in Euripides' old men, and their ridiculous attempts to dance and to fight [1], show the popular feeling about them to have recognised this weakness. But apart from these peculiarities of race, the feverish and agitated condition of Greek politics, the perpetual wars and civil conflicts must have made prompt action and quick decision all-important, and so the citizens could not brook the slowness and caution of old age, which often mistakes hesitation for deliberation, and brands prompt vigour as rashness.

There yet remains the idea of *loyalty*—I mean hearty and unflinching allegiance to superior authority, or to the obligations taken by oath or promise. The idea is not unknown to Homer's men and women. Achilles and Penelope (more especially the latter) are in the highest sense loyal, the one to his friend Patroclus, the other to her husband Ulysses. But in the Greek camp the chiefs in general are wofully deficient in that chivalrous quality. I will not lay stress on their want of conjugal loyalty, a point in which Menelaus, according to the scholiasts, formed an honourable, but solitary exception. In those days, as in the times of the Mosaic law,

---

[1] In Euripides' *Heraclidæ* and *Bacchæ*.

absolute fidelity was expected from women, but not from men. In their own homes, indeed, scandals of this kind were avoided as the cause of ill-will and domestic discomfort. It is specially observed (α 433), that Laertes avoided these relations with Euryclea from respect for his wife's feelings, and the misconduct of the suitors in the same direction is specially reprobated; but when the chiefs were away at their wars, or travelling, the bard seems to expect no continence whatever. The model Ulysses may serve as an example, *instar omnium*.

But it is in their treatment of Agamemnon that the want of loyalty is specially prominent. Achilles is quite ready to insult him, and but for the promptings of Athene (that is, of prudence), who suggests that he may play a more lucrative game by confining himself to sulkiness and bad language, is ready even to kill him. The poet, too, clearly sympathises with Achilles. He paints Agamemnon as a weak and inferior man, succeeding by fortune to a great kingdom, but quite unfit to govern or lead the turbulent princes whose oath had bound them to follow him to Troy. It is in fact Ulysses, Diomede, and Nestor who direct him what to do. It may be said that we might expect such insubordination in the case of an armament collected for a special purpose, and that even the mediæval knights did not escape this disgrace in the very parallel case of the Crusades. I will not, then, press the point, though Agamemnon's title to supremacy is far different from that of Godfrey de Bouillon. Take the case of Peleus, which

I have already mentioned (p. 32). Take the case of Ithaca in the absence of its king. We are told repeatedly that he treated his people like a father, and yet only a few old servants seem to side with him against the worthless aspirants to the throne.

The *experimentum crucis*, however, is the picture of the gods in Olympus. We have here Zeus, a sort of easy-going but all-powerful Agamemnon, ruling over a number of turbulent self-willed lesser gods, who are perpetually trying to evade and thwart his commands. At intervals he wakes up and terrifies them into submission by threats, but it is evident that he can count on no higher principle. Herè, Poseidon, Ares, Aphrodite, Pallas, all are thoroughly insubordinate, and loyal to one thing only, that is, their *party*. Faction, as among the Greeks of Thucydides, had clearly usurped the place of principle, and we are actually presented with the strange picture of a city of gods more immoral, more faithless, and more depraved, than the world of men.

This curious feature has much exercised critics, and caused many conjectures as to the real moral attitude of the epic poets. I think the most natural explanation is based upon the notorious levity and recklessness of the Ionic character, as developed in Asia Minor[1]. We know from the lyric poets, we know

---

[1] We have ample evidence that the more serious of the Greeks regarded the matter in the same light. Xenophanes, for example, was known as a severe critic of Hesiod's *Theogony*, as well as of Homer, and Sextus Empiricus has preserved for us his bitter utterance :

πάντα θεοῖς ἀνέθηκαν "Ομηρός θ' 'Ησίοδύς τε
ὅσσα παρ' ἀνθρώποισιν ὀνείδεα καὶ ψόγος ἐστὶν

from the course of history, how the pleasure-loving Ionians of Asia Minor seem to have lost all the stronger fibre that marked the Greeks of Hellas. Revelling in plenty, associating with Asiatic splendour and luxury, they very soon lost those sterner features—love of liberty, self-denying heroism, humble submission to the gods—which still survived in Greece; and thus I conceive the courts at which the bards sang enjoyed a very free and even profane handling of the gods as a racy and piquant entertainment, so that presently it was extended even to the so-called Homeric hymns, which, of all Greek poetry, treat the gods in the most homely and even sensual way. The Hymn to Aphrodite, detailing her amour with Anchises, and that to Hermes, detailing his theft and perjury, are exact counterparts to the lay of Demodocus, which treats both Ares and Aphrodite in the same way.

This bold and familiar attitude was narrowly connected with another leading feature in the Greeks— their realism in art. There is nothing vague, or exaggerated, or incomprehensible, tolerated by their chaste judgment and their correct taste. The figures of dogs or men, cast by Hephæstus, are specially remarked for being *life-like* throughout the Homeric

---

οἱ πλεῖστ' ἐφθέγξαντο θεῶν ἀθεμίστια ἔργα
κλέπτειν μοιχεύειν τε καὶ ἀλλήλους ἀπατεύειν.

The discussions upon epic poetry which Plato has left us in his *Ion*, and in the second book of his *Republic*, point in a similar direction, and even show how the strange utterances were explained as the result of direct inspiration, and not the natural outcome of the poet's mind.

poems. They actually walk about, and are animated by his peculiar cunning. This, as Overbeck has well observed, is merely the strong expression of the object proposed to himself by the Greek artist, in contrast to the cold repose and mute deadness of Egyptian sculpture. The Egyptians seldom meant to imitate life in action. The Greeks, from their very first rude essays, set before them this higher goal. Like the statuary, so the poet did not waste his breath in the tiresome and vague adoration of the Egyptian psalmist, but clothed his gods in the fairest and best human form, and endowed them with a human intellect and human will.

Homer's gods are, therefore, too human to embody an abstract principle, and so this side of their religion the poets relegated to certain personified abstractions, which seldom appear, and which seem to stand apart from the life of the Olympic gods. Perhaps Zeus himself, in his Dodonean character, has this impersonal aspect as the Father of light and of good. But Zeus of Olympus is quite a different conception. So there is a personified or semi-personified Αἰδώς, and an Ἄτη, and Λιταί, and an Ἐρίνυς, which represent stern and lasting moral ideas, and which relieve the Olympic gods from the necessity of doing so, except when the poet finds it suitable to his purpose. But as these moral ideas restrained and checked men, so the special privilege of the gods seems to be the almost total freedom from such control. The society of Olympus, therefore, is only an ideal Greek society, in the lowest sense,—

the ideal of the schoolboy, who thinks all control irksome, and its absence the *summum bonum*,—the ideal of a voluptuous man, who has strong passions, and longs for the power to indulge them without unpleasant consequences.

It appears to me, therefore, that the Homeric picture of Olympus is very valuable as disclosing to us the poet's notion of a society freed from the restraints of religion. For the rhapsodists were dealing a death-blow (perhaps unconsciously) to their religion by these very pictures of sin and crime among their gods. Their idea is a sort of semi-monarchical aristocracy, where a number of persons have the power to help favourites, and thwart the general progress of affairs; where love of faction overpowers every other consideration, and justifies violence or deceit. It will quite satisfy our present object to select the one typical character which both the poems place in the foreground as the Greek ideal of intelligence and power of the highest order.

The leading personage in Homer's world of men and gods is undoubtedly Pallas Athene. She embodies all the qualities which were most highly esteemed in those days. She is evidently meant to be the greatest and most admirable of the deities that concern themselves with men. Yet, as Mr. Hayman has truly observed, she is rather infra-human than super-human. There is no touch of any kindly feeling, no affection or respect for either God or man. There is not even a trace of sex, except in her occasional touches of spite. 'Her character is without tenderness or tie of any sort; it never owns obligation, it never feels pain or privation, it is pitiless; with no gross appetites, its activity is busy and restless, its partisanship unscrupulous, its policy astute, and its dissimulation profound. It is keenly satirical, crafty, whispering base motives of the good (indeed she comprehends no others), beating down the strong, mocking the weak, and exulting over them; heartless—yet staunch to a comrade; touched by a sense of liking and admiration for its like, [she accounts expressly for her love of Ulysses by his roguery and cunning,] of truth to its party; ready to prompt and back a friend through every hazard.' Such is Mr. Hayman's picture, verified by citations for each and every statement[1].

This very disagreeable picture is not, as he would have it, an impersonation of what *we* call the world. Surely the modern world at least professes some high motives, and is touched by some compassion. But it is the impersonation of the Greek world, as conceived by Thucydides in his famous reflections on the Corcyræan massacre. He was mistaken indeed, profoundly mistaken, as we shall often see in the sequel, in considering this hard and selfish type a special outcome of the civil wars. No doubt they stimulated and multiplied it. But here, in the Iliad and Odyssey, in the days of Greek chivalry and Greek romance, even here we have the poet creating his ideal type—intellect and energy unshackled by restraints—and we obtain a picture which, but for the total absence of sex,

[1] Cp. Hayman's Odyssey, i. p. 73, Appendix E.

might be aptly described as a female Antiphon. The great historian, despite his **moral** reflections, speaks of Antiphon, the political assassin, the public traitor to his constitution, as ἀρέτῃ οὐδένος ὕστερος—'in general merit second to none[1].' The great epic poet silently expresses the same judgment on his own Pallas Athene. Were it not impossible to assign so late a date to the origin of the Iliad and Odyssey, we should be compelled to consider this impersonation of the patron goddess as suggested by the grasping policy and astute intellect of imperial Athens. Had the Athenian envoys who took part in the mythical Melian dialogue[2] chosen to assert mythical precedent for their conduct, they might have cited the Athene of Homer as their patroness and forerunner in a heartless and brutal policy.

[1] I ought in fairness to mention that some old grammarian notices in the early orators, from whom Thucydides learned his style, a peculiar use of ἀρέτη for *general reputation*. Thus Hesiod, Ἔργ. 313, πλούτῳ δ' ἀρετὴ καὶ κῦδος ὀπηδεῖ, and Theog. 933. This would give the passage an easier sense, for Antiphon was certainly the most prominent man of Athens at that time. I am not sure that the usual rendering should not be amended in this way, but yet, as none of the lexicographers have noticed it, I leave what I had written in the text.

[2] I perfectly agree with Grote that this celebrated dialogue at the close of Thucydides' fifth book is not only imaginary but historically absurd. Most German historians have accepted it as strictly historical. A. Holm, as usual, views it in the light of common sense.

CHAPTER III.

THE HOMERIC AGE (*continued*).

THE foregoing general reflections on the Homeric age have necessarily detained us, as being essential to the better understanding of the permanent features in the Greek character. I still owe such readers as are not intimate with Greek literature some details which may help them to picture to themselves the society of those long-past days.

Homer introduces us to a very exclusive *caste* society, in which the key to the comprehension of all the details depends upon one leading principle—that consideration is due to the members of the caste, and even to its dependants, but that beyond its pale even the most deserving are of no account save as objects of plunder. So the Homeric chieftain behaves even in battle with some consideration to his fellow chieftain; in peace and in ordinary society he treats him with the most delicate courtesy and consideration. To his wife and to the wives of his friends he behaves with similar politeness, though in a less degree, and with a strong sense of their inferiority. To his own slaves, who are as it were dignified by being attached to him, he conducts himself with consideration, as he does even to his horses and his dogs for the same reason. But there is evidence enough that the stranger who was not a guest friend, and the free labourer who was unattached to his household—these, as well as all women not belonging directly to the governing classes, were treated with reckless brutality, and in disregard of the laws of justice and mercy. A few illustrations on each of these points will be sufficient to establish the principle, and so give us a clue to gathering up details under its special heads.

The Greeks and Romans always laid great stress on the habits of the table as indicative of civilisation, and it was specially noted of such mythical humanisers as Orpheus, that they had induced men to improve the tone and manners of their feasting. The Greeks of historic times not only contrasted themselves in this respect with their semi-barbarous neighbours, but even (as we shall see) estimated the comparative culture of the Greek cities by this sensitive social test. From this aspect, then, the Greeks of Homer and of Hesiod occupy a very definite position. The appointments of their feasts seem simple, but not unrefined. Each guest generally had a small table to himself (α 106–112) well cleansed with sponges, and a special supply of bread. The washing of hands before eating was universal. With the exception of the large cup (κρητὴρ) for mixing, which was often embossed, and the work of a famous artist, we hear of no

plate, or other valuables to ornament the room.
This neat simplicity, however, does not correspond
with the extraordinary quantity and rudeness of
the food, and the barbarous sameness in the
victuals and their preparation. The Achæan heroes seem always ready to join in a meal of great
roast joints, and they hardly ever meet on any important occasion without forthwith proceeding to such
a repast. Nor do we see any refinement or variety
in either cooking or materials. We hear of no
vegetables except among the peculiar Lotos-eaters
(οἵ τ' ἄνθινον εἶδαρ ἔδουσιν, ι 84), or of fish, except
indeed that the latter is mentioned by Menelaus [1]
as the wretched sustenance of his starving comrades
when wind-bound off the coast of Egypt! Here is
indeed a contrast to the Attic banquet, where large
joints were thought coarse and Bœotian, while fish
was the greatest and most expensive of luxuries.

Yet withal the primitive and primitively cooked
materials of the banquet, in themselves no better
than the 'mutton and damper' of the wild Austra-
lian squatter, were accompanied by evidences of high
refinement and culture. There was ruddy sweet
wine, mellowed by age, and esteemed for its *bouquet*
as well as its flavour [2]. And yet good as the Greeks
thought it, they tempered it with water, for drunken-

[1] Cf. δ 368, and Mr. Hayman's instructive note on the passage.

[2] The eating of cheese, and general *Milch-speise*, as the Germans call
it, which we find to be the habit of the Cyclopes in the ninth book of
the Odyssey, was evidently the habit of pastoral tribes, or of the lower
classes similarly occupied. Still Ulysses and his companions seem to
enjoy it thoroughly, though they prefer meat diet.

ness was in all ages an offence against Greek taste; it was even by the immoral suitors considered fit for Centaurs, and by later Greeks for Thracians : αἴσιμα πίνειν (φ 294) was an universal rule of society. There was also present the reciting bard, who aided and was aided by the generous wine in raising the emotions of the guests to a warmer and loftier pitch, for he sang the deeds of men of old renown, the ancestors and models of the warriors who sat before him at their tables. This was truly the intellectual side of the Homeric banquet, a foretaste of the *Symposium* of Plato. But the Homeric Greeks were still far below the stage when intellectual conversation, in which all took part, was considered essential to social enjoyment ; for the most cultivated of the heroes, Ulysses, describes it as his notion of the highest enjoyment (ι 7) to sit in a row of silent guests and listen to a bard singing, with ample meat and drink upon the table. There were sometimes ladies present also, as we see in the case of Helen and Arete at their respective courts, and the strong intellect and high qualities of such ladies are plainly seen in the leading part which they take in the conversation.

The current news of the day seems to have been the chief topic, whenever strangers were present, and we can imagine the eagerness with which men inquired concerning absent friends, when they had no other means of hearing of their welfare. So much was the want of regular communication felt, that wandering beggars evidently attained an importance similar to

that of the beggars and also of the pedlars in Scott's
novels, who combine with the trade of selling goods that
of carrying news, and were even at times employed as
confidential messengers.   These vagrants, in Homer's
day, either carried or invented news, and obtained
their living in reward for it.   Thus Ulysses, in this
disguise, asks his swineherd (§ 118) what sort of man
his lost master was, perhaps he may have met him in
his wanderings.   And the swineherd replies :—

'It were vainly striven,
Old man, with news to cheer his wife and child,
Oft needy wandering men, to fraud much given,
Have for a lodging many lies compiled:
These far too much whileome have my dear queen beguiled.

Such she treats tenderly, enquiring all,
And in heart-bitterness doth weep and wail
As should a wife, whose lord far off doth fall.
Thou too, old man, wouldst quickly forge some tale;
But as for him, long since his life did fail;
Dogs must have torn him, and wild birds of prey;
Or, as the dead form drifted with the gale,
Fishes devoured him, and his bones this day,
Wrapt in the cold sea-sand, lie mouldering far away [1].'

In so similar a state of society to that of old Scotland, I fancy that the Phœnician traders may have
corresponded somewhat to the pedlars, as the beggars
were so analagous.   The Homeric beggars do not,
however, seem to have made so much money as those
of Scotland and Ireland in the last century.

The great courtesy and hospitality shown to strangers, even of the lowest type, nevertheless appear to
me rather the remains of a more primitive state of

[1] Worsley's transl.

things, than the natural outburst of Homeric generosity, for even in the ideal society depicted by the
poets, there are many passages where the close
shrewdness and calculating generosity of the Greek
mind break out naively enough through the curtain
of nobler feeling which only disguised them. I lay
no stress on the absence of that modern sentiment
which values a gift as a keepsake, and will not part
with it even for greater value. The Homeric heroes
readily gave away the gifts of respected guest friends.
But this was probably because the absence of coined
money had not made the broad distinction now
universally felt between the market value and the
sentimental value of a present. The main Homeric
personalties consisted of arms, cups, and ornaments.
These were obtained by barter, and taken in payment, and so even the gifts of friends were not considered in any different light from a mere money
present.

But in other points hospitality was, I think, decaying. Though every chief was bound to receive a
stranger, and though the more noble of them did so
readily, yet there are hints of some compunctions in
accepting hospitality, and some merit claimed by the
host for granting it. Mentor and Telemachus (γ 343)
rise up from Nestor's feast, and intend to return to
their ship, when the old hero lays hold of them, and
exclaims, 'Zeus and the other immortals forbid that
you should leave me and go to your ships as if I
were a man short of clothing, or poor, who had no
wrappers and rugs for himself and his guests to sleep

E

in comfortably.' And so when Telemachus arrives at Sparta, Menelaus' confidential servant (θεραπὼν) asks, 'Tell me, shall we take round the horses of these noble strangers, or send them on to some one else, who may befriend them?' But Menelaus answers in great anger : 'You used not to be a fool; but now you are talking silly nonsense, like a child : as if we ourselves had not before reaching home enjoyed the hospitality of many!' Both Nestor and Menelaus were gentlemen of the old school; so that when the question is raised, they hesitate not in their answer. But another hero speaks out more naively : 'Of course you must receive a stranger, when he comes ; but who would be so foolish as to *invite* a man of his own accord, except it were a skilled artisan'—who of course would more than repay his host by his services.

We hear too that the presents generously bestowed by the kings were recovered by them subsequently from their people, and yet this homely arrangement seems fairer and more satisfactory than the habit of modern times, when people give their kings a large income beforehand, in the vain expectation that they will spend part of it at least in hospitality. The Homeric Greeks were too shrewd and wide-awake a people to sow where they did not reap, and the increase of communication, and consequent frequency of visitors, were sure to close quickly the open door, and bar the right of entering unasked. The anxious precautions of Ulysses on entering the house of Alcinous, so similar to the acts of the exile Themistocles at the hearth of the Molossian king, show that there was risk, even in peace, for travellers; and it may be that the generous hospitality of the nobler Homeric chiefs was even then not the general rule, but the mark of a higher and more refined nature. So we find the elder Miltiades, in historical times, sitting at his open door and receiving strangers in contrast to the general selfishness of his neighbours. Homeric politeness seems, then, in this respect also, a forerunner of the later Greek courtesy, that it consisted rather in good taste and in tact than in reckless extravagance or in self-denial for the sake of others. Thus we find Homeric men avoiding to press an unwilling guest — a piece of good taste unknown to many of our middle classes; and evading all unpleasant subjects—a piece of tact requiring subtlety of mind and quickness of perception. The mediæval baron, or the old Irish squire would readily fight a duel for a friend from mere politeness, they would not have comprehended the points on which the Greeks laid stress.

Indeed no one can read the account of the games in the Iliad (Ψ), or that of the courts of Alcinous and of Menelaus in the Odyssey, without being greatly struck with the gentleness and grace of the ideal life portrayed by the Homeric poets. The modern betting man will be surprised to see the open and gentlemanly way in which the races and other contests were conducted. Of course there was a little jostling, and some cheating, especially on the part of the gods who befriended each competitor; but then we find a man's word believed that he had no unfair intention—a piece of open dealing which would hardly answer among the *habitués* of our race-courses. Above all, the conduct of Achilles is marked throughout by the finest and kindliest feeling ; indeed, in no other part of the poem does he appear to nearly such advantage.

The court of Menelaus is a worthy counterpart to this picture. No doubt this hero is always represented in a very favourable point of view socially, and Helen is acknowledged to have charms not only of person, but of intellect, beyond all other women, so that this court may be regarded as the poet's ideal of refinement and politeness. But admitting this, we must also admit that the ideal is very high. There is nothing inferior to the tone of society in our best circles in this picture. The presence of Helen among the company, her luxurious elegance, her quick tact and ability—all these features show how fully the poets appreciated the influence of female society in softening the rude manners of the pugnacious heroes. So at the court of Alcinous we are especially introduced to Queen Arete (η 66 sqq.) as a lady honoured by her husband above the honour given to other ladies by their husbands, and greeted with kindly words by her people whenever she went out through the city, 'for she was not wanting in good sense and discretion, and acted as a peacemaker, allaying the quarrels of men.'

We have thus been passing insensibly from the Homeric hero's treatment of his fellows, to his treatment of the ladies of his family. The cases I have already cited show how high was the position of married women in the royal houses. The charming portrait of the Princess Nausicaa corresponds with it perfectly—and in all these ladies' habits we find the greatest liberty of demeanour, and all absence of silly jealousy on the part of their relatives. Arete, as we have just seen, was in the habit of going, apparently on foot[1], through her city. Nausicaa thinks that if her gossiping townsmen see her passing through the streets with so handsome a stranger as Ulysses, they will at once set him down as her intended husband, and censure her behind backs for despising all her Phæacian suitors. And when Ulysses has apparently forgotten her, and she feels somewhat heartsore about him, she does not think it unmaidenly to lie in wait for him where he cannot pass her, and gently cast up to him that though now honoured and courted by all the nation, yet to her he once owed his rescue from want and hunger. These and many other passages show that the Homeric ladies enjoyed a liberty unknown in good society at Athens, though perhaps allowed in other parts of Greece; and it will be a question for special discussion hereafter, why the Athenians, of all Greeks, retrograded most from the higher attitude of the epic age. More especially, the abduction of Helen and the seduction of Clytemnestra seem to imply a very free intercourse among the sexes, even to admit of such attempts being made. From this point of view Æschylus felt with a true instinct the independent and free attitude of a reign-

---

[1] στείχῃσ' ἀνὰ ἄστυ. η 72.

ing queen when her husband was from home. So
Penelope entertains even wandering strangers, and
has long interviews with them, in the hope of hearing
of Ulysses, and there was nothing unseemly in doing
so. Sophocles, in his dialogues between Clytemnestra
and Electra[1], was misled by the customs of his own
day, and did not feel the epic freedom of women sufficiently. It is also important to note that this liberty
was not the privilege of the higher classes, as might
possibly be supposed ; for a remarkable simile[2] says,
'Why should we now revile one another, like women
who in some angry quarrel go into the middle of the
street and abuse each other with reproaches both true
and false?' We shall find the same license implied
in many of the lyric poets.

But I do not feel at all sure whether the very mild
censure expressed against infidelity is to be regarded
as a trustworthy reflex of the morals of the times.
No doubt the painful facts which I have noticed
above (p. 31) must have blunted the moral sense of
men on these delicate relations. Though we now-
a-days rate personal purity so highly, that the loss
of it by misfortune is hardly less excused by society
than its abandonment through passion, yet in the
Homeric times, when the compulsory infidelity of a
wife as a prisoner of war was openly recognised, and
in no way reprehended, this callous attitude may
have reflected its influence upon cases of voluntary
sin, and so they came to be regarded with much in-

---

[1] ἀνειμένη μὲν, ὡς ἔοικας, αὖ στρέφει. Soph. *Elect.* v. 516.

[2] Υ 251 : cf. σ 27, in support of it.

dulgence. All this is possible, and may be allowed, I think, some weight. So also the open concubinage allowed to married men often afforded a plea for retaliation, and a justification in the case of crime.

But yet, after all these allowances, I think we must still consider the most important reason for the apparent leniency with which the adultery of princesses is regarded to be the poet's own social position, and the audience before whom he sang. Doubtless noble ladies were present at his songs; he owed to their favour many precious gifts, and perhaps a comfortable retreat in the precincts of the palace. It was necessary then to treat them, as he does the kings, with peculiar leniency, and to set down their delinquencies to the special temptations of the gods, rather than to their own wickedness.

It was, I think, for this part of his audience that the poet inserted the list of celebrated ladies whom Ulysses met in the lower regions. I hardly think the male part of the audience felt sufficient interest in them. If they did, it would be an additional proof of the prominence of noble ladies in their society, and of the celebrity which a lady of exceptional beauty and rank might attain. There can be no doubt that this passage was very similar to the fuller catalogue of female worthies known as the 'Hoîαι and ascribed to Hesiod.

Despite all that the advocates of Homeric morals may say, we but seldom find throughout the poems a really strong reprobation of Helen's adultery, even in her own mind[1]. She is never spoken of by others as disgraced in the eyes of men, she is never regarded as a castaway, or unfit to return to her position in Menelaus' palace. If she had not caused bloodshed and misery by the Trojan war, I see little reason to think that her crime would have been regarded much more seriously than that of Aphrodite in the lay of Demodocus.

The treatment of Clytemnestra is, I think, equally lenient, if we consider her more violent character, and that she added the crime of murder to her adultery (γ 263 sqq.). She is specially said to have been of a good disposition, and to have stood firm as long as the old bard whom Agamemnon had left in charge of her was there to advise her. The shade of Agamemnon of course (in λ) speaks more sharply; but the advice put into his mouth shows how strong was the influence and intimate the relation of married women as regards their husbands: 'Take care not to speak your whole mind to your wife, but keep back something'—an advice which is sometimes given in the present day by people who pretend to be practical men, and who have never heard of Agamemnon. Noble ladies then came strictly within the limits of the exclusive caste, they were treated with courtesy, and even too great leniency, and occupied a very important position in aristocratic society.

The very same remark will hold good of the ser-

[1] Some of my generous critics (in the *Academy* and *Saturday Review*) pointed out that I had expressed myself too strongly on this point in my former edition. I have accordingly qualified what I there said.

vants attached to noble houses. They were often, as we are told, children of good birth, brought up with the children of the family, after they had been bought from the vagrant pirates who had kidnapped them. In fact, there appears to have been no traffic such as afterwards existed, which brought slaves of inferior races, usually Thracians and Syrians, into Greek ports. There was, in Homer's day, no feeling of shame at enslaving other Greeks; nor, indeed, had the Greeks separated themselves in idea from other nations under the title of Hellenes. So the slave was, or at least might be, socially his master's equal; and I think the bards take pains to tell us that those who distinguished themselves by fidelity to their masters were, after all, of no common origin (like the wretched day-labourers who worked for hire), but were really, though lowered by misfortune, members of the same caste society of which I am now speaking.

These confidential servants were, perhaps, exceptions; for we find the faithlessness of the mass of Ulysses' household coupled (ρ 319) with the general reflection 'that Zeus takes away half a man's virtue in the day that slavery comes upon him.' If we wish, however, to see the good side of the matter, we need only read what is told of Euryclea, and of Eumæus the swineherd, to see how thoroughly they belonged to the family, and felt with it against the lower domestics. Eumæus tells the disguised Ulysses the history of his life, and of his intimate relations to Laertes and Anticlea. He speaks with gratitude of the comfortable position which he holds, but nothing

can compensate for the exile in which his circumstances have placed him. He longs to see his old
patrons, to talk with them, be entertained by them,
and to carry back to his country home some token of
their affection in the shape of a present [1]. Euryclea,
who plays a leading part through the poem, is clearly
one of the mainstays of the house, and so self-devoted
in her conduct that we feel hurt with Ulysses as
we do nowhere else in the whole poem, when he
threatens her, should she be wanting in discretion
(τ 487). There is a curious combination of harshness
and of high feeling in this passage, which is one of
the finest in either poem. The old nurse, recognising
him suddenly by his scar, lets everything fall, and the
bath pours over the floor. Overcome by a burst of
mingled joy and grief, she cries out and looks round
to Penelope, whose eyes are darkened, and her mind
distracted by Athene that she may not perceive it.
Ulysses seizes her by the throat, and whispers vehemently: 'Nurse, why will you destroy me—you
that nursed me at your breast—now that I am come
home a wayworn sufferer after twenty years? But
since god has allowed you to recognise me, silence!
and let no one in the house know it, (for if you
do) I solemnly declare that I shall not spare you,
though you are my nurse, when I am putting to
death the other handmaids in my house.' And she
answers: 'Child, how could you say such a thing?
you know how staunch is my resolve, and that I shall
keep the secret, like some hard stone or mass of iron.

---

[1] Not a keepsake, as I have already explained.

But when the day of vengeance comes, I can tell you who are the women that are dishonouring your house.' He answers: 'Nurse, why should *you* tell of them? 'tis not your business, I shall find them out for myself. Keep you silent, and leave it to the gods.' Such slaves differed in social standing but little from the free attendants (ὀτρηροὶ θεράποντες), who held a very honourable position in the retinue of the chiefs, just as well-bred gentlemen and men of respectability are now not ashamed to perform menial duties at the courts of kings and governors.

As I have touched upon the slave-nurse in the Odyssey, I will for completeness sake, cite another very ideal description of a hired nurse from the hymn to Demeter, more especially since this beautiful poem is almost unknown to, or neglected by, our Greek scholars [1]. Although the date of this poem may be later than the Odyssey, it breathes the true spirit of the epic age, and reflects epic social life. I must abridge the passage considerably, and therefore premise that the following paraphrase gives a very inadequate notion of the original. But this is so markedly the case with all translations from Greek, with or without abridgment, that the translator's despair almost makes him callous.

The goddess is described (vv. 92, sqq.) as departing in bitter wrath from the assembly of the gods, because they would not restore her lost Persephone. 'And

---

[1] It was indeed altogether lost till its discovery in a single MS. at Moscow in the last century. I had the privilege of handling this precious relic at Leyden, where it is now preserved.

she came to the cities of men and their rich farms,
disguising her form a long time, nor did any mortal
recognise her, till she reached the house of the warlike
Celeus, who was lord of Eleusis.   And she sat by the
way, grieved in her inmost heart, at the Parthenian
well, whence the citizens drew water, in the shade
of an olive that grew above her head; and her form
was like an aged crone, who is past child-bearing
and the gifts of wreathed Aphrodite, such as are the
nurses of the children of ruling princes, and have
charge of their echoing mansions.   Her did the
daughters of Celeus see as they came for water, that
they might bear it in pitchers of brass to the house of
their father.'   'And standing near they addressed her:
Who art thou, aged woman, and why dost thou keep
away from the city, and not go among the houses,
where there are many women through the chambers
both old, as thou art, and younger, who will friendly
entreat thee in word and deed?'   So the goddess,
professing to tell them the strict truth, invents a fable
about her own history.   'Thus I came here in my
wanderings, nor do I know what land this is, or who
be the men that dwell therein.   But may the gods
give you youthful husbands, and to bear children,
as parents desire, so pity me, that I may come to the
house of some man or woman, where I may do for
them diligently the work which an aged woman can
perform.   Well could I carry in my arms a young
child, and nurse it, and take charge of a house; and
I could make the bed of my masters in the recess
of their chamber, and teach their work to the maids.'

The eldest maiden, Callidice, answers her courteously that her mother, or any of her three aunts, would doubtless be very ready to engage her. 'Not one of these would despise thy looks at first sight, and send thee away, but receive thee, for thou art indeed like unto a goddess. But if thou wilt, wait till we go home, and tell all to our mother, Metaneira ; perhaps she will ask thee to come to us, and not seek a place in the houses of others. For she has a late born son in the house, the child of many prayers, and much loved. Wert thou to nurse him through his infancy, and if he attain maturity, well mightest thou be the envy of other women, such wages would she give thee.'

So they fill their pitchers and hurry home, and their mother bids them run and fetch her without limiting wages. 'And they like fawns gambolling through a spring meadow, rushed down the hollow way, holding up the folds of their lovely garments, and their hair waved about their shoulders like saffron-coloured bloom. And they found her by the road, where they had left her, and brought her home,' wrapped up, and covered from head to foot, so that her dark robe clung to her as she walked. She is received by Metaneira, who is nursing her boy, and who is awe-struck by her dignity. But she repeats the promise held out by the maidens, if she will rear the child. To this the goddess consents, adding that she knows means of averting charms and evil eye ; and she proceeds to feed him upon ambrosia, and at night to prepare him for immortality by putting him, like a billet of wood, into the heat of the fire. But Metaneira, who was watching to see how the child was made to thrive so marvellously, sees him in the fire, and cries out in anguish; 'so Demeter in wrath dropped the dear child whose birth had surprised the house upon the ground,' and bursts out upon Metaneira, declares herself, and changing into her proper majesty, passes through the chamber, and vanishes. The mother sinks speechless to the ground, ' nor did she think of lifting the child of her later years from the ground. But his sisters heard his piteous voice, and started from their beds, and one taking up the child hugged him in her lap, another kindled the fire, the third ran barefooted and raised up her mother. And they bathed and nursed the gasping child, but could not quiet him, for far inferior nurses now tended him.'

It will be seen from this picture that, in the days of this Hymn, hired nurses were employed, as well as slaves; and also that the position of such a nurse was closely similar to that of Euryclea in the Odyssey. She had a very different social rank from the out-door hired labourer, and seems quite adopted as one of the intimate dependants of the ruling caste, so enjoying many comforts and privileges.

Even the animals, such as horses and dogs, which were attached to the Homeric chief, enjoyed their privileges accordingly. The horses of Achilles, with their human sympathies and their human voice, remind us of Balaam's ass, and her friendly relations with the prophet. Indeed, throughout the whole

Iliad, the poets seem to be full of sympathy with the energy and fire of the war-horses. In the Odyssey the dog Argus takes the place of the horses of Achilles. The island was rugged, as Telemachus says to Menelaus, when he offered him a chariot and pair as a present, and chariot-driving was consequently not in fashion. But the dogs, chosen for both speed and scent, the faithful companions of the young men in hunting, must have been as highly esteemed as they are now, and they must have attained, through constant intercourse with human society, that intelligence which now makes certain breeds so interesting. The wonderful picture of the old broken-down hound recognising his master after twenty years, and dying of joy on the dunghill, where he had lain helpless with age and neglect—this affecting trait could never have been drawn except by men who themselves knew and loved dogs, and appreciated their intelligence.

I can show even more cogent proof in a phrase not observed by the commentators. When Telemachus (β 11) sets out, in full state, for the public assembly in Ithaca, where he is to appear for the first time, and declare his wrongs, the poet describes him as proceeding '*not alone*, for two sharp-toothed dogs accompanied him.' It is quite true that to us a dog is a real companion, and we hardly feel ourselves alone if the trusty comrade of our sports is with us; but still even we should hardly say, ' I met such an one walking yesterday. He was not alone, for he had his dog with him.' So the wild beasts

of Circe are compared (κ 216) to 'the dogs that fawn
about a chief coming from his dinner [it appears they
were not allowed into the house], for he never forgets
to bring them morsels that delight them.' Notwithstanding, there is a passage which describes the dogs
of the swineherd Eumæus in exactly the terms in
which our sporting men describe the fierce dogs of
the same coast and country which they meet when
shooting. The Epirot shepherds will not call them
off; they are very savage, and if strangers kill them
all the country rises up in arms. Eumæus, when the
dogs rush out at the ragged Ulysses, is obliged to
run out and pelt them with stones to drive them off,
and observes that had he not been there to do so the
stranger would have been roughly treated. This is
the lower side of the Homeric dogs. The highest side
is the passage where they, by their instinct, recognise Athene as present, and cower in fear, while their
masters are unconscious of her presence (π 162), again
reminding us strongly of the story of Balaam's ass.

This sympathy for the lower animals reaches even
farther. The monster Polyphemus, who had no dogs,
and who neither feared god nor regarded man, shows
no trace of friendliness, or of any humane feeling,
except in his pathetic address to his ram, who had
been detained last by Ulysses, instead of leading out
the flock from the cave of the Cyclops as usual. The
blinded savage pours out his griefs to the animal,
which he thinks affected by his master's misfortune,
and longs that the ram had a voice to tell him the
hiding-place of the miscreants who had deprived him

of his sight. We shall meet again this sympathy, with dogs at least, in later Greek history.

What consideration those received who lived apart from the reigning caste, or made themselves obnoxious to it, appears painfully enough in the Homeric poems and in Hesiod. If we consider the punishment of his rebellious household by Ulysses, or the fate threatened to Irus by the suitors[1], if he declines to fight with Ulysses, we see what treatment rebellion or disobedience met at their hands. The Greeks were always a passionate people, and wreaked fierce vengeance to satisfy their wrath. Thus men did not abstain altogether from mutilation of the living; thus Achilles keeps insulting the dead body of his foe, and thus even queens desire to eat the raw flesh of their enemies.

But the utterance of Achilles in the nether world is still more remarkable on the position of the poor, who were unattached to the houses of the great. 'Talk not to me,' says the hero, 'of honours among the dead; I would rather be a hired servant on earth, and that to a poor man, than rule as a king among the shades.' In other words, I had rather choose the most wretched existence conceivable on earth than rule beneath[2]. Accordingly the hired

---

[1] σ 83. They threaten to send him in a ship to king Echetus, the general mutilator of men (βροτῶν δηλήμονα πάντων), who will cut off his nose and ears and other extremities. This personage is twice again mentioned with the same epithet, and in similar connection. We have no farther information as to his intention, or why this brutality was tolerated.

[2] βουλοίμην κ' ἐπάρουρος ἐὼν θητευέμεν ἄλλῳ

servants (θῆτες) of poor farmers are selected for this
distinction. Is not this hint thoroughly borne out
by the state of things we meet in Hesiod? If the
poor-farmer class, though personally free, had such
a hard life as he describes, how wretched must have
been the hired servant, whom the poet recommends
his hearers to turn out as soon as the press of farm
work was over[1]. There must, then, have been an
abundance of such servants, since they could be
again procured at pleasure, and we can conceive
how miserable must have been their pay and lodging
on Hesiod's farm.

But the poet Hesiod himself had no enviable days.
And of all his griefs, undoubtedly the foremost was
a patent fact seldom alluded to by the polite Homeric bards[2]—the gross injustice of the chiefs in

> ἀνδρὶ παρ' ἀκλήρῳ, ᾧ μὴ βίοτος πολὺς εἴη,
>
> ἢ πᾶσιν νεκύεσσι καταφθιμένοισιν ἀνάσσειν. λ 489.

It is worth while to suggest as a parallel picture the γυνὴ χερνῆτις
ἀληθὴς of M 433, who, by toiling night and day, earns an ἀείκεα μίσθον,
miserable wages, wherewith to feed her starving orphans. She is described just as we should describe the most oppressed sempstress,
striving to rival with worn-out fingers the machine which she has no
means to buy.

[1] I adopt Grote's rendering of the words θῆτα ἄοικον ποιεῖσθαι in
preference to that of Göttling and others. Cf. a similar expression in
Sophocles, Œd. Rex, 1029, ἐπὶ θητείᾳ πλάνης.

[2] There is only one definite allusion, that in Π 384, where the onset
of Hector is compared to the dreadful torrents sent in late autumn by
Zeus to punish the men who by sheer might decide crookedly in the
agora and banish justice, not reverencing the gods. The very phrases
used are so thoroughly Hesiodic as to suggest to sceptics the rejection
of the passage from the Iliad. I can see no reason for doing so, especially
as the allusion is perfectly general, and could not be taken by any noble

deciding lawsuits, and their readiness to devour bribes. The fable he adduces ("Ἔργ. 184) implies plainly enough that they felt a supreme contempt for the lower classes and their feelings; they openly proclaimed the law of might, and ridiculed the lamentations of the ill-used and injured husbandman. The repeated reminder to the people of Ithaca that Ulysses had not thus treated them, but had been considerate to them as a father, almost implies that he was exceptional in his justice. And indeed what could we expect from a society which regarded the Pallas Athene of the Iliad and Odyssey as its ideal of intellect and virtue? But in Homer we see only the good side (if we except the Ithacan suitors, who are described as quite exceptional); in Hesiod we are shown only the bad side. The wretched farmer looked on the whole class of aristocrats as unjust and violent men, that cared not at all about his rights and his interests.

Perhaps if we strike an average or balance, we shall obtain a fair view of the real state of things in these old days. Possibly the aristocrats who managed the states after the abolition of monarchy in Bœotia were worse than the single kings; for we know now-a-days that boards and parliaments have neither conscience nor human feeling, so that they commit injustices almost impossible to individuals, and moreover they are deaf to the appeal that touches

hearer as a personal reflection. But as heavy autumn rains were an ordinary phenomenon, so I believe the crime which they punished to have been ordinary also.

a single heart. But it is surely a certain proof of the
antiquity of Hesiod's poems, and perhaps the most
hopeless feature in his difficulties, that there seems no
redress possible for the injustice of the nobles, except
the interference of the gods whose duty it is to punish
wrong among men[1]. The poet insists that the gods
do see these things, and that they will interfere ;
but this very insisting, coupled with the desponding
tone of the whole book, lets us see plainly what was
the general feeling of the lower classes. For as to
obtaining help from public opinion of any sort, even
from the χαλεπὴ δήμου φῆμις (ξ 239) of Homer, or the
grumbling in the ἀγόρα to which Telemachus appeals—
there is no trace of it. The earnest and deeply outraged husbandman never dreams of a revolution, of
calling the assembly to declare its anger, or even of
enlisting some of the chiefs against the rest. It speaks
well for the sterner and sounder qualities of the Bœotian farmers that such circumstances did not induce
despair, but rather a stern resolve to avoid the wicked
judgment-seats of the aristocrats, above all things to
keep clear of litigation, and to seek the comforts of

[1] So again in Hom. (A 142 and π 384 sq.) and Hes. Ἔργ. 260, the
people have to suffer *en masse* for the king's crimes; this is recognised
far more bluntly by the kings in recovering gifts and extravagances from
their people (cf. Ameis on ξ 81). The principle of the people paying
for the waste of kings was exemplified even in English history not very
long ago; and as to people suffering for their rulers, it not only appears
in later Greek authors, such as Pindar, Pyth. xii. 12, but (of course) in
Oriental nations, such as the Jews, where plagues are openly sent on
David's people because he chose to number them (2 Sam. 24). This
is perhaps the most explicit example to be found in early history.

hard-earned bread and of intelligent husbandry. This, then, is the isolated position of the works of Hesiod —the poet of the Helots—of which I have spoken already.

And yet in the moral parts of his writings the Greeks of later ages found much that was attractive. The 'Works and Days' became even an ordinary handbook of education. This fact will not surprise us, when we consider that in one broad feature the moral lessons of Hesiod run parallel with the pictures of Homer, in this the exponent of the most permanent features in Greek character—I mean that combination of religion and shrewdness, that combination of the *honestum* and the *utile*[1], which, though it often jars upon us, yet saved the Greeks, one and all, from sentimentality, from bombast, and from hypocrisy. The king Ulysses and the farmer Hesiod have the same respect for the gods, and the same 'eye to business,' the same good nature and the same selfishness, the same honour and the same meanness. Perhaps the king was laxer in his notions of truth than the husbandman; just as the Cavalier thought less of lying than the Roundhead. But perhaps this arose from his greater proximity to the gods of the

---

[1] I have perhaps spoken too favourably of Hesiod's ethics in the text, seeing that an appeal to pure justice only takes its place in regard of the high-handed violence of the nobles. In all the rest of his book, and especially throughout his ethical maxims, the *utile*, the πλείστη χάρις as he calls it, is the only sanction applied to actions. This cannot be asserted of Homer, or even of Theognis in later days. There are some good remarks on this subject in Steitz' Hesiod.

epic poets, who had no difficulty at all in practising falsehood.

In another point, however, the king, owing to his manifold pursuits and interests, escaped a grave danger. No ambition whatever lay open to Hesiod and his fellows, save the making of money, and laying up stores of wealth, as he says (686), χρήματα γὰρ ψυχὴ πέλεται δειλοῖσι βρότοισι [1]. In those depraved days, when a verdict could be bought under any circumstances from the corrupt chiefs, money was power, even to a greater extent than in more civilised conditions. Hence the natural tendency among the lower classes must have been to postpone everything to the amassing of wealth—nay, rather, there was no other occupation open to them. So we find that both Tyrtæus and Solon, early poets and political reformers, set down φιλοχρηματίη as the real cause of the disorders in their respective states [2]. The same tendency is plain enough in king Ulysses and shows itself even ludicrously in the midst of the deepest melancholy and the greatest danger; as, for example, when he finds himself cast upon a desolate shore and abandoned (ν 215), and when he

---

[1] When I speak of money I do not prejudge the question whether coined money was in use in Hesiod's day. Probably not; but the precious metals in their rude state, or worked into cups, answered the purpose equally well. Men had got beyond the stage of counting their wealth exclusively by sheep and oxen, and by changes of raiment.

[2] So Theognis bitterly exclaims (v. 699), 'the mass of men know but one virtue—to be rich':—

> πλήθει δ' ἀνθρώπων ἀρέτη μία γίνεται ἥδε
> πλουτεῖν.

sees Penelope drawing gifts from the suitors: but his lofty and varied sphere of action forces it back into a subordinate place. Yet I would have the reader note this feature carefully, as we shall meet it again in many forms throughout later Greek society.

There is another point on which Hesiod is vastly inferior in social attitude to Homer; I mean in his estimate of women. But the plain-spoken bard was not singing at courts, where queens sat by and longed to hear of worthies of their own sex; nor did he contemplate the important duties of the house-mother in the absence of her husband in wars and on the service of his state. Hence it was that Æschylus, though living in a democracy where women fared badly enough, yet found and felt in the epic poets such characters as his Clytemnestra, a reigning queen, invested with full powers in the king's absence—free to discuss public affairs, to receive embassies, and act as her judgment directed her. All these things were foreign to Hesiod's attitude; yet surely it is strange that in describing farm life and farm duties, he should not have thought more of the important duties of the house-wife—duties which throughout all Greek and Roman history raised the position of the country-woman above that of the towns-woman, whose duties were less important, and whom the jealousy of city life compelled to live in fear and darkness[1]. Yet the first allusion in the 'Works and Days' is rude

---

[1] εἰθισμένον δεδοικὸς καὶ σκοτεινὸν ζῆν is Plato's expression.

enough : 'You must start with a house, a wife, and
an ox to plough, and have your farming implements
ready in the house[1].' There is, I believe, no farther
notice of the woman till the short advice concerning
marriage; and here too nothing is stranger than the
brevity with which the subject is noticed, and the
total silence concerning the all‑important duties
which even Homer's princesses performed, and which
were certainly in the hands of the women of Hesiod's
acquaintance. We might almost imagine that some
sour Attic editor had expunged the advice which
Hesiod owes us on the point, and had justified him‑
self with the famous apophthegm of Pericles (or
rather of Thucydides), that 'that woman is best who
is least spoken of among men, either for good or
for evil.' Hesiod implies, indeed, that a man may
know something of the young women in the neigh‑
bourhood, and this supposes some freedom of inter‑
course; yet he seems to consider the worst feature
of a bad wife her desire to sit at meals with her
husband, an opinion which in his age, and his plain
and poor society, seems very harsh indeed[2].

However, then, I may be accused of having drawn
Homeric society in darker colours than it deserves,
though I have given authority for every charge, yet

[1] Of course Aristotle's authority is decisive for the meaning of the
verse (375), οἶκον μὲν πρώτιστα, γυναῖκά τε, βοῦν τ' ἀροτῆρα, as well as
for the spuriousness of the false commentary added in the next line.

[2] I am not satisfied with the epithet δειπνολόχου (649), or with the
rendering of the old Commentators, and think some corruption must
have crept into the text, though the MSS. do not vary except in the
termination, and the editors seem satisfied.

on the Hesiodic society all intelligent students of
the 'Works and Days' are pretty well agreed. It
pictures a hopeless and miserable existence, in which
care, and the despair of better things, tended to
make men hard and selfish, and to blot out those
fairer features which cannot be denied to the courts
and palaces of the Iliad and Odyssey. So great, indeed, is the contrast, that most critics have assumed
a change of things between the states described
in Homer and in Hesiod; they have imagined that
the gaiety and splendour of the epic bard could
not have coexisted with the sorrows and the meanness of the moral teacher. But both tradition and
internal evidence should convince us that these poems,
if not strictly contemporaneous, are yet proximate
enough in date to be considered *socially* pictures
of the same times, differing, as I have explained,
in the attitude of the poets, but not in the men
and the manners which gave them birth [1]. If so,
Hesiod has told us what the poor man thought

---

[1] The usual theory makes the authors of the Iliad and Odyssey
Asiatic Greeks, living among the Ionians, though of Æolian extraction.
If this were so, the contrasts of Asiatic luxury and Greek poverty might
be brought in to explain the striking differences between the two poets.
For we know that the Asiatic Greeks attained to wealth and luxury
long before their brethren in Greece. Mr. Gladstone, however, in the
Contemporary Review for June 1874, contends earnestly that Homer
composed his poems in Greece, and both Sengebusch and Professor
Geddes assert it of the earliest part of the poems. To any who may
adopt this theory, my argument in the text will be even more pointed,
and the contrast more remarkable, between the refinement of the noble
and the rudeness of the peasant, in immediate contact throughout the
same, or adjoining, districts.

and felt, while the Homeric poet pictured how kings
and ladies ought, in his opinion, to have lived and
loved. And with all the contrasts, I think we can
see conclusively that the fundamental features were
the same, and that they were the legitimate seed
from which sprang the Greeks of historic times.

I may add, in conclusion, that this great contrast
between the fair exterior and the misery and injustice
within, though it has been now put very strongly in
the case of the Greeks, was not peculiar to them, but
has probably existed in all history where a favoured
caste has ruled in its own interest, and to the exclusion of the general mass of the people. It was so
in ancient Egypt, it was so in ancient India—indeed,
in India at all times,—and it was so in mediæval
Europe.

But in most of these cases the stronger classes
write their own history and sing their own praises,
while the wrongs and troubles of the poor transpire
but rarely and by accident. So, the miseries of the
old Egyptian poor are only transmitted to us by the
boasts of reckless kings, who so loved their own
glory, and to magnify their deeds, that they confessed
the ruthless waste of human life with which they
completed their eternal monuments. And again, the
letter of a scribe has reached us, calling on a friend
to embrace a literary life, and contrasting the poverty
and the oppression under which the farming class suffered, with the comforts of his own calling[1]. These
chance pieces of evidence lay open to us great social

[1] Cf. my *Prolegom. to Anc. Hist.*, p. 327.

sores, great sorrows of humanity covered with a surface of unjust and heartless splendour. Can we imagine that in the Middle Ages, in the days of trouba-
dours and tournaments, of moated castles and rich
abbeys, when the rude baron and the wily abbot
divided the spoil—that the lower strata of society
fared in proportion? and can we imagine them sharing the splendour and the refinement told in old
romances and ballads? I need not speak of persecuted races like the Jews, who were so barbarously
treated that injustice towards them lost its very meaning to their oppressors, who have vaunted their own
rapine and murder as the execution of Divine commands, and as the spreading of the gospel of mercy
through the world. But even in the case of the poor
and the unprotected, the orphan and the widow, the
sick and the destitute, it is but too certain that all
the earth was full of violence; and that hearts were
broken and honour trampled in the dust with little
compassion, when no law was found to punish transgression.

Feudal times may be brilliant, they may produce
both sentiment and heroism in the baron; to the boor
they are days of turmoil and misery, of uncertain and
scanty comfort, of certain oppression and wrong.
What are the social pictures drawn of these times in
the novels of Sir Walter Scott—books which contain
more and truer history than most of the dry annals
professing to be such? Consider *Ivanhoe*, or *Quentin
Durward*, or the *Fair Maid of Perth*, are they not all
darkened with the cry of the poor for justice and

mercy, while the rich and powerful are made by the
novelist only to suffer the punishments which they
escaped in real life? These things should moderate
our contempt for the Homeric Greeks, even though I
have stripped off the husk, and shown the bitterness
of the fruit within. They were unjust and cruel and
coarse below the surface; but so were our ancestors,
ay, within a century of to-day. After all it is the
democratic spirit — vulgar, unsentimental, litigious
spirit that it is—which first overthrew this feudalism
in the world; and which, in ancient Greece, in Rome,
and in the Europe of to-day, has redressed social
grievances, forbidden injustice, and punished violence
and wrong.

CHAPTER IV.

THE GREEKS OF THE LYRIC AGE.

WHEN we pass the great gap that separates Homeric from historical Greece we find ourselves in presence of a very different type of literary men. The tooth of time has eaten their works into fragments. We can find no continuous picture, no complete sketch of life, in these scanty remnants; but still there is a something in the briefest of them that speaks to us in a different tone from that of the smooth and courtly rhapsodists. The lyric poets had lost interest in old kings and byegone glories; they wrote about the present, they told about themselves, they spoke out the plain truth. We can see in the earliest of them, such as Archilochus, a clear reaction against the perpetual singing of antique glory, and the false palliation of heroic crimes. 'Had not the poet himself told us,' says an old writer[1], 'we should never have known that he was the son of a slave, and that he was driven from his country (Paros) by poverty and want, to Thasos, where he became

[1] Critias, quoted by Ælian, in Bergk, *Fragg. Lyric. Græc.* p. 724, from which I quote throughout.

very unpopular; nor should we have known that he abused friends and foes alike, nor that he was an adulterer, except from his own words, nor that he was sensual and insolent, nor, worst of all[1], that he threw away his shield. Archilochus, therefore, was no good witness concerning himself.'

And yet this poet was unanimously placed by the Greeks next to Homer in popularity. We are, therefore, no longer in the presence of Greek Spensers and Miltons, who forgot themselves and their age to sing about gods and heroes, but in the presence of a Greek Byron, who not only applied his transcendent genius to satirise the men and the social laws of his own time, but who flaunted before the world the worst passages of an evil life, and, as a *fanfaron de vices*, gloried in violating the holiest obligations which restrain ordinary men in every civilised community. The same outspokenness, though it did not reach the same extremes, marks the fragments of Alcæus, of Sappho, of Theognis, and of Solon. They stand totally apart in spirit from the old rhapsodists, and in contact with the moderns. They were strict realists in their art, not approaching the ideal save in the hymns they composed for the public worship of the gods.

The self-assertion of cowardice in so many of these poets is a feature well worth noticing more particularly. Not only have we the evidence just quoted about Archilochus, but Herodotus (v. 95), and afterwards Strabo (xiii. 600), tell us a similar story of Alcæus, who actually wrote a poem to a friend, and

---

[1] Observe this Greek gradation of crimes.

published it, detailing how he had thrown away his shield in battle, and how the Athenians, with whom he had fought, had hung it up as a trophy in Sigeum. We are not surprised, when such statements were made by turbulent and warlike poets, to find allusions in the fragments of Anacreon which seem to point to some similar story (*frags.* 29, 30). I argued above (p. 21) that the Greeks were not a courageous nation, in the sense now accepted, and I think these additional pieces of evidence, from a later age, corroborate what I have said. The attitude of Pindar towards war is quite similar to that of other Greek poets. His style and subject-matter do not admit of confessions like those of Archilochus and Alcæus. He says (*frag.* 74) that only the inexperienced love war; a sentiment likely enough to be strongly felt in the days of the disastrous, though glorious, Persian invasion, just as we often heard it expressed by German soldiers and officers after the late war in France. But still it is evidence of a feeling in Pindar different from, and more modern than, the valour of the knight-errant and the crusader.

Plato, in his *Laws*[1], has a very Greek theory to account for the decay of valour in modern times, as compared with the valour of the ideal Homeric hero and the old Spartan citizen. He notices that the Athenians were subject to Minos[2], and obliged to pay him a tribute of human lives, because he pos-

[1] Jowett, vol. iv. p. 227.
[2] This is probably the mythical account of the old Phœnician supremacy in the Greek waters. Cf. above, p. 16.

sessed a naval power, and they did not. 'Better for them,' he adds,. 'to have lost many times over the seven youths, than that heavy-armed and stationary troops should have been turned into sailors, and accustomed to leap quickly on shore, and again to hurry back to their ships'; or should have fancied that there was no disgrace in not awaiting the attack of an enemy and dying boldly; and that there were good reasons, and many of them, for a man throwing away his arms, and betaking himself to flight, which is affirmed upon occasion not to be dishonourable. This is the language of naval warfare, and is anything but worthy of extraordinary praise. For we should not teach bad habits, least of all to the best part of the citizens. You may learn the evil of such a practice from Homer, by whom Odysseus is introduced, rebuking Agamemnon, because he desires to draw down the ships to the sea at a time when the Achæans are hard pressed. 'For,' says he, 'the Achæans will not maintain the battle, when the ships are drawn into the sea, but they will look behind and cease from strife.' You see that he quite knew triremes on the sea, in the neighbourhood of fighting men, to be an evil; lions might be trained in that way to fly from a herd of deer. Moreover, naval powers, which owe their safety to ships, do not honour that sort of warlike excellence which is most deserving of honour. For he who owes his safety to the pilot, and the captain, and the oarsman, and all sorts of rather good-for-nothing persons, cannot rightly give honour to whom honour is due.

Plato has not the smallest notion of real sailor courage, such as we have inherited from the Norsemen ; he does not know that such courage may be higher than that of any landsman, for he only had before him the wretched coasting and plundering sea warfare of the Greeks. His evidence, however, on the small valour of the Greek marine is most valuable.

But to return : there are ample historical reasons to account for the blunt realism of the lyric poets. The main interests of the Hellenic nation, after the wars and adventures occasioned by their colonising epoch had passed away, were centred not on foreign affairs, or external wars, but on the internal conflicts of their cities. The great social struggle between the higher and lower classes had commenced, and so the aristocracy became naturally separated in most of the cities into close factions, with common interests and common principles of action. The early lyric poets, as a class, were members of this society, and spoke as equals to intimate equals, not as paid inferiors to please their employers, till the epoch of the tyrants came, when a few of the later lyrists fell back socially into a position somewhat analogous to the rhapsodists. Since these things are so, the scanty and dislocated lyric fragments are worth far more, historically, than the more consecutive but more imaginary pictures of the epic poems. They disclose to us a society of men of like passions with the later Greeks, but more reckless and violent, inasmuch as men whose old privileges are for the first time attacked are more bitter than those who have become accustomed to this ungrateful reform.

When Thucydides tells us that the moral depravity so graphically described in his third book came in with the civil war, it is surprising that this assertion has been adopted by historians without large qualifications. It may possibly be true that democracies, being more thoroughly organised and firmer in their claims, began to develope these vices more manifestly at this time, but *it is plainly false to say that the Greek aristocrats did not openly act on all the principles indicated by Thucydides long before his day.* As I have already shown, even Homer's Gods and Hesiod's Iron Age possess all these disagreeable features. Were we to seek an historical illustration of the same thing, it would rather be found in the poems of Theognis (v. 1182) or Alcæus than in any other portion of Greek literature.

But we must look more to Hesiod than to Homer for the antecedents of the moral darkness of lyric Greece. We now see, not the oppressed farmer suffering from injustice and violence, yet still in awe of the divine right of his princes, but these very δωροφάγοι βασιλῆες quarrelling, as we might expect, over their ill-used privileges, and over the booty they had plundered from their people. Greek history, too, makes it plain that the lower classes did not awake spontaneously to their rights, and put forth one of themselves to vindicate and lead them ; but that the noble who failed in the struggle with his brother aristocrats—this was he who taught the δῆμος their rights, and offered to lead them against their former oppressors. The Hesiodic boor was thus awakened to his claims, and entered into the conflict with the vigour of his race. But of course he was duped by his leader, who only wanted him as a tool, not as a friend, and who reduced both his former equals and his former supporters to one level, as soon as he was able to establish his tyranny.

Thus there arose a certain phase of Greek society, called the age of the Tyrants, which has hardly received fair treatment at the hands of historians. Politically, indeed, as regards the development of written laws, and the habits of public debate, it must be regarded as an epoch of stagnation, or of retrogression in Greece; but socially and æsthetically, nay even morally, in spite of the vices of many Greek despots, I hold it to have been not only an age of progress in Greece, but even a necessary prelude to the higher life which was to follow. For if we regard carefully the attitude of Hesiod, Theognis, Alcæus, and other such poets, we shall find that in the aristocratic stage, in which the proper history of Greece opens, the degradation of the lower classes and the undisguised violence of the nobles made all approach to a proper constitution impossible. The Bœotian farmer thought that he must suffer for the sins of his princes, and never thought it possible that he should reject the responsibility. He regarded this Jove-sprung pestilence as a sort of iron necessity that brought him unavoidable suffering. In like manner the aristocrats could never endure to see the men who lived like wild beasts in skins, and were timid as deer [1], claiming privileges, and discussing rights with their noble selves. 'Between us and you there is a great gulf fixed'—this was the watchword of their policy. And so the nobles in Athens, in Megara, in Lesbos, and probably in Sparta, quarrelled among themselves with great violence, but never thought for one moment of bettering the condition of the δῆμος.

When the tyrants arose, they forced these widely separated classes into the same subjection. There is ample evidence that they systematically raised the common people, and lowered the nobles. There is equally ample evidence that they enforced order, and in some cases put down with a strong hand open immorality [2], so that cities which had been racked with revolution and violence for generations, first came to feel the blessings of a strong government, and the benefits of a peace to which they had been total strangers. This gave them time to develope commerce and to cultivate art—the latter specially encouraged by the tyrants as a class. I hold, then, that Greece, when the tyrants passed away, was in a condition vastly superior to its aristocratic age—in fact, in a condition fit to develope political life. This

---

[1] I quote this from Theognis, v. 55.

[2] This is certain from the evidence we have in the fragments of Theopompus (cf. *frag.* 252) about the tyrants of Mitylene. Curtius has an ingenious theory that the tyrants were the evidence of a mercantile Ionic reaction against the aristocratic Doric ascendancy brought about by the greatness of Sparta. This theory, if proved, does not contradict what is said in the text, but concerns the political side of a question, which I am regarding from a social point of view.

would have been impossible but for the fusion of classes and the development of culture produced by the tyrants.

One memorable example will suffice by way of illustration. What was the state of Athens when Solon arose? It had been torn by factions for years. The country was languishing. Men were weary of turmoil and confusion. At last this great genius was entrusted with the regulation of public affairs. He tells us plainly enough in extant poems that he endeavoured to lay down a fair constitution, raising the lower classes gradually, curbing the violence of the nobles, tempering all the extremes into a great whole in which all should have an interest. Here, then, was a fair and just constitution offered to a city in the pre-despotic stage. What was the result? In spite of all his efforts, in spite of his self-imposed absence, and the oath taken to avoid changes, the aristocrats could not be restrained. They openly ridiculed Solon, as he tells us, for not grasping the tyranny, in fact they could not conceive his declining to do so; even the lower classes seem not to have understood his great benefits, for the noble legislator complains, in language which still touches us across the great gulf of centuries, how he stands alone without friend or support in the state [1].

---

[1] The ridicule of his aristocratic friends appears in quotations from Solon's own poems by Plutarch in chap. xvi. of his precious *Life of Solon.* 'But his intimates more particularly depreciated him, because he thought ill of monarchy on account of its name, as if it did not forth-

It is to be observed, farther, that the lessons which he taught, and the ideas which he strove to instil into the Athenian mind, were no obscure metaphysics, no lofty flights of fancy, but the plainest homespun morality, so plain indeed that his practical lessons appear to us mere truisms. His moral attitude differs *toto cœlo* from that of Æschylus, and stands so close to that of Hesiod and Theognis, that they dispute with him the authorship of sundry reflections.

This very plain teaching, and this great moral and political pre-eminence of Solon, were nevertheless to all appearance useless. No sooner had he completed his work and left Athens, than the old strife of parties revived. His return made no change in this wretched state of things. His laws were powerless, his lessons were unheeded. He had cast his pearls before swine, and they were ready to turn again and rend him. His solution of the problem was no

with become a kingship [instead of a tyranny?] by the merit of the holder, and as they had the precedents of Tynnondas in Euboea and Pittacus in Mitylene. None of these things made Solon to swerve from his policy, but he said to his friends that a tyranny was a fair position with no escape from it. . . .' He has thus described the ridicule of those who derided him for avoiding the tyranny : 'Solon is no man of sound sense or counsel, for when God gave him a fine chance he himself would not take it; but when he had made a miraculous draught, in amazement he did not haul in the great net, through want both of spirit and of sense. He should have been well content, having got power and abundant wealth, to be tyrant of Athens for a single day, even were he then flayed alive and his race destroyed.' It is with reference to such friends that Solon speaks of himself (*frag.* 37) as a wolf worried by dogs crowding about him.

doubt theoretically excellent, but practically it was a decided failure. Peisistratus, a man of inferior genius, but of greater vigour and boldness, saw better how to solve it. Of course Peisistratus had private ends, like Julius Cæsar, like Alexander, like Napoleon. But when a great man's private ends happen to coincide with the good of the state, he ought not to lose all credit because he happens to benefit himself. There is ample evidence that Peisistratus was not only a wise but a humane and orderly ruler. Despite the violent opposition of the aged Solon, he treated him with respect, and is said to have strictly observed his laws. This shows his estimate of Solon's theory. But if he did approve of Solon's laws, he introduced the new element in which Solon was wanting. After all, the aristocrats who had ridiculed the lawgiver for not turning tyrant, had some wisdom in their taunts. Laws must not only be made, they must be enforced. Peisistratus enforced Solon's laws[1]. He was not content with laws punishing neutrality during insurrections. He insisted on peace and order in the city. He stopped by main force the perpetual political agitation which is the ruin of any commonwealth. He developed the tastes of the lower classes, giving them intellectual and social pleasures to compensate for the loss of higher but more dangerous excitement. The reading

---

[1] See the remarkable passage in Plato's *Laws*, iv. 711, in which he shows how rapidly a tyrant was able, even by merely setting the fashion, to alter the laws and customs of a state. He is distinctly of opinion that there is no other means at all so rapid and complete.

of Homer, the feasts of Dionysus, the newest lyric poems, attracted the attention of the public, and weaned them from the wild fever of conflicting rights and opposing privileges. Of course the great nobles found the change intolerable. They retired, like Miltiades, to their country mansions. They gladly left the country to found colonies, and regain as foreign princes the importance they had lost at home. Athens stood still in political training, but she gained immensely in culture. Let the reader remember that without sound intellectual culture all political training is and must be simply mischievous. A free constitution is perfectly absurd, if the opinion of the majority is incompetent. Until men are educated, they want a strong hand over them—a fact which very few in this country will be disposed to dispute. I fear it is almost hopeless to persuade English minds that a despotism may in some cases be better for a nation than a more advanced constitution. And yet no students of history can fail to observe that even now very few nations in the world are fit for diffused political privileges. These nations are so manifestly the greatest and best, and consequently the most prosperous, that inferior races keep imitating their institutions, instead of feeling that these institutions are the result and not the cause of true national greatness. Of course the result reacts upon the cause, and becomes itself a cause in due time, but only where it has grown up naturally, not where it has been superinduced artificially. Thus the attempts at democracy of the Spaniards, of the American negroes, and of all such non-political races, must for generations to come end in failure. The case of the Irish is still more remarkable. The English nation has in vain given them its laws, and even done something to enforce them. The nation will not thrive, because this is the very constitution not fit for it. I believe even a harsh despotism would be more successful, and perhaps in the end more humane.

When the Greek tyrants had done their work, the day of liberty came, and with it a great struggle, which nerved and braced the people's energies against an outward foe. The literature of free Athens shows us a perfectly new attitude. Of course it were absurd to attribute this memorable national development — the most miraculous the world has ever seen—to any single cause. A concurrent number of great causes could alone have produced such an effect. But I claim as one cause the literary culture which Athens received at the hands of Peisistratus and his sons. The hearers of Æschylus were intellectually men widely different from the hearers of Solon, nay even from the early hearers of later lyric poets, like Pindar and Simonides. There is a depth and a condensation of thought in Æschylus which would have made him perfectly unintelligible to men who appreciated the stupid saws of Hesiod and Solon, even when obscured or polished by Pindar and Simonides. The fact that Æschylus was appreciated proves that Athens had attained the intellectual culture fit for a great democracy. I believe that she owed this culture mainly to her tyrants [1].

But of course the tyrants had their bad effect on literary men, even while they promoted culture. For their position and their policy led them to encourage smoothness and elegance rather than originality and vigour. Archilochus and Aristophanes could not have been tolerated among them, and there were certain species of poetry, like the comedy of the latter, which though born, lay dormant till their control had passed away. So then the lyric poets, who have been divided in numerous cross divisions, as regards dialect, metre, country, and subjects, may be divided for our present purpose into the poets of free states, and the poets at the courts of tyrants.

The characteristics of the former and the value of the evidence they afford us are sufficiently obvious from the foregoing remarks. I shall only here call attention among the latter to the attitude of Pindar, who appears from his poems to have been more a courtier than an honest man. I take his moral reflections, and those of Simonides, to be far less sincere than those of Solon or Theognis. But unfortunately, the high popularity of the earlier gnomists made it impossible to keep their works

---

[1] In corroboration of this view of the literary influence of the tyrants, I may quote the curious case of Magna Græcia, where the Achæan confederation, which excluded tyrants, also exhibited no literary genius, though Tarentum and Rhegium and the Sicilian cities bore their full share, often under tyrants. Cf. Mommsen's *Rom. Hist.* i. 143, Eng. Trans.

pure and undefiled. Later moral teachers added
to the older reflections various new saws and
maxims, and these, especially when they were
of high merit [1], took refuge under the name of
Hesiod, or of Solon, or of Theognis, even where
they seem to us in direct contradiction to these
authors' opinions. Accordingly there is no more
hopeless task than the critical expurgating of such
texts. The interpolations are often as old as the
circulation of the poems, and usually of equal merit
as to thought and diction. These additions are
flagrantly obvious in our extant remains of Theognis,
and have been there since the fourth century B.C.,
at all events, for Plato criticises them in his *Meno* [2]
as part of the received text. The curious *saltus*
from subject to subject, the constant and direct in-
consistencies, the total absence of continuity in the
fragments, tell but too plainly the history of their text.

It is beyond the scope of a general sketch to
attempt a notice of all the individual peculiarities

---

[1] This consideration shows the folly of a very common procedure
among the German critics, of determining by their own taste (generally
a very capricious one) what lines are of inferior merit, and excluding
them as unworthy of the genuine poet. The supposed defect in the
suspected passage often arises from a want of comprehension on the
part of the critic. Choice specimens of this sort of restitution may
be seen in Steitz' otherwise valuable book on Hesiod, and still better
in Lucian Müller's papers on some of Ovid's *Heroides* in the twenty
third vol. of the *Rhein. Mus.* In proverbial poetry at all events, neither
commonplace nor disconnection are sufficient proof of spuriousness, and
again no line is more likely to be foisted in than a really good and striking
line. There is indeed no reason why the interpolated lines should not be
superior to the original poem.   [2] Jowett, vol. i. p. 286.

scattered through the widely severed fragments of the
lyric poets.   Where the germ was developed in later
Greek society we shall notice it in our more special
consideration of the Attic age.   But there are a few
general features, repeated in many of the fragments,
despite of contrasts in time and place, in metre and
in dialect.   These must here occupy us a brief space.

There is, for example, a peculiar uniformity in
many of them as to their religious views—I mean
their views of Divine Justice and Benevolence, of
Providence and of Fate.   Solon and Theognis, Archilochus and the earlier Simonides, the later Simonides and his contemporary Pindar, all agree in their
general theory of life.   They were led by bitter experience to assert, what had never been dared by
Homer and only hinted by Hesiod, that goodness
and justice among men were often without reward,
and that the wicked did flourish as a green bay tree ;
and yet, for all that, they never advanced even to the
most distant hint of atheism, or to a denial that the
gods could and did interfere in human affairs.   Had
such a notion been within their horizon, it must
have come into sight when we find such almost
comic appeals as this of Theognis :—'Dear Zeus, I
wonder at thee : for thou rulest over all, having in
thine own hands honour and great power and of men
thou knowest well the heart and mind of each, and
thy strength is over all, O king !   How is it then that
thy mind can tolerate to hold transgressors and the
just in the same lot ?'   And so the conclusion appears
briefly in the succeeding lines, 'there is nothing de-

cided for mortals as regards the Deity, nor what path he must tread to please the immortal gods.' This is their common attitude. They feel the presence of the Deity; they believe that human happiness and misery are bestowed by him; but though their deepest instinct tells them that virtue must be his law, and justice his principle, they cannot reconcile with it the facts of common life. They conclude, therefore, that the ways of God are inscrutable, and his paths past finding out. Thus Solon, in the most famous of his fragments (No. 13, ed. Bergk), where he tells us the results of his deepest reflections on human life, after asserting in the strongest terms a ruling Providence, which though often tardy, yet never fails to seek out and punish vice, it may be in the sinner himself, it may be by visitations upon the third and fourth generation—after this dogmatic teaching, Solon goes on to show how men are carried about, each by his own vanity and his peculiar ambition, and how not one of them can see what dangers and what successes are before him. In the words of another fragment (17) πάντῃ δ᾿ ἀθανάτων ἀφανὴς νόος ἀνθρώποισιν.

The lines of Theognis (vv. 133 sq.) are still stronger:—'No one, Cyrnus, is himself the cause of his misfortune or his gain, but the gods are the givers of them both; nor does any man work with a sure knowledge whether the result will be good or evil. For often when he thinks he is producing evil, he produces good, and again thinking to produce good he produces evil. Nor does any man

attain his expectations, for the limits of stern ina-
bility restrain him (ἴσχει γὰρ χαλεπῆς πείρατ' ἀμηχανίης).
For we men form idle opinions, knowing nothing,
but the gods accomplish all according to their mind.'
It must be observed that, by way of antidote, the
succeeding lines tell that he who deceives a stranger,
or a suppliant, never escapes the immortal gods.
The gloomy lines of Archilochus (*fr.* 56), and Simonides of Amorgos (*fr.* 1), of Simonides of Ceos
(*fr.* 5), and of Pindar's twelfth Olympian Ode,
repeat the same disappointment and the same despair ; nay, their very language is so similar to that
of Solon and Theognis, that they seem but evident
repetitions of the common wisdom of the day,
couched in the tritest and most homely words [1].

It is worthy of remark that these poets were far
too philosophic to account for their difficulties, as
Homer would do, by the conflicting passions of independent deities. This vulgar polytheism had long
passed away from educated minds, and the poets
speak of the Deity, for the most part, impersonally,
or as one almighty Zeus.

The vague and negative attitude of their religion

---

[1] I quote the words of Pindar *instar omnium* :—

σύμβολον δ' οὔ πώ τις ἐπιχθονίων
πιστὸν ἀμφὶ πράξιος ἐσσομένας εὗρεν θεόθεν·
τῶν δὲ μελλόντων τετύφλωνται φραδαί.
πολλὰ δ' ἀνθρώποις παρὰ γνώμαν ἔπεσεν,
ἔμπαλιν μὲν τέρψιος, οἱ δ' ἀνιαραῖς
ἀντικύρσαντες ζάλαις ἐσλὸν βαθὺ πήματος ἐν μικρῷ πεδάμειψαν
χρόνῳ.   *Ol.* xii. 7-12.

These poets add but little to Hesiod, Ἔργ. 83 sqq.

naturally coloured their practical ethics, and so we here find many conflicting apophthegms, as is wont to be the case in all proverbial philosophy. According to the writer's momentary attitude, according to the subject in hand, the preacher frames his parable, without regard to consistency. This peculiarity is indeed so salient in the extant works of Theognis, that it seems impossible to deny extensive interpolations ; and there can be little doubt that here, as in Hesiod, the use of the author as a schoolbook induced men to smuggle in foreign morality under the shelter of a great name. It is of course impossible to gather such teaching under general heads, or present it as a connected system.

But there are some points on which lyric poets as widely apart as Tyrtæus and Pindar agree, and this because they have both inherited them from the Ionic and Bœotian Epos. They both think, for example, that the best way of inculcating heroism is not by sentimental appeals, but by showing the solid advantages to be derived from it. It is far better, says Tyrtæus (*fr.* 10), to die in battle, than to be driven from one's city and rich fields and have to beg, going about with one's aged father, one's wife and little children. For a man is hateful to those whom he visits in his poverty and dire distress, and disgraces his race and his own respectability. 'If then,' the poet proceeds, 'there is no regard for a wandering man, nor respect, nor consideration, nor pity, let us fight with courage, and not spare our lives.' This picture of the contempt in which a vagrant beggar is held, even if sprung from gentle blood, reminds us of the anxious hurrying of Ulysses to the asylum of the hearth, it literally repeats Hesiod's advice to Perses (v. 367), and reminds us of the sad words of Andromache, in describing the lot of her orphan child (above, p. 41).

Pindar, whose evidence is not quite so valuable, inasmuch as he wrote in the interest of his profession, repeatedly tells us that the satisfaction of doing great things is nothing, if the glory of being publicly praised does not attend it. We saw above that this worship of success was quite Homeric, being the counterpart of the contempt of failure, and equally prominent in the Greek mind. To the passages already quoted I may add one in Pindar, which shocks us in comparison with the gentleness and sympathy of Achilles towards the vanquished at the games. He says that the Deity has given to the four lads, whom Alcimedon conquered, a most hateful return from the arena, a cowed voice, and a sneaking along unfrequented paths [1]. The same idea is found in one of his fragments (150). A very remarkable historical parallel is to be read in Herodotus (vi. 67), where the new king of Sparta sends a messenger to ask his deposed rival, out of insolence and derison, how he liked being a magistrate after being a king. I think, therefore, that in this respect, the Greeks of the lyric age were hardly gentlemen in our sense. Another feature may, perhaps, be regarded

[1] νόστον ἔχθιστον καὶ ἀτιμοτέραν γλῶσσαν καὶ ἐπίκρυφον οἶμον.

Ol. viii. 68.

as at that epoch (if not, indeed, at all epochs) really national and Hellenic. Their usual teaching, which was in theory sound, and based upon the excellence and the satisfactions of virtue, did not extend to political life, or at least was confessedly to be there overridden by the pressure of circumstances. This inconsistency was the natural outcome of their religion. As they believed in a Providence, and in this Providence rewarding virtue, so they taught that men should follow virtue. As they also held that the reward was often withheld, and that dishonesty and craftiness were constantly successful ; so they did not expect men to be proof against pressure, but advised them to follow the stream of fortune, and, above all, not to miss the satisfactions of love and of revenge[1]. They were, like Machiavelli, more outspoken than we are on this side, as many of them were scarcely moral teachers, and were more intent on painting life as it is, and as they found it, than on raising the standard of actions. But I hardly know whether we should not note the same kind of inconsistency in our own professed Christian, who exhorts his neighbour to turn the other cheek to him who has smitten one, and to give his cloak to the man who has taken his coat, and yet this same adviser upbraids and scorns his friend if he brooks an insult without instant satisfaction.

The party struggles of the Greek cities made the aristocrats, who were in the end for the most part defeated, far more vindictive than ever Greek nature

---

[1] Solon, *fr.* 13 ; Archil. *fr.* 65.

could have been originally, and the poems of Theognis, which were general favourites among the nobles throughout Greece, show a mixture of contempt and hatred against the lower classes that excludes all generous and even honest treatment. It was openly recommended to fawn upon your enemy, to deceive him till he was in your power, and then wreak vengeance upon him. It is usual among critics to speak of this as the attitude of Theognis, and of the special aristocracy to which he belonged. They forget that we find the same attitude in the moral Pindar (*Pyth.* ii. 84).

> φίλον εἴη φιλεῖν·
> ποτὶ δ' ἐχθρὸν ἅτ' ἐχθρὸς ἐὼν λύκοιο δίκαν ὑποθεύσομαι,
> ἄλλ' ἄλλοτε πατέων ὁδοῖς σκολιαῖς.

It is expounded by Hesiod ("Εργ. 165, sqq.) as proximate, by Thucydides as universal, at a later epoch.

I cannot but dwell for a moment on this painful feature, inasmuch as it is so closely paralleled in the Ireland of to-day. Theognis is full of exhortations against making friendships, against trusting in any way the lower classes, who will ever be found false and ungrateful. 'Make none of these townspeople (vv. 60 sq.) your friend for the sake of your need; rather seem to be friendly with them all in words (ἀπὸ γλώσσης), but communicate not at all with them any serious matter whatever, or you will know the minds of these miserable men, how they have no honour (πίστις) in their actions, but they love wile and stratagem, and tortuous ways, like men despairing of security' (μηκέτι σωζόμενοι). Many other passages[1] repeat this doctrine. It is precisely the feeling entertained towards Roman Catholics by the old-school Orangemen of Ireland. Hundreds of times have I myself been warned not to trust the 'false papists,' whose religion was full of lies, and whose word could not be believed, who had been known to betray their best friends, and to violate the holiest ties[2]. Unfortunately, there are real facts sufficient to vamp up such a frightful theory. In the first place, the pure Celt, who is always a Catholic, has less regard for truth than the Protestant, with his touch of Saxon breeding. Secondly, the long oppression of the Roman Catholics, and their enforced separation from Protestant society, has created a clan feeling, which, in times of great bitterness and bloodshed, has been known to outweigh even the closest ties of friendship toward the enemies of the clan. In this way, what one side translate as faith towards country and religion, the other call traitorous betrayal of friends

[1] vv. 279, 847, 853.

[2] This antipathy sometimes assumes a very grotesque form. 'How are you getting on, James?' said a friend of mine to one of these Orangemen. 'Badly enough, your honour; sure the country is gone to the divil.' 'Why do you say that? I see your farm in good order, with plenty of stock on it.' 'What matter about that, doesn't your honour know that if you shot a Papist now you'd be *tried* for it?' When my friend looked amused, the Orangeman added with much warmth: '*Well, with the blessin' o' God, I'll have one day's fowlin' among them before I die.*'

Another was known to object vehemently to controversial sermons, whereby the Papists might be converted. 'Till hell with them,' he exclaimed, 'I wouldn't convert them.' Such anecdotes might be multiplied *ad libitum*. The Roman Catholic party have just as strong sentiments, but do not express them so boldly.

and relations. Thus any thoughtful man who has lived in Ireland comes to understand Greek political hate with peculiar clearness.

Theognis has various theories to explain the meanness and falseness of the lower classes, all of them more or less true, and all of them verified by the modern parallel I have cited. He says (v. 279) that these people have to live from hand to mouth, and therefore are trained to disregard and forget just requital, if future. He says (v. 305) that they are not all bad from the mother's womb, but are brought up in bad society, and so all degenerate to a low level. Crush them under your heel, and drive them with a sharp goad (v. 847), for they are slavish. Finally (vv. 383, 899), he speaks very strongly on the degrading effects of poverty, which drag even a fine and noble mind into meanness and cowardice; for strong necessity compels him to look to his daily bread, and not to endanger it by pride and independence.

If we weigh the evidence on these great problems in the lyric fragments, as compared with the epic poems, we shall say that while on the question of religion men had begun to see and appreciate difficulties, and to repudiate low and childish views about the gods, in morals there was neither much advance nor marked retrogression. The collapse of the popular religion, which was even then in process, ought to have made men more reckless, for many are totally unhinged when old beliefs fall away from them; they have bound together all their morals with their dogmas, and cannot sustain the one without the other. But a deeper sense of moral obligation, and a sounder and stronger conviction of the duties each man owes to society—these counterbalancing forces saved the higher and purer minds, and gave them a surer and better reason for honesty and goodness than the wrath of Athene or Apollo ; and so in some minds, and those the highest, a better and nobler morality took the place of the religion of olden days. This development would doubtless have borne good fruit, and shown us the lyric age far superior to Homer's, had not the almost universal and chronic civil wars in the Greek cities embittered every relation of life, and sown the growing mind of Greece with hate and with revenge. It is to this melancholy social state— a state first checked by the tyrants—that we must ascribe the smallness of the moral progress among the Greeks of this age. I pass to kindred, but lighter topics.

CHAPTER V.

THE GREEKS OF THE LYRIC AGE (*continued*).

SOCIAL intercourse appears to have stood far apart from the older times, and in close relation to the manners of the later Greeks, as we shall have ample occasion to notice hereafter. In feasting especially, moderate eating and drinking, combined with good conversation, had assumed in the minds of educated Greeks the prominence which they now have in intellectual society. Of course all noise and clamour, such as is the fashion among our students, were intolerable to Greek refinement[1]. 'Come, now,' says

[1] Tennyson has well contrasted (*In Mem.* lxxxvi.)

> ' the noise
> Of songs, and clapping hands, and boys
> That crashed the glass and beat the floor,'

with that higher society which Xenophanes and Plato enjoyed ages before him.

Even the reckless suitors of Penelope (σ 401) are disgusted with the brawling of Eurymedon, when he hurls the footstool at Ulysses, and hits the attending herald, and exclaim to one another: 'Would that this stranger had perished elsewhere in his wanderings, before he came hither, and so had saved us this disturbance. But now here we are brawling about beggars, nor is there any pleasure in the goodly banquet, since the worse prevails.'

Anacreon, 'let us no longer with this clatter and din of voices (πατάγῳ τε κἀλαλητῷ), practise Scythian toping at our wine, but drinking to the sound of sweet hymns' (*fr.* 64). Yet even this is rather Homeric, and reminds us of Ulysses declaring that the highest delight is to sit at a plentiful table and hear a bard singing a pleasant lay. Other lyric poets are more advanced in their notions. Phocylides recommends light and good-humoured banter (ἡδέα κωτίλλοντα) over the wine-cup. Theognis wishes that he may sit at table beside some wise man, by whose conversation he will profit (v. 563) while in another passage (v. 295 sqq.) he complains of the nuisance of a chatterbox, whom all hate, and whom no one will meet at a feast if he can help it—

> ἐχθαίρουσι δὲ πάντες, ἀναγκαίη δ᾽ ἐπίμιξις
> ἀνδρὸς τοιούτου συμποσίῳ τελέθει.

The *locus classicus*, however, of this epoch is the great fragment (No. 1) of Xenophanes, where he describes the requisites of an elegant and refined feast, and, being a reformer not only in religion but in society, specially inveighs against rhapsodising bards. He wants to hear a man talk from his own resources, either drawing from his experience, or suggesting moral discourse, and 'not one who marshals for you (διέπει) the battles of the giants or the Titans, or those of the Centaurs, inventions of the ancients— in such things there is no profit.' This is quite a Platonic or Attic attitude.

With the sustained lay, it is evident that the

groaning board and the unmixed wine departed
from society, and there is no subject on which the
lyric and gnomic poets have left us more copious
advice than on the proper use of wine. They loved
pleasure, and understood life too well ever to recommend water-drinking. But they understood it also
too well to tolerate surfeiting and drunkenness.
While they personified wine (Ion, *fr.* 9) as 'an un-
tamed child and daring, young and yet not young,
sweetest minister of boisterous loves, wine that ele-
vates the mind, the president of men,' yet they know
(Euenus, *fr.* 2), 'that if out of measure he was the
cause of grief or madness. In company with three
(water) nymphs he is most suitable. But should he
blow a full gale, he is hostile to love, and steeps
us in sleep the neighbour of death.' So Critias tells
us the Lacedæmonians would not allow each guest
to pledge his friend in separate cups, for that this
drinking of healths was the fertile cause of drunkenness. As might be expected, of all the lyric remnants, the poems attributed to Theognis contain the
most numerous reflections on this subject—reflections,
I mean, of a gnomic character, as contrasted with the
wild license of Alcæus[1].

But in an elegy, of doubtful authorship, addressed

---

[1] Dicæarchus (Müll. *Fragg. Hist.* ii. p. 247) says that Alcæus drank
watery wine out of small cups; but the extant fragments tell us that his
mixture was one to two, therefore stronger than that of Euenus just
quoted, and that he began early, and had one cup following close upon
another (ά δ' ἐτέρα τὰν ἐτέραν κύλιξ ὠθήτω), thus compensating for the
smaller size.

to Simonides[1], and apparently the work of no mean poet, the duties of a Greek gentleman as to wine drinking are perhaps most accurately and elegantly expounded. 'Wake not the friend, Simonides, among us whom soft sleep may overcome when he has indulged in wine, nor ask the waking man to sleep against his will : everything compulsory is offensive. But to him who will drink let them pour out without stint, it is not every night that we enjoy such luxury. But I—for I am moderate in honey-sweet wine—will court soothing sleep when I have gone home, and will show you how wine is most pleasant for men to drink. For neither am I too sober a man, nor am I very intemperate. But whosoever exceeds a measure in drinking, is no longer master of his tongue or his mind, and talks recklessly of things disgraceful to the sober, and is ashamed of nothing, though modest when he was sober. Now you, perceiving this, drink not to excess, but either retire before you are drunk— let not your lust compel you, like some wretched journeyman—or else stay and do not drink. But you are ever babbling that silly word " fill your glass," and so you get drunk. For first comes the health of the guests, and then a second cup is left ready before you, and a third is for the libation to the gods, and another you keep before you, and so you

---

[1] Bergk thinks to Simonides of Amorgos, and that the author was an early Euenus, not the Sophist alluded to by Aristotle; cf. *Fragg. Lyr.* p. 515, note. The fragment has reached us in the collection attributed to Theognis. It is corrupt in several places, and the meaning not certain.

know not how to refuse. He is indeed invincible,
who can drink many cups and say nothing foolish.
But do you promote good conversation sitting round
the bowl, restraining one another from contention,
addressing individuals so that the company may join
in[1], and so our feast will not want in refinement.'
In other fragments of Theognis, and these genuine,
we see the same conflict between good sense and
good fellowship. ''Tis a shame to be drunk among
sober men, 'tis also a shame to stay sober among
men that are drunk'; and, again, ' O wine, in some
things I praise, in others I blame thee; nor can I
ever altogether love thee or hate thee. A good art
thou and an ill. Who might blame thee, who might
with a fair share of wisdom praise thee[2]?'

In all these quotations we see a moral attitude
which is about the same as that of average society
in our day. But intellectually the bright and pleasure-loving Greek would have hated the heavy pomp
and stupid sameness of our large dinner parties.
Athenæus however observes, on the evidence of

v. 495, ἐς τὸ μέσον φωνεῦντες ὁμῶς ἐνὶ καὶ συνάπασιν. On no point
were the Greeks more particular as regards their dinner parties, than
that the conversation should be general. As soon as the common
listening to a reciting bard became obsolete, it is the serious discourse of
a leading guest which is prized, as in this fragment and that of Xenophanes above quoted. It is the λεγόμενον ἐς μέσον at Cleisthenes'
banquet in Herodotus; it is the demand in Plato's *Symposium* that
Socrates shall not whisper—this is in fact the universal feature of the
Greek banquet. We stupid moderns seem to be specially providing
against it in our large dinner parties, where people are broken up into
couples, and so restrained from general talking.

[2] Cf. Theog. vv. 510, 627, 836, 873.

Anacreon, that they still at this period maintained the habit, afterwards only to be found among barbarians, of crowding their tables all through the feast with dishes. In fact, they had not yet introduced their *dîner à la Russe*[1]. But that they had already begun to give attention to cooking in the lyric age appears from fragments of Solon (*fr.* 38) of Simonides of Amorgos (*fr.* 23, 24) and of Hipponax (*fr.* 35). To the Greek, brilliant conversation was not an accident, but a necessity in society, and wine was chiefly prized as promoting this end. He was intensely fond of good cheer and of elegant dishes, but the cooks and the vulgar people who made this the end of banquetting were always despised and ridiculed. He compensated, too, for the frequent absence of the female sex from his feasts by that romantic friendship which subsisted between young men in ancient Greece—a friendship which absorbed all the higher affection now felt only towards the opposite sex. On this question the second book of Theognis' elegies gives ample and curious information, and those who compare it (especially vv. 1260, and 1313 sqq.) with the allusions in the courtly Pindar[2] will be struck with the free and manly tone of the old aristocrat, and how completely faithful friendship comes into the foreground, while the court poet, who was living like Anacreon among tyrants and their minions, pictures the sensuous beauty alone, and so degrades his higher genius to a baser level.

---

[1] Athenæus i. 12 A.

[2] *Ol.* i. 40; xi. 105 ; *Isthm.* ii. 1 ; and *fr.* 2 of the Skolia.

But these considerations lead us on to a more interesting question, and one on which modern critics have gone almost uniformly astray, the question of the position of women in the Lyric, as opposed to the Heroic and the Attic ages. It is not true that in this period women had been degraded, and that the Homeric poems afford models and characters superior to those of the Lyric poets. Take the feeling of maternal love, as shown by Andromache and Penelope. The celebrated passage in which the former appears is one of the very best in the great Iliad, and yet I hesitate not to say that an extant fragment of Simonides containing the lament of Danae is not a whit inferior either in sentiment or in diction. In this, the most exquisite of all the lyric fragments, the purest maternal love and the noblest resignation find their most perfect expression, and we may safely assert that the poet, and the age which produced such a poem, cannot have been wanting in the highest type of female dignity and excellence.

I quote it in Dean Milman's version; but even that excellent poet's version falls vastly short of the great original.

> 'When rude around the high-wrought ark
> The tempests raged, the waters dark
> Around the mother tossed and swelled;
> With not unmoistened cheek she held
> Her Perseus in her arms, and said:
> "What sorrows bow this hapless head!
> Thou sleepst the while, thy gentle breast
> Is heaving in unbroken rest;

In this our dark unjoyous home
Clamped with the rugged brass, the gloom
Scarce broken by the doubtful light
That gleams from yon dim fires of night.
But thou, unwet thy clustering hair,
Heed'st not the billows raging wild,
The moanings of the bitter air,
Wrapt in thy purple robe, my beauteous child!
Oh! seemed this peril perilous to thee,
  How sadly to my words of fear
  Wouldst thou bend down thy listening ear!
But now sleep on, my child! sleep thou, wide sea!
  Sleep, my unutterable agony!
Oh! change thy counsels, Jove, our sorrows end!
And if my rash intemperate zeal offend,
For my child's sake, his father, pardon me!"'

There are other, though less prominent, indications in the other poets, not less clear and convincing. We are told that Stesichorus composed a poem called Calyce, which was highly popular among the ladies of ancient days. Aristoxenus has preserved to us the mere outline of the plot, which shows it to have been the forerunner of the novels or love stories afterwards fashionable at Miletus. The maiden Calyce, having fallen madly in love with a youth, prays to Aphrodite that she may become his lawful wife, and when he continued to be indifferent to her, she committed suicide. It was specially noticed by ancient critics how the poet had drawn the character of the maiden as exhibiting the greatest purity and modesty under this sore trial, and we are told, or we can at least plainly infer, that this noble feature was the great cause of the popularity of the poem.

A careful consideration of the fragments of Sappho

will, I think, lead to the same conclusion. There appears to have been, in her day and in her city, both great liberty for women to mix in general society, and a bold independent way of asserting their rights and their dignity. She versified, we are told, a dialogue, by some suspected to have taken place between Alcæus and herself, in which the lover says to his flame, 'I have something to say to thee, but I feel confused and ashamed.' Whereupon the girl in answer to him, says: 'Wert thou a good man, and were the thing thou hast to say to me a good thing, thou hadst not felt this shame and confusion, but hadst said it freely, looking me straight in the face without blushes[1].' She went so far as openly to censure in another poem her own brother, who was in the wine trade between Lesbos and Egypt, and having gone to Naucratis, there fell in love with a lady of beauty, but unworthy of him in moral character; and this poem was celebrated and much quoted by the ancients.

A less remarkable poet, Simonides of Amorgos, has left us a more complete fragment on this question— the celebrated poem in which the various tempers of women are shown to result from a kinship with various domestic animals. There are so many curious indications of manners in this poem, that I shall here extract the substance of it. I do so the more unre-

---

[1] Cf. Bergk, pp. 887 and 919. The passage is one of the innumerable instances in which ἀγαθός was used in a strictly moral sense by the early Greeks; for the quotation makes it plain that the word occurred in the original text.

servedly as the exigencies of our modern universities, with their fixed or traditional courses, are such that even good Greek scholars may not be familiar with it. We are too apt to go round the ordinary course of well-known Greek authors, and neglect these fragments, which surely merit our attention as much as anything in Greek literature.

The poem begins with the untidy woman, whose mind is said to be akin to that of a pig : and next, the curious and tell-tale woman is compared first to a fox, and then to a dog[1]. She wishes to hear and to know everything, and goes about looking out for news, and retailing it. 'Nor can her husband make her stop even with threats, though in a rage he should knock her teeth out with a stone, nor though he speak to her gently, even when she is sitting in company with guests.' Next comes the dull woman without sensibility, whose mind is of the earth, earthy, 'who cares not for good or evil; the only work she does is to eat, and not even when God sends a hard winter, does she draw her chair nearer the fire.' We can hardly conceive a more telling or truthful picture. People without sympathy for others are sure to have no taste for comfort themselves, for comforts are essentially social things, and imply a pleasure in other people's happiness.

We next come to the fickle woman, who is like the sea. One day she is laughing and joyous, and the guest seeing her in her house will praise her, and say 'there is not in all the world a better or fairer woman

[1] There appears some inconsistency or confusion in the text here.

than this.' But next day she is furious and unapproachable, alike to friends and enemies. There
follows an elegant parallel description of the sea,
alternately smiling to the sailor's delight, and again
raging with loud-sounding waves[1]. Then follow the
ass-like and ferret-like women, with details showing
that these domestic animals were esteemed then exactly as they are now.

Presently we come to the luxurious and extravagant woman, whose mind is akin to a horse. She
avoids all slavish work and toil, and will not touch
the grinding-stone, nor clean up the house, nor sit at
the kitchen-fire. Such a woman makes her husband
intimate with necessity. She washes herself twice a
day or even three times, and uses unguents. She
wears her hair always combed and in tresses (βαθεῖαν)
shaded with flowers. Such a woman is a fair sight
for other people, but to him that owns her an evil,
except he be some tyrant or ruler, who delights his
mind with such things by way of luxury. Then
comes the ugly woman, akin to the ape, who is of
course most objectionable to the Greek moralist.
'Such a woman goes through the town a regular
laughing-stock to all men.'

But the last has the nature of a bee; happy the

[1] Cf. *fr.* 7, v. 37 sq. :—

> ὥσπερ θάλασσα πολλάκις μὲν ἀτρεμὴς
> ἕστηκ᾽ ἀπήμων, χάρμα ναύτῃσιν μέγα,
> θέρεος ἐν ὥρῃ· πολλάκις δὲ μαίνεται
> βαρυκτύποισι κύμασιν φορευμένη
> ταύτῃ μάλιστ᾽ ἔοικε τοιαύτη γυνὴ
> ὀργήν.

man that obtains her, for to her alone no blame attaches. Under her care his living prospers and increases. She grows old, a loving wife to her loving husband, the mother of a fair and praised race. Distinguished is she among women, and divine grace clings to her (θείη δ' ἀμφιδέδρομεν χάρις); nor does she delight in sitting among women, when they are talking of intrigues (ἀφροδισίους λόγους). The poet ends with some general remarks, one of them very modern in tone, the other strange and opposed to our ideas. He says that when there is a lady in the house, 'the guest is not received with the same open welcome,' alluding, I suppose, to the friend of bachelor days; and then, that it is the habit of every man to praise his own wife, and abuse those of others, not reflecting that all are under a like misfortune.

I call the reader's attention particularly to the fact that the public appearance in society of married women is so openly recognised throughout this poem. He will also see how heartfelt and earnest is the praise of the virtuous woman, in spite of all the poet's cynicism. It is moreover evident that he does not speak of the higher classes exclusively, but rather of those middle ranks, in which the lady of the house is expected to do such house-work as is now performed by the corresponding class in Germany.

Yet withal the age was not behind the epic age in sentiment. Far from it. These historical Greeks, for example, fell in love as no Homeric hero ever could. When we read the precious fragments of burning complaint left us by Archilochus, by Sappho, by

Anacreon, and by Ibycus, we feel that we stand close to them, while the epic heroes are afar off and have not yet entered into the real atmosphere of that great emotion. The aged Ibycus dreads another visitation of Eros, as the old racer dreads a new contest, when he feels that his limbs have lost their vigour, and will not carry him as of old to victory. When Sappho sits in presence of her lover, her eyes grow dizzy, and her tongue refuses utterance, her heart flutters, and her ears are full of confused din, her mind wanders, and her cheek becomes pale [1]. I need not comment how truthfully these great poets felt the facts of human nature as the young now feel them, and as the old remember to have felt them. And I need not point out to the student of the Odyssey how differently the Homeric Greeks endured the same trial. Only one Aeschylean tragedy (the *Myrmidons*) equals in its reality these lyric poets; and till we descend to the pathetic Euripides, no like sympathy with this, the largest of human feelings, rewards our search.

So also the respect for the holiest of human emotions, the mother's love for her child—which had been so ex-

[1] *Fr.* 2 (according to Bergk's reading):—

ὡς γὰρ εὔιδον βροχέως σε, φώνας
        οὐδὲν ἔτ᾽ εἴκει·
ἀλλὰ καμ μὲν γλῶσσα ἔαγε, λέπτον δ᾽
αὔτικα χρῷ πῦρ ὑπαδεδρόμακεν,
ὀππάτεσσι δ᾽ οὐδὲν ὄρημ᾽, ἐπιρρόμ-
        βεισι δ᾽ ἄκουαι.
ἀ δέ μ᾽ ἵδρως κακχέεται, τρόμος δὲ
πᾶσαν ἄγρει, χλωροτέρα δὲ ποίας
ἔμμι, τεθνάκην δ᾽ ὀλίγω ᾽πιδεύης
        φαίνομαι ἄλλα.

quisitely painted in the Homeric poems in the person of Andromache among nobles, in that of the wretched widow among the poor, who toils at her wool for miserable fare, and wears out her life in support of her helpless children—this great and beautiful emotion is brought out in the lament of Danae over the infant Perseus, which I have already quoted.

But having noticed these points of social and moral advance, I desire to recapitulate a few others in which the lyric Greeks were strictly the successors of the Homeric heroes. In the matter of cowardice, our evidence is curiously precise. We are no longer told by a courtly bard that the gods sent fear into the heart of a warrior ; but the poets themselves, men fond of war, and perpetually engaged in it, tell us themselves in express terms, that they ran away and threw away their arms. Archilochus says so, and so does Alcæus, and so does Anacreon. One of them even jokes about the shield that once belonged to him being hung up as a proud trophy by one of his enemies. Stesichorus and Pindar (*Ol.* xi. 15) told how even the great Heracles, when Cycnus was helped by his father Ares, fled in fear[1]. Pindar makes elsewhere (*Nem.* ix. 27) similar statements.

These passages, especially the confessions of the cowards themselves, strike us as very curious. Of course they tend to corroborate what was said above about Homeric valour ; but I hardly think they can simply be explained by a low standard of courage, for all through Greek history the loss of the shield

---

[1] ἔφυγε δείσας, Bergk. p. 978.

certainly was considered a disgrace. We must, in addition, not fail to keep in mind the intense realism with which these men appear to have led a reaction against the smooth ideal courtliness of the rhapsodists. They caught the public ear by a new and welcome sound—the sound of plain straightforward reality. Intense it was, and therefore brimful of passion, and of the beauty and interest which passion lends to every product of human art, but homely too and truthful, not shirking poor admissions nor disguising vulgar notions.

We saw above, how the *advantages* of heroism were put forward as the proper inducements to valour; how on the valiant side of their character the Greeks were not less homely in stating their motives. The very passage of Tyrtæus which suggested these reflections (*fr.* 10) is equally remarkable for its want of compassion to the poor, as the reader will see by referring back to the passage (p. 95). This attitude is strictly Homeric, there is neither advance nor decay in this side of Greek nature. It is corroborated by numerous reflections of Theognis and Solon, where poverty is reckoned the worst of evils, especially the poverty of exile, so much so that the promises or the friendship of an exile were held of no value when he returned. He would do anything to obtain that result, and felt justified in any deceit to obtain it.

As to the sympathy with lower animals, on which the epic poetry yielded us a good deal of evidence, hardly a notice has reached us in the lyric fragments. One distich, attributed to either Theognis (**v.** 1252)

or Solon, speaks of horses and dogs, as well as
foreign friends, as essentials to a man's happiness.
Nor did the great Simonides scorn to write an epitaph
(*fr.* 130) on a famous hound[1], probably belonging
to the Thessalian Scopadae, his patrons. I have no
doubt his namesake would have compared some class
of women to dogs, but that his plan admitted of only
one good kind, as opposed to various bad types ; and
perhaps the Homeric epithet κυνῶπις influenced him
in the same direction.

If we turn to the more serious feature of avarice,
it seems to me that the Greeks of the lyric age
were the direct successors of the Hesiodic Greeks
certainly ; probably therefore of the Homeric Greeks,
did we know more of the poorer classes in that
society. It was hardly the love of wealth for its own
sake, an artificial vice rare in early times, and still
rarer in a people who loved natural enjoyments so
keenly as the Greeks. It was rather as a means to
power and pleasure that the Greek loved money, and
the reflections of Solon and the advices of Theognis
only repeat literally what had been said before by the
sour and practical Hesiod. To Solon, indeed, the
love of money is the root of all evil, the real parent of
that selfishness which thwarted and ridiculed his
earnest and philosophical reforms ; to Theognis,
poverty—hereditary poverty—is the source of the
meanness of the lower classes ; its pinching grasp
is now laying hold of the nobles in defeat and exile,
it is to them the cause of faithlessness, and is

[1] This Simonides indeed often mentions dogs.

breaking up the old loyalty and the old exclusiveness.
With the rise of trade and of shipping, riches have
made themselves a place beside ancient lineage, and
the bankrupt noble will not blush to ally himself with
the base but wealthy merchant.   These things are
all common now-a-days, and we look upon the
grumbling of the Greek aristocratic moralist just as
we look upon the pompous absurdity of the en-
cumbered Irish squire, who has retained of all his
heirlooms nothing but the old contempt for trade,
and who still reconciles himself with grief and shame
to the marriage of his ignorant and spendthrift son
with some respectable shopkeeper's daughter, who
will not only, by her fortune, save him from immediate ruin, but is also likely to introduce a sober
strain into the race, and be the parent of wiser
and more reasonable children.

But I repeat that the Greeks never sank to the
stupidity of our day, when wealth is eagerly sought
by people who can never enjoy it ; when the addition
of thousands does not add one enjoyment to their life,
save the barren consciousness of importance.   The
Greeks loved wealth because it obtained for them all
the great enjoyments of this life—success in love, success in revenge, success in politics ; and, as we can see
clearly, money was then more effectual in procuring
all these blessings than it has been in almost any
other nation at any epoch of its history.   This keen
love of pleasure was one of the indelible characters in
Greek human nature, reappearing at all times and in
all ranks of society ; so much so that Aristotle notices

the defect even of a term in the language to denote
that blunt and stolid nature, which is not strongly
affected by this motive, and feels fully justified in
calling such a man a sort of inanimate or non-per-
cipient creature—ἀναισθητός τις [1].

It is to this same source that we may trace the
reappearance of another Homeric feature in the lyric
fragments, I mean the horror and *hatred of old age*.
The beautiful lines still left us of Mimnermus have
it as their marked characteristic. He tells us to enjoy
the delights of love (*fr.* 1), 'but when old age with its
pains comes upon us, which mars alike even the fair,
ever do wretched cares besiege his mind, nor does he
delight in beholding the rays of the sun, but is hateful
to boys and despised among women, so sore a burden
has God made old age.' He comes back upon this
γῆρας ἀργαλέον repeatedly, a gift worse than death, as
the wretched Tithonus had found it:—'When youth
has fled, short-lived as a dream (*fr.* 5), forthwith this
burdensome and hideous old age looms over us, hateful and dishonoured; which changes the fashion of
a man's countenance, marring his sight and his mind
with its mist.' Theognis makes similar complaints
(vv. 526, 567) and Pindar, in his first Olympian ode
(v. 82), asks why those who must of necessity meet
the fate of death, should desire to 'sit in obscurity,
vainly brooding through a forgotten old age, without
sharing a single blessing.'

---

[1] Simonides of Amorgos, by the way, describes just such a character
in one of his general types of bad women, as I have above remarked
(p. 112).

These quotations, which might easily be multiplied, show clearly a feeling quite foreign to our own literature, and to that of the Germans, where, no doubt, the commonplaces about age do occur, but where altered conditions of society, and the late growth of republican ideas, have left both honour and power to old age, and have thus, as it were, compensated socially for its great physical disabilities. Among the Greeks, on the contrary, in addition to these latter, there were arrayed against old age a rude assertion of superior force, and, with the rapid intellectual development of the nation, a strong consciousness of the greater force and knowledge of youth. Old men had to contend with the rising generation upon even terms, and without those large allowances conceded to them by modern sentiment and modern good manners. There were isolated peoples in the classical epochs who felt this sentiment. It was well known throughout Greece that at Sparta the reverence for age, as such, was a strict prescription of Lycurgus, and even the Athenian theatre honoured this feeling as an evidence of refinement. The Romans, ruder and coarser than the Greeks in almost every respect, in this stand closer to us moderns, that they shared with the Spartans the conservative respect for age.

But the most enlightened Greeks stood nearer, I fear, to the savages of the present day, who regard without respect or affection any human being who has become useless in the race of life, or who even impedes the course of human affairs. We know that, at Athens, actions of children to deprive their parents

of control of property were legal and commonly occurring, nor do we hear that medical evidence of
imbecility was required.   It was only among a few
conservative cities, like Sparta, and a few exceptionally refined men, like Plato, that the nobler and
kindlier sentiment prevailed.   The philosopher, indeed, has applied to it his finest metaphor :—' Some
of the gods we see with our eyes, and honour them ;
of others, we honour the images, raising statues of
them, which we adore ; and, though they be lifeless,
yet we imagine that the living gods have a good will
and gratitude to us on this account.   Now if a man
has a father or mother, or their father and mother
treasured up in his house stricken in years, let him
consider that no statue can be more potent to grant
his requests than they are, who are sitting at his
hearth ; . . . whom, when a man honours, the heart
of the God rejoices, and he is ready to answer their
prayers[1].'

The reader however who has not forgotten what
was said above (p. 41) concerning Pallas Athene, as
a Homeric ideal, will see that the ingrained *selfishness* of Greek character was the active and perpetual
opponent of all such sentiment.   This selfishness was
nourished by the perpetual conflicts and vicissitudes
of the Greek cities.   Even the closest and most sacred
bond of Homeric days, that of party, which had alone
been able to sway the hard hearts of Athene, and
Here, and Poseidon, — even this bond was being
loosened, for Theognis' bitterest lamentations are on

[1] Jowett, iv. 442.

this very decay; how the exile would promise anything to return, and then betray his friends; how the
magistrate would endeavour, by any deceit, to overcome
his old fellows, and reduce them to a level with the
townsmen under his tyranny.

It is fashionable in certain philosophies, long since
exploded, but of late showing signs of new life, to
attribute all human action to selfishness, and to
translate the plain facts of passion and of principle
into involved and subtle deductions from this idea.
I am very far from advocating such an absurdity, but
am ready to admit, with Bishop Butler, that except
stronger motives supervene, this is ever present and
constantly asserting itself. In Greek politics, as in
ours, principle did at times, though rarely, suppress it,
as we may see from the case of Solon. Passion, too,
silenced it, and far oftener than it does now, because
society had not settled down into a calm and equable
state from its troubled and violent beginnings. Yet
these were intermittent agents, and made but a small
figure in the fragmentary history of old days beside
the constant workings of selfishness, on which we
chance to have three very adequate witnesses —
Hesiod, Theognis, and Thucydides.

Selfishness is akin to *dishonesty*, and thus we are
led to the consideration of another disagreeable feature, on which the Homeric age gave us considerable
materials. Here again we have a permanent Greek
feature, and one recognised, as well in old times as
in modern, both by the better Greeks themselves, and
by their more respectable neighbours. Herodotus no-

tices, in evident contrast to his own nation, the care with which Persian boys were taught to speak the truth. Cyrus is said, in the same spirit[1], to have expressed his open contempt for men who met in a fixed marketplace daily to lie, and cheat one another. Darius caustically calls Scythes the justest of all the Greeks he ever knew, because he kept a single promise. So much for earlier days. Thucydides and Aristophanes are home witnesses for the dishonesty of Greek life at a later epoch. Then we come to days when the somewhat brutal Romans were able to assert their own superiority, in this respect at all events. *Græca fide mercari* is a proverb in the older comedy. Cicero, in his oration *Pro Cæcina*, turns aside to apologise for doubting generally the veracity of Greek evidence. He claims to know more of the Greeks than any man of his day; he confesses his love and admiration for their genius; he concedes to them all the high qualities they choose to claim, save one—that of truthfulness[2]. I need not descend to the *Græcia mendax* of Juvenal and Persius, when the Greeks in Rome may have been, like the Irish in America, the mere offscourings of home society.

---

[1] Herod i. 153.

[2] 'Verumtamen hoc dico de toto genere Græcorum; tribuo illis litteras, do multarum artium disciplinam, non adimo sermonis leporem, ingeniorum acumen, dicendi copiam; denique etiam, si sibi alia sumunt, non repugno; testimoniorum religionem et fidem nunquam ista natio coluit; totiusque hujusce rei quæ sit vis, quæ auctoritas, quod pondus, ignorant.' I think almost the same remarks might be applied to the lower-class Irish, if we substitute a mere capacity of literary excellence for the developed genius justly ascribed to the Greeks.

Apart then from any exaggeration, without denying
to many of the philosophers the highest feelings of
honour, without denying to the lower classes much of
that respect for truth without which constitutional
government is impossible, we cannot claim for the
Greeks a high place for honesty among civilised
nations. In Athens the demos indeed, upon one
memorable occasion, adhered to its oaths of amnesty,
and allowed murderers and informers under the tyrants to return unmolested, and dwell among the
children of their victims. But such instances are
noted as rare. I have no doubt that many, even of
the Athenians themselves, regarded this noble self-
denial as a Quixotic display of honour, and counted
it among those excesses of doing good which Aristotle afterwards classed among vices, and among
which he deliberately ranked excess in speaking the
truth. Socially, no doubt, we all agree with Aristotle;
society cannot subsist without polite suppressions of
truth, but, in a moral treatise, the admission points
to a different standard from that of the old Persians
and Germans. The main point on which I here insist is, that dishonesty was not an occasional symptom
in the worse epochs of Greek history, but a feature
congenital in the nation and indelible—waxing and
waning, no doubt, but always at a tolerably high
level.

Let us pass to a pleasanter topic, and cast a glance
at the *hospitality* of the lyric days, as compared with
that of the Homeric epoch. The reader will remember that there were symptoms of the decay of this

virtue, which naturally flourishes among primitive
societies, when means of communication are difficult,
and the providing of food and shelter for travellers
has not yet become a matter of commercial speculation. It appeared that the Homeric Greeks were at
the close of that condition in which men keep open
house for strangers, and that they were beginning to
estimate the cost and convenience of having to do so.
We can hardly fancy Hesiod welcoming a stranger
with much cordiality : he objects to spending time in
idle talk, and would ill brook the interruption of his
field work to amuse vagrants.

Of course the lyric poets, being aristocrats, have
more gentlemanly notions ; but the princely incomes
of the old kings and chiefs had gone in the party
struggles, the confiscations, and the exiles which distracted the Greek cities. When a single ruler or
tyrant attained to wealth and power, there is reason
to believe that he was as hospitable as his suspicions
would permit, but the average aristocrat was seldom
in a position to practise Homeric hospitality. Miltiades the elder, indeed, who was a sort of prince or
dynast in Attica, is described by Herodotus, at the
close of this period, sitting at his door, like Abraham,
and ready to bring in every passing stranger. Yet
this was in the power of but few, and perhaps in the
inclination of but few also.

We have in Theognis a kindly and interesting
passage on the point, which is worth quoting (v. 511
sqq.) : ' Thou hast come here, Clearistos, having accomplished thy voyage through the deep sea, with

nothing, wretched man, to me who also have nothing; we will place supports (ζυγὰ) under the sides of your ship such as we have and such as the gods give us; and we will afford you the best of what we have, and if any friend of yours arrives, he shall sit down with us in as friendly a way as yourself. Neither will I reserve any of my goods, nor will I bring from another house any greater display for the sake of my friendship with you. But if any one asks what is my life, you may tell him that for an easy life it is hard, but though hard yet easy enough[1], so that I need not abandon a *single* hereditary guest friend, though unable to afford hospitality to any larger number.' He repeats almost the words of Telemachus receiving the suppliant seer (ο 280), ' Come into the ship, and then you shall be friendly entreated with the best that we can afford.'

There are certainly two points of great importance already mentioned,—points upon which the lyric age had made a decided advance, if not an improvement, on the Homeric range of feeling and sentiment. The first is the emotion of love, which is described as quite a different passion in its manifestations by the lyric poets, and is frequently excited by different objects. It is difficult to handle such a subject freely, but it is far too important in any social sketch of the Greeks to bear being omitted. I will merely indicate points of view and materials which may guide the student who seeks to comprehend this aspect of Greek life more thoroughly.

---

[1] ὡς εὖ μὲν χαλεπῶς, ὡς χαλεπῶς δὲ μάλ᾽ εὖ (v. 520).

In the first place, as I said above, the lyric poets describe the emotion of love with a depth and an intensity quite foreign to the rhapsodists. Even when Agamemnon and Achilles quarrel fiercely about a fair captive, there is hardly one word about their love for her. Nay, the peerless beauty Helen excites mere vulgar passion in her seducer; nor do we hear of any deeper and nobler feeling in Menelaus, whose private emotions are kept out of view by the poet, to be developed with full richness and beauty by Æschylus and Euripides in a later age. The marital affections of Hector, Ulysses, and their wives, are deep and lasting, but there is nowhere any hint of that sort of all-absorbing influence which we meet in Archilochus and Sappho, just as we meet it in all the great modern poets. It is there in Archilochus, even in the wretched scraps left us by jealous time: 'I lie wretched and lifeless with desire (*fr.* 14), pierced to the inmost marrow by the potent pang of the gods,' says he; and there is no doubt what pang he means, if we compare *fr.* 103, where he speaks of 'the desire of love pouring a mist over his eyes and stealing away his heart.' No Homeric hero would have understood such poignant feelings on the score of a woman. There was, no doubt, desire, but desire such as that of Aphrodite in the song of Demodocus, or of Paris in the third book of the Iliad, of Penelope's suitors, or of the same Aphrodite in the famous Homeric Hymn addressed to her. There was love of home, and with it of wife and children, but no passion other than the lowest, and that treated rather as a mere appetite, than as anything high or worthy of poetic glory.

But in the lyric age we have Archilochus, we have, above all, Sappho, whom I have above quoted (p. 114), we have Ibycus, we have Anacreon, devoting all their genius and their art to portray this potent master of human happiness and misery.

There is yet a greater change in the objects towards which it was felt. Here first in Greek literature we meet with that strange feature which reached its climax in later times, and centred upon beautiful boys affections as romantic as those which we naturally feel between opposite sexes, and opposite sexes only. The reason of it is obvious enough. It is only when mental refinement is added to physical beauty that the love of lyric poet, and mediæval knight and troubadour, becomes possible—that love rises from an appetite to a sentiment. If this be so, I am convinced that the deeper and fuller awakening to love in *our* sense among Greek hearts was closely connected with the custom of strong attachments among men. The change in the object of their love was the cause of the ennoblement of that feeling itself. The generous affection for an intellectual equal displayed in the second part of Theognis' Elegies, the various stories of heroism and self-devotion which were familiar to Greek historians—these were not possible in early Greek society, except under the conditions to which I have adverted. We have as yet no Aspasia to advocate the higher education of women. We have in many cities a tendency to seclude women, and prevent them from being companions to their lovers. Thus their natural place was invaded by those fair and stately youths, with their virgin looks, and maiden modesty, who were the delight of Solon and Theognis, and Socrates and Epaminondas—in fact, almost every great Greek in the greatest days of Greece.

There remains but one more topic to complete our review—the moral and religious progress of the lyric age as compared with the boasted excellence of Homer. Here there was indeed a change of vast importance. Of old, the poet had been the only accredited preacher, expounding the brief and obscure responses of the oracles, describing the lives of the great men of old, then advancing to personal reflections, to gnomic wisdom, and to terse summaries of human experience. In these various functions the poets had been, if I may so say, the established clergy of the older Greeks. But now there sprang up a new class of teachers, the philosophers, who emerged from the wretched polytheism of the Epos, with its shameful immoralities, and taught a larger creed and purer morals. Of course the old poets were at first contemptuous, then disgusted, then abusive.

This is the old contest between poetry and philosophy of which Plato speaks (*Rep.* p. 607, C): 'of which there are many proofs, such as the saying [of the poets] of "the yelping hound howling at her lord," or of one "mighty in the vain talk of fools," and "*the mob of sages circumventing Zeus*," and "the subtle thinkers who are beggars after all"; and there

K

are ten thousand other signs of ancient enmity
between them.' 'Such studies,' he says again, in the
Laws (p. 967 C), 'gave rise to much atheism and
perplexity, and the poets took occasion to be
abusive—comparing the philosophers to dogs, uttering vain howlings, and saying other nonsense of the
same sort. But now, as I said, the case is reversed.'
Of course it was reversed gradually, and so Plato
is able in the *Protagoras*[1] to speak of the old poets
as really the forerunners of the Sophists, and thus
opposed to true and philosophic teaching.

But the struggle was long, though never doubtful.
Xenophanes, writing in verse no doubt, but still
decidedly a philosopher, as opposed to the professed
poets, decries the singing old theologies about gods
and Titans. Pindar, a poet, though affecting to be
a philosophic teacher, shows constant traces of the
struggle. But he is clearly on the defensive. Though
he reviles the philosophers, he is obliged to manipu-
late and palliate the myths. He speaks contemptuously (*Nem.* iii. 40) of artificial wisdom, which
attempts a thousand virtues and attains none : Ἀτελῆ
σοφίας καρπὸν δρέπειν is his expression (*fr.* 124) for
philosophy. Yet he is elsewhere obliged to deny the
poets' stories of murder and adultery among the
blessed gods. He tries to mediate between faith and
rationalism, but of course in vain. He may accommodate some isolated legends, he may even venture
to deny others, but no piecemeal criticism, no sur-
rendering of outworks, no attempted truce with the

[1] Jowett, i. p. 125.

enemy, could save the old Greek religion. Even those poets who professed to find in the myths a solid creed, and who claimed to be the accredited moral teachers of the nation—even they owed their noblest thoughts and their loftiest poetry, not to the Epos, but to the contact with their opponents. Thus in Pindar, of whom we can speak most confidently, we are not attracted by his long mythical narratives, or by his moral lessons drawn from these models, in any sense as we are attracted by those splendid passages where he shows contact with the Orphic mysteries, or whatever theosophy had brought into life the reward of the good and the punishment of sinners in a future state. Here is a doctrine absolutely foreign to the gods of Homer, foreign to the gloomy justice of Providence in Hesiod ; and yet in Pindar it makes the poet soar above his ordinary course into a higher and purer air:

> ' To them the sun, in radiant might,
> Lights up the subterranean night.
> In meads empurpled o'er with roses
> They take their calm suburban ease,
> While over them the fragrant shade reposes,
> When golden fruits weigh down the loaded trees.
> Some in the chariot's rapid flight,
> Some with the dice indulge, or in the harp's soft delight.
> And still luxuriant all around
> The universal plenty blooms;
> And over all the holy ground
> Float evermore the incense-fumes,
> When from the altars of the gods arise
> The far-seen fires of constant sacrifice.'

(Milman's transl.)

So too we find him compelled to assert the moral

side of the old religion. He must select those instances, exceptional as they are, which show the
ruling of Providence over men, which show the punishment of guilt, which show the difficulties and
trials of virtue rewarded in the world. It is indeed
true that the poet was able to say but little upon
morals which was not the tritest commonplace. Di-
vest his maxims of their stilted diction, and you will
find the saws of Hesiod, of Theognis, and of Solon,
neither deepened nor enlarged. It is all mere
children's prattle beside the deep speculations of
Æschylus, his younger contemporary. But Pindar
and Æschylus may be contrasted as Herodotus and
Thucydides, the former perhaps more antique and
childlike than his age, the latter so advanced as to
outrun even his successors, and stand out a monument
of genius apart from or beyond the natural development of things.

Here then I pause, at the threshold of a new epoch,
in which our materials are no longer too scanty, but
too full, and where our difficulties do not arise from
doubtful inferences and uncertain hints, but rather
from the great multiplicity and variety of the materials
before us.

CHAPTER VI.

THE GREEKS OF THE ATTIC AGE.

THE epoch of which we are now to treat is that in which Athens took such a lead as to be presently considered the head of Greece, if not from a military, yet at least from a social and literary point of view. It may indeed be said, that her empire in this latter sense was not accomplished until she had been compelled to abandon her claims to rule Greece by her arms as well as by her arts. For though, during her first and most brilliant career as a conquering state, she had produced literary men who were never equalled, and works of art which were never rivalled, yet it seems to me that her real empire over the manners and minds of the other Greeks dates rather from the days of Plato and Menander than from those of Thucydides and Sophocles. Euripides lived, indeed, in the former epoch, but his works had hardly attained their full popularity until its very close, and until, after the disastrous end of the Peloponnesian War, *culture*, rather than naval and military power, became her pride. I am disposed, therefore, to separate this

Attic epoch for my purpose into three subdivisions: the first, extending from the repulse of the Persians to the end of the great civil war and the capture of Athens (in 403 B.C.); the second, from her liberation to the battle of Chæronea (in 338 B.C.); the third, the close of her greatness, comprising the age of the New Comedy, the days of Epicurus and Menander, and extending till the days when Alexandria and Rome supplanted her as the centres of the world's thought. To the first two epochs I shall adhere proximately, claiming however that freedom which is due to a mere social sketch as opposed to strict history. Nor do I think the distinction between the second and third epochs very vital or deeply marked in Greek life.

But to any one intimate with Attic literature, the general contrasts of these epochs will at once be felt, and perhaps more easily felt than demonstrated by special citations. Thus the remains of the first epoch are the tragedies of Æschylus, Sophocles, and Euripides, the earlier Comedy down to Aristophanes' old age, the histories of Herodotus and of Thucydides, and the fragments of the earlier orators (Antiphon and Andocides). If we add the fragments of Greek historians, chiefly preserved in the anecdotes of Athenæus, Plutarch, and other such later compilers, we have before us a considerable body of various literature, marked by several distinct features, and by certain contrasts to succeeding ages. It was an age of great hurry and prodigious development, when event after event so came crowding upon the people, that they were under the perpetual excitement of some new acquisition or some unexpected danger. A great public enthusiasm laid such hold of every Athenian, that private life was despised, and private comforts set aside, while every man devoted himself with all his might to advance his city, and to sacrifice private ends to the calls of state service. I need but refer to the remarkable picture attributed to the Corinthians, or to Pericles himself, in Thucydides (i. 70, and ii. 66), and fully borne out by the historical facts of the previous generation.

It is perhaps a mistake to look upon this apparent self-sacrifice as patriotism in our modern sense—as the same feeling which prompts noble natures to postpone their private comforts to great public ends. If my estimate of Greek character hitherto be just, this will seem highly improbable. I am rather disposed to look upon the undeniable public spirit of the Athenians as that of men who, seeing a great future before their country, rise from a paltry ambition after private wealth and comfort to a higher—though still selfish —ambition after public fame, and the glory of leading the course of public affairs. So they became a city full of public men, if I may so say, engrossed with state service, and with politics, men of little leisure, and of small curiosity in speculating upon the reasons of things, in fact no theorists, but stern men of action, full of earnestness in their lives, and allowing themselves little relaxation. I am here speaking of the general tone of Periclean society, for I know well that Pericles himself, and some of his familiar friends, such as Anaxagoras, formed marked exceptions to this rule[1]. So also Euripides, who in this as in other respects marks a transition to the succeeding age, shows many traces of pure philosophy, of speculative thinking, as opposed to practical politics. But the timid and fragmentary philosophical teaching of this great poet shows how a man who wrote for the Periclean public was obliged to conceal his speculations, and put on the stage plain practical politics and plain human passion.

Thus even when their relaxation came we see that it bore the deep impress of their hurry and their public cares. The Old Comedy was essentially political, and directed to satirising public affairs and public characters, so that the Athenian statesman might well have complained that even in his leisure hours the strife of party and the fever of public life did not depart from him. In another respect, too, this Comedy was the relaxation of busy men, in the full flavour of its wit and the grossness of its vigorous satire. This is, I think, an universal feature in human nature. Men that live lives of excitement and exceeding fatigue, whether it be professional, or political, or commercial —men that are wild speculators in the market or in public affairs, cannot afford time and attention for

[1] Stesimbrotus tells us, as quoted by Plutarch, that Pericles used to discuss subtleties with Protagoras, and that they disputed for a whole day in the case of a fatal accident at an athletic contest, whether the dart which inflicted the wound, or the thrower, or the arrangers of the contest, were truly the *cause* of the accident. This case is discussed in Antiphon's second tetralogy, and seems therefore to have been a favourite subject for casuistry.

gentle and soothing recreation, for the so-called Attic salt of mere leisure conversations, for philosophical disquisitions and for long rambles in the country. They will generally plunge from one excitement into another, and will not rest their minds save with such engrossing bodily pleasures as expel all thought of serious things. They too often rest the man by indulging the beast within them. No one who has observed our great centres of life and business in the present day can have missed this prominent feature. I think this may be the reason why the Athenians of the first epoch, men of far more seriousness in many respects than their successors, delighted in public exhibitions which became coarse and unseemly in the eyes of their gentler but weaker successors. There was no time for Platonic dialogues, no taste for the quiet comforts of home life. The ribald scenes in Aristophanes were meant to satisfy far different wants.

But who would have expected from this picture that, among these busy, hard, realistic politicians, art or literature would have prospered? Do not all the features adduced rather point to a state of things in which the leisure enforced by the tyrants, and their enlightened patronage, must be felt by the artist an irreparable loss? I am convinced this was so, and believe that, *throughout Greece generally*, the age following the time of the despots, which I call the Periclean age, but which reaches far beyond his death, was in literature decidedly an age of decline. There is no other reason why the lyric poetry, which was

flourishing at the opening of the period, should have
decayed, and almost vanished from Greece. Up to
the rise of the Athenian and other democracies, we
have art centres for sculpture, poetry, and architecture
throughout Greece, at Samos, at Lesbos, at Corinth,
in Sicily,—we may say wherever there was a court.
And so lyric poetry, like the epic which preceded it,
was the general property of all Greece, sung and read
everywhere, speaking to the heart of every Greek.
All this now vanishes[1]; the plaintive Mimnermus and
the fierce Tyrtæus, the passionate Sappho, and the
turbulent Alcæus, the voluptuous Anacreon, and the
bombastic Pindar,—all these have left no successors.
But this great and melancholy void is hidden from
us by the dazzling splendour of Athens. And the
exception is so great that it has obscured the rule
and made historians speak of the Attic period as the
most brilliant in Greek literature.

This was due to two special causes: first, to the
discovery of the drama, by which a poem could be
produced before king Demos, as well as king Peisistratus, thus giving back to the poets a many-headed
and wealthier patron than the friendly despots.
Secondly, to the substitution by Pericles of a presi-
dency over subject states, for a tyranny over subject
citizens. This great man was in many respects the
direct successor of the older despots. He had the
blood of despots in his veins, and their instincts in his

---

[1] Thus even Eupolis, early in the Attic age, speaks of Pindar's poems
as ἤδη κατασεσιγασμένων ὑπὸ τῆς τῶν πόλλων ἀφιλοκαλίας (*Athen.* i. 4).
He seems to assert a degradation in taste.

heart, but he contrived, with extraordinary genius, to combine these instincts with a democratic policy. He made all his fellow-citizens into one great despot, subject to his own influence, taxing other states, and applying the proceeds just as Polycrates or Peisistratus would have done, to the beautifying of his city and the active patronage of literature. Thucydides was not blind to this curious combination [1]. He saw that Athens was under Pericles a democracy only in name; he felt the concealed despot in him; but it is in Plutarch's life that we find all the details about sculptors, and painters, and architects, and poets, which show how thoroughly the Athenian prime minister had combined the tyrant's patronage of literature with the political life of a free constitution. Thus under this man, and owing to his

---

[1] As Mr. Müller Strübing observes (*Aristoph. u. d. hist. Kritik.* p. 82), this idea of Athens as a tyrannis is put forward in express terms in the speech of Pericles (*Thuc.* ii. 62), and that of Cleon (iii. 37), by Thucydides. He might have added *Aristoph. Eq.* 111 :—

> ὦ Δῆμε, καλήν γ᾽ ἔχεις
> ἀρχὴν ὅτε πάντες ἄν-
> θρωποι δεδίασί σ᾽ ὥσ-
> περ ἄνδρα τύραννον·

also that Demosthenes (*in Lept.* p. 478) alludes to the Lacedæmonian rule in similar terms, ἡγοῦντο γὰρ οὐ μικρὰν τυραννίδα καὶ τοῦτον, τὴν Λακ. ἀρχὴν καταλύσαντα, πεπαυκέναι, when speaking of Conon, and comparing his merits with those of Harmodius. The administrators of the common fund were Athenian citizens responsible to Athens alone. The tribute was fixed and assessed by the Athenians, who divided their empire into four provinces, comprising about 180 cities. The lists and amounts have now been recovered from inscriptions, and published with a most instructive map, in Kirchoff's collection (vol. i. Berlin, 1873).

exceptional genius, Athens enjoyed the advantages of both conditions, and consequently strode ahead of all the rest of Greece. But I repeat that it was at Athens alone, and for these special reasons, that civic democracy was compatible with an advance in literature. We look for it in Samos, in Mytilene, in Syracuse, in vain. Throughout the rest of Greece the fever of politics, and the hardships of war, had acted fatally on literature [1].

[1] Though I freely confess the transcendent genius of Pericles, I see no reason for following the modern German school in the extravagant estimate of his moral character, which they have borrowed from Thucydides' *History*. There are not wanting evidences, to any one who will read the work, not in blind admiration, but with a critical sense, that it is to a great extent what the Germans call a *Tendenz-schrift*, intended to magnify Pericles and his policy, while it traduces Cleon and others who succeeded the great statesman. This sort of party-history has been written by Sallust, and detected by modern critics, who hold his two treatises to be political pamphlets, concealed under a garb of severe narrative. Perhaps Thucydides was to Sallust a more exact model than that historian suspected. Pericles (and Thucydides) stood to Cleon and his party in somewhat of the relation of the old Whigs in English politics to the modern Radicals. The former were great noblemen, who took up the cause of the people, and opposed the Tories, and so far the Radicals are their direct successors, just as Mr. Grote has shown that Cleon succeeded to the policy of Pericles. But nevertheless there are many old Whigs whose rank and traditions lead them to despise and dislike their modern allies, to claim a distinct name, and assert on many points a distinct policy. Thus Thucydides, a follower of Pericles, certainly intends us to believe, and even insinuates strongly, that Cleon's policy was not the continuation of that of Pericles. But it is really strange how the genius of the historian has carried with him all the moderns, though he is almost the only contemporary, or nearly contemporary, authority who estimates Pericles so highly. Thus, for example, the opinions of the two greatest Greek thinkers, Plato and Aristotle, which are fortunately preserved, are apparently against him.

But I must not let these political considerations draw me away from my proper subject. I urge them to show that the exaggerated esteem for Pericles and for the Athens of his creation should not blind us to the defects which were very plain to the philosophical critics of his own and succeeding generations. I am persuaded that as the age of the tyrants in Greece generally, and of the Peisistratids at Athens, was an age of political stagnation, but of social and artistic advance, so on the contrary, the age of Pericles, including the whole period between the battles of Plataea and Ægospotami, was an age of rapid political development, possibly also at Athens of literary and certainly of artistic development; but at Athens, and perhaps throughout Greece, one of social and moral stagnation. And as my present

Though the former was a decided aristocrat, and the latter a Liberal Conservative, and so opposed in principle to Pericles' Radicalism, as they thought it, yet as they judged him long after his death, when all personal bias had long passed away, their opinions are too weighty to be summarily set aside. Plato (*Gorgias* 515–18) does not indeed insist upon what seems to have been the usual aristocratic judgment, that Pericles had made the people lazy, idle, and grasping, but he does insist that he merely gratified their desires, and was their servant for popularity's sake. This view, however, appears to have been modified by Plato in his *Phædrus*, where he speaks of him very respectfully. Aristotle's opinion may be gathered from two passages quoted by Plutarch, the first in his life of Pericles, cap. 9, where Aristotle gives a sketch of his policy very similar to that attributed to Caius Gracchus at Rome. The second is an indirect notice of equal value, in Plutarch's *Nicias*, where he enumerates from Aristotle the three best public men of Athens —Nicias, Thucydides (ὁ Μελησίου), and Theramenes—and where the omission of Pericles is very striking. The evidence of the Old Comedy, were it of any value, agrees with these judgments.

object is to regard the Greeks in this latter point of view, the Periclean epoch, so brilliant in other respects, will be that from which we can draw but scanty materials. There was in social life even retrogression.

The attitude, for example, of women in imperial Athens was lower than we have yet found it in Greece. A certain contempt for them seems to have become the fashion. As if in contrast to the old-school Herodotus, in whose delightful pages women occupy a due place, and come before us in very distinct characters, Thucydides is pointedly silent upon them, and makes his silence the more speaking by the aphorism put into the mouth of his ideal hero—'That woman is best who is least spoken of among men, whether for good or for evil[1].' There is no modern reader who will not confess that the practical adoption of this sentiment in his history is one of its main defects, as compared with the truer and more artless picture of the great Herodotus. Posterity owes the dry Athenian a grudge that he has not deigned to break his studied silence on that remarkable woman, who is said to have had no mean influence on the course of public affairs. Had he condescended to vindicate her true position against

---

[1] I have elsewhere (*Proleg. to Ancient History*, pp. 10, sqq.) shown additional reasons for Thucydides' silence, as antagonistic to the prominence given to Aspasia by the comic writers, and also how this particular point in Pericles' speech specially intends to repress a second outburst of the enthusiasm shown on a previous occasion, which was doubtless disagreeable to his cold and distant dignity.

her comic slanderers, or to endorse it with his sober judgment, we might have well excused him his digressions about Hipparchus and Hippias, valuable as they are to modern historians. In this, as in other respects, my former judgment of his work, as a 'great but defective history,' has been confirmed, not only by farther reflection, but by a valuable ally, Mr. Müller Strübing, whose *Aristophanes und die historische Kritik* shows, with great power, how wretchedly poor and starved are the allusions of Thucydides to the attitude of parties at Athens. We are, in fact, reduced to doubtful inferences from the ribald joking of Aristophanes, and to the scanty evidence of a few recovered inscriptions, for explanations of what he saw, and could have told us in a few of his pregnant clauses, had not his intention been otherwise. His very contemporaries were obliged to write books supplying his omissions [1].

From this important writer we accordingly gain but scanty light as to social and private life at Athens. There are, however, a few indications of old simplicity in manners and luxury in dress deserving of notice, which cast special light on the peculiar and somewhat repulsive features of Athenian life, as we find it in this epoch. Thucydides (ii. 15–17) mentions that, up to the outbreak of the Peloponnesian war, many of the citizens had still preserved the ancient custom of living in the country,

---

[1] Cf. Dionysius Halicar. περὶ Θουκυδ. c. 16, who mentions Cratippus as ὁ συνακμάσας αὐτῷ καὶ τὰ παραλειφθέντα συναγαγών. (Müller's *Frag. Hist. Græc.* ii. p. 75.)

and only visiting the city on business—a condition
of things reminding us of Hesiod, who regards these
visits as only compelled by vexatious lawsuits; and
blames his brother for wasting his time, and fre-
quenting the town. If we combine this notice of
the old country life in Attica with another remark
on the elegant dress of the older citizens, who wore
from luxury linen tunics, and fastened their hair
with a golden tettix (i. 6), and then compare the
picture in Herodotus of the elder Miltiades sitting
before his door, and offering hospitality to passing
strangers[1], these indications show us a state of society
in which the Athenian women held a very different
position from that conceded to them under the developed democracy. Nothing was more depressing
in ancient times to the freedom of women than city
life, for the absence of proper police regulations made
it not easy for them to go abroad; and besides, the
duties or responsibilities of a town household are as
nothing for a housewife compared with her importance

---

[1] Herod. vi. 35: 'When Peisistratus was autocrat at Athens, Miltiades, the son of Cypselus, also was a man of great importance
(ἐδυνάστευε), being of a house that kept a four-in-hand, and by remote
descent a scion of the Æacidæ of Ægina, but now an Athenian. This
Miltiades, sitting in his verandah, and seeing the Doloncian envoys
coming by dressed in foreign garb and carrying spears, called out to
them, and when they approached offered them lodging and hospitality.'
They had previously gone along the sacred road through Bœotia
and Phocis, but had met with no such treatment. The hospitality
and plenty of ancient days was a favourite topic with the old comic
poets, as may be seen from the numerous citations on this point in
Athenæus (vi. p. 267 sqq.), especially from Teleclides, Cratinus, and
Aristophanes.

in a country establishment[1]. Although, therefore, the surly Hesiod complains that one of the grievances of having a wife is her insisting on joining her husband at meals, I suppose the nobler Athenians (as the lower classes certainly did) acted very differently; and how sharp this contrast between their town and country life appeared to Athenian women can be proved from the affecting utterance of Xenophon, in a tract which will hereafter occupy us, when he speaks of the moving out to the country as 'delightful to the wife, and longed for by the children.'

This contrast was very essential in Greek life; for we see so late a writer as Polybius struck by it, when he comes to describe the Eleians (iv. 73). This people had even then preserved an old-fashioned and luxurious country life, very like that of early Attic days. There were rich families, he tells us, who had not visited the city for several generations, and who lived a quiet life free from all politics. This arose partly from the rich soil, partly from a wise policy in the city, but most of all from the sacrosanct character of Elis, on account of the great Olympic festival.

Had, therefore, no other concomitant changes occurred at Athens, I hold that this transference of residence from the country into town must have affected private life severely.

There were added even more important political

---

[1] The model husband Ischomachus, in Xenophon's Œconomics, advises his wife to obtain bodily exercise by folding up and sorting clothes in her various presses! (Xen. *Œcon.* cap. x. § 11.)

L

causes. With the progress of the age, the aristocratical tone of Athenian life, lasting, no doubt, far
longer socially than it did politically, gave way before
the invading democracy, and the political centre of
gravity changed from the side of the nobles into the
midst of the whole male population. The result of
this equality upon the position of women is obvious.
I have shown before that, in Homer's day, the wives
and daughters of the chiefs were respected and influ-
ential because they were attached to the centre of
power, because they influenced the king more than
free men did, and because they belonged to an exclusive caste society which despised all beyond its pale.
The same thing holds good, though perhaps in a lesser
degree, in the aristocratic days of historical Greece.
As long as the Eupatridæ held the sway, their noble
ladies held a high position in Attic society ; and it
is doubtless from such that Æschylus has drawn his
figures of Clytemnestra and Electra—figures full of
grace and refinement, and very different from the
coarser and harder heroines in the works of Sophocles. Accordingly, when the power passed from
the special class of the nobles the consideration felt
for all their *entourage* would also pass away. A
common man, with an actual vote, would become
of more importance thán an Alcmæonid lady, who
might possibly of old have swayed her ruling husband ; and so with the development of political
interests, gradually absorbing all the life of every
Athenian, there came, in that deeply selfish society,
a gradual lowering in the scale of all such elements

as possessed no political power. Old age and weaker sex were pushed aside to make way for the politician—the man of action—the man who carried arms, and exercised civic rights.

Yet even these weighty causes seem to me inadequate to explain the really Asiatic jealousy with which women of the higher classes were locked up in imperial Athens, and the contempt with which they were systematically treated. Of course, these very feelings have hidden from us their full explanation, but I think we should not fail to remember a certain reaction of Ionia upon Attica, which must certainly have been produced by the development of the Athenian marine, and by the closer relations of the various members of the Delian Confederacy. There seems no doubt that even about Solon's time educated Athenians considered a visit to Asia Minor, and to the splendid court of Lydia, just as necessary as our young noblemen once considered a visit to the French court, then the perfection of refinement and elegance. It is also well known that the wealth and the luxury of the Asiatic cities far exceeded those of their Hellenic sisters. It seems, therefore, more than probable that the Asiatic tinge which the Ionic Greeks received both by their contact with Lydia, and by the Persian conquest of Ionia, as it certainly introduced lower notions concerning the social position of women, so it also affected fashionable life at Athens[1]. There is nothing so infectious

---

[1] There is distinct evidence that Polycrates, for example, modelled all his city and its habits after the luxurious Sardis. Clearchus of Soli,

among imitators as the contempt and the sneers of
a fashionable man, and I can well conceive the young
Athenian who went to see the world at Miletus and
Sardis, coming home with an altered view on the
rights and privileges of women, and thinking that
after all the hareems of the Asiatics were the best
arrangement for men, inasmuch as it left them full
liberty to follow their own pleasures, without hindrance and without criticism from mothers, and
wives, and sisters[1].

I think that some such influence as this should
be conceded, and it will help to explain the extraordinary phenomenon before us; I mean, how imperial Athens, the home of the arts and of literature,
the centre perhaps, even then, of social refinement
in Greece (though this is doubtful)—how this Athens,
which had thoroughly solved the problem of the extension of privileges to all citizens, had retrograded as to

quoted by Athenæus (xii. p. 540, E), describes how the morals of all
Greece were corrupted by these imported customs. There was a street
at Samos devoted to debauchery of all kinds, called the λαύρα στενή.

[1] The fair and gentle attitude towards women in Herodotus, and the
great influence he is disposed to allow them in modifying the greatest
historical events, show that mere contact with Asia Minor did not
produce this degradation of women, which seems peculiar to Athens,
and induced by Asiatic models grafted on Athenian city policy.
Eupolis (Meineke's *Com. Frag.* ii. p. 529) speaks of Ionian women
following their husbands when on military service (ὥσπερ λεχώ στρα-
τιῶτις ἐξ ᾽Ιωνίας), which is inconsistent with strict seclusion, and the
girls of Miletus and of Ceos are well-known to the comic writers as
temperate, and of refined manners at table. But these things may refer
to the lower classes, who were at Athens sufficiently free. The Asiatic
character of the Greeks, as compared to the western Aryans, should also
not be overlooked.

women, and if not in practice, yet certainly in theory, denied them that reasonable liberty which all the older Greek literature shows them to have hitherto possessed. Many effects of this injustice are apparent in Athenian literature.

But it is high time to escape from generalities, and examine in detail our individual authorities. Hitherto almost all our evidence was in the epic age anonymous, in the lyric fragmentary, so that the mental bias of the writers could not be ascertained, or if so, criticised with any certainty. The case is now widely different. The personal characters of Herodotus, Thucydides or Euripides, are quite essential in considering the information they convey to us, and the neglect of this obvious point has occasioned innumerable errors. As my conclusions are in many points singular, owing to the weight which I allow to this disturbing element, I must examine each of the Attic authors separately, and in some detail. In following out this plan, the social points will be elicited disconnectedly, but I trust so fully that a short summary at the close (p. 233) will give clearness and consistency to a long and irregular exposition.

It is to be remarked that for the earlier part of the present epoch we have but little direct evidence. Æschylus and Herodotus can alone be said to throw any light upon the state of Greece immediately after the Persian wars ; and unfortunately for our purpose, the latter, as to facts, is engaged with the previous generation as his special subject, and the former was a man of that peculiar genius which is little coloured

by the current of every-day life around him, and
which centres itself upon those great eternal world-
problems, whose features are ever the same, and
which are not changed with the changing fashions of
men's lives.   Thus in the extant tragedies of Æschylus, the interests are, if I may so say, too colossal
to admit of much delineation of character ; amid the
crash of armies, and the mightier 'shocks of doom,'
these purely human features fall into the background.
I know not that he has left us distinct pictures of any
heroes or heroines save those of Agamemnon and
Clytemnestra, and that of Electra in his *Choephoræ.*
The rest are general types, such as that of a warrior
king (Eteocles), of a patient sufferer (Prometheus), of
an overbearing herald (Hermes, in the same play), of
an anxious suppliant (Orestes and Danaus).   It is in
respect of the development of personal character that
the great trilogy of Æschylus stands far in advance
of his earlier plays; and the combination of this feature
with the great laws of destiny and the gloomy lowering of an ancestral curse over a great regal house—
this combination it is which makes the *Agamemnon*
of Æschylus, in my opinion, far the greatest of extant
Greek tragedies.

It is, however, not my intention to give an æsthetical
analysis of this Greek masterpiece, in so many features
analogous to Shakespeare's *Macbeth*, but rather to indicate what sort of characters are implied among the
actual contemporaries of Æschylus by the features in
which he has clothed his characters on the stage. The
γυναικὸς ἀνδρόβουλον ἐλπίζον κέαρ (v. 11) of the queen is

far removed from the weak though complimentary picture of the Homeric bards [1]. She is a ruling queen, like the Artemisia, whom the poet might have seen commanding her ship in battle; she sways her husband's sceptre, and even when unfaithful to him, is able to suppress the discontent and the murmurs of her subjects. She is a far stronger character than either Agamemnon or Ægisthus, and it is with a deep psychological instinct that the poet has portrayed her as such, and yet wasting her attachment on unworthy and insignificant men—a case so common in our, as in every, society. She shows no inferiority in reasoning power or in resource to the men around her, and while boldly asserting as a queen her right to take vengeance on her husband, is very anxious to justify it by subtle arguments about blood-guiltiness and about fate. The same equality between the sexes is shown in the second play of the trilogy, where Electra is the more leading character. The feminine side of both these characters in Æschylus will be better discussed in contrast with the very different women of Sophocles.

The principal result attained for our social sketch from the works of Æschylus is the high conception he forms of the ability and of the importance of women, and how large a part they play in human history.

[1] She is there described as a person of excellent disposition, who only yielded to a long course of temptation, when her good advisers were removed. I have explained (p. 56) that this estimate may have been partly due to the position of the rhapsodists, who sang for queens, and who wished to magnify the good influence of their own order.

The pictures he draws, in the mouth of Clytemnestra, of the faithful wife waiting for her husband's return, and of the husband's anguish at the loss of the wife he loved, cannot be passed over as evidences of the social relations of married people. In the first (*Agam.* 855 sqq.), Clytemnestra, after excusing herself for telling in public of this longing for her husband—a modesty which is effaced by long continuance of her desire—paints how distressing are the many vague reports carried at second-hand into the retirement of the palace, how many times Agamemnon had been killed according to them, and how often she had rushed in despair to commit suicide upon hearing them ; how to this source of anguish was added the danger of revolution, or an outbreak of popular fury, if any grave mischance befel the army. ‘For you indeed the rushing fountains of my tears have run dry, and there is no drop left. But in my eyes, worn with late watching, you may see how I sorrowed for the signals of your victory that ever tarried ; and in my disturbed sleep I started at the faint buzzing of the gnat's wing, for I dreamt of you long tales of woe, crowded into a short moment of repose.’ In the second, the chorus, in the same play, is describing the feelings of Menelaus, when Helen had fled [1]. The

---

[1] The long and beautiful recognition scene between Menelaus and Helen, in Egypt, where Euripides brings them together in his *Helena* (vv. 625 sqq.), shows how the later poet fully appreciated this most honourable of human affections. Sophocles was too exclusively *Athenian* to leave us any similar picture. The translation which follows above is quoted from Dean Milman's version of the *Agamemnon.*

tender and uxorious character is well marked in the Homeric poems, and the tragic poet has only added depth and subtlety without modifying the main features (vv. 412 sqq.).

> 'Silent there she stood,
> Too false to honour, too fair to revile;
> For her, far off over the ocean flood,
> Yet still most lovely in her parting smile,
> A spectre queens it in that haunted spot.
> Odious, in living beauty's place,
> Is the cold statue's fine-wrought grace;
> Where speaking eyes are wanting, love is not.
> And phantasms, from his deep distress unfolding,
> Are ever present with their idle charms;
> And when that beauteous form he seems beholding,
> It slides away from out his clasping arms:
> The vision, in an instant it is gone,
> On light wing down the silent paths of sleep.'

Quite apart from the refined and delicate relations of the sexes in marriage, which these splendid passages imply, we are struck forcibly throughout all the seven tragedies, as I have elsewhere remarked, with the extraordinary depth, subtlety, and boldness, both of the conceptions and of the language of Æschylus. When we reflect upon the fact that these poems were brought out upon the stage, and acted in connected series before an audience without printed texts, or previous knowledge of the treatment, we find ourselves in the presence of a society which in intellectual culture must have been vastly superior to the best and most critical modern audience[1].

---

[1] According to Aristophanes (*Ran.* 760), even the Athenians found

No doubt the Athenian public was by no means so
learned as we moderns are, they were ignorant of
many sciences, of much history—in short, of a
thousand *results* of civilisation, which have since ac-
crued. But in civilisation itself, in mental power, in
quickness of comprehension, in correctness of taste,
in accuracy of judgment, no modern nation, however
well instructed, has been able to equal by laboured acquirements the inborn genius of the Greeks.
Let me add that no modern theology has taught
higher and purer moral notions than those of Æschylus and his school, developed afterwards by Socrates and Plato, but first attained by the genius of
Æschylus. Thus he censures high-handedness even
in the gods (*Prometheus*), so laying the foundation
for that great doctrine of immutable morality which
is the basis of modern ethics. Again, he shows the
indelible nature of sin, and how it recoils upon the
third and fourth generation, thus anticipating one
of the most marked features in Christian theology.
Nay, even involuntary transgressions of the moral
law are followed by dire consequences. The agreement of Sophocles (in his *Œdipus*) shows that these
deep moral ideas were no individual feature in

Æschylus hard to appreciate, though his many victories are good
evidence that they succeeded:

>   οὔτε γὰρ Ἀθηναίοισι συνέβαιν' Αἰσχύλος,
>   λῆρον δὲ τἄλλ' ἡγεῖτο τοῦ γνῶναι πέρι
>   φύσεις ποιητῶν.

Other Greeks were accordingly thought quite incompetent, the Athenians
partially so. but this of course applies to a newer generation.

Æschylus, and that there must have been a sober earnestness at Athens very far apart from the ribaldry of Aristophanes. Such immorality as that of the modern French stage was never tolerated among the Greeks, in spite of all their license. In respect then of deeper ethics, Æschylus, and consequently the society in which he lived, rise far above the lyric age, and to us the so-called flights of the inimitable Pindar, which astonished the Latin imitators of Greek poetry, are as the efforts of a weak fledgeling leaving his warm nest with fear, compared with the bold eagle that swoops from his unapproachable λισσὰς αἰγίλιψ ἀπρόσδεικτος οἰόφρων κρεμὰς γυπιὰς πέτρα. This intellectual power and acuteness, presupposed by Æschylus in his audience, was in prose just as fully taxed by Thucydides, of whom I shall speak at greater length presently.

But we must first pause before the social pictures of Herodotus, the younger contemporary of Æschylus, the personal friend of Sophocles ; yet as Æschylus may be considered the old school poet, so he is called the old school prose writer of the period. I think that this common remark has been exaggerated, and that it is rather in the choice of subject than in his handling of it, that Herodotus really represents the 'good old times.' The facts which he relates are more properly discussed in our sketch of social Greece in the lyric age, but the dramatised dialogues, and the vivid pictures which adorn his incomparable history—these must be coloured by his own imagination, and must therefore necessarily

show the complexion of the society in which he lived.
Thus, for example, his theory of the Deity as a *jealous*
God, visiting the sins of the fathers upon the children
—this theory, though not so deeply or morally worked
out, decidedly reminds us of the theology of Æschylus, and not of the views expressed in any lyric
poet, though it might be gathered indirectly from
Theognis. It is, like most ideas of deities, the reflex
of a leading feature in the people's mind, and noticed as such. Thus Herodotus himself introduces
Xerxes' brother as advising him, that ' it is on this
principle that the Greeks delight to act, they grudge
good fortune, and hate superiority [1].'

Those who think of the sharp contrast we find in
Thucydides, and how modern the latter appears in
comparison with Herodotus, should not consider Herodotus, as is usually done, exceptionally old-fashioned,
but rather Thucydides as exceptionally advanced.
He belonged, as I believe, to a small set of hard
sceptical politicians who clustered about Pericles and
Anaxagoras at Athens, who were not in sympathy
with even the Athenian, far less the Greek public,
and who have therefore no right to be thought the
representatives of Greek opinion or of Greek social
life in those days. Some small sections of Greek
society, or Greek society under some peculiar strain,
may have assumed the repulsive features which Thucydides describes, but there is in my mind no doubt
whatever that the ordinary Greeks of the Periclean

---

[1] καὶ γὰρ δὴ καὶ τρόποισι τοιούτοισι χρεόμενοι οἱ Ἕλληνες χαίρουσι·
τοῦ τε εὐτυχέειν φθονέουσιν καὶ τὸ κρέσσον στυγέουσιν (vii. 236).

age were rather the Greeks of Herodotus, than the Greeks of Thucydides.

The broadest and deepest reason for this assertion is that the Greeks of Herodotus have all the universal features of the race, stamped upon them in all ages, while Thucydides pretends that in his day the face of society changed to a totally different type. As if the evidence of Aristophanes and Euripides his contemporaries, of Antiphanes and Alexis in the next generation, of the patriots Epaminondas and Demosthenes—as if in fact all the evidence we can get in all Greek history and literature did not contradict him! The Greeks before his day, even in Homeric and Hesiodic days, had been often treacherous and cruel, generally dishonest and selfish, but withal often generous and gentlemanly, always clever and agreeable, and always carried away by a love of beauty more than by a respect for truth[1]. All these features, the heritage of early days, are found in the men of Solon and Theognis, in the men of Pindar and Simonides. They are also found in the men of Herodotus and of Euripides, whose portraits are far more faithful than those of the dry and surly Thucydides.

Let me verify my assertions by a few citations from Herodotus on each of these somewhat contrasted features. As to the meanness and lying of

[1] Thus the Egestæans of Sicily, even in Herodotus' time, had a shrine at the tomb of the Crotoniate Philip, and offered sacrifices to him as a hero, *on account of his extreme beauty* (Herod. v. 47). At Athens, even old men were selected for their beauty to take part in public processions.

the Greeks in Herodotus, I may select their relations
with the Asiatic monarchs, especially with Darius,
as a feature which remained unchanged in the historian's own day, and for generations to come.

There was at Athens a clan of Alcmæonidæ, into
whose history Herodotus goes at length (vi. 121,
sqq.) owing to an allegation that they had attempted
to betray their city to the Persians after the battle
of Marathon. This story seems to Herodotus incredible, owing to the high respectability and known
anti-tyrannism of the family. ' For,' says he, ' there
were no men more highly thought of among the
Athenians, or more highly honoured.' He tells us
how one of this famous old clan, who had been of
service to Crœsus, was invited to Sardis, and promised
as much gold as he could carry away on his person.
Whereupon this great Athenian nobleman puts on
a very wide tunic, with hanging folds, and the very
largest top-boots he can procure. Proceeding to the
king's treasure-house he at once sets to work upon
a heap of gold dust, and having stuffed his boots full,
he next puts as much into the folds of his tunic as
it will hold, and then having crammed his mouth
with more, and having sprinkled it through his hair,
emerges so stuffed out as to be hardly like a man.
Crœsus bursts out into laughter, but like a thorough
gentleman, adds as much more to his gift, so that
Alcmæon, out of the proceeds, was able to breed
horses, and conquer at Olympia.

This story, which was told, as I suppose, to Herodotus by the Alcmæonidæ themselves, shows what

notions they had of gentlemanly conduct. But the
story is by no means isolated. All through the reign
of the Achæmenid dynasty, the Greeks, and Greeks
of all cities, were going up to Susa on all manner
of pretexts, promising the great king all manner of
easy conquests, begging for restoration to their homes,
asking for money, and paying him with perpetual
ingratitude. Nothing is more striking than the good-
natured and gentlemanly contempt of Darius, who
never shows vindictive feeling, but always, apparently
to Herodotus' surprise, pardons, and even favours,
rebels and traitors. Thus the Milesians, who had involved him in a bloody and expensive war (vi. 30),
the son of Miltiades, his false friend, and bitter enemy
(vi. 41), and the people of Eretria, who had burned
wantonly his Lydian capital (vi. 119), when brought
before him as prisoners, are treated kindly, and
settled in his country. It is evident that the great
king appreciated their talents and activity, though
he evidently despised their treachery. I have no
doubt the Persian grandees only shared with him this
latter feeling[1], and to this, as much as to the love

---

[1] To what pitch of meanness the Greek, even of those days, could
descend in making money, appears from the disgusting story of
Panionius the Chian, told by Herodotus (viii. 105 sqq.). The longing
to return to Hellenic life is well described by Andocides (pp. 3, 58,
ed. Blass). 'Why,' say his adversaries, 'will you await trial and
danger here, when you can go to Cyprus, and there enjoy wealth and
tranquillity; see you not the wretched state of our city?' 'But I,
gentlemen, am of a far different mind. For I would not choose all the
good things of the world, to live away from my country; and were it
even in such a plight as my enemies allege, far rather would I be a
citizen of it, than of others, which perhaps seem to me at present very

of Hellenic society, and city politics, do I attribute
the fact that no Greeks, however magnificently treated,
could ever content themselves at Susa; they all
sought to beg or to embezzle the treasures of the
great king, and bring them to Hellenic homes.   There
was, indeed, a single exception—Scythes, tyrant of
Zancle—who asked leave to visit Sicily, and returned
to die in Persia.   ' Him Darius considered to be the
most righteous of all those who had gone up to
him from Greece, in that he kept his promise to the
great king.'

What an evidence of Greek dishonesty! We can
well fancy the Aryan barons of Darius' court speaking
in the tone of the Roman Juvenal. To them, too,
the *Græculus esuriens* was but too well known—with
his fascination, his cleverness, and, withal, his mean
and selfish knavery. I need hardly remind the Greek
scholar that all through the Ionic revolt, and through
the Persian wars, this treachery and this selfishness
were the mainstays of the Persians; in fact, had
they depended upon these more completely, the sub-

prosperous.' I cannot refrain from adding a parallel piece of evidence
from a different and little known source. ' It happened to the people
of Posidonia,' says Aristoxenus (Athenæus, xiv. p. 632, A), ' who were
sometime Greeks, that they were utterly barbarised, and became Tyr-
rhenians or Romans, so that they changed their language and the rest of
their customs; but they even now still observe one of the Hellenic
feasts, in which, coming together, they call to memory their old names
and customs, and having bewailed them to one another and wept their
fill of tears, they separate.' How strange and affecting an evidence of
the deep hold which Greek culture had taken even on those who were
compelled for generations to abandon it !

jugation of Greece would have been a mere question of time. The several states were always intent upon their own interests, always ready to betray their neighbours and allies for material advantages ; and had not the satraps, who held them in special dislike because of their personal influence with the King, treated them with severity, doubtless much more could have been effected by combined bribery and pardon. The Ionic cities were, perhaps, injured in political morality by the prevalence of tyrants, who were generally paid, or at least supported, by the Persians : but still among the Æginetans and the Argeians, and even among the Athenians and Spartans, there are not wanting melancholy instances of the same defects [1].

So far, then, Herodotus agrees with Thucydides' picture, though describing the generation preceding the men of the Peloponnesian war ; so far, too, I am certain that both rightly felt the salient weaknesses of the Greek character. But Herodotus makes these baser motives give way at times to real patriotism and kindly justice. Most men are, with him, selfish and hard ; yet it is not unusual to find a just man. There is, too, a Providence rewarding goodness, and thus higher principles have their weight in Greek

---

[1] How lax or peculiar must Herodotus' own notions have been, when he tells us (vii. 164) that Cadmus, tyrant of Cos, without pressure or danger, *and merely from a love of justice*, surrendered his tyranny ; and yet that this same Cadmus went with the Samians to Sicily, *where with them he seized and held the city of Zancle*, thenceforth called Messana, one of the most scandalous pieces of injustice and treachery in all Greek history (vi. 23).

M

society.　Here, then, Herodotus openly asserts what
Thucydides denies in spite of facts, and here he is
in harmony with the tragic poets, with the higher
aspirations of the Old Comedy—in fact, with human
nature as opposed to the refinements of the selfish
moralists.　With most men the oracles, though
Thucydides and his set despised them, commanded
veneration and respect, nor did the contempt of the
Periclean party overthrow them, seeing that in after
days such men as Xenophon condescended to consult
them.　Now there can be no doubt that as the
confessional of the Roman Catholic is mainly a moral
engine for good, so the oracles, especially that of
Delphi, were the priestly guide to many troubled
consciences, and 'led into the way of truth those that
had erred, and were deceived,' especially by their
own interests.　The greatness of this moral force is
proved by the fact that even some acknowledged
cases of bribing the oracle did not destroy its popularity or its use.

We do not realise what a great moral engine was
here at work, for we have but few of the private
responses preserved.　But here is an example [1].　It
occurs in a speech of the Spartan king to the
Athenians, when they refused to surrender some
hostages whom they were keeping for the Spartans.
There was a certain Glaucus at Sparta, celebrated
for justice (like our friend Cadmus, just cited), as
well as in other respects, to whom a Milesian, who
had heard of his fame, came and entrusted a treasure,

[1] Herod. vi. 86.

wishing, as he said, to get the benefit of his justice, since Ionia was disturbed. Of course, such a temptation was too much even for this paragon of Greek honesty. When the heirs of the Milesian came with their tokens, and claimed the treasure, he professed to know nothing of the affair. But when they had gone away baffled, Glaucus, who had a conscience, was afraid to spend the money without asking the oracle whether he could safely do so. Whereupon he received an answer telling him that he might, himself, escape [1] the consequences, but that the family of perjurers should suffer vengeance and be exterminated. This is not all. When Glaucus begged pardon for his indiscreet question, the Pythia declared *that making trial of the god, and committing the crime, were of equal guilt*, and though he sent for the Milesians, and gave back the treasure, his house, says the king, is now desolate.

When the great oracle of Greece gave such moral responses, nay more, when they were still quoted with faith, there must still have been much sound moral feeling in Greece.

Allied to sound morality we may expect to find tender and kindly feeling, and of this there are some remarkable examples in the stories with which Herodotus adorns his narrative. I know none more striking than the love of children which breathes through many of his dramatic anecdotes, and which I believe, in spirit and in form at all events, to be

---

[1] The same view is put strongly by Lycurgus in his great speech against Leocrates (cap. 19) in a later generation.

his own, or that of his age, even though the naked
facts may be the heritage of a previous society. He
is here, as in many other points, the direct successor
of the epic poets (cf. above, p. 30).

We have, for example, the story of the birth of
Cypselus (v. 93), afterwards tyrant of Corinth.

The oligarchs knew by oracles that this child
would be dangerous to them, so they watched for its
birth, and when this occurred they sent ten men to
the deme, or townland, where its father Eetion lived,
to slay the child. 'These men coming to the house
of Eetion, went into the courtyard, and asked for the
child ; so its mother, Labda, knowing nothing of their
intentions, and *thinking that they had come to see it
out of friendliness to its father*, gave it into the arms
of one of them. Now they had determined, on the
way, that the first of them who got the child into his
hands should dash out its brains (προσουδίσαι). But
when Labda brought it to him, *by God's providence,
the child smiled at him as he took it*, and a pang
of pity as he perceived this prevented him from
slaying it ; and so, with a soft heart, he handed it
to the second, and he to the third. Thus the child
passed through the hands of all the ten, and none
of them would murder it. So giving back the child
to its mother, and going out, they stood and began
to reproach one another, and especially the first who
had taken it, that he had not carried out their resolution, until, in time, they made up their minds to
go back and accomplish the deed.' Meanwhile the
mother had hidden it in a chest (κυψέλη), and, after

a half-hearted search, they go home to say that their duty has been performed.

This picture of the mother naturally expecting her husband's friends to walk out into the country, in order to see and admire her new-born baby, shows a pleasant contrast to the darker features we have been discussing, and the pity of the miscreants, and their hesitation, shows how strong a hold the helpless innocence of an infant had upon them, as upon all civilised men. I believe the notion of exposing infants, from *economical* motives, not to have prevailed till later times; and it is possibly to the same age that we may refer the interesting notice of Aristotle [1] about the Malians, that an oracle having commanded them to love the dearest of the dear [2], they used to carry round their little children naked at their feasts and kiss them. It must have been an usual fashion in later days at Athens to send for them after dinner, for Theophrastus notices, as one of the features of the Flatterer, that he asks for the children, plays games with them, and lets them sit on him and molest him without grumbling. Thus also we find, going back to Herodotus, that the Peisistratidæ, when they were in a good condition to resist and conquer the Athenians in revolt, 'had all their affairs thrown into

---

[1] Müller, *Frag. Hist.* ii. p. 150.

[2] φιλεῖν τῶν φιλτάτων τὰ φίλτατα. To reproduce the alliteration, and to render the double meaning of φιλεῖν (to love and to kiss), as well as the emphasis of the double superlative, is impossible in English; nor would it be easy to find a shorter and more obvious example of the power of the Greek language.

confusion,' and agreed to evacuate the country in
five days, because their children, whom they were
sending out secretly to a foreign place of refuge, were
captured by the Athenians. A *bon mot*, pointing in
the same direction, is preserved in Plutarch's life of
Themistocles (c. 18), who used to say 'that his boy [1],
who bullied his mother, was the greatest power in
Greece: for the Athenians ruled the rest of Greece,
he (Themistocles) ruled the Athenians, his wife ruled
him, and the boy ruled her'—a charming piece of
humour, but showing a deep feeling for the power of
little children in the house.

I will quote yet another anecdote on this feature,
and, for variety, from Sparta. It occurs (vi. 61, sqq.)
in Herodotus' account of the ungentlemanly trick by
which the king Aristo obtained from his dearest
friend a beautiful wife whom he coveted. He proposed that each of them should give the other whatever that other desired—a proposal which Agetus,
who knew that Aristo was already married, and who
had no suspicions of his intention, readily accepted.
However, the lady (whose name, strange to say, is
not mentioned) 'was the fairest woman in Sparta,
and this, too, after having been the most hideous
child; and her nurse, seeing her ugliness, and that
she was the child of wealthy parents, though so ugly;
and, moreover, that her parents thought her appearance a misfortune,' went daily to the temple of the
heroine Helen, and prayed that the goddess would

[1] His name was Cleophantus; he was a famous horseman, but otherwise insignificant. Cp. Plato, *Meno*, p. 93.

take away the hideousness of the child[1]. At length a lady meets her going out of the temple, 'and asks her what she is carrying in her arms; but she answers, "a child": and the lady (who is the heroine herself) asks to see it, but she refuses, *for she had been ordered by its parents to show it to no one;* however, the lady persists, and, stroking its head, predicts it will yet be the fairest of Spartan women.' So from that day the child's appearance began to amend.

Such was the interest which Herodotus and his age felt in little children. It was accordingly mentioned as one of the greatest calamities that befell the

---

[1] The reader who wishes to see the Greek ideal and epical nurse, should consult the exquisite narrative in the Homeric hymn to Demeter (vv. 113, sqq.), part of which I have quoted (above, p. 59). Æschylus, on the contrary, lofty tragedian as he is, has given us a picture too realistic to bear translation of the duties and troubles of the ordinary historical nurse, who upon hearing the death of Orestes, weeps over the recollections of all her idle toil. Her avocation is in no respect different from that of our own nurses.

τὰ μὲν γὰρ ἄλλα τλημόνως ἤντλουν κακά·
φίλον δ' Ὀρέστην, τῆς ἐμῆς ψυχῆς τριβήν,
ὃν ἐξέθρεψα μητρόθεν δεδεγμένη,
καὶ νυκτιπλάγκτων ὀρθίων κελευσμάτων . . .
καὶ πολλὰ καὶ μοχθήρ' ἀνωφέλητ' ἐμοὶ
τλάσῃ· τὸ μὴ φρονοῦν γὰρ ὡσπερεὶ βοτὸν
τρέφειν ἀνάγκη, πῶς γὰρ οὔ; τρόπῳ φρενός.
οὐ γάρ τι φωνεῖ παῖς ἔτ' ὢν ἐν σπαργάνοις,
ἢ λιμὸς ἢ δίψ' εἴ τις ἢ λιψουρία
ἔχει, νέα δὲ νηδὺς αὐτάρκης τέκνων.
τούτων πρόμαντις οὖσα, πολλὰ δ', οἴομαι,
ψευσθεῖσα παιδὸς σπαργάνων φαιδρύντρια,
κναφεὺς τροφεύς τε ταὐτὸν εἰχέτην τέλος.
ἐγὼ διπλᾶς δὲ τάσδε χειρωναξίας
ἔχουσ' Ὀρέστην ἐξεδεξάμην πατρί.

Chians (vi. 27), how the roof fell in upon 120 children
at their lessons in a school, and only one escaped
alive. Even the cold Thucydides confesses that in
after days the greatest and deepest sympathy excited
by any incident in the Peloponnesian war was the
massacre of a school-full of little children, at Myca-
lessus, by some Thracian savages, who passed through
when returning home from mercenary duty. His
own feelings are pretty well concealed under the
most violent contortions of grammar[1]. Thus Euripides, who appealed to the emotions of ordinary
men, heightens the pathos of his *Andromache* by
putting her child Molossus on the stage — no easy
matter in a Greek theatre. The pathetic appearances
of Astyanax in the *Troades*, and of Orestes in the
Iphigenia in Aulis, though they are silent, have not
escaped the observation of intelligent critics.

Before leaving Herodotus I must add a word on
the sociality and *bonhommie* which his whole work
breathes. However dishonest and selfish, the Greeks
were always pleasant and conversational. This appears even in his pictures of the tyrants, a class whom
he detested politically, and regarded as one of the
greatest of human evils[2]. In telling us the story of
Polycrates and the ring, he describes the fisherman
(iii. 42) bringing the fine fish he had caught *to Polycrates' door, and asking to see him.* And when he
was admitted, he says: 'O king, when I caught this,

---

[1] vii. 29: καὶ ξυμφορὰ τῇ πόλει πάσῃ οὐδεμιᾶς ἥσσων μᾶλλον ἑτέρας
ἀδόκητός τε ἐπέπεσεν αὕτη καὶ δεινή.

[2] v. 78; vi. 104, 134.

I would not bring it to market, though I live by my trade, but it seemed to me worthy of you and your greatness, I accordingly bring it a present to you.' The tyrant is delighted, and says, 'You have done right well, and I thank you twice, first for your deed, and next for your (pleasant) words, *so join us at supper.*' This Polycrates, it must be remembered, was the greatest and most powerful Greek sovereign of that age, perhaps excepting the tyrants of Syracuse (Herod. iii. 60, 125); and the habit of the Asiatic monarchs was to see no such people, but to receive their messages, as Herodotus well knew (iii. 119). Yet here we have a certain simplicity of life very peculiar for a man who aspired to the sovereignty of the sea.

The same friendliness, combined with much refinement, comes out in the story of the famous marriage of Agariste (vi. 126, sqq.), which I believe Herodotus to have heard at Athens from the Alcmæonidæ, whose family history he knew so well. Its peculiar features are decidedly Athenian. For the tyrant Cleisthenes of Sicyon entertains for a year in his palace all the great lords of Greece, who are suitors for his daughter's hand. With great tact, if it be not historically accurate, Herodotus does not introduce a Spartan among these suitors, as his exclusiveness and boorish manners [1], if they did not prevent him from aspiring to the Corinthian tyrant's daughter, would

---

[1] He gives an account of Spartan boorishness again, when certain envoys were required to prostrate themselves before the king of Persia. and refused (vii. 160).

certainly have totally unfitted him for the competition which ensued. For they were tested as to disposition and temper and education and manliness, in gymnasia if they were young, but in any case and particularly he tested them by *social entertainments*[1]. When the deciding day came, there was a feast of a hundred oxen, and after (late) dinner, the suitors endeavoured to outshine one another in matters of music, and in *general conversation* (τῷ λεγομένῳ ἐς τὸ μέσον), when of course the two Athenians excel the rest. But Hippocleides takes to dancing and then to standing on his head, and Cleisthenes for some time, though he loathed the idea of having a son-in-law so shameless, *refrained from breaking out upon him*, but when he saw him standing on his head, and gesticulating with his legs, he could not help calling out, 'O son of Tisander, you at all events have danced away your marriage.' And then he selects the other Athenian, Megacles, an Alcmæonid.

Nothing can exceed the gentlemanly conduct of the tyrant all through this affair, who, by the way, on choosing Megacles, apologises to the suitors for the necessity of choosing one among so many whom he would all gladly favour. In fact throughout his history, Herodotus, with true tact, contrasts the manners of the despots with the manners of such free Greeks as the Spartans, whom he evidently respects, but thinks very disagreeable. Thus when the joint

---

[1] καὶ τό γε μέγιστον, ἐν τῇ συνιστίῃ διεπειρᾶτο. Here I think I see the Athenian touch of the story coming out.

embassy of the Greeks goes to Gelon of Syracuse to ask for aid, and he offers it, but claims the command on the ground of his superior force, the Spartan envoy (not like Cleisthenes) at once bursts out into invective ; but Gelon answers, ' Spartan stranger, reproaches are wont to excite anger in him who receives them, but you, though you showed yourself insolent in your speech, will not persuade me to make an unseemly reply '—a sentiment more like those of Menander than those of the age of Euripides.

These dialogues, which I quote rather as evidence of Herodotus' own culture than of that of the men whom he introduces as his speakers, show that there was throughout Greece, and especially among the states which had been ruled by tyrants, a great deal of social culture, and a great deal of gentleness and good breeding. The Athenian society in which he mixed was, I think, of this kind, and the many obligations of Sophocles to his immortal history show how much in sympathy he stood with the foremost men of his age. Nay, even in one respect he seems to me clearly in advance of the hard, grasping, and shortsighted selfishness of the Greeks of Thucydides. In the exquisite passage which gave to Sophocles the germ of his finest chorus, Herodotus has attained to that Indian summer in human experience, where the fading leaf and the ripened fruit with all their richness suggest the winter of decay, and remind us that however sweet is life, it has been doled out in scanty measure. Nay, even the end that comes so soon, comes not so soon as we pray for it, and bitter as it is, there are few who have not longed that it might cut short their earthly miseries. From this deeper reflection flow the gentleness and the unworldliness of the man who loved and enjoyed the world so keenly.

I will cite the famous passage in detail (vii. 46). Xerxes, having ordered a review of all his forces at the Hellespont, and seeing the sea hidden with ships and the coast swarming with men, at first was over-joyed, but presently burst into tears. Whereupon his uncle Artabanus observed to him : ' O king, what a sudden change there is in your conduct ; just now you were congratulating yourself, but now you weep. But he said : it occurred to me, when I thought thereon, to pity human life, how short it is, since of all this multitude not one will survive in one hundred years. But the other answered : There are other things harder in our lot than the mere shortness of life. For in this so brief span there is no mere mortal born throughout all the world so happy, that he does not once and again come to wish for death rather than life. For misfortunes falling upon him and diseases troubling him make this life, short as it is, seem full of weariness. Thus death has become a very chosen refuge to man from so sorry an existence, and the God who has given us a sweet taste of it in our generation, is found grudging in his dole [1].'

---

[1] This is the germ of Sophocles' famous chorus, *Œdip. Col.* 1242, sqq., to which I shall refer hereafter, also anticipated by Mimnermus.

CHAPTER VII.

THE GREEKS OF THE ATTIC AGE (*continued*).

I NEXT take up Thucydides, the most misleading, and therefore the most misunderstood, of our
authorities.

His general account of the Greek character in his
own times (to which he distinctly limits himself, by
contrasting the older days of simplicity and honesty)
is clear, hard, and unpleasing. He describes the
Periclean Greeks as differing from their fathers in
possessing a greater political insight, in habitually
hearing and using argument, in understanding a far-
seeing policy, and estimating the balance of complicated and conflicting interests. But most critics
have failed to observe that in these features he makes
the Corinthians, and Corcyræans, and Sicilians, not
a whit inferior to the Athenians; and there is here,
to my mind, a great want of dramatic power in the
author, or else an absence of that finer perception
which is so prominent in Herodotus. The speeches
in Thucydides are so completely cast in the same
mould as to be obviously rhetorical exercises of his
own, and not honest attempts to dramatise the

critical moments in his history. Yet there is about this dull sameness an element of truth. As the small territories of so many enterprising cities, and their consequent proximity, made isolation wellnigh impossible, so their complicated relations and constant wars made politics an all-absorbing pursuit The notion of an empire of intellect and of taste without political supremacy, had not yet dawned even upon the Athenians. Consequently politics corroded the social life, as well as the literature, of Periclean Greece.

There resulted, farther, a greater simplicity of dress and life[1], and probably some carelessness as to home comforts and material luxury. There followed thirdly a harder view of life and of men; a more daring assertion of self-interest as opposed to principle, of force as opposed to justice; and often a habit of casuistic dispute and of subtle equivocation. These painful moral features, which are patent enough through all his history, are saliently brought out not only in his speeches, but in an imaginary dialogue which he has composed between the Athenians, when they proceeded to force the island of Melos into their naval confederacy, and the unfortunate Melians, who plead that they have broken no treaty, violated no obligation, and therefore incurred no lawful hostility. The Athenians are here represented as laying aside all that speciousness which was their known characteristic. They brutally assert that justice is only

[1] Cp. above p. 144.

invoked by the weaker side, and that superior force asks no justification for asserting itself [1].

Another passage, in which Thucydides turns aside to reflect upon similar ideas, but quite generally, is the famous compendium of Greek politics appended to his account of the Corcyræan massacre.

The substance of what he says is as follows : That according as the war progressed, the general state of society became gradually worse ; men became what the French call *effarouchés*, and sought out new schemes of overthrowing their enemies, and new cruelties in wreaking their vengeance upon them. Even the very signification of ordinary terms changed. Rash boldness came to be considered loyal friendship, and wise caution specious cowardice. Men were expected to stop at nothing for their party ; and if they did hesitate, they were cast aside as worthless and unfaithful. For party became the paramount bond, and overrode the ties of blood. Its object was not to abide by the law, but to evade and violate it. Oaths and promises were indeed given and taken, but had not a particle of force if interest opposed them. And the one interest which swallowed up every other feeling was the lust of power—of ruling in the state, some as aristocrats, some as leaders of a democracy, but even then only so long as no more complete victory, such as a tyranny over both friends and foes, was in view. Thus every form of villainy became prevalent in the Greek world on account of their internal factions. Simple honesty was laughed out of

[1] Cp. the whole dialogue at the close of the Fifth Book.

society, and guarded mistrust took its place. There was no superior power to arbitrate, and men were so trained to forecast unexpected dangers, that they were unable to feel confidence in either oath or promise[1].

I am not the least disposed to question the accuracy of the *facts*, which suggest to him these reflections. Such cruelties as the Corcyræan massacres are unfortunately not uncommon in Greek history. The murder of the Platæan prisoners in cold blood by the Spartans (iii. 68), and the vote passed at Athens against the conquered Mityleneans (iii. 36), of whom the ringleaders were executed, while perhaps 5,000 more escaped with much difficulty—these are, within Thucydides' own volume, sad corroborations of his statements. There are not wanting other witnesses. Heracleides Ponticus[2] tells us that 'the city of the Milesians met with misfortune through their luxury and their political enmities, since they were not content with what was reasonable, but destroyed their foes utterly. For the rich and the poor (who were called Gergithæ) being in conflict, the demos was at first victorious, and having expelled the rich, collected the children of the fugitives into threshing-floors, and bringing in oxen had them trampled to death, destroying them with unnatural cruelty. Accordingly the rich having in turn got the upper hand, burnt in pitch all whom they got into their power, along with their children.' These horrible facts exceed any of the cruelties so commonly attributed to individual

[1] Thuc. iii. 82, sqq.   [2] Athenæus, xii. p. 523.

despots, such as Phalaris, or Pheretime[1], and should not be forgotten in our admiration for Greek culture and for Greek refinement. On this subject I shall make farther remarks in the sequel.

But in his *inferences* Thucydides is, I think, unfair. He supplies indeed a true, but partial apology, when he says that 'war is a stern schoolmaster, and makes men's tempers as hard as their circumstances.' We have ample evidence in our own day, how nations as civilised as, and far more humane than, the Greeks become cruel not only through revenge, but more inevitably through fear[2]. This partial defence should not be forgotten. Yet Thucydides has overlooked or concealed another most important consideration. It is this, that if a nation fall into a policy of faction, if the public men begin to act in cabals, the politics of these factions or cabals will always be far worse than those of the average individuals who compose them[3]. A glance at the leading politicians of Greece, even as Thucydides himself is obliged to portray them, will prove this fact, however we may explain it. Not to speak of Aristides, we have Cimon, and Archidamus,

[1] Heracleides, Κυρηναίων πολ. (Müller ii. p. 212), and Herodotus lib. v. sub. fin.

[2] There is no more striking ancient example than the treatment of the Athenian senator, who at Salamis or Trœzen proposed submission to the Persians. The exiled people stoned him forthwith, and their women hearing the tumult, and learning its cause, set upon his wife of their own accord, and stoned her *and her children.* Such conduct was rare among Athenians at any epoch.

[3] It seems a parallel fact, that Boards consisting partly at least of honest and respectable men, are often guilty of mean and even dishonest acts.

and Nicias, and Brasidas, men of honour and probity, and universally respected as such, Nicias indeed disastrously so, as Mr. Grote has amply shown in his history of the Athenian defeat in Sicily.

Our first impression, when we come to weigh these facts, is that Thucydides has been guilty of gross exaggeration in his political reflections above cited; and no doubt he *has* exaggerated, though all modern historians quote him with more confidence than they would quote the Gospels; yet he has not necessarily exaggerated so much as we at first surmise. For it is a certain fact, that considerable personal probity may be combined with political rascality, when that rascality is the act or policy of a party and not of an individual. We see it in our own day in a milder form. How many members of the House of Commons vote with their party, and feel themselves obliged to do so, though they disapprove of the action of the party, and even tell their friends that they would gladly see it defeated? It is only with exceptionally bold as well as honest men that conscience at once overrides political ties, and so a scrupulous man, in Thucydides' time, as now, was unfit to join any party [1].

But I must hasten to add that the Greek parties in his day were very unlike the great constitutional parties of our House of Commons, and should be rather called factions and cabals. They were of small compass, occupied, for the most part, in the struggles of small societies, where all the members

[1] τὸ πρὸς ἅπαν σύνετον, ἐπὶ πᾶν ἄργον, was the general opinion.

were personally known as friends, and all the opponents personally hated as enemies. Thus the bitterness, the rancour of faction, was intensified to a degree
hardly known among us. The nearest parallels are
the Italy of Macchiavelli, and the Court of France in
La Rochefoucauld's day. The *maxims* which these
writers drew from their observation are accordingly
very similar to those of Thucydides[1].

Such factions are only joined from motives of interest, and abandoned when these motives cease, for
factions have no other attraction. Thus it may happen, and, indeed, generally does happen, that a number
of fairly respectable men join together in a cabal *so
far as they are actuated by selfish interest;* and, ac-

---

[1] Manzoni in his *Promessi Sposi* (ed. Flor. 1845, p. 15) depicts a very
similar state of things throughout North Italy even in the 17th century.
'L'uomo che vuole offendere, o che teme ad ogni istante d'essere offeso,
cerca naturalmente alleati e compagni. Quindi era in quei tempi por-
tata al massimo punto la tendenza degli individui a tenersi collegati
in classi, a formarne di nuove, e a procurare ognuno la maggior
potenza di quella a cui apparteneva. . . . Ognuna di queste piccole
oligarchie aveva una sua forza speciale e propria; in ognuna l'individuo
trovava il vantaggio d'impiegare per se, a proporzione della sua au-
torita, e delle sua detrezza, le forze riunite di molti. I piu onesti si
valevano di questo vantaggio alla difesa loro; gli astuti e i facinorosi ne
approfittavano per condurre a termine ribalderie,' &c. The reader will
find similar phenomena within the limits of a single court admirably
sketched by Géruzez, 'Cours de Littérature Française,' vol. ii. p. 191.
Cp. also Plato's *Phædo* (Jowett i. 438), and Mill's *Autobiography*, p.
104. But I would call particular attention to Demosthenes *in Leptinem*,
p. 499, whose argument proceeds on the very point I have been urging.
He protests against the Athenian assembly proposing to do publicly
what they would not think of doing individually, and speaks as if such a
thing were not possible, but likely.

cordingly, the public action of the cabal represents the combined meanness and rapacity of all its component members, without at all representing the good qualities they possess. In fact, these good qualities are the strongest disintegrating forces in such a combination, and must be treated in the secret counsels of the faction as indecision and weakness.

This is the very aspect of things described by Thucydides. His history being strictly political, and his only consideration of men being their political side, he has noticed clearly enough the hard and cruel characteristics of the Greek political factions of his day, but has completely exaggerated his account by making it a general picture of the Greeks, instead of confining it to the Greeks as politicians. When he says that 'frankness, a prominent quality among honourable men, was ridiculed out of society[1],' he says what is true of the politics of faction, but false of the Greeks as a people, of the Greeks as private men and women, and certainly false of all the purer and more honourable men amongst them. It is surprising, among all the critical estimates of Thucydides' history which have occupied European scholars, that this very obvious one-sidedness has hitherto escaped notice[2].

[1] Cp. ii. 83: καὶ τὸ εὔηθες οὗ τὸ γενναῖον πλεῖστον μετέχει καταγε-λασθὲν ἠφανίσθη.

[2] I suppose the reason of this omission with many critics is that no man is absolutely sceptical. However he may assail ancient documents, and disbelieve legends, there is some point at which his doubt ends and his faith begins. Even Sir George Lewis, one of the most consistent and absurd unbelievers the world has yet seen—even Sir G. Lewis is

But as private life was reduced to a minimum of importance in this epoch, so the realistic pictures of private life, and therefore of women, which we meet in earlier literature, and again in Euripides, are well-nigh wanting to us here. We must rely on the ideal pictures of tragedy for the higher side, or the ribald travesties of comedy for the lower side of Greek home life during the early part of this brilliant period. Herodotus is, no doubt, a partial exception, and would have been a striking one had his subject led him to paint, in greater detail, this side of human nature. But the female characters in Herodotus may fairly be classed, as I class them, with the heroic characters of the dramatic poets. For, as his great historical epic brought him into bygone days, and into distant courts of foreign rulers, so the painting of his

conservative on the origin of the Homeric poems! So it is that most of the Germans, and with them Mr. Grote, having doubted or rejected older evidence, when they come to Thucydides, begin to exercise their faith. And this long pent-up virtue then bursts out with a certain strange fervour. As if to compensate for the long and painful exercise of scepticism, these men, like new converts, take up their long-sought idol, their model of historic accuracy, with a vehemence more generous than prudent. Everything that Thucydides says is to be right and accurate; though all our other authorities differ he is to be placed above them; not even a mistake in judgment is to be imputed to him. I think this is unsound criticism, and likely to mislead us on the subtler phases of Greek life. The older writers and the later compilers are in my mind more trustworthy than they are commonly thought; Thucydides is less so, not because he was dishonest, but because he was throughout all his work one-sided, and in some places, as I have elsewhere shown, partial. Cp. my *Prolegomena to Ancient History*, Essay 1; cp. also Mr. Strübing's work on Aristophanes and his age.

women, where we should expect hints as to social life, was rather ideal and artistic, than copied directly from models around him. The pictures he draws of the Persian queens, such as Amestris, are more analogous in gloom and cruelty to the portraits of Æschylus than to those of his own friend Sophocles, though such a figure as Artemisia might well take its place in any tragedy. But, in some smaller touches, Herodotus shows, as we should expect, a sympathy with female excellence deeper than that of Attic tragedy before the days of Euripides. Apart from the personal geniality of the man, which is in itself sufficient reason, we may attribute the good effect to his colonial origin. where the Athenian seclusion of women was not practised, and to his cosmopolitan education. But as I believe the morals of Herodotus represent far better than those of Thucydides the average condition of Greece in those days, so I have no doubt that the role played by women at the same date, throughout Greece generally, was rather such as is implied by Herodotus than by the surly silence of Thucydides.

Returning to the tragic poets, I have before hinted that the women of Sophocles are very degenerate and poor as compared with those of the older Æschylus. The latter has left us, in his extant plays, only three of any import—Clytemnestra, Cassandra (in the *Agamemnon*), and Electra (in the *Choephoræ*). Cassandra's magnificent scene is mainly due to her tragic situation—a clear-sighted but despised prophetess, seeing a hideous crime impending, and unable to avert it. Of Clytemnestra I have spoken above. She is one of those great figures that stand out in the dramatic literature of the world. I shall only here remind the reader of the feminine features in her character (as compared with the Clytemnestra of Sophocles), a certain tenderness, a want of resolution, which no inferior poet would have conceived as combined with the commission of wild and daring crimes. The poet has here departed widely from the insignificant character presented to us in the *Odyssey.* Thus, again, the Electra of Æschylus, in the midst of all her determination to have vengeance, does not court the sight of blood, and takes no part in the actual scene of retribution, where she does not appear. The Electra of Sophocles, on the other hand, cries out to her brother twice to slay his mother, and would, doubtless, ask to see the slain, like Penelope in the *Odyssey.* She shows, too, a certain hardness and bitterness in altercation, which the consent of Euripides proves to have been borrowed from actual life[1]. Æschylus is altogether free from this defect. The altercations are, in his plays, short, and always strictly necessary to the plot. Such are the dialogue between the Egyptian herald and Pelasgus in the *Supplices,* that between Antigone and the herald at the close of the *Septem,* that between Orestes and the Furies in the *Eumenides.* Far different, and truly Euripidean, are the almost comic scenes in Sophocles' *Electra, Ajax,* and *Œdipus Rex,* where

[1] Cp. on these points V. Courdaveaux's inaccurate but clever book on the genius of Æschylus, and his contrasts with Sophocles, pp. 209, sqq.

the constant sparring between the members of the same family (mother and daughter in *Electra*) occupy a disproportionate place, and prove to us that such wrangling did not produce on the Periclean Athenians the impression it produced upon Menander, or upon us. When Aristophanes, accordingly, marshals all his strictures on Euripides, in *The Frogs*, and in other plays, this feature, to us so vulgar, and which Æschylus had avoided, is hardly mentioned[1].

As in the case of Sophocles' Electra, so in his Antigone, there are, I think, some disagreeable features. There is something masculine in all her actions, and hard in her words. The way in which she repels the sympathy of the gentle, but common-place, Ismene, is very unpleasing, and shows a heroism vastly inferior to that of Euripides' Alcestis, or Iphigenia, where, as we shall presently see, equal courage was not sustained by the excitement of a violent conflict, or by that αὐθαδία which is anything but feminine. So, again, the coldness of her relations to Hæmon must strike every modern critic — a defect which Euripides very naturally avoided when he wrote his own Antigone[2]. I am not insensible to the grand side of her character, upon which Mr. Evelyn Abbott has lately insisted with much eloquence[3]. But still I cannot see in her any peculiarly feminine greatness.

The women of Sophocles are not skilfully drawn, and were I to select any favourites, I should certainly

[1] v. 728.

[2] Cp. the description of the argument in Dindorf's edition of the *Fragments*.

[3] *Journal of Philology*, viii. 96.

pass by his first-class heroines, and name Dejanira and Tecmessa, who though subordinate, are truly 'female women,' as Homer would say, gentle and loving, not above jealousy, but, for that reason, a finer and clearer contrast to the heroes than the coarser and more prominent heroines.

If these criticisms be just, they will show that, in the most perfect and exclusively Athenian society, that is to say among Thucydides' and Sophocles' set, the ideal of female character had degenerated ; that to these men, whose affections were centred on very different objects [1], the notion of a true heroine was no longer natural, but was supplanted by a hard and masculine type. The old free noblewoman, whom Æschylus had, in early days, still known, was banished from their city life to make way for the domestic slave of the Attic household, called, indeed, *mistress*, but, as such, contrasted with the *companions* (ἑταῖραι) who gradually supplanted her in Athenian society. To this all-important social subject I shall often return, according as each successive author adds to our evidence. It gives us another strong line in the hard features of Periclean Athens—in that Athens which considered political life as the only life worth having, and despised the age and the sex that were excluded from its privileges.

But however scanty the social evidences left us by Æschylus, however narrow and Athenian the sym-

---

[1] Σοφοκλῆς, says Athenæus, φιλομεῖραξ ἦν, as opposed to Euripides being φιλογύνης, a statement which I believe on the internal evidence of their works

pathies of Sophocles, when we come to Euripides, we find ourselves on different ground. This great poet, whose popularity stood the test of Aristophanes' travesties—a trial which must have ruined any smaller man—this poet, whom the Athenians, the best judges of poetry and of tragic poetry too, loved and delighted in, whom the philosopher Socrates acknowledged his favourite, and whom Aristotle calls of all poets the most tragic, had been of late years so depreciated by the Germans, that it seemed revolutionary to say one word in his favour. I prefer however the judgment of the Greeks, to that even of Schlegel and O. Müller. Our best English poets have of late years done much to rehabilitate this most human of writers, and I trust that the good sense of English scholars may lead them to estimate the jibes of Aristophanes at their true value, and judge Euripides fairly through his own works.

But I am not here concerned with the reputation of Euripides as a poet, and desire rather to examine how far his plays give us an insight into the social life of his times. This is indeed a most interesting question, for he certainly differs widely from the tone and manner of his rivals, who nevertheless were true and real enough to carry with them public sympathy and approval. Yet a saying attributed to Sophocles indicates the true relation between these poets. 'I have represented,' said he, 'men as they ought to be, Euripides men as they are.' Sophocles therefore did not lay claim to the same realism as his younger rival, though his notion of what men ought to be was rather a narrow Athenian ideal, than one which we, or any other civilised society, could heartily admire. His heroines, if not masculine heroines, with hard features and with no dislike for blood, are insignificant, his heroes are often querulous in misfortune, and almost always given to wrangling; as to slaves and nurses, if in Æschylus they are vulgar and comic, in Sophocles they play no prominent part at all. This is quite the attitude of Thucydides, in fact of the strictly Periclean Athenian, who with much praise of antique days [1], really invented an antiquity in character with the advanced and exclusive democracy in which he lived. The splendour of Agamemnon's court, and the queenly character of Clytemnestra are foreign to him ; even the dependants of the court, which have in Æschylus some significance, are to his democratic mind as nothing. But the wrangling and *dicastic* habits of his countrymen appear everywhere, and extended in Athens to the women as well as the men, if we may judge from these tragedies.

I have returned for a moment to the peculiar features of Sophocles, in order to qualify his statement that he painted men as they ought to be, which perhaps means no more than that he only put upon the stage such personages, and such events in their lives, as were worthy of the drama. I also desire to show by contrast the altered attitude of Euripides. Painting no ideal situations, no imaginary society of grandees, he rather felt that even the heroes of the old legends were men of like passions as he was,

---

[1] Soph. *fr.* 267, quoted by Schol. on Aristoph. *Pax,* 530.

and that to make people interest themselves really and deeply in tragedy apart from mere antiquarian curiosity, he must attribute to his characters the passions and faults of ordinary men. Of course heroism in the highest sense was not excluded, for Euripides was too thoroughly and deeply human not to know that the most ordinary civilised society produces grander and truer heroism than any primitive conditions. But his heroism is the heroism of civilised life—that of self-sacrifice and of patience rather than that of extraordinary valour.

If then Euripides drew his tragedies from the Athenian life of his own day, we must materially modify the notions still prevalent among scholars, owing to the exclusive study of Thucydides, of Sophocles, and of Aristophanes. In the first place he agrees with Sophocles as to the wrangling instincts, nay even goes so far as to make the chorus a sort of jury or dicastery which listens to the arguments on one side, and then demands to hear the other[1]. In *The Wasps* Aristophanes ridicules the same weakness, and shows us that the habit of sitting in judgment, imposed on the whole Athenian population by their extended empire, invaded social life, and that the method of Socrates was only a modification in form of the prevalent practice of arguing and discussing everything which came before them. But in this the women and the slaves are not behind their masters. To the slaves indeed Euripides, in contrast with the older poets, gives important parts,

[1] *Hel.* 945 sqq., *Elect.* 1051 sqq.

and often makes them the vehicles of his deepest
reflections: 'All the life of man,' says the nurse in
Hippolytus, 'is full of pain, and there is no respite of
toil; but whatever state there may be better than
life, shrouding darkness hides it with its clouds. We
seem indeed sorely fond of this life, with its glitter
upon earth, through want of trial of another life, and
of proof of what there is beneath the earth; but
on myths we drift about at random.' (v. 190 sqq.)
There are many other passages, such as the fine
speech of the slave in *Helena*[1], of like merit, and we

[1] vv. 711 sqq. The old servant has just discovered that his beloved
mistress is free from guilt, and that all the long disgrace of years is
now wiped away. His speech is full of tender and deep feeling,
mixed with philosophical aphorisms, as is usual with Euripides.

ὦ θύγατερ, ὁ θεὸς ὡς ἔφυ τι ποικίλον
καὶ δυστέκμαρτον· εὖ δέ πως ἀναστρέφει
ἐκεῖσε κἀκεῖσ' ἀναφέρων· ὁ μὲν πονεῖ,
ὁ δ' οὐ πονήσας αὖθις ὄλλυται κακῶς,
βέβαιον οὐδὲν τῆς ἀεὶ τύχης ἔχων.
σὺ γὰρ πόσις τε σὸς πόνων μετέσχετε,
σὺ μὲν λόγοισι, ὁ δὲ δορὸς προθυμίᾳ.
σπεύδων δ', ὅτ' ἔσπευδ', οὐδὲν εἶχε. νῦν δ' ἔχει
αὐτόματα πράξας τἀγαθ' εὐτυχέστατα.
οὐκ ἄρα γέροντα πατέρα καὶ Διοσκόρω
ᾔσχυνας, οὐδ' ἔδρασας οἷα κλῄζεται.
νῦν ἀνανεοῦμαι τὸν σὸν ὑμέναιον πάλιν,
καὶ λαμπάδων μεμνήμεθ', ἃς τετραόροις
ἵπποις τροχάζων παρέφερον· σὺ δ' ἐν δίφροις
ξὺν τῷδε νύμφη δῶμ' ἔλειπες ὄλβιον.
κακὸς γὰρ ὅστις μὴ σέβει τὰ δεσποτῶν
καὶ ξυγγέγηθε καὶ ξυνωδίνει κακοῖς.
ἐγὼ μὲν εἴην, κεἰ πέφυχ' ὅμως λάτρις,
ἐν τοῖσι γενναίοισιν ἠριθμημένος,
δούλοισι, τοὔνομ' οὐκ ἔχων ἐλεύθερον,
τὸν νοῦν δέ.

find no more common assertion both through plays
and fragments than that slavery, while affecting the
body, leaves the mind untouched (*fr.* 828, &c.).
When he desires to represent a low character of this
kind, as in *Orestes,* he carefully denominates him
a *Phrygian,* so as to leave our impression undisturbed, that in his mind slaves were unfortunate but
not degraded.

An historical reason for this altered attitude is not
far to seek. The great civil war in Greece must have
multiplied enormously the number of free and educated Greeks, who were sold as prisoners of war;
and as I suppose that for years after the Persian invasion the slaves whom Æschylus knew were chiefly
barbarians, like the policemen and public menials long
afterwards, so in Euripides' day, and especially in his
old age, I fear Athens had returned to the condition
of the Homeric poems, where piracy and kidnapping,
like civil war made free-born or even noble slaves by
no means unusual. This sympathy then of Euripides
for the slaves around him shows a gentle and humane
spirit towards these unfortunate people, who, having
been torn from their homes and separated, were subject not only to all the injustice of harsh masters, but
even to torture at the hands of the law, if their evidence was required. It is a curious circumstance
that this upholder and preacher of slave virtue
effected results, as regards slaves, beyond his wild-
est hopes. We are told that when the Syracusans
took prisoners the remnants of the great Athenian army in the Sicilian disaster, they freed from

slavery those who could recite the verses of Euripides. We can well imagine that many of these unfortunate men had of old crowded with delight to join in Aristophanes' jeers against the poet, and we can imagine them thinking with remorse how their laughter and their ridicule had saddened the days of their now greatest benefactor. And so Plutarch tells us, at the close of his *Nicias*, that many of them, when they returned home at last, went to see Euripides, and thanked him, I have no doubt with tears, for having saved them from hopeless misery.

There can be no doubt that this equality in race, and often in culture, among all the members of the house had no mean influence on Greek life, and that the women in particular, who were so secluded from free male society, must have been anxious to obtain educated and companionable slaves. Some of the characters indeed in our poet[1] complain that this very intimacy led to evil results, as the inmates of the house were apt to conspire in deceiving their master; but of course this objection would apply more strongly to ignorant and degraded servants.

Akin to this sympathy for slaves, and advocacy of their mental equality, we find in Euripides a respect for the poor, and a disregard of the accessories of poverty, which seem to have greatly shocked the old-school frequenters of the tragic theatre. I do not merely allude to the constant assertions by his characters that mind and morals, not birth, are man's true nobility (especially *fr.* 53-6), but to the utterly

---

[1] *Hipp.* 645 sqq., and *fr.* 49.

novel and bold conception of introducing heroes in the garb and condition of penury upon the stage, and (apart from special misfortunes), to such scenes as that with which he opens his *Electra*[1]. This scene, much ridiculed by the Germans, speaks to me with the deepest feeling and the greatest pathos, but, as I observed, it is a totally new and curious conception in Greek tragedy.

Electra, whom Ægisthus, her mother's paramour, had desired to slay, was saved from death by the remaining compunctions of her mother, whom Euripides with great psychological acuteness represents as boasting of and justifying her husband's murder, and yet fearing the vengeance of the gods if she illtreats her children. She therefore fears to murder Electra, but refuses her in marriage to all her noble suitors, and still fearing some clandestine amour with them (a very curious touch), gives her in marriage to a peasant, of good family, but poor. This man, with great nobility of character, will not treat her as his wife, knowing as he does the motives of her mother, and being besides attached to the murdered king and his house. We find Electra and her peasant husband at the opening of the play, living in this unusual relation, full of mutual respect and affection, both performing their daily labour willingly and honestly, but Electra with the additional stimulus of raising odium against Clytemnestra by her condition.

[1] Aristophanes, as usual, speaks of this as being a peculiarity of Euripides, and a special fault in him, whereas the *Philoctetes* of Sophocles offers us as strong a case as any in Euripides both of a hero in rags, and a hero in villainy (Odysseus).

The peasant begs of her not to work so hard in carrying water and performing other menial duties for his sake, as there is really no necessity, and he has often dissuaded her from it. She answers with great feeling (v. 67 sqq.), 'I consider you a friend equal to the gods, for in my misfortunes you have not insulted me. A great boon is it to mortals to find a healer like you in their misfortunes. Surely it is my duty to strive unbidden, as far as I can, to lighten your toil. You have enough to do in outdoor work, it is my part to keep the house in good order; when the labourer returns he is pleased to find his home comfortable.' 'Well then, go if you will,' he says; 'the well is not far, and I with the break of day must go to plough and sow my seed; for no idler by talking about Providence will earn a livelihood without labour.' On his return, I suppose towards noon[1], he finds two young strangers (Orestes and Pylades) talking to his wife, and is surprised, as it was unseemly for a Greek woman (of Athenian habits) to be seen so employed. But she at once sees and removes his suspicions by telling him that they have brought news of her brother (v. 345 sqq.). 'Then you should long since have thrown your door open. Come in, strangers, and I will give you what hospitality my house can afford in requital for your good news. Make no difficulties, ye come welcome to me from a dear friend, and though I be poor, you will not find me mean.'

'Is this,' asks Orestes, 'the husband who has treated

---

[1] Probably for his ἄριστον, or late breakfast.

O

you so nobly?' and he turns to the audience in a splendid monologue, which I hold to be Euripides' deepest reflections on the true causes of honour among men. His characters, in fifty places, assert the strange power of an ancient lineage in maintaining under the greatest misfortunes a noble and princely bearing; in as many more, they assert that the poor and despised, nay even the slaves, have in them these virtues beyond their station; so true and human and many-sided was he, in contrast, I believe, to most of his contemporaries.

Here then is the sum and substance of these true, but partially conflicting facts in human nature. 'There is no plummet line to measure excellence, for the varying natures of men confuse our reckoning. Oft have I seen the son of an honourable father nothing worth, and again good children sprung from evil parents; I have seen leanness in the soul of the rich, and a large heart in the body of the poor. How then can we surely discriminate the good? Is it by the test of wealth? Then should we indeed employ an unjust judge. Is it by poverty? But this too has its weakness, and makes men mean by its necessities. Shall I take the test of arms? Who, looking to the array of battle could testify to real worth? It is better to leave these things undetermined; for here is a man, not great among his fellows, nor supported by the pride of family, yet he has been found among the crowd a man of the most sterling worth. Will not ye learn wisdom, that speculate full of vain theories, and will ye not judge men by personal experience, and the noble by their characters?'

I cannot but translate the sequel (404 sqq.), where the painting is intensely modern and human. '*El.*— My dear fellow, when you know the indigence of your house, why have you invited these guests who are beyond your station? *The Peasant.*—Why not? if they are well born, as they seem to be, will they not be as well satisfied with scanty fare?' She then urges him, if he will have it so, to send to an old retainer, who has been dismissed from the palace, and feeds cattle at the boundaries; he will bring with him some provisions. 'Very well,' he answers, 'but do you go in and make ready. When a woman tries, she can find many little additions to a dinner. But there is surely in the house at least enough to satisfy these men for a day. When I turn to think of these things, I see how valuable money is to entertain strangers, or to spend upon yourself when you fall sick; but for our daily sustenance, it matters little, when each has had enough the rich man and the poor are after all on an equal footing.' Nothing can be more natural than this scene; how often even now-a-days does the careful wife protest against the husband's reckless hospitality, on the very ground that they have no proper means of entertaining, and does not the husband answer with the same off-hand vagueness, thinking that a hearty welcome and good intentions are a sufficient substitute for scanty fare?

The play is not less striking for our purpose when Clytemnestra (v. 998 sqq.) comes to pay the young people a visit. She orders her Phrygian attendants to get out, and give her a hand while she steps out of her carriage, which Electra spitefully offers to do, being, as she says, just as great a slave as they. This leads to some mutual recriminations between mother and daughter, which Euripides with his Athenian notions extends beyond the limits of modern taste. Clytemnestra tries to end it amicably (v. 1100 sqq.) by saying that by nature some children are devoted to their fathers, some to their mothers, and that therefore she cannot blame Electra. She then (v. 1135) orders her attendants to bring round her carriage to the stables, and to have it ready when they think her business is completed. When she is entering the house, Electra tells her 'to take care *that the smoky cabin does not soil her robes,*' an advice which many an Irish lady has received in our day without irony.

These accessory parts of the tragedy give us, I conceive, an excellent sketch of lower-class life in the outskirts of Athens in the poet's day, and it is here— in such scenery and in his *characters*—that we must seek for evidence of social life and habits [1]. It has been, I know, the habit from the days of Aristophanes to the present to quote the utterances of

---

[1] This is indeed what Aristophanes makes him say (*Ran.* 912): οἰκεῖα πράγματ' εἰσάγων, οἷς χρώμεθ', οἷς ξύνεσμεν, and the women who accuse him in the *Thesmoph.* comically amplify this, stating that, owing to his teaching, old men would not marry young wives; that others had got safe locks with many wards for their store-rooms, and kept the keys; that others had fierce dogs which kept away clandestine visitors.

Euripides' heroes, *spoken in character*, as the poet's own sentiments. The celebrated line ἡ γλῶσσ' ὁμώμοχ' ἡ δὲ φρὴν ἀνώμοτός—'My tongue has sworn, but my mind is free,' which is ridiculed by Aristophanes, is for example, in its place, perfectly just and harmless ; 'You have bound my tongue, but my mind, which was deceived as to the circumstances, has not consented to the oath.' And these words, harmless as they are, but spoken in a burst of wrath, are retracted by the very speaker a few lines farther on, when he says, that had he not been deceived into taking an oath he would certainly have told what he is now bound to conceal. There is no clearer and better specimen than this of the sort of criticism which suited Aristophanes well enough, and of which he knew the effect, but of which modern critics ought to be ashamed. Thus for example, on the goodness or badness of women, on the value of high birth or its worthlessness, on aristocracy or democracy, on almost any social question, we can put together series of quotations on opposite sides. Of course there are German critics whose inner consciousness tells them exactly when the poet is speaking for himself ; but for my part, except in such cases as Orestes' monologue above cited, which contains a mediation between two series of contradictory passages of equal weight, I cannot lift the veil which the poet has not chosen to withdraw. In some of his choruses, which he certainly made the vehicle of philosophical reflections often loosely connected with the action of the play, we may perhaps find an index of his thoughts, but from his dialogues, which are highly dramatic, we can for this very reason draw no sure conclusions.

The *characters*[1] of Euripides, on the contrary, are all-important, as he confessedly drew them from real, and even ordinary life; and they are therefore necessarily fair specimens of what might be found in Athenian society. We even have complaints that he drew his characters meanly and shabbily, nor is there the smallest hint or suspicion that he made bright pictures or took sanguine views of human nature. We may, therefore, perfectly trust his kindly attitude to the slave world, on which something has already been said; but I am doubtful whether we may also trust him in his general estimate of the men of his day, who are in his plays with rare exceptions, such as Achilles and Theseus, not gentlemen in our sense, but litigious, mean, quarrelsome and selfish[2]. There is in fact no single hero, in all Euripides' plays, who has laid hold of the imagination of the world like the Ajax and Œdipus, or the

[1] It is very curious, and has not been, I think, sufficiently observed, that Greek tragedy differed widely from the modern in not preserving the same type for the same hero throughout different pieces. The Creon of Sophocles' *Antigone*, is not the same character as the Creon of the *Œdipus*, and if it be argued that royalty had spoilt him—a very true Greek feature—I can show unmistakeable cases in Euripides. The Menelaus and Helen of *Orestes* are the very opposite of those of *Helena*; the Odysseus of the *Cyclops* is quite at variance with the Odysseus of *Hecuba* and other plays. I do not know the reason of this indifference to fixed types, fixed too for all time and for every spectator, in Homer, when the very nature of Greek tragedy was unity and fixity of type in a formal sense.

[2] Cp. the chapter on these characters in my *Euripides*, pp. 101 sqq.

Philoctetes and Neoptolemus of Sophocles[1]. No doubt several second-rate figures, the peasant in *Electra*, the Achilles in *Hecuba*, and still more in *Iphigenia in Aulis*, the Menelaus in *Helena*, are all respectable and brave men : the dialogue of Achilles with Clytemnestra[2] is even very gentlemanly, so far as it goes; but considering the great number of heroes in his plays, nothing is more surprising than the want of depth or variety in their natures. Ion is perhaps the purest and most loveable among them, yet it is not depth and greatness, but grace and innocence which makes him so pleasant an exception to the Euripidean heroes. It was surely not for want of striking men, nor for want of striking misfortunes in their lives, that they are so insignificant ; we must rather seek the explanation in a peculiarity of the poet himself, who deliberately preferred to make women his chief study, and who, perhaps owing to the neglect of them in the older tragedy, found here a new field for his genius, as well as a new means of advocating an unpopular but righteous cause. Considering the contemptuous attitude of Thucydides, and the scurrility of Aristophanes, his contemporaries, I see in this leading feature of Euripides plain indications of a great social controversy, in which the tragic poet maintained against the aristocrats, that woman was no cipher in society, but able to do and to suffer great things[3].

---

[1] Even here Œdipus and Philoctetes are rather heroes of *situation* than of *character*. [2] *Iph. Aul.* 819 sqq.

[3] It seems possible, from the part played by Aspasia in the dialogues

If we take all the plays and fragments of Euripides together, and collect from them a general view of his treatment of women, we shall see that while he is perpetually putting into the mouths of his heroes the most virulent abuse of them, yet the majority of his heroines—nay the great majority of them— are the noblest and best of women. There are in fact very few contemptible and frivolous characters among them, such as his Hermione (in *Andromache*), or purely vindictive, like his Medea. Even his much-abused Phædra (*Hippolytus*) is a noble and pure nature, wrestling in vain with a passion directly inflicted by the spiteful Aphrodite—who is really the lowest character in all his plays. So Creusa (in *Ion*), though she attempts a great crime, is a much-injured and heart-broken woman, with whom we cannot but feel deep sympathy.

But what shall we say of his Alcestis? Where has either Greek or modern literature produced a nobler ideal? She is not, like the Antigone of Sophocles, stimulated by the excitement of altercation with her advisers and opponents, and by the assertion of independence in violating a harsh law. Neither is she, as Sophocles' Antigone almost seems to be, of too strong and masculine a fibre to yield to the influence of love. Devoted to her husband and children, beloved and happy in her palace, she sacrifices her life

of the Socratic Æschines, that she was an advocate of the same cause, and brought women to her house, in order to educate them, and teach them their higher duties. (Cp. Becq de Foucquières' *Aspasie de Milet*).

calmly and resignedly—a life which is not, like Antigone's, encompassed with afflictions, but of all the
worth that life can be, and of all the usefulness which
makes it precious to noble natures. The narrative of
her farewell is one of the finest in Euripides, and I
am happy to be able to quote it from a version which
all my readers can study—a poet's version of a poet,
and no poor prose traduction.

> ' For when she felt the crowning day was come,
> She washed with river-waters her white skin,
> And taking from the cedar closets forth
> Vesture and ornament, bedecked herself
> Nobly, and stood before the hearth and prayed:
> " Mistress, because I now depart the world,
> Falling before thee the last time, I ask—
> Be mother to my orphans! wed the one
> To a kind wife, and make the other's mate
> Some princely person: nor, as I who bore
> My children perish, suffer that they too
> Die all untimely, but live, happy pair,
> Their full glad life out in the fatherland!"
> And every altar through Admetus' house
> She visited and crowned and prayed before,
> Stripping the myrtle-foliage from the boughs,
> Without a tear, without a groan—no change
> At all to that skin's nature, fair to see,
> Caused by the imminent evil. But this done,—
> Reaching her chamber, falling on her bed,
> There, truly, burst she into tears and spoke:
> " O bride-bed, where I loosened from my life
> Virginity for that same husband's sake
> Because of whom I die now—fare thee well!
> Since no wise do I hate thee : me alone
> Hast thou destroyed : for shrinking to betray
> Thee and my spouse, I die : but thee, O bed,
> Some other woman shall possess as wife—
> Truer, No! but of better fortune, say!"

—So falls on, kisses it till all the couch
Is moistened with the eyes' sad overflow.
But when of many tears she had her fill,
She flings from off the couch, goes headlong forth,
Yet—forth the chamber,—still keeps turning back
And casts her on the couch again once more.
Her children, clinging to their mother's robe,
Wept meanwhile: but she took them in her arms,
And, as a dying woman might, embraced
Now one and now the other: 'neath the roof,
All of the household servants wept as well,
Moved to compassion for their mistress; she
Extended her right hand to all and each,
And there was no one of such low degree,
She spoke not to nor had an answer from [1].'

If, as I have said, it is agreed on all hands that Euripides took his characters from real life, must there not have been, among the despised and secluded Greek women, uneducated and ill-treated as they were, great examples of real heroism, which caught the sympathy of the most tragic of poets? For the Alcestis is no exceptional type, since we have it, under varying circumstances, in the splendid though little known Macaria of *the Heracleidæ* [2]. We have another modification of it in the better known Polyxena (*Hecuba*), who is indeed doomed to die, but who meets her death with great nobility. We have the type of Polyxena carried out with infinitely more grace and beauty in *Iphigenia* (*in Aulis*), the poet's last play, and so far as it is genuine, far his greatest and most dramatic piece. For here the innocent girl

[1] R. Browning, *Balaustion's Adventure*, pp. 36 sqq. Her parting address to Admetus (pp. 48 sqq.) is equally fine, but I have already made too long a quotation.

[2] Cp. vv. 474 sqq. especially, and my *Euripides*, § 65.

has been decoyed to Aulis under the pretence of a marriage with Achilles, and only discovers her fatal delusion by an accident. Then follows a great scene, in which the young and happy creature, just blooming into life, begs and entreats for mercy with all that horror of death, which age and troubles can but gradually blunt.

> ' Had I the tongue of Orpheus, O my Sire,
> To wile away the rocks to follow me,
> And with my words to charm the rugged will,
> I had been here. Now all the arts I know
> Are artless tears—I have no power but this—
> And suppliant at thy knees I fondly twine
> The form which she, my mother, bare to thee.
> O blast me not untimely, for the light
> Is sweet to look on, and compel me not
> To peer into the darkness underground.
> I was thy first-born—first I called thee Sire,
> And sat, thy child, upon thy knees the first;
> And we exchanged sweet charities of life;
> And this was thy discourse with me—" My child
> Shall I behold thee happy in the home
> Of thy liege lord and husband, as befits?"
> And nestling in the beard, which now I clasp
> A suppliant, I made answer unto thee;
> "I too will welcome thee when grey with years
> In the sweet shelter of my home, my Sire,
> And with fond fostering recompense thy love."
> Such were our words, which I remember well;
> But thou forgettest, and wouldst take my life.
> Be not so cruel! By thy father's love
> I beg of thee, and by my mother's throes,
> Who in her anguish feels those throes anew.
> Say, what have I to do with the false vows
> That Paris pledged to Helen—to my bane?
> Look on me! give one parting look—one kiss,
> That when I die I may remember thee,

> Though with my words I may not bend thy will.
> My brother, feeble infant as thou art,
> Let thy tears flow with mine! Entreat our Sire,
> If so thy sister may escape her doom.
> The speechless infant hath a sense of ill;
> See how his very silence is a prayer—
> Have pity on me, father! spare my life!
> 'Tis sweet to gaze upon the blessed light:
> The grave is nought! The fool resigns his breath;
> The sorriest life is better than the noblest death [1]!'

Yet even she, when she stands out with majesty from her former self, will not allow her mother to revile the weak and stricken Agamemnon ; she will not allow the gallant Achilles to risk his life for her; she will not even allow her household to put on mourning, since she has entrusted to her the high mission of dying to save her country.

These are the women who have so raised the ideal of the sex, that in looking upon them the world has passed from neglect to courtesy, from courtesy to veneration ; these are they, who across many centuries, first of frivolity and sensuality, then of rudeness and barbarism, join hands with the ideals of our religion and our chivalry, the martyred saints, the chaste and holy virgins of romance—nay more with the true wives, the devoted mothers of our own day, whose loyalty and self-sacrifice in a cold and selfish generation, sustained through years of commonplace duties and amid careless ingratitude, show with no uncertain sound that they too are heroines of the first order, if society did but require of them more splendid, and therefore easier sacrifices !

[1] This translation was made for me by Professor Webb.

When we read the systematic charges of Aristophanes against such a poet, that he traduced and blackened the female sex, that he hated women, that he delighted to represent their guilty passions on his stage ; when we read these charges, made by the poet who of all others has spoken most vilely and scurrilously of the whole sex, and who of all known authors is the most open to the charge himself,—we are led to wonder at his audacious buffoonery, and how a sense of common justice did not set his audience against him. But if we can explain this from the great popularity of his brilliant wit—and in no case is injustice more readily condoned—what shall we say of modern critics, who are led by the jeers of Aristophanes, who speak of Euripides as the painter of woman's passion and her crime, and who, in total oblivion of the splendid figures in his greatest tragedies, speak with pity and disgust of the immorality of Athenian women, and actually believe that the greatest and most refined civilisation of the world coexisted with the lowest and most brutal demoralisation of home and family relations[1]? As if the portraits of Cleon, and of Socrates, were not ample proof how totally Aristophanes disregarded truth for the sake of the theories of his party, and the exigencies of his boundless and uncontrolled humour[2]!

[1] E g. Mr. Symonds, in his *Greek Poets*, p. 273.

[2] I am quite aware that there is a picture of Socrates very different from that of Plato and from that of Xenophon, handed down to us in the fragments of Eupolis (*Frag. Incert.* 10, ed. Meineke, vol. ii. p. 553) and of the serious and learned Aristoxenus, who says he obtained

One is almost tempted to believe that the ordinary critics of Euripides have studied him in Aristophanes alone, and are ignorant that we have before us ample and clear refutations, not in the praise of partisans, not in the faint echoes of scattered fragments, but in a long series of plays, expressing his views on life and character, and above all establishing what might else have been fairly doubted, that the ideal woman of his day was as noble and as natural as those of the best and most approved epochs of human morals. I have since brought together the evidence more fully, and given what I believe a just estimate of Euripides in a special monograph, to which I refer the reader for a fuller discussion of the poet's genius, and his peculiar position in relation to his age.

his information from a personal friend of Socrates (Müller, *Frag. Hist. Græc.* ii. p. 280). But even this adverse picture is not in the least like the grotesque distortion in Aristophanes.

CHAPTER VIII.

THE GREEKS OF THE ATTIC AGE (*concluded*).

BUT let us proceed to a closer examination of this Attic comedy. We look throughout it, in vain, for noble qualities, or even for refinement of feeling in the characters. The poet does indeed in some of his splendid *parabases*, strip off the veil of buffoonery and of satire to give serious advice to the assembled people, and there are not wanting pathetic touches in his rudest scenes. But, with these exceptions, coarseness and vice are perpetually before us. Women, for example, are almost invariably treated by Aristophanes and his fellow-poets with ridicule and contempt. They are derided for immorality and drunkenness, and such a picture is drawn of them as is quite appalling, if we are foolish enough to take it as evidence of Attic home life. The legion of critics who have made this mistake, in drawing inferences from Greek tragedy and Greek comedy, have ignored a remarkable feature in Greek literature, which I must again bring before the reader with fuller illustrations.

While we, both in strict history and in historical

fiction, think it essential to adhere closely to traditional or well-attested types in describing celebrated
characters, the Greeks did not feel themselves so
bound, but consulted rather the artistic proprieties
and the requirements of the special occasion. Thus
the artistic type of a hero, or of a class, was with
them often consciously different from the received or
real one, without shocking that tame and strict sense
of accuracy which, in the English, is a most serious
hindrance to all imaginative art. Consider, for example, in such a history as that of Thucydides, the
introduction of speeches which cannot pretend to be
real; which are often in a dialect foreign to the
speakers, and which so manifestly represent the
theories of the writer and his mere notions of dramatic propriety, that such biographers as Plutarch
totally ignore these harangues placed in the mouths
of the men whose lives they are compiling from this
very history. Thus of Pericles, who has several long
speeches attributed to him in Thucydides, Plutarch
says that he left nothing written, and that of his
sayings hardly any are preserved [1].

In the dialogues of Plato, the next great prose
writer, the same feature has been often noticed, and
of late with great force by Mr. Jowett. Though

[1] I am not aware that this remarkable evidence against Thucydides'
speeches, as historical, has yet been noticed. It were superfluous to
cite it, but that the most prominent historians of Greece, Curtius, and
even the great Grote, still long to accept Pericles' speeches, and evidently desire their readers to accept them, as genuine historical documents.

celebrated names are introduced — men known to many of his readers—Plato is not at all careful of historical accuracy, nay even violates it so as to show plainly that he did not aim at the mere reproducing of known and ordinary men. The case is more remarkable, as I have shown above, in the tragedians. For here not only do the types vary widely from the well-known originals in the old epic poems, *but these types vary in different plays of the same poet.* This is, indeed, a feature which must be insisted on, as quite peculiar to Greek tragedy. Thus, in Sophocles, his earlier Creon and Antigone, and those of the *Œdipus at Colonus,* are not at all the same. Similarly in Euripides, if we compare the Menelaus and the Helen of the *Helena* with those of the *Orestes,* or with the Menelaus of the *Andromache,* the contrast is startling. So the Odysseus of the *Cyclops* and of the *Hecuba,* the Heracles of the *Alcestis,* and of the *Hercules Furens,* as well as many others, make good my statement.

With these examples before us, we need not be surprised that the comic poets used even greater license, and travestied known characters so as to make them hardly recognisable. The Euripides presented to us on the comic stage, as well as the Socrates of the *Clouds,* were so unlike the well-known and respected originals, that if the plays of Aristophanes had made the smallest pretensions to accuracy, they must have totally failed in their success. We may, therefore, confidently assert that in all such matters he is no historical authority whatever, and that to draw inferences from his statements, proved to be false in so patent a case as that of Socrates, is nothing better than establishing a fact upon the evidence of a convicted perjurer[1].

It is, however, only a lawyer who will argue that a perjurer is totally unworthy of credit. Ordinary men know that even *he* must speak the truth generally, and especially when off his guard ; it may, therefore, be argued that, apart from special characters, the general tone and plot of Aristophanes' plays must be good social evidence. Admitting this, there are plays of Aristophanes, such as the *Lysistrata* and *Thesmophoriazusæ*, of which the plot could not be here even explained, and which represent the body of Athenian women, even mothers of respectable families, in such hideous colours as to be thoroughly disgusting. Pictures so exaggerated are simply in- credible in a generation which produced and handed down untarnished the most refined and brilliant civilisation the world has yet seen. It may be also urged that when Aristophanes' portraits of known and celebrated men were so audaciously false, he is not to be trusted where his falsehoods could easily escape confutation, and where his sweeping charges fell in with those suspicions common to all men who are themselves prone to immorality. I suspect, how- ever, that his three plays on women might be ex-

---

[1] This point is at last put in its proper light by Mr. Müller Strüb- ing, in his remarkable work, *Aristophanes und die historische Kritik* (Teubner 1873). I may add that Aristophanes himself confesses great obligations to Euripides, Σκην. Καταλαμβ. *fr.* iv. (Meineke, ii. p. 1142). There is even a special compound word pointing to the fact—εὐριπιδα- ριστοφανίζων. Cp. also *Ranæ*, 1334.

plained from quite a different cause ; not from a low
opinion of women in the poet, not from any desire
of scourging a great rampant evil, as we find it done
in Juvenal's sixth satire, but rather from the remnant
of some old religious customs, where women met
apart, as we know they did, and also where mimic
choruses, during the feasts of such goddesses as Demeter and Cora, devoted themselves to licentious
abuse of women, at times even exclusively.   There
is not evidence enough to prove the custom at Athens,
and to show the filiation of Aristophanes' comedies
from these choruses, though choruses were undoubtedly the origin of all developed drama in Greece.
My hypothesis rests on the fact that Aristophanes
perpetually rails at Euripides for this very feature,
that his other comedies are nearly free from it, and
that the custom, which I presuppose at Athens,
certainly did exist at Epidaurus, connected with the
worship of Damia and Auxesia, which are probably
local names for Demeter and Cora.   Herodotus tells
us (v. 83) θυσίησί τέ σφεα καὶ χόροισι γυναικηΐοισι
κερτόμοισι ἱλάσκοντο, χορηγῶν ἀποδεικνυμένων ἑκατέρῃ τῶν
δαιμόνων δέκα ἀνδρῶν, κακῶς δὲ ἠγόρευον οἱ χοροὶ ἄνδρα
μὲν οὐδένα, τὰς δὲ ἐπιχωρίας γυναῖκας.   Possibly, therefore, these famous ribaldries about women are not
meant to convey any bad impression of them by
the poet.   But quite apart from any such special
reason, the general grounds above adduced, and the
evidence we have found in Euripides, show that on
this large question the evidence of Aristophanes is
hardly of any value.

My general observations, however, which apply to the comic estimates of women, as well as those of men, are of peculiar importance when we come to consider the most prominent woman of the day— Aspasia. This lady, being a Milesian, with whom no Athenian citizen could contract any but a morganatic marriage, was readily and generally identified with a class of people somewhat outside the pale of society, and peculiarly open to gross charges —the *hetairai*, afterwards so celebrated as the most witty and brilliant talkers at Athens. In the absence of cultivated society at home, Greek gentlemen often betook themselves, in later days, to the houses of such ladies, whose manners are sufficiently described in the thirteenth book of Athenæus. These were the days of Epicurus and Menander. There is no doubt that men like Socrates and Xenophon went, in like manner, for the purpose of serious mental improvement, to the house of Aspasia, who even received ladies and appears to have discoursed much upon the duties of married life. But there is no evidence of a society of cultivated *hetairai* at Athens in Pericles' day. I say, advisedly, at Athens, for there is evidence of a large and prominent class of this kind at Corinth as early as the Persian wars. We still possess a fragment of an ode specially composed for them by the poet Pindar, whose time and talents were in such demand among tyrants and free cities, that they must have paid him a large fee. These same ladies were celebrated through Greece for their public prayers and votive offerings in behalf of the Greeks during the invasion of Xerxes. This shows public spirit and patriotism among them. But I am not aware that in any poet of the Old Comedy, save Pherecrates (who is a notable exception, and rather belongs to the Middle Comedy), a character of this kind is mentioned upon the stage [1], if we except Aspasia, who certainly held a peculiar position. Not only is she said to have risen from a disreputable past, but she is openly accused of still pursuing the vilest of professions— that of promoting vice in others—and an action in open court charged her with the *impiety* of making her house a place of assignation for Athenian ladies of position.

This charge, were it true, would give us such a picture of Athenian life in the house of Pericles, the greatest of Greeks, that we ought to shut our Greek books, and refuse further intercourse with people whose best society was worse than the lowest stratum of modern life. Of course the charge was false ; of course the home of Pericles was not a house of this description ; but the meetings of married ladies for discussion, such as that alluded to by Cicero, where Xenophon and his wife (according to the Socratic philosopher Æschines) were present —these meetings naturally gave rise, *at Athens*, to grave suspicion, and Pericles was not the man to

---

[1] Of course I do not include those open bad characters of the lowest type, who sometimes appear upon the stage of Aristophanes (*Achar.* and *Thesmoph.* sub. fin.). These people are in no sense ἑταίραι, and are never called so by the Greeks.

trouble himself with refuting them. Possibly Aspasia was a free-thinker, at least on those points where the every-day religion was base and immoral, and hence arose another stone of stumbling. Even if her early life had not been free from blame, there is no absolute proof of her want of dignity and morality[1]; nor can I conceive Socrates constantly visiting her, and advising his friends to send their sons to her to be educated, if the charges of Aristophanes and his fellows were in any sense true. No doubt many Athenian citizens were very jealous of the position of this foreigner—a position which one of their own daughters ought, by right, to have held—and the conversations at her house, which brought ladies there from their dull and secluded homes. were to the old-fashioned Athenian dangerous innovations[2].

We have some very instructive parallel cases,

[1] I cite with reluctance a modern parallel. There are few men who have been forced into contact with the pariahs of our society by professional duties, such as medical practice, who will not testify that among these outcasts they have found great generosity, self-denial, and even purity of motives. A celebrated French author, Dumas, has ventured to assert this in his great and affecting novel, *La Dame aux Camélias*. Yet even such a suggestion is deemed dangerous by our respectable people, and this remarkable play could not be represented in England without being concealed by an Italian translation, and Verdi's music (*La Traviata*).

[2] The whole question about Aspasia has been discussed with great ability by M. Becq de Fouquières in his very interesting monograph *Aspasie de Milet*. If his enthusiasm leads him too far, he has nevertheless brought out the main points, I think rightly. He need not have dogmatised about her life before and after Pericles' union with her.

which, I think, can be fairly cleared up, and which will show the nature of the comic charges against Aspasia and Pericles. The very same charge of making his house a meeting-place for Pericles and his lady friends, is preferred against the sculptor Phidias, who was, if I may so say, the minister of art under Pericles. We also hear, strangely enough, accusations of Pericles having induced another friend, who possessed peacocks, to make presents of them to these ladies. Peacocks had then been lately introduced into Athens, as we know from allusions in Antiphon. One Athenian gentleman, who kept them, had an open day every new moon, on which the public might come to see them freely, but he refused all admission at other times. Their screaming is complained of by the comic poets. The gift of a peacock was therefore a handsome present, as the bird could not be bought for money, owing to its rarity. To those who will not believe that the great Phidias, and the greater Pericles, combined for the lowest and most scandalous purposes, an explanation of these suspicions and charges readily presents itself. The Greek sculptors and painters must have required, like our own artists, suitable models. We know of only one *hetaira* at Athens thus employed; if there had been many, the comedy would certainly have told us of it. Whoever thinks for a moment of the pure and noble types of female beauty in Greek art, can hardly conceive the models to have been anything but the very highest and best of society. I imagine Pericles and Phidias to have been under great difficulties in procuring the best models, owing to the seclusion of women at Athens, and I conjecture that they were induced with difficulty to come to the sculptor's studio, where Pericles no doubt often met them, and that they were rewarded upon some few occasions with the present of a peacock, as money payments would have been unseemly. Thus I conceive the suspicion of the Athenian public to have been excited. We know that Phidias copied himself and Pericles on the shield of Pallas. Of course he must have copied some fair woman of Athens for the goddess herself, though he dared not confess it to the public.

We chance to have from the same epoch a strictly parallel case. Plutarch tells us[1] that the celebrated sister of Cimon, Elpinice, who appears from various anecdotes to have gone about Athens with some liberty, is said to have transgressed with the painter Polygnotus, and that accordingly when painting the Trojan women (in his famous portico called ποικίλη) he made his figure of Laodice a portrait of Elpinice. This Polygnotus was the Phidias of Greek painting. Here, I take it, there can be no doubt, that Elpinice was a model to Polygnotus, and we see her charged with the same suspicions as the ladies who went to Phidias' studio. These considerations are, in my mind, quite sufficient to overthrow the bare presumption against Aspasia, raised by the comedians' scurrilous buffoonery.

I turn with more pleasure to the casual glimpses

[1] *Cimon*, c. 4.

given us into her home life with Pericles. We are indebted to the invaluable Plutarch for having collected from numerous anecdotists these slighter touches in the portraits of the great Periclean Athenians. From him we can quote something on the aristocratic side of Athenian life to compare with the homely scenes in the *Acharnians* and *Wasps*. Several of the anecdotists, such as Ion of Chios and Stesimbrotus of Thasos, were contemporary with the men they described, and are trustworthy in some details ; while in others Plutarch's notice of their bias enables us to doubt and to criticise. They agreed in making Pericles haughty and cold, avoiding society altogether, and hardly to be seen except on the way from his house to the assembly. He had once condescended to go to a cousin's wedding-feast, but left the moment grace was said, I have no doubt to the great relief of the company. This cold contempt of men appeared plainly enough, we are told, in his speeches, and was, I think, transmitted by him, without his dignity and soberness, to his ward Alcibiades. It was clearly this feeling, and not pressure of business, which kept Pericles from going into society. Nicias, on the contrary, a stupid but excellent and high-spirited man, felt himself bound to deny access to his friends, and to avoid society, on account of the pressure of public business, which he performed most conscientiously, but, like many conscientious men, stupidly and slowly[1]. They both were very careful of their private affairs and of the

[1] Cp. Plut. *Nic.* chap. **v.**

management of their income, but Pericles had the
sense to find a trusty person to whom he committed
them, just as he committed routine business in the
assembly to friends ; whereas Nicias, as Thucydides
says of him, with deep insight, in the last great crisis
of his life (vii. 69) was ever thinking that things were
not perfectly ready and complete, or had not been
sufficiently explained, and so wearied himself in doing
other people's work as well as his own. But there
was a gap in Pericles' cares, when he was at home
with Aspasia, whom he never left in the morning,
they tell us, without affectionately kissing her, and in
whose brilliant conversation he found better solace
and recreation than in men's wine parties, or in the
excesses with which he has been falsely charged.

Cimon and Alcibiades, on the contrary, though
both public men, were essentially men of society,
indulging in all the amusements of Athenian life,
and not free from stain in their morals. But Cimon
was rather a general than a politician ; he was not
oppressed, when at Athens, with the burdens of the
Home Office and the Exchequer. He was reckless
in expenditure, and was often to be met in society,
where Ion of Chios, when a youth, had met him,
and whose interesting account of him is preserved by
Plutarch. Cimon, who was, of course, the great man
of the party, was asked to sing, and did it so well
and pleasantly, that some of the company politely
observed how in this he had beaten Themistocles,
who was no doubt an equal politician, but no musician. Cimon then begins to tell of his military

experiences, apparently to show that he was not deficient in cleverness like that of Themistocles.

The conversation seems to have turned exactly on the line suggested in a pleasant passage in Aristophanes' *Wasps*, when Bdelycleon is teaching his father how to behave in good society (vv. 1174–1264). The old man is exceedingly rude and boorish, and suggests coarse and vulgar subjects of conversation, whereupon the son objects, and suggests fine talk, 'about your being at a show-embassy along with Androcles and Cleisthenes.' 'But I was never at a show, save once to see Punch and Judy, and that for a fee of two obols.' 'Well then, you should tell how, for example, Ephudion fought a fine *pancratium* with Ascondas, though already old and gray-haired, but showing great form and muscle. This is the sort of talk usual among refined people. But come to another point. When you go out into society in the evening among strangers (παρ' ἀνδράσι ξένοις πίνων), what manly act of your youth can you relate?' 'Oh! that was the bravest of my acts when I stole Ergasion's vine-stakes.' 'Will you kill me with your vine-stakes? I want you to tell how you chased a boar or a hare, or won a torch race by some bold device.' 'I know, then, my greatest act of youthful boldness, when I won a suit for abusive language from the runner Phayllus.' 'Stop, but come and lie down here and let me teach you to be convivial and pleasant over your cups.' 'Show me how to lie down;—will this do?' 'Not at all. Straighten your knees, and throw yourself in a graceful and easy way on the couch.

Then make some observations on the beauty of the appointments, look up at the ceiling, praise the tapestry of the room[1].' He then proceeds to instruct the old gentleman how to take his part in the *scolia*, or catches, in which one guest started a line, and challenged some other to go on in the same metre and construction, giving, of course, the most amusing turn he could to the sense[2]. The old man makes such good political cuts in this game that the son is satisfied, and proposes to bring him out to dinner, where they can have a good carouse. 'Oh, no,' says the old man, 'for from wine-drinking come assault and battery, and then having to pay money next day after your drinking bout.' 'No,' says the son, 'at least not if you mix in good society (ἢν ξυνῇς γ' ἀνδράσι καλοῖς τε κἀγαθοῖς), for either they pacify the offended man, or you say something clever to him yourself, some good thing of Æsop's, or from Sybaris, which you have learned at the feast, and then you turn the affair into a joke, so that he lets you off and goes his way[3].'

This passage, agreeing so well with the anecdote about Cimon, is full of interest. It shows the high-class Athenian not ashamed of showing off consciously before strangers, a feature very strongly marked even

[1] To do this too eagerly is noted by Theophrastus as one of the features of the Flatterer in his *Characters*.

[2] Cf. also Νεφ. 649: πρῶτον μὲν εἶναι κομψόν ἐν ξυνουσίᾳ ἐπαίονθ' ὁποῖός ἐστι τῶν ῥυθμῶν, κ.τ.λ., where the amusement is rather a discussion on forms of poetry than actual extemporising.

[3] Demosthenes (ii. p. 163) notices the habit of doing this very thing in court, and so escaping the legal consequences of violence.

in Alexander the Great, who indeed damaged the
conversation at his table by his exceeding self-con-
sciousness [1]. We also see how highly cleverness in
conversation was prized. The allusion to the dis-
orderly conduct of the guests in the later part of
evening reminds us of the appearance of Alcibiades
in Plato's *Symposium*, which is quite a scene of the
same kind, except that Plato makes Socrates so influence the conversation as to give it a deep and
solid value. But there can be no doubt that such
men as Alcibiades and Callias were often guilty of
gross violence in their drinking bouts, and that they
escaped punishment partly by the means above
suggested, partly also by intimidation. The portrait
we have of Alcibiades in Plutarch and elsewhere is
hardly of any use as a specimen of manners, for we
are told that he was in every way exceptional, though
in immorality and in home scandal Callias was perhaps his solitary equal.

But in one respect I do think the excesses of
Alcibiades instructive, in showing how far the most
aristocratic, handsome, fascinating man at Athens,
the idol of the mob, the autocrat of society—how far
this man was removed from the modern English gentleman. He is accused of having brought women of
the lowest character so constantly into his house that
his wife, an excellent young lady of high family, fled
from home and took refuge with the Archon, who

---

[1] Plutarch's *Alexander*, c. 23: καὶ τἆλλα πάντων ἥδιστος ὢν βασιλέων
συνεῖναι καὶ χάριτος οὐδεμιᾶς ἀμοιρῶν, τότε ταῖς μεγαλαυχίαις ἀηδὴς
ἐγίνετο καὶ λίαν στρατιωτικός.

was by law the protector of married women. But when she was obliged to come forward in person to prove her case for a divorce, Alcibiades appeared with a band of friends and carried her off (we are told) by force, nor did the unhappy woman ever again appear against him. This violence is characterised with the strongest epithets by the orator who has left us the speech against Alcibiades among the remains of Andocides. Again, he seized a painter, who refused to decorate his house owing to previous engagements, and kept him a prisoner till he had no longer need of him. Worse than all, after having supported in the assembly the ruthless massacre of the men of Melos, he bought one of the captive women and had a child by her, thus imitating one of the worst and lowest features to be found in the Homeric age [1].

The case of Callias, told by Andocides (περὶ Μυστ. p. 46), is, if possible, worse. Having married a respectable and blameless girl, he within a year took her mother into his house as a second wife. The poor daughter attempted suicide, but was prevented,

---

[1] ἐκ ταύτης γὰρ (says the orator Andocides, p. 88, ed. Blass) παιδοποιεῖται τῆς γυναικός, ἣν ἀντ᾽ ἐλευθέρας δούλην κατέστησε, καὶ ἧς τὸν πατέρα καὶ τοὺς προσήκοντας ἀπέκτεινε, καὶ ἧς τὴν πόλιν ἀνάστατον πεποίηκεν. I fear such acts were not, as the orator implies, extraordinary. The affecting story about Pausanias' murder of a girl at Byzantium implies in the Spartan an equal recklessness and villainy. When there, as generalissimo of tne Greek forces, after the retreat of Xerxes, he demanded from her parents that this young girl should visit him; they were afraid to refuse, and sent her in the dead of the night. When she came in, Pausanias, who was asleep, started up, and thinking some assassin was upon him, struck her with his dagger, and killed her. Her ghost was said to have haunted him ever after. Cp. Plutarch, *Cimon*, cap. vi.

and fled from the house, being turned out by her mother. Of course Callias soon got tired of her too, but took her back after she had borne him a son. 'being again in love with this most daring old woman' (ὑστέρῳ πάλιν χρόνῳ τῆς γραὸς τολμηροτάτης γυναικὸς ἀνηράσθη). This deed too is spoken of as extraordinary; but is it not an index of the manners of Athenian aristocrats?

The anecdote about Alcibiades' dog points in the same direction, and proves the man, to my mind, not to have been a gentleman. The Periclean Greeks, with all their faults, were very fond of dogs. The dog of Eupolis is said to have died of grief on its master's tomb[1]. In Plutarch's *Themistocles* there is a remarkable passage, in which he describes the tame animals, of course chiefly dogs, crowding to the shore and howling when their masters were leaving for Salamis on the approach of the Persians. The dog of Xanthippus, Pericles' father, not able to endure the separation (οὐκ ἀνασχόμενος τὴν ἀπ' αὐτοῦ μόνωσιν), leaped into the water, and swam alongside the ship to Salamis, where it is said to have died of exhaustion. These legends show the deep sympathy of the Athenians for dogs[2]. It was an old custom,

---

[1] λύπη καὶ λιμῷ ἑαυτὸν ἐκτήξας ἀπέθανεν ἐπὶ τῷ τροφεῖ καὶ δεσπότῃ λοιπὸν μισήσας τὸν βίον ὁ κύων. Aelian x. 41.

[2] In the picturesque account of Aratus' attack on Sicyon, dogs play a great part. The chief difficulty in surprising the city are the dogs of a market gardener, 'which were small, but very pugnacious and uncompromising' (μικρῶν μὲν, ἐκτόπως δὲ μαχίμων καὶ ἀπαρηγορήτων). They accordingly give tongue, and challenge a great sporting dog, kept in the tower on the wall, which had not perceived the noise, 'whether from

says an Attic antiquary, that no dog should go up
into the Acropolis, a prohibition which shows how
constantly they accompanied their masters. So, then,
this dog of Alcibiades, for which he is said to have
paid four minæ (reading Δ for the incredible O (70)
was remarkable for size and beauty, and generally
admired for its tail. Alcibiades cut the tail off, and
when his friends scolded him, and said that *everybody was vexed about the dog and was abusing him*,
he answered with a laugh, 'That is what I want ; I
wish them to talk about this, that they may say
nothing worse of me.'

I fear this set of men, despite of the graceful conversation attributed to them by Plato, were reckless
and unfeeling to all around them, nor do I see that
it made much difference to Alcibiades or Callias who
or what was ill-treated—dog, wife, or neighbour. But
as to the wife, they were the very set against whom
I believe Euripides to have written, that society of
men who upheld with Thucydides the complete
seclusion and insignificance of women, and that 'she
was best who was least spoken of among men,
whether for good or for evil [1].' Yet, when these very
men got into trouble, the despised women were their
comforters. 'When,' says the aristocrat Andocides

natural sluggishness, or from being fatigued during the day.' It answers
with a vague and uncertain sound (ὑπεφθέγγετο τυφλὸν καὶ ἄσημον τὸ
πρῶτον). Plut. *Arat.* v. viii. Wicked dogs were logged, cp. Xen. *Mem.*
II. iv. § 41.

[1] It is probably for this reason that Thucydides is silent on the
outrage committed by Paches at Mitylene, on his accusation by the
women, and his death in court. He probably thought it (as Plutarch
does) a scandalous ill-treatment of a general, for the sake of such a trifle.

(περὶ Μυστ. p. 20), 'we had all been bound in the
same chamber (on the capital charge of impiety), and
it was night, and the prison had been closed (apparently to visitors or legal advisers), there came to
one his mother, to another his sister, to another
his wife and children, and there was woe and la-
mentation as they wept over their misfortunes.'
So then these much-abused and ill-treated women
were after all, then, as now, the faithful and self-
denying helpers of men [1].

In the lower classes there is evidence, even among
city people, of a community of life and interests quite
analogous to the scenes between Electra and her
peasant husband, above described. In the *Wasps* of
Aristophanes, the old juryman, whose education we
have already been discussing, tells how when he
comes home his children run to kiss him, and how
his wife sets before him a dainty dish, and sitting
down beside him, coaxes him to eat (v. 583). He
says it is for the sake of his salary, but this is the
comic reason, the facts are probably real and ordinary. The humorous scenes at the opening of
the *Ecclesiazusæ* testify to the same friendly intimacy
between men and their wives, and I must add, to
very good temper among the men. In ordinary life
the men were obliged to get up before dawn, and set
out for the assembly, trudging along with a stout
stick and humming a tune. The women could stay
in bed, and avoid this great hardship (v. 461). On

---

[1] There is a parallel passage in Lysias (p. 103, ed. Teubner), when the
citizens were being imprisoned and put to death by the thirty tyrants.

Q

this occasion the women plan an early meeting in the assembly to discuss their rights, and set out in their husbands' attire. When the men awake they cannot find their clothes, and yet when the women come in they show excellent temper, and put up with very lame excuses. They allude to their wives going out to breakfast with friends, and one woman says she was called to see a sick friend, and took the first garment she could find, and her husband's shoes. If Aristophanes is not making the men gentler and quieter than they really were for the purpose of comic contrast (and this is quite possible), the whole tone of the play implies far truer and better relations among married people than the facts known to us about the aristocrats.

There are indeed dark spots here too, not merely in comic writers, but in the orators. The story told in Antiphon's first oration (p. 113) seems bad enough. The speaker's father had a country friend, Philoneos, a man, he says, who was a perfect gentleman. This Philoneos had the use of an upper chamber in his friend's town house, when he came in from the country, and here he kept a concubine, whom, for no cause assigned, he was about to treat with great harshness and injustice (ἐπὶ πορνεῖον ἔμελλε καταστῆσαι). The wretched woman is accordingly induced by the lady of the house, who wants to poison her own husband, to administer a pretended love-potion to her master and his friend, when they went one day to the Peiræus to dine together. But she apparently had no redress from the fearful treatment intended by her master, which is called indeed (in the oration) injustice, but seems not in the least otherwise reprehended. We have also an oration written by Lysias for an Athenian gentleman, who had a quarrel with another concerning the affections of a woman which they had originally agreed to share. The woman preferred the other man, and eloped with him, and so there was a quarrel, which was the occasion of the action. The speaker actually proposes and urges that the woman to whom he had stood in such peculiar relations *should be tortured* to elicit the real facts of the case, and this in the very same speech in which he relates his intimacy with her. I do not know in all Greek literature a more painful and morally grating passage than this proposal, made in open court by a man whose interest it was to represent himself as a fair and honourable man to the jury [1].

These, as I have said, are dark spots, which remind us of the old Homeric recklessness and cruelty of the higher classes toward those outside pale or privilege, and might be corroborated by the *mise en scène* of Plato's *Euthyphro*, where a wretched tenant farmer, a free dependent of some sort, is cast bound into a ditch, and allowed to die of hunger and exposure. But I am strongly of opinion that these cases are all special, and concern, not the relations of citizens to citizens, but of citizens to inferior and non-privileged classes. I here mention them by way of parenthesis, as they support the main theory of this book—I mean

---

[1] Cp. Lysias, p. 38, ed. Teubner.

the *sameness* of Greek character and Greek social ideas through all periods of Greek literature.

It is therefore unsafe to take Pericles, the highest specimen of Periclean Athens, or Alcibiades and Callias, morally the lowest, as average examples of manners and morals among men. As I believe that in estimating women at this time, the Alcestis and Macaria of Euripides are too high, and the women of Aristophanes too low; so I think in the case of men, we should choose neither the best nor the worst, but judge the age by an average standard. As it would be very easy, but highly reprehensible, to consult the Newgate Calendar for a few years, and estimate from it English morals—a course pursued by Mr. Froude in estimating Irish morals in the last century—so it is uncritical to judge an age by its greatest men, since they are always exceptional, and come under no general rule. Unfortunately the exclusively political or ideal literature of the day, devoted either to the heroic ages, or to the public life of the present, gives us little light on the average men of that epoch. I suppose the old gentlemen in Aristophanes and Euripides, who are not travesties of some particular public man, are the truest representatives of what we now wish to find. There is the anxious father in the *Clouds*, the angry countryman in the *Acharnians*, the independent Trygæus in the *Peace*, the contemptible old dicast in the *Wasps*, all of whom seem to my mind of a definite and easily grasped type. I cite them with greater confidence in this work, as ordinary readers can refer to Mr.

Frere's and Mr. Rogers' translations of most of these plays—translations which have not been excelled, so far as I know, in any language.

Any one who will examine with care these characters will find them, I think, not gentlemen in our sense [1], or even in Plato's sense. They are old-school men, one of them rich and well bred enough to have married an Alcmæonid noble, and to have sons addicted to horses—a most aristocratic taste in Athens; they are intelligent too, and shrewd, if not highly educated, but still they seem to me of a coarse fibre, and not gifted with much refinement or delicacy of feeling. In broad comedy, we must confess, there is not much room for these traits of character, so that we cannot expect them to be prominent. Still there *is* room for them, as we can see in the comedy of other nations, or in the middle and new comedy of the Greeks, in which, as well as in Plato and Xenophon, we shall find ample evidence of good breeding. The contemporaneous tragedies bear out this view in one point strongly, inasmuch as they cannot avoid attributing a disagreeable, and in our minds somewhat ungentlemanly practice even to their heroes and heroines—I mean the practice of perpetual wrangling.

---

[1] Euripides, whose average characters were of the same kind, makes Menelaus, (in *Iphigenia in Aulis*) take by violence and break open a letter sent by Agamemnon. It is remarkable that the messenger, and Agamemnon when he finds it out, speak of such an act very much as we should. They consider the breaking of a seal, and reading another man's letter a gross breach of manners, and even of common honesty.

There are indeed in Greek tragedy few characters
which we can call especially *gentlemanly*, perhaps
only Neoptolemus in the *Philoctetes*, and Euripides'
Achilles. Both Ajax and Theseus are to Sophocles
rather heroes than men of refinement, and I have
already commented on the general feebleness of
the men of Euripides. The old comedy agrees
in these features with the tragedies. The worthy
Dicæopolis in the *Acharnians*, when celebrating his
country Dionysia, indulges in language to his daughter
as jocose as, and even a little coarser than the
humour of Squire Western to his daughter Sophia
in Fielding's *Tom Jones*. But the resemblance is
striking enough, especially when we remember that
in the *Plutus* (971, sqq.) there is a young gentleman
who makes his livelihood by the very same trade
which Fielding attributes to his hero, apparently
without censure. This coarseness is testified by the
very comedy itself, religious though it may have been
in origin, by the Phallic processions, such as that
just alluded to in the *Acharnians*, and by the Hermæ
that stood in every street.

We can find many other points, where the Athenians showed a rudeness very striking in the midst
of so great artistic and literary refinement. Thus for
example, though they had attained to a notion of an
absolute umpire (ἐπιστάτης) in the palæstra, as we can
see from Antiphon, they had not in their public
assemblies arrived at that remarkable invention in
our public life, the fictitious omnipotence of the
speaker or chairman, who by his ruling commands

more absolutely than a judge in a court of law. At Athens, if any speaker was troublesome, the πρυτάνεις or presidents ordered the police to drag him off the *bema*. We hear too of impertinence on the part of Cleon to the assembly, which could hardly be received with laughter among us, as it was by the Athenians [1]. It was a very different thing when the handsome and fascinating Alcibiades was passing by, and heard the clamour of the assembly, and on enquiry was told that voluntary contributions were being asked for the state. 'He forthwith,' says Plutarch [2], 'came forward and contributed, but when the people loudly applauded, he was so pleased that he forgot a (fighting) quail, which he was carrying under his cloak.' When it fluttered out and escaped from him, the Athenians applauded still louder, and a general chase ensued (πολλοὺς δὲ συνθηρᾶν ἀναστάντας), the man who caught it for him earning his lasting friendship.

Here we have a genuine spirit of fun. But as to rudeness of manners, what shall we say of a man of position strewing before his door the feathers of expensive birds used at his feast in order to display his wealth [3]? They had another habit, now found in lanes and alleys of towns, among the lower classes, of throwing out their dirty water into the street, but crying ἐξίστω (out of the way!) to warn passengers

---

[1] Plut. *Nic.* c. 11.   [2] *Alcib.* c. 10.

[3] Aristoph. *Ach.* 989, τοῦ βίου δ' ἐξέβαλλε δεῖγμα τάδε τὰ πρὸ τῶν θυρῶν. There is a somewhat similar mark of ostentation mentioned by Theophrastus

of their danger[1]. I fear even their town life may
have been, as Aristophanes says of their country
life, εὐρωτιῶν ἀκόρητος εἰκῆ κείμενος. The whole opening
of Aristophanes' *Clouds* shows how strongly this contrast of town and country was felt, and the contempt
of Socrates for the old country gentleman was no
doubt the expression of a general feeling[2]. But
nevertheless, in their daily life, and in some of the
arrangements which we consider most essential to
decency and comfort, the Greeks were, like many
otherwise cultivated European nations, very much
behind their own level.

I say this, despite of the many evidences of refined
tact and politeness which they show in other respects.
Take, for example, the ordinary forms of courteous

---

[1] Aristoph. *Ach.* 616 and Schol. According to Plutarch's anecdotes,
even noble boys played in the streets. Thus Alcibiades was once playing at dice (I suppose our *pitch and toss*) in a lane, with some other boys,
and his turn was just come, when a man came up with a cart.
Alcibiades called to him to stop till he had done throwing; 'but the
fellow was rude enough not to mind him' (a curious view of things).
Thereupon the other boys gave way, but Alcibiades threw himself on
his face before the cart, and dared the man to pass; so that he
backed his cart in fear; and the bystanders were terrified, and rushed
up screaming to save him.

[2] So Euripides says of Hippomedon (*Supp.* 882, sqq.)

> παῖς ὢν ἐτόλμησ' εὐθὺς οὐ πρὸς ἡδονὰς
> Μουσῶν τραπέσθαι, καὶ τὸ μαλθακὸν βίου,
> ἀγροὺς δὲ ναίων, σκληρὰ τῇ φύσει διδοὺς
> ἔχαιρε πρὸς τἀνδρεῖον.

Cf. also Lysias (p. 157, Teubner).

> ὁ μὲν γὰρ ἐν ἀγρῷ πένης ὢν
> ἐποίμανεν, ὁ δὲ πατὴρ ἐν τῷ ἄστει
> ἐπαιδεύετο.

refusal which they used[1]. 'I praise your remark,'
(but don't agree with it). ''Tis well' (but I do not
need it), and 'what a busybody I am'! (I beg your pardon)—these are the forms used by Aristophanes and
the tragedians. Probably the Spartans, whom Herodotus takes care to paint as very rude and coarse
in every-day intercourse, would despise these ameni-
ties, but at Athens, notwithstanding the hurry and
hardness of the times, the features already exist
which make the society of Plato and the new comedy
so charming. How much conversation was already
prized appears both from Herodotus' account of the
marriage of Agariste, and from the remark of Plutarch about Phæax, a leading rival of Alcibiades. He
says that he was persuasive and powerful in private,
but unsuited to public haranguing, and he quotes a
remarkable line of Eupolis about him[2]. He was,
I conceive, the exact opposite of Demosthenes in
talent.

On the whole, an accurate and calm review of the
old comic fragments, and of Aristophanes, of the
orators Antiphon and Andocides, of the striking
sketches left us by Plutarch of the six prominent
Athenians of this epoch—these varied documents,
socially considered, may bring us somewhat to lower
the estimate usually formed of Periclean Athens, and
to consider that both the incomparable literature and
the incomparable art then produced were to some extent the work of a select few, who stood apart from

---

[1] ἐπῄνεσα, καλῶς, and τῆς πολυπραγμοσύνης.
[2] λαλεῖν ἄριστος, ἀδυνατώτατος λέγειν. Plut. *Alcib.* c. 13.

the crowd, as they have done in other golden periods, and who in many respects owed their success to the patronage, first of the tyrants, and then of the tyrants' successor, Pericles.

I have spoken before, in connection with Thucydides, of the cruelty prevalent through Greece during the Peloponnesian war. It was not merely among Corcyræans, or among Thracian mercenaries, but among the leaders of Greece that we find this disgusting feature. The Spartans put to death in cold blood two hundred and twenty-five prisoners, whom they took in Platæa after a long and heroic defence—in this very different from the so-called barbarian Persians, who years before had done all they could to save alive a brave man, Pytheas, who fought against them[1]. But this is a mere trifle, when we hear from Plutarch that Lysander, after the battle of Ægospotami, put to death 3000 prisoners[2]! Greek historians are too much in the habit of passing carelessly over such scenes as this. The appearance of Coomassie struck with horror all our troops who entered it, and afforded to the papers a subject which even the *Daily Telegraph* failed to exaggerate. What can Coomassie have been compared to Ægospotami, where 3000 men, not savages, not negroes, but Athenians, men of education and of culture, were butchered with swords and spears[3]? What are we to think of

---

[1] Cf. Thuc. iii. 68 with Herod. vii. 181.

[2] τῶν δ' ἀνθρώπων τρισχιλίους ἑλὼν ζῶντας ἀπέσφαξεν ὁ Λύσανδρος, *Alcib.* c. 37, cp. the details in his *Lysander* c. 13.

[3] We are told, and this was a point which did strike the Greeks

the men who ordered this massacre, of those who executed it, of those who looked on ? I do not believe that there is now a sovereign in the world, even the King of Dahomey or King Koffee, who would execute such a horrible and bloodthirsty deed. If our soldiers found the smell of blood and of decay horrible among the Ashantees, what would they have found it on the shore of Thrace, where Lysander celebrated his victory in rivers of human blood ? And yet I believe this atrocity, seldom paralleled in human history, called forth no cry of horror in Greece. The unfortunate Athenian general, according to Theophrastus [1], submits with dignified resignation to a fate which he confesses would have attended the Lacedæmonians had they been vanquished.

For the Athenians with their boasted clemency and culture, were very nearly as cruel as their enemies In the celebrated affair of the Mitylenæans, which Thucydides tells at length in his third book, the first decree of the Athenians was to massacre the whole male population of the captured city. They repented of this decree, because Diodotus proved to

with horror, that on this occasion the bodies were left unburied, so that the resemblance to Coomassie is quite complete. When the habits of the Ashantee people became known, we were all filled with horror, and there were loud appeals made by the public to put down such depraved and abominable barbarism. Good people in Europe seem to think that a nation which is cruel and executes large numbers of people must be savage and degraded. Let me point out the striking example of Greece in its palmiest days in disproof of such hasty generalisations.

[1] Plut. *Lys.* 13.

them, not that it was inhuman, but that it was in-
expedient[1]. The historians, and especially Grote,
contrast the conduct of the Athenians—full of bloody
impulses but quick repentance—with the colder and
more heartless cruelty of the Spartans at Platæa,
and even speak of the feeling of pain which was felt
when they came to refleet on the *details* of such a
scene as the massacre of 6000 unarmed men. I believe this account of the Athenian feelings to be
false. They pardoned the population of Mitylene,
from no feelings of humanity, but from feelings of
expediency, which Diodotus explains, and from feelings of justice. For these people, as soon as they had
obtained arms, rose against the revolting aristocracy,
and gave themselves and their city up to the Athenians. But I argue, in opposition to Grote, how could
the *imagined details* of the massacre of 6000 men *in
Lesbos* have been a motive, when the Athenians did
at the same time have the ringleaders executed *at
Athens*, and *they were more than one thousand men*[2]!
Such is Thucydides' cold remark, which the historians
pass by without comment, but which again reminds
us of Coomassie : we have here, not on the coast of
Thrace, not in distant islands, but in Athens, the
centre of refinement and of humanity, *more than one
thousand men executed together by the hands of Athenians*, not with fire-arms, but with swords and knives.
A few years after, the inhabitants of Melos, many

---

[1] Cp. Mr. Grote's excellent discussion in his *History*, vi. 343, &c.

[2] ἦσαν δὲ ὀλίγῳ πλείους χιλίων. Thuc. iii. 50. I now read Λ (30) instead of Α, as 1,000 ringleaders seems to me absurd.

hundreds in number, were put to the sword, when conquered after a brave resistance[1], and here I fear merely for the purpose of making way for a colony of Athenian citizens, who went out to occupy the houses and lands of their victims!

Such are the facts, admitted by all, and so far as I know never protested against save in a single passage of Euripides[2]. I know that in the Middle Ages re- fined and cultivated men sanctioned great atrocities, and even witnessed voluntarily hideous tortures as well as executions. I know that Roman Popes ordered wholesale massacres. But they did it not through defect in the love of men, but through excess in the love of God, and perhaps of human souls. Theology had expelled ordinary humanity from their hearts, in order to install in its place theological humanity—a love of men's souls at the expense of their bodies and their feelings. These cases are therefore not parallel to the inhumanity of the Greeks. There is no excuse for their barbarity. It is but one evidence out of a thousand that, hitherto in the world's history, no culture, no education, no political training, has been able to rival the mature and ultimate effects of Chris- tianity in humanising society.

There appears however to have been one limit to these horrors. Women and children were never massacred, nor even (I think) treated with outrage or

---

[1] Thuc. v. 116.

[2] *Heracleidæ*, 961 sqq. The poet speaks as if it were against the habit of the Greeks to slay a captive taken alive in battle, and Alcmene, who persists in doing it, is threatened with the vengeance of the Gods.

insult beyond that of being sold into slavery. On
the very occasion of which I have just now spoken,
the same Athenians who voted the actual massacre of
many prisoners at Athens, are said to have received the
complaint of two married women against the Athenian
general Paches with such an outburst of indignation,
that he committed suicide in open court to avoid
their sentence. We have here a strange inconsistency.
The honour of two women, who were condemned to
be sold as slaves, and who were in any case prisoners
of war, stands at Athens on the modern basis, and is
even treated there with far more severity than it would
be now-a-days, while a wholesale massacre of men
excites not one word of pity. We know also that the
massacre of a school of children by Thracian savages
is really regarded as a horrible atrocity by Thucydides,
and, he tells us, by the Greek world. These then were
the limits of cruelty in Greek war at this epoch—limits
often exceeded in more modern times.

But it will perhaps be more interesting to examine
what evidences there are of this feature in the peaceful
and home life of the Greeks. War is no doubt a stern
taskmaster, and it may seem unfair to estimate a people
from the excesses instigated by the fear and the fury of
a protracted civil strife. Are there any parallel cases
in the course of ordinary Athenian life?

It is well known that at the beginning of the
epoch under discussion human sacrifices had hardly
disappeared from Greece. Plutarch tells us that
Themistocles was forced by the acclamations of the
army to sacrifice three Persian prisoners of distinction,

brought in just before the battle of Salamis, though
he was greatly affected at the terrible nature of the
sacrifice[1], so that it appears to have been then unusual. But Aristophanes, long after, makes allusions
to what he calls φάρμακοι, as still remembered at
Athens, if not still in use[2], and which the scholiasts
explain, chiefly from Hipponax, as a sort of human
scapegoat, chosen for ugliness or deformity (a very
Greek standpoint) and sacrificed for the expiation of
the state (κάθαρμα) in days of famine, of pestilence, or
of other public disaster. I think that Aristophanes
alludes to this custom as by-gone, though the scholiasts do not think so[3], but its very familiarity to his
audience shows a disregard of human life strange
enough in so advanced a legal system as that of
democratic Athens.

But however this may be, we have full and clear

---

[1] ἐκπλαγέντος δὲ τοῦ Θ. ὡς μέγα τὸ μάντευμα καὶ δεινόν. Plut.
Them. 13.

[2] *Ran.* 732, (πονηροὶ) οἷσιν ἡ πόλις πρὸ τοῦ
οὐδὲ φαρμακοῖσιν εἰκῆ ῥαδίως ἐχρήσατ' ἄν.

[3] Besides the fragments of Hipponax (*fr.* 4-9, ed. Bergk), and of
Archilochus (113), the Scholiasts seem to rely on the antiquary Ister,
who, writing at Alexandria in Callimachus' days, mentioned among
his collection of the ancient customs and feasts of Attica, the habit of
sacrificing two φάρμακοι yearly at the *Thargelia* (cp. *fr.* 33, ed. Müller).
But there is no evidence that this lasted into Periclean times, and
Plutarch's mention of Themistocles' horror at the proposal of a human
sacrifice seems to me inconsistent with it. Curt Wachsmuth, indeed
(*Stadt. Athen.* i. p. 439), thinks the sacrifice at the *Thargelia* was merely
symbolical, but if so, why were the victims carefully selected for vice
and ugliness? The once equivalent word κάθαρμα is known to have
been used in later Greek (from Lysias onward) in the general sense of
'miserable wretch,' with an implication of depravity.

evidence in the common practice of torture in the
Athenian law-courts, and possibly even in the assembly, which has not been recognised by the panegyrists
of Periclean Athens. We find evidence through all
the extant orators on this question, but especially
Antiphon, in whose speeches on cases of homicide
this feature constantly recurs. It is well known that
in such cases the accused might offer his own slaves
to be tortured, in order to challenge evidence against
himself; and it was thought a weak point in his case,
if he refused to do so when challenged. It is also well
known that the accusers were bound to make good
any permanent injury, such as maiming, done to these
slaves.

But there were both restrictions and extensions of
this practice as yet but little noticed. It was not the
custom to torture slaves who gave evidence to a fact,
but only if they denied any knowledge, or appeared
to suppress it in the interest of their master[1]. On the
other hand, it was common enough to torture female
slaves, and also free men. There is a remarkable case
in Antiphon's speech about the murder of Herodes[2],
in which the conduct of a slave and of a free man
under the same torture are contrasted. The slave
gave in and confessed what his persecutors wanted.
The free man held out. No doubt in another place[3]
Antiphon contrasts the coercing of free men by oaths
and solemn pledges, which are to them the strongest
bonds, with that of slaves by torture, '*by which they*

---

[1] Antiphon, *Tetral.* A, γ; also Lycurgus *in Leocrat.* § 31 sqq.
[2] pp. 72, 135, ed. Blass.   [3] περὶ τοῦ χορευτοῦ, pp. 100-101.

*are compelled to speak the truth, even though they must
die for it afterwards* (at the hands of their master),
for the present necessity is to each stronger than the
future.' He argues in the former passage about the
absurdity of the thing, and yet in the latter he adopts
it completely, so leaving us a picture of the treatment
of slaves almost grotesque in its absurd cruelty. The
slave had his choice of death from his master if he
confessed anything, of continued torture on the rack
if he refused to confess.

I delay on this as the only case of real *stupidity*
I can bring against the Athenians. Almost all the
orators speak of it as an infallible means of ascer-
taining the truth. Demosthenes says it has never
been known to fail. It is considered one of the wisest
institutions of Athens. I know not whether the free
man cited in Antiphon's speech was submitted to
torture because he belonged to a subject state—I fear
this may be the reason. But in Andocides there are
distinct parallels to it—in fact whenever any great fear
or crisis came upon the Athenians they were always
ready to extend the treatment to freemen. We have
first a proposal to force masters to give up their slaves
for torture[1] against the usual practice, and then the
presidents (πρυτάνεις) of the assembly take away Andocides' *female slaves* (p. 25) for the same purpose.
But still farther Peisander (p. 18) proposes to suspend
the decree of Scamandrius (against torture I suppose)
and put on the rack (ἀναβιβάζειν ἐπὶ τὸν τροχὸν) forty-
two free citizens, who had been accused of mutilating

---

[1] p. 10, περὶ Μυστ.: τοὺς δὲ μὴ θέλοντας ἀναγκάζειν.

R

the Hermæ, and violating the mysteries ; and we know
from Plutarch (*Nicias* sub. fin.) that the unfortunate
barber, who heard the awful news from Syracuse from
a stranger in Peiræus, and ran up to tell it to the
magistrates, was tortured for a long time, because he
could not give any further evidence for his statement.
Aristophanes[1] even characterises business days in the
law-courts as opposed to holidays by torturing as an
ordinary feature, so that we have here detected in
Periclean Athens a point of similarity, not with
modern, but mediæval times. I must however add
in justice to Athens, that the torture was never inflicted for torture's sake, as among Oriental despots
and Roman Catholic Inquisitors, but from a blunder-
ing desire to elicit truth in evidence. I can also find
no trace of ingenuity or variety of tortures, save in a
comic passage of Aristophanes (*Ran.* 619) : the ordinary rack is the universal engine of the Attic courts.
It appears also from a passage in Isocrates (p. 361)
that torturing was only permitted when inflicted by
state-torturers, who were called δημοκοίνοι. For when
the defendant Pasion, after many delays and sub-
terfuges, had agreed to produce a slave required to
give evidence, and when his opponent came with his
torturers to the temple of Hephæstus, Pasion objected
that they were not state-torturers, and told them
merely to question the slave. It appears that these
men accordingly would not venture to torture him
on their own responsibility, and so the prosecutor's
project broke down.

[1] *Nub.* 620: στρεβλοῦτε καὶ δικάζετε ; cp. Aeschines, παραπρεσβ. § 126.

Nevertheless the ordinary occurrence of such scenes in the every-day life of the Athenians is sadly in harmony with the hideous execution scenes in the civil wars, and shows us that with all their intellect, and all their subtlety, the Greeks were wanting in heart. Their humanity was spasmodic, not constant. Their kindness was limited to friends and family, and included no chivalry to foes or to helpless slaves. Antiphon, in speaking of the danger of convictions on insufficient evidence, mentions a case of the murder of his master by a slave boy of twelve years old, when *the whole household would have been put to death* [1], had not the victim cried out when struck with the knife, and the little boy discovered himself by running away. Otherwise so young a child could never have been suspected. We have here the same savage law which in the pages of Tacitus and of Dion so deeply affects us with pity and horror, and against which even the Roman populace revolted. It is not easy to despise human rights and human tears in one relation, without running the risk of general hardness of heart, and so the men who murdered their prisoners in war, and sold noble women and children into slavery, were not likely to treat with mercy and consideration those dependent on them at home and in the days of peace [2].

The strongest case, however, against the Periclean Greeks, and one which marks their parentage most clearly from their Homeric ancestors, is the treatment

---

[1] ἀπώλοντ' ἂν οἱ ἔνδον ὄντες ἅπαντες.

[2] See also the cases quoted above (pp. 226, 227) from Lysias, Antiphon, and Plato.

of their old men. For here it is no inferior class, but
their own equals, nay even those to whom they directly owed their greatness, whom they cast aside
with contempt when their days of usefulness had
passed away. The reader will remember the same
feature alluded to in a former chapter, and how
Achilles assumes that his aged father will be treated
with violence and injustice because he has no son
at home to help him. In Ulysses' household we see
the aged Laertes cast aside, like the old dog Argus,
and pining for the return of the son who alone
honoured him and recognised his position. The
Greek lawgivers were accordingly most explicit in
enjoining upon children the nurture and support of
aged parents, who could otherwise expect little from
the younger generation. The Attic law alone added
a qualification, that the children were to be without
responsibility if their parents had neglected to educate them. It should also be remarked that in
theory the Greeks, like all other civilised nations,
respected age, and that in conservative Sparta this
theory was strictly enjoined by law, and carried into
practice.

But unfortunately the practice at Athens differed
widely from the theory, and both tragedy and
comedy agree in painting the contempt in which old
men were held, and the consequent misery of their
position. Aristophanes, in the Parabasis of the
Acharnians, makes a special complaint to the assembled people of the treatment of the older men
by the newer generation (v. 676 sqq.) :—

'We, the veterans of the city, briefly must expostulate
At the hard ungrateful usage which we meet with from the state,
Suffering men of years and service at your bar to stand indicted,
Bullied by your beardless speakers, worried and perplexed and frighted,
Aided only by their staff, the staff on which their steps are stayed;
Old and impotent and empty; deaf, decrepit, and decayed.
There they stand, and pore, and drivel, with a misty purblind gleam,
Scarce discerning the tribunal, in a kind of waking dream.
Then the stripling, their accuser, fresh from training, bold and quick,
Pleads in person, fencing, sparring, using every turn and trick;
Grappling with the feeble culprit, dragging him to dangerous
    ground,
Into pitfalls of dilemmas, to perplex him and confound.
Then the wretched invalid attempts an answer, and at last
After stammering and mumbling, goes away condemned and cast,
Moaning to his friends and neighbours, "All the little store I have,
All is gone! my purchase money for my coffin and my grave." ' [1]

And then the chorus speaks with much pathos of
the days of old, when they could have made short
work of such adversaries. There is much similar
complaint in the *Wasps* of the same author, where
the old dicast declares that his only chance of respect
or even safety is to retain the power of acting as
a juryman, so extorting homage from the accused,
and supporting himself by his pay without depending
on his children. When he comes home with his fee,
they are glad to see him, in fact he is able to support
a second wife and younger children, as the passage
(605 sqq.) plainly implies, whereas otherwise the
father must look towards his son and his son's
steward to give him his daily bread, 'uttering imprecations and mutterings, lest he knead me a deadly

[1] Frere. iii. p. 36.

cake [1],' a dark insinuation, which opens to us terrible suspicions, and which would hardly have been ventured by the poet, were the idea quite foreign to the minds of the audience.

The indications in the tragedies are not inconsistent with these passages. There are often (especially in Euripides' plays) old kings introduced, who in the absence of their sons endeavour to guard the dominion which has already passed into stronger hands, and almost invariably these old men are represented as acquiescing, though with complaints, in the weakness of their position, and submitting to much insolence from foes and rivals. There seems no such thing as a patient submission to an aged sovereign, nor did his old experience, or the scars of former battles, secure to him the allegiance of his people, when his vigour had passed away.

It is easy to see the grounds of this harshness in the Greek mind. Sentimentality was to them almost unknown. In spite therefore of that respect which they could not but feel for age, the violent nature of Periclean politics, as well as the warlike temper of earlier days, made vigour in their leaders an absolute necessity. The nation was a stirring nation, always seeking advance and enlargement in some direction, and therefore not tolerant of the sleepy and effete governments which are often popular, and still more

---

[1] ἄλλην μή μοι ταχὺ μάξῃ. The habit of old men marrying again after their children were grown up, was not uncommon. As might be expected, they were often guilty of great folly on these occasions, and selected very unsuitable and improper persons.

often tolerated, in modern Europe and among anti-quated orientals. One terse line of Hesiod expresses the Greek attitude in all history[1]: Work for youth, counsel for maturity, prayers for old age—such are the duties of life as expressed in this untranslateable apophthegm. It was left for other nations, such as the Chinese and ourselves, to tolerate, nay rather to honour governors who are long past their usefulness, to have great offices of trust filled by timid and hesitating old men, whose incapacity often ruins great interests, and breaks the hearts of the earnest workers who see their way clearly, but cannot lead or command till the same terrible disease has dimmed *their* vision, and made them in turn a burden and a drag on the progress of a younger generation.

But in these safe and quiet times, we can afford without absolute ruin generals and judges and bishops whom five years of life like old Greek life would sweep to the winds. The Periclean Athenians were too acute to be imposed upon by the absurd, but still potent maxim, that quantity of experience in itself increases our wisdom; they saw that when maturity of age is passed, and the power of decision begins to wane, this very burden of long experience perplexes the mind, and engenders doubt and fear instead of confidence. Euripides often puts forward the ridiculous and feeble aspects of old age, and makes them the comic element in his tragedies. Thus Horace, painting his typical old man, doubtless from Greek models, puts before us, not his venerable

[1] ἔργα νέων, βουλαὶ δὲ μέσων, εὐχαὶ δὲ γερόντων.

aspect, and his wise authority, but rather his weakness and querulousness :—

> ' Multa senem circumveniunt incommoda, vel quod
> Quærit, et inventis miser abstinet, ac timet uti:
> Vel quod res omnes timide gelideque ministrat:
> Dilator, spe longus, iners, avidusque futuri ;
> Difficilis, querulus, laudator temporis acti
> Se puero, censor castigatorque minorum.'

It is but fair to urge these points in defence of a hard feature in Greek life, which even reached such a pitch, that by a law commonly acted upon, old men could be brought into court by their children[1], and if found incapable of managing their property, it was taken from them and transferred to their heirs. Such an attitude of public opinion would go far to explain the strange account given us of the old people in Ceos, who when they came to the age of sixty or upwards, and felt themselves growing useless, drank hemlock, and left the world in which they were becoming a mere incumbrance[2]. How desirable

---

[1] Cf. Ar. Νεφ. 845.

[2] Müller, *Frag. Hist.* ii. p. 214. In more barbarous nations, the same results are attained, despite the want of public spirit in the old people, who put their relations to the trouble of deciding the question of a rude but effective test. Waitz, in his *Anthropology* (vol. v.) tells us of people in Borneo, who when they think their elders have lived a reasonable time, and show signs of decay, put them up into trees, and then dance round the tree, shaking it violently, and singing in rude refrain: ' The fruit is ripe, the fruit is ripe, 'tis time for it to fall.' When the fruit does accordingly fall, it is cooked and eaten. We are not informed what happens when it does not. Probably the old man has proved his farther usefulness by his literal and not figurative tenacity of life. The Chinese, with the oldest civilisation in the world, and perhaps the most effete, have gone into the other extreme even beyond ourselves, and honour

would such a practice appear in some of our public services and institutions !

But though from the practical side it is possible to offer these explanations, from the poetical we cannot be surprised at the extreme horror of old age felt by the Greek poets, how they loaded it with imprecations, and reviled it as the most certain and most awful of human miseries. With their keen love of enjoyment, and appreciation of beauty, we can well imagine how bitterly they felt the passing away of youth, and on no subject have they at all times spoken with more heartfelt utterance. I have spoken above (p. 119) of this sentiment among the lyric poets. Everybody knows the great chorus in Sophocles' later *Œdipus*, which has been so often translated, and will ever be tempting other hands to essay the mastery of its Protean beauties. I prefer to conclude this chapter with an English version of a less known, but not less characteristic chorus, that in Euripides' *Hercules Furens* on the miseries of old age. I have again to thank my friend Professor Webb for having translated it especially for this place. It speaks the same language which we find in Mimnermus, in Solon, in Theognis—that ingrained horror of a keen sensitive race against the condition of life which destroys beauty and mars enjoyment. It is thus one of those passages in Euripides which are in peculiar relation and in intimate sympathy

a man in direct proportion to his age. This seems to have been the case in ancient Egypt also, as appears from various documents. (Cp. my *Prolegomena to Anc. Hist.* p. 280.)

with the whole nation, and which secured his wide-spread and lasting fame :—

'If the high Gods would give me a guerdon,
    Be it youth ere its forces are fled;
For age is a wearisome burden,
    An Aetna that lies on the head,
A robe of the blackness of darkness, that over the eyelids is spread.

Tell me not of the Asian Tyrant,
    Or of palaces plenished with gold;
For such bliss I am not an aspirant,
    If youth I might only behold—
For in weal 'tis a halo of glory, and in woe it is riches untold.

But sombre and stained as with slaughters
    Old age is a thing I abhor;
Oh! would it were swept o'er the waters
    To plague home and city no more:
Oh! would it were swept through the Ether, and cast on some nameless shore.

If the high Gods would only assert you
    Their wisdom and goodness, I trow,
As the manifest impress of virtue
    A renewal of youth they 'd bestow,
And the path of descent would revert, and restore the blest shades from below.

And the dead and the living would mingle,
    And bask in the beams of the sun;
But the life of the bad would be single,
    And the death of the wicked be one;
And there would be a symbol for ever, that the good from the evil were known.

In the sky, though the cloud-rack may dim it,
    Each star by the sailor is seen,
But the high Gods have fixed not a limit
    The good and the evil between;
And still as the tide of time floweth, wealth all that is noble outgroweth.'

CHAPTER IX.

ATTIC CULTURE.

I DO not think any strict subdivision into epochs is necessary in a social point of view, when we have once passed through the fever of the Periclean age. To this I have above (p. 134) alluded. The century which followed the collapse of the Athenian empire was no doubt one of great political vicissitudes, seeing that the centre of gravity in politics moved from Sparta to Thebes, then perhaps to Athens, for a moment to Phocis, and lastly to Macedonia. There were doubtless grave changes also in literature and in philosophy, but yet no *revolution*. The forms and kinds of literary composition, as of the other arts, were fixed for ever. The inventive genius of the Greeks, which had allowed no previous century to pass without new and strange developments, seems now changed into a critical spirit, perfecting and developing the established types. Thus Menander, Epicurus, and Demosthenes are the direct inheritors of the art of Aristophanes and Plato and Pericles—tamed down, no doubt, in some respects, and modified to suit lower politics and higher culture, but yet after all the same art, and addressed to almost the same society. With the conquests of Alexander, and the tumultuous epoch of the Diadochi, there arose a really changed society; but this is beyond our present scope, for these turbulent days have left us few traces of their peaceful pursuits, amid the dreary and confused annals of their wars and revolutions.

I desire now to discuss Greek culture in its highest development at Athens, and in the age when men had learned to rate culture above the hard business of politics, when in fact their highest social refinement was built upon the ruins of their political greatness.

The first point I would urge upon all those who desire to form a true notion of Athenian culture in these palmy days, is the limited size of the city, and the fact that from the smallness of its population and its habits of leisure, every man of any mark was known to all the citizens, if not personally, at least by name and character. 'It is impossible,' says Hypereides in a speech written for Lycophron, 'for any man to be either a miscreant or a man of good character in this city, without all of you knowing it[1].' It was in fact *as to size* a society far more like that of Dublin or Edinburgh, than that of the vast modern capitals, where even neighbours are perfect strangers, and where a diversity of pursuit severs men more

---

[1] Cp. Hypereides, pp. 28, 39, ed. Blass: λαθεῖν γὰρ τὸ πλῆθος τὸ ὑμετέρον οὐκ ἔνι οὔτε πονηρὸν ὄντα οὐδένα τῶν ἐν τῇ πολεῖ οὐδὲ ἐπιεικῆ. Cp. also Lysias, p. 177.

effectually than miles of distance. Thus Socrates, coming home from the campaign at Potidæa, is represented, at the opening of Plato's *Charmides,* asking eagerly what new beauties had appeared in the Gymnasia, just as we should ask what new belles had appeared at the balls of the season in Dublin. He takes it for granted that his friend will be sure to have seen them, for at Athens they did not observe the strict Spartan rule, which ordered that all who came in to see the sports should either 'strip or depart.' The appearance of Charmides is described just as we describe the reigning belle at a flower show—surrounded by a crowd of gentlemen in attendance, and causing quite a sensation when she comes in [1].

So again at the opening of the *Laches,* there is an old man introduced, who had been a friend of Socrates' father Sophroniscus, but who, living in an uneducated set of people, has lost sight of Socrates. He has however constantly heard his sons and their friends talking of him, and is quite surprised that it never struck him that Socrates might be the son of his old neighbour [2].

I think this limited size of Athens—a feature which both Plato and Aristotle seem anxious to retain in

---

[1] See Jowett's *Plato,* vol. i. pp. 8–10.

[2] Prof. Jowett (*Plato,* i. p. 74) draws exactly the wrong inference from this passage. He takes it to imply that this old man has never heard of Socrates. This is exactly what the old man (p. 79, Jowett) does not say. He says he has constantly heard of him, but did not before meet him, being in a different set.

their ideal commonwealths—had a marked effect in producing a certain unity and harmony in Athenian culture. It was like that uniformity of type, produced in such a society as the old Universities of our own day, where the men are not too many to be in some sort influenced by one another, and all to attain, amid decided differences, a certain sameness, which though undefinable, strikes every intelligent observer. In art we may find something similar in the effect of residence at Rome on a painter or sculptor, perhaps a still closer analogy would be the society of painters and literary men gathered together in Munich by that modern Pericles (as to art) King Ludwig I. In such societies, where master spirits can really reach and influence the whole mass, there arises an uniform standard of criticism, recognised laws of taste, and a form at least in art and literature secured from rudeness and extravagance.

There is no greater contrast between Greek and modern civilisation than this, and no plainer cause of the greater perfection of Greek culture in some respects— I mean the severance of cultivated Greeks into separate small cities, like the Bonn, Weimar, and Dresden of former Germany, where intellectual life gathered about independent centres, and where men were not, as they now are in Great Britain and France, looking ever to an overgrown capital, and in vain, for standards of perfection.

When we read the comedies of Aristophanes, or even the dialogues of Plato, we feel that they were

addressed to the whole of Athens, though also to a
highly intelligent audience, and so it is that modern
historians have come to attribute so extraordinary
an average culture to the Athenians. An authority
on old Greek history says[1], and in my opinion
rightly, that the average *intelligence* of the assembled
Athenian citizens was higher than that of our House
of Commons. Without doubt each citizen, at all
events, lived in an atmosphere far more stimulating
than that in which our mercantile members are
brought up. He enjoyed the contemplation of the
highest art, the performance of the greatest tragedies,
the delivery of the most refined orations. He and
his fellows were all exercised as jurymen in deciding
political and social disputes, nay even in awarding the
prizes for tragedies and comedies. Nor do I find any
trace of that severance of amusements which is one
of the saddest features of modern life, where refined
art and high excellence are only exhibited under
such restrictions (especially pecuniary) as to exclude
the masses, which are now so brutalised that they
require a separate literature, as well as a separate
art, if art it can be called, to amuse them in their
rapidly increasing leisure. We hear of no Liberties,
or Seven Dials, at Athens. We hear of no hells,
or low music halls, or low dancing saloons. Even
such vice as existed was chiefly refined and gentlemanly.

I fancy that to some extent this was due to a
fortunate accident in the situation of Athens. The

[1] Freeman, *Hist. of Federal Government*, i. p. 37 sqq

refinement of the people themselves was of course
the great and primary cause, but nevertheless we
should not forget to notice how circumstances cooperated. I allude to the separation of the sea port
of Athens, the Peiræus, by four miles from the city.
The character of the sailor mob, the ναυτικὸς ὄχλος,
which dwelt there, is plainly enough indicated in
scattered hints throughout the literature of the day.
Thus in Plato's *Phædrus* [1] the 'haunts of sailors' are
spoken of as a place where good manners are unknown. Even the merchant ship-captains are spoken
of in another place (*Laws*, iv. p. 165) as of low social
standing, and on a level with retail shopkeepers.
Later on in the same dialogue (p. 226) there is a
striking passage on the character of sea towns, which,
as I believe Plato had the Peiræus before his mind,
I shall here quote. 'Had you been on the sea, and
well provided with harbours, and an importing rather
than a producing country, some mighty saviour would
have been needed, and lawgivers more than mortal,
if you were to have a chance of preserving your state
from degeneracy and discordance of manners. . . .
The sea is pleasant enough as a daily companion,
but has also a bitter and brackish quality, filling
the streets with merchants and shopkeepers, and be-
getting in the souls of men uncertain and unfaithful
ways—making the state unfriendly and unfaithful
both to her own citizens, and also to other nations.'

To this description may be added the striking
passage in the *Critias*, where the din and noise of

[1] Jowett i. p. 577.

the harbour in his Utopia is evidently borrowed from the sea-port he knew so well. 'The entire area was densely crowded with habitations, and the canal and the largest of the harbours were full of vessels and of merchants coming from all parts, who, from their numbers, kept up a multitudinous sound of human voices and din of all sorts night and day.' Aristophanes describes with great vigour the Peiræus when an expedition was ordered out (*Acharn.* 54 sqq.) :—

> 'You would have launched at once three hundred galleys,
> And filled the city with a noise of troops :
> And crews of ships, crowding and clamouring
> About the muster-masters and pay-masters ;
> With measuring corn out at the magazine,
> And all the porch choked with the multitude ;
> With figures of Minerva newly furbished,
> Painted and gilt, parading in the streets ;
> And wineskins, kegs, and firkins, leeks, and onions ;
> With garlic crammed in pouches, nets, and pokes ;
> With garlands, singing girls, and bloody noses.
> Our arsenal would have sounded and resounded,
> With bangs and thwacks of driving bolts and nails,
> With shaping oars, and holes to put the oar in ;
> With hacking, hammering, clattering, and boring,
> Words of command, whistles, and pipes, and fifes [1].'

---

[1] Frere, iii. p. 27. Among the various characters that thronged the quays, Heracleides Ponticus (Athen. xii. 5, § 2) speaks of a certain Axoneus, 'who was subject to this peculiar madness, that he thought all the ships that came into the Peiræus were his own, and so he wrote down their names, and sent them out, and directed them, and hailed them when they arrived with all the joy of a man who was possessed of all this wealth. Of those that were lost he took no account, while he delighted in those that came in safe, and so he lived in great contentment. But when his brother Crito, having come over

I think this accident, as I call it, of Athens being
situated some miles from the sea, which is rather the
consequence of its being a very ancient site, when
men were as yet afraid to venture down from the hill
forts to the seaboard, for fear of piracy—this feature
was of great importance in keeping the society of
Athens pure and refined. No doubt there was constant intercourse with the port, there was always
business-traffic, there were often shows and processions which brought crowds from either town to
the other, rich men possessed houses in each, nay the
road between the long walls was so recognised a
promenade for Athenians, that Plato speaks of it[1]
as 'made for conversation.' Yet, notwithstanding,
the populations were evidently quite distinct; there
were even distinct boards of magistrates for the
Peiræus, as we can see from the fragments of
Aristotle's *Politeiai*; there was a distinct tone of life,
and probably a distinct society. So then a certain
aristocratic flavour must have ever dwelt about the
Athenian, and led to a general feeling of selectness
and refinement.

Acting in unison with this special feature, was that
other general one, which applies to all Greek towns
—I mean the existence of a large class of slaves to
do all the drudgery of life, and to leave the dominant class free for higher pursuits and higher amuse-

on a visit from Sicily, brought him to a physician, and had him cured,
he used to say he had never spent a happier time, for he had felt no
troubles, but an excess of pleasures.'

[1] *Symposium*, Jowett i. 490.

ments. Thus it is that the Athenian people had such
leisure to pursue politics, and when their empire
diminished, to pursue art and literature. The
characters in Plato's Dialogues always seem to have
time at their disposal, they seem to spend but little
care upon any professional or private concerns. they
are in fact wholly devoted to conversation and society.
It must not be forgotten that Socrates was specially,
and I believe justly, criticised by his contemporaries[1]
for encouraging among young men these vices of
talking and of idleness, λέσχης τέρπνον κακὸν, as
Euripides calls it. Yet he could never have *created*
this peculiarity, and had he attempted his peremptory
'Ancient Mariner' habits of stopping men in a really
busy place, such as our modern Liverpool or Man-
chester, he would doubtless have been rudely thrust
aside, even by intellectual merchants.

But one of the leading features of Attic culture
was the contempt of trade[2], or indeed of any occu-

---

[1] Cp. Meineke, i. p. 287, and among the middle comic poets Amphis
(iii. 301), Ephippus (p. 332), Epicrates and Alexis perpetually. In the
old comedy cp. Arist. *Ran.* 1410, and Eupolis (Mein. ii. 553).

[2] This feeling was of course even more strongly developed in the aristocratic cities of Greece. It was a law at Thebes, says Aristotle (*Pol.*
vi. 4), 'that a man could not hold office for ten years after he had been
in trade (ἀπεσχημένον τῆς ἀγορᾶς). The Thessalians went farther, and
had an ἐλευθέρα ἀγορά, a *free meeting place*, where no mechanic (βά-
ναυσον) or field labourer (γεωργὸν) could enter without being specially
summoned by the magistrates. In Plato's *Phædrus* (Jowett i. 582) there
is a scale of professions, which shows *his* opinion clearly, but seems
otherwise untrustworthy as a general index: (1) philosophers, artists,
and musicians ; (2) kings and warriors ; (3) politicians, economists, and
traders ; (4) gymnasts and physicians ; (5) prophets and hierophants ;

pation which so absorbed a man as to deprive him
of ample leisure. Though architects were men of
great position, and obtained large fees, yet in Plato's
Gorgias we have even so, intellectual a trade as that
of an engineer despised, and in Aristotle's *Politics*
(p. 1340) we find the philosopher with deeper wisdom
censuring the habit of aiming at perfection in instrumental music, as lowering to the mind, and turning
the free gentleman into a slavish handicraftsman.
Possibly we may have this feeling rather strongly
represented by aristocratic writers, like Plato and
Aristophanes, who felt hurt at tradesmen coming
forward prominently in politics ; but the tone of
Athenian life is too marked in this respect, to let
us mistake the fact [1]. Hence came the favour and
indulgence shown to handsome aristocrats like
Alcibiades, hence too the excesses of men like Demosthenes' opponent Meidias, who evidently trusted
to this sentiment, which, though distinctly repressed
by the strict impartiality of Athenian law, yet swayed
the juries, and often retarded or mitigated a just
sentence.

Considering then this leisure, and considering the
selectness of Athenian society—which was not only
free from the vulgar and turbulent classes, but was

(6) poets and imitators; (7) artisans and husbandmen ; (8) and (9)
are classes whom he personally hates. In the *Laws* he classes retail
traders and captains of merchantmen together.

[1] Mr. Strübing (*Aristoph. und die Kritik*, p. 235) shows that a wealthy
middle class could not arise till the trade of Athens developed on sea.
Hence these people were despised by the old landed gentry. Plato
repeatedly speaks of the captains of merchant ships as a low class.

not burdened with an aristocracy of mere birth, overriding that of intellect—we have before us in Plato's Dialogues, and in the numerous fragments of the Middle and New Comedy, a life not inferior to the best society of our own day. The instances of delicate tact and of graceful refinement in Plato's Dialogues especially are so numerous that there is great difficulty in making choice among them. Thus as to deportment, in the *Lysis*, and indeed elsewhere, we find it held impolite either to whisper or to monopolise attention in company[1]. On the other hand, loud talking or hurried walking was thought equally improper—I need only mention the frequent apology of the Messengers in the Tragedies, that they had important reasons for coming θᾶσσον ἢ μ᾽ ἐχρῆν[2]. Of course rudeness and violence in conversation were not less censured than in outward demeanour, and nothing pleases us more in the Platonic or Xenophontic Socrates than the gentleness and irony with which he meets and quiets the few opponents who lose their temper, and attack him with impolite vehemence.

We have indeed in the fragments of Aristoxenus, a very serious authority, grave charges against Socrates himself for this very infirmity of violence in temper.

[1] E. g. *Sophist* (iii. 476): 'I feel ashamed, Socrates, upon coming into a new society, instead of quietly conversing, to be spinning out a long oration, which even if adapted to another, would seem a kind of display.'

[2] Thus Sophocles, *fr.* 234 b (ed. Dind.):

Ὡς νῦν τάχος στείχωμεν, οὐ γὰρ ἔσθ᾽ ὅπως
σπουδῆς δικαίας μῶμος ἅψεταί ποτε.

But though I have great faith in Aristoxenus' seriousness, it seems hard to reconcile his statement, which he bases on direct information from a friend of Socrates, with the evidence of Xenophon, whose realistic and historical account of Socrates agrees with Plato's ideal picture. However, the exact truth as to Socrates really matters little from our point of view. There can be no doubt as to what Plato thought admirable, and what he required from a perfect gentleman in society. Whether attributed rightly to Socrates or not, the very prominence of these features in any ideal sketch shows the estimation in which they were held.

There is a very different point suggested by the death of Socrates, which proves the refined culture of the Athenians from another side. It is an universal contrast between civilised and semi-civilised societies (not to speak of barbarians), that the penalty of death, when legally incurred, is in the former carried out without cruelty and torture, whereas in the latter the victim of the law is farther punished by insults and by artificial pains. The punishments devised by kings and barons in the middle ages, the hideous torments devised by the Church for the bodies of those whose souls were doomed to even worse for ever and ever—these cases will occur to any reader from the history of semi-civilised nations. It will not perhaps strike him that our own country was hardly better even in the present century, and that the formula now uttered by the judge in sentencing to death suggests by its very wording horrible cruelties threatened almost within the memory of living men. 'That you be hanged by the neck, *till you are dead*,' points to the form uttered in the courts of Dublin within this century in cases of high treason, though not then literally carried out. It ran thus: 'It is therefore ordered by the Court that they and each of them be taken from the bar of the Court where they now stand, to the place from whence they came—the gaol: that their irons be there stricken off, that they be from thence carried to the common place of execution, the gallows; and that there they and each of them be hanged by the neck, *but not until they be dead, for whilst they are yet alive, they are to be taken down, their entrails are to be taken out of their body, and whilst they are yet alive, they are to be burned before their faces;* their heads are then to be respectively cut off: their bodies to be respectively divided into four quarters; and their respective heads and bodies to be at His Majesty's disposal [1].'

Let us now compare these formulæ, used by the most cultivated and humane European nation in the

[1] I quote this from the original warrant issued for the execution (for high treason) of Henry and John Sheares in July 1798, now in the possession of my friend Mr. T. T. Gray, of Trin. Coll. Dublin. The same form was of course used in 1803, in the case of Emmett, and may be the legal form now, for all I know. I cannot ascertain whether it was carried out literally since the Restoration. In the Sheares' case the decapitation on the gallows was, I think, the only addition to the hanging, for these men were buried in S. Michan's Church, and were to be seen, with their heads beside them, in good preservation about twenty-five years ago.

nineteenth century, with the enactments of the
Athenian democracy four hundred years before
Christ. In the first place, there was no penalty permitted severer than a quiet and painless death.
There were no antecedent insults and cruelties, no
aggravations, no exhibitions before a heartless and
ribald mob. Even in his day, Herodotus, in describ·
ing the death of Artayctes (ix. 120), evidently regards the manner of it as required for a special
atonement to the hero Protesilaus. In the next
generation care had even been taken to ascertain
the most easy and gentle death, as Xenophon distinctly implies (*Apol. Socr.* § 7), and for this reason
death by poisoning with hemlock was introduced—
at what exact period we cannot say.   Here again
the Athenians were in advance even of the present
day, when death by hanging, in the hands of ignorant
and careless officials, is often a slow death, and a
death of torture [1].   But all this is to my mind far
less significant than the *manner* of Athenian executions, as compared with those even of our day. We
have fortunately in Plato's *Phædo* a detailed account
of this scene, which, however imaginary as to the
conversations introduced, must have lost all its dramatic propriety and force to Plato's contemporaries,
had not the details been reproduced from life with
faithful accuracy.

There is I think in all Greek literature no scene

---

[1] This has been shown by the researches of my friend Prof. Haughton,
who has indicated the means of avoiding such results.   Cp. his *Animal
Mechanics*, p. 7 sqq.

which ought to make us more ashamed of our boasted
Christian culture.   The condemned, on the day of
execution, was freed from his chains, and allowed
to have his family and friends present in his cell,
as they had already been during the nights of his
imprisonment [1].   I suppose the state would then have
been slow to build great gloomy fortresses, whose
massive walls and iron gates mock the prisoners'
attempts, and render chains an idle precaution and
an additional cruelty.   At all events, the chances of
escape, considering the many friends who visited the
prisoners, were such as to render them necessary [2];
yet I feel very sure that any one who could try
both alternatives would without hesitation choose
the chains of the Athenian prison, in preference to
the solitude and gloom of the modern cell.

The condemned then was left with his family and
friends, to make his arrangements and bequests, to
give his last directions, to comfort and to be com-
forted by those dearest to him.   When the hour of
death approached, the jailor came in, and left the
cup of poison with the victim, giving him directions
how to take it, and merely adding that it must be
done before a certain hour.   He then retired and
left the prisoner in his last moments to the care of

---

[1] This appears from Andocides, p. 20.

[2] There is evidence in Lysias (pp. 67, 100) that escape from an impending sentence was openly recognised.   It is evident that exile was
in itself regarded a penalty sufficient for grave crimes, and one which
most people would not accept, if there was any chance of an acquittal.
However, the *Eleven* used to issue a *Hue and Cry* proclamation, when
any one escaped.

his friends. They sat about him as life gradually
ebbed away, and closed his eyes in peace. In the
absence of contrary evidence, it is certain that his
body was restored to his relatives, when death had
been officially testified, and the funeral obsequies
were decently and privately performed by his family.
The omission of any direct mention of them in
Socrates' case, shows that public and ostentatious
mourning was not allowed, while on the other hand,
had the body been buried without ceremony or cast
into the *barathrum*, Socrates would not have omitted
to argue against the supposed injury which such
treatment was held to inflict on the deceased, and
show that the moral laws of God could not allow the
dead to be punished for the acts of the living.

As this interesting question has not been discussed,
so far as I know, by Greek antiquaries, I may observe
that though in Socrates' case (who speaks of *saving
the women trouble* by taking a bath before his death)
and in the case of several victims of the thirty tyrants, who were put to death merely for the sake of
their property, the bodies of the executed were given
back to their relatives, yet we have other cases mentioned by Lysias, when there was added to the simple
sentence of death the refusal of funeral rites, and there
was a place outside Athens, probably the *barathrum*,
also called ὄρυγμα, where the bodies were cast out,
having been carried out from prison by the ἱερὰ πύλη, or
accursed gate[1]. It appears that in cases of public in-

[1] This gives the point of the *Stupid Man's* answer in the *Characters*
(pseudo-Theophrastus?), when asked how many corpses had been

dignation against a culprit this harsh proceeding was carried out (below, p. 391), the psephism of Cannonus makes treason an offence for which it should be inflicted. It also appears that those convicted by an εἰσαγγελία were refused burial in Attic soil, and this was probably a humane or sanitary substitute for casting into the *barathrum*. If this be so, we may suppose that the additional penalty was inflicted according to some precedent, if not according to some strong feeling, outside the strict letter of the law, which commanded death only [1].

Let us compare all this humane and kindly feeling with the gauntness and horror of our modern executions, as detailed to us with morbid satisfaction by the daily newspapers. We are informed that the prisoner's relatives came to see him the previous evening, but were not allowed to stay with him during the last dread hours of his life—during that awful silence of the night, when each tolling hour reminds him of the march of time, and when loneliness and desolation, following upon the tears and the sympathy of those who are torn from him, seem

carried out through this gate. Mr. Jebb (p. 115) translates 'Sacred Gate,' and is evidently puzzled by the passage, which other editors have endeavoured to amend, from an ignorance of the true meaning of the phrase. This is due to C. Wachsmuth (*Stadt Athen.* i. 346), who is more doubtful about it than he need have been.

[1] The facts above stated follow partly from a comparison of the following passages in Lysias, pp. 79, 80, 92, 94, and 143, ed. Teubner. Mr. H. Hager has since shown (*Journal of Phil.*, viii. 1–13) further evidence on this interesting point. It is not discussed in the books upon Greek antiquities with which I am familiar. Cp. also Hypereides, *Pap. Arden.* col. xvi.

as it were so pre-arranged as, if possible, to drive him mad. Sometimes, if the chaplain be very zealous, these awful hours are relieved by religious exercises, in which the danger of hell and the heinous nature of sin are so prominently put before him, that God's mercy, if extended to him, is held a miracle, and God's vengeance the natural and proper issue of his evil life. If he has fallen asleep from the exhaustion of despair or of long devotions, he is roused in the gray morning by the jailor and told to prepare for death at that hour of the day when the spirits are most depressed, when the temperature is most comfortless, and when we hear with surprise that he 'partook of a hearty breakfast.' I cannot bring myself to follow out the hideous details farther. The pinioning, the procession, the crying of the anxious chaplain for Divine mercy, the masked executioner—there is no single detail which is not hideous and harrowing. Were not the old Greeks vastly superior? Even their very executioner, instead of being a masked villain, who shuns the light of day, is a respectable and kindly official, of whom Socrates speaks with great friendliness, and who sheds tears at the execution of the sentence, remarking how rationally and amiably Socrates had behaved. He adds an interesting trait of manners, that many prisoners were wont to curse him when he brought in the poison, and execrate him as if he were the author of his misfortunes; and yet he seems to have borne all this, and to have been a respectable and respected member of society. This social position of the executioner, as

well as the whole scene in Socrates' prison, is the
greatest proof I know in Greek literature of a culture
exceeding in refinement and humanity that of our
own day.

But to any one who compares the Platonic with the
Periclean generation, there will gradually come into
sight a greater gentleness and softness, a toning down
of the hard features, a nearer approach to the greater
humanity of Christian teaching. It was impossible
that this should not be. The fearful civil war, increasing yearly in cruelty and heartlessness, ended
with the most horrible massacre in Greek history—
the cold-blooded execution of three thousand Athenian prisoners at Ægospotami. We are told that the
Athenian general Philocles, who was the first to
suffer, had proposed, if not carried a vote, to ampu-
tate the right thumbs of all the prisoners taken by
Athens, in order that they might henceforth be unable
to wield the spear, and be only fit for rowing.

After all this barbarity, Athens was conquered, and
obliged to turn for years to her internal concerns. So
there arose a new generation, not nurtured amid raid
and rapine, but taught to live at home; to learn from
the lips of the great teachers who had been hitherto
more admired than obeyed; above all to live in re-
conciliation with political foes, and to feel that even
civil strife should be forgotten, and that men who had
stood behind lines of hostile shields, and met one
another with the spear's point, could settle down into
quiet and orderly citizens. The great misfortunes of
the state had taught the Athenians that citizen life

was too precious to be poured out in wrath, and so we see with wonder and respect the restored democracy passing their great Act of Amnesty, whereby as the orators assure us, many murderers and other miscreants of the deepest dye were enabled to come back to the city, and live under the eyes of their victims' families [1].

I do not remember in any of the later wars atrocities such as those which we have discussed hitherto. Xenophon tells us that Agesilaus, after the fearful struggle with the Thebans at Coronea, received the news, when lying wounded, that eighty Thebans were cut off from the rest, and had taken refuge in a neighbouring temple with their arms. He ordered them to be escorted in safety to their camp. For he was wont to exhort his soldiers at all times 'that prisoners in war were not personal enemies,' and should not be treated with cruelty. Still earlier, the noble Callicratidas had inaugurated the same high principles, and refused to sell as slaves the Greeks whom he had captured. Under Epaminondas, under Iphicrates,

[1] This is sometimes the case in Ireland, where cold-blooded murderers return, through the clemency of the English Government, and resume their residence near the scene of their crime. An Irish judge once told me that on a journey he suddenly found himself sitting opposite a man whom he had himself sentenced to be hanged some few years previously. There is, indeed, one contrast between Athens and Ireland. At Athens the returned miscreant was in disgrace, and apparently often threatened and molested. In Ireland it is the returned murderer who threatens the remaining members of his victim's family, and tells them 'he will serve them the same way, *even if he was to get two years for it!*'

and under Phocion, we hear of no massacre of prisoners,
and though the enslaving of women and children
was still common, yet we hear from Demosthenes
and Æschines how sad a sight the gangs of slaves
from Olynthus appeared when passing into Greece—
a feeling unknown in the Peloponnesian war. The
extreme barbarities of war had passed away with the
cruel Lysander.

I must add, however, that here as elsewhere, in
Greek benevolence, duty chanced to coincide specially with interest. When wars came to be carried
on chiefly by mercenaries, all extremities in treatment of the vanquished in battle must necessarily
be abandoned. For these men will only fight on
such terms, and though they will stand the chance
of battle, they cannot in fairness be supposed to
participate in the personal hates which have given
rise to the struggle. The aversion which the Spartan
felt for the Athenian could not in fairness be transferred to his paid representative—more especially
when this representative would take service for
money against his old employer, and become useful
to his captor. Thus mercenary wars, for many independent reasons, cannot be carried on except on
terms of reasonable humanity to the vanquished
army, and this circumstance cooperated with the
growth of real humanity and justice in the Greek
mind [1].

---

[1] Cf. Plutarch, *Pelop. and Marcelli Comp.*, also *Timol.* capp. 20, 80.
Prof. Barlow suggests an interesting parallel, which he copied for me
from Ordericus Vitalis (xii. 18). This author, in describing a battle

There are indeed not wanting hints that in private life men had not attained to the Christian or modern sentiment of regard for life. The cool way in which Plato in his *Republic* (p. 461) speaks of exposing children, shows that, as we should expect, with the increase of luxury and the decay of the means of satisfying it, the destruction of infants came more and more into fashion. What can be more painfully affecting than the practice implied by Socrates, when he is comparing himself to a midwife (*Theæt.* 151 B): 'And if I abstract and expose your firstborn, because I discover that the conception you have formed is a vain shadow, do not quarrel with me, *as the manner of women is, when their first children are taken from them.* For I have actually known some men ready to bite me when first I deprived them of a darling folly.' So then after the exposure of a first child, the unfortunate mother became comparatively reconciled to it! Is this what he implies?

Again, at the opening of the *Euthyphro* there is a story told, which is not intended to be anything exceptional, and which shows that the free labourer, or dependent, had not bettered his position since the days when Achilles cited him (p. 65) as the most miserable creature upon earth. 'Now the man who is dead,' says Euthyphro, 'was a poor dependent of

between Henry I of England and Louis VI of France observes : ' In the battle between the two kings, in which nearly 900 knights were engaged, I have ascertained that *three* only were slain. This arose from their being covered with steel armour, *and mutually sparing each other for the fear of God, and out of regard for the fraternity of arms.*'

mine who worked for us as a [free] field-labourer at Naxos, and one day, in a fit of drunken passion, he got into a quarrel with one of our domestic servants [slaves] and slew him. My father bound him hand and foot and threw him into a ditch, and then sent to Athens to ask of a diviner what he should do with him. Meantime he had no care or thought of him, deeming him a murderer, and that even if he did die there would be no great harm. And this was just what happened. *For such was the effect of cold and hunger and chains upon him*, that before the messenger returned from the diviner, he was dead. And my father and family are angry with me for taking the part of the murderer and prosecuting my father.' I greatly fear that such doings were not uncommon, and that the treatment of poor members of the subject cities by Athenians was not so gentle as Mr. Grote would make us believe [1]. Nevertheless when we remember the absence of wholesale massacres, and the humanity of Agesilaus to the wounded and to little children, even in war, isolated cases of cruelty will not overthrow the assertion of a real improvement; and so capital a fact as the amnesty of Eucleides at Athens shows plainly that the moral teaching of Euripides, of Socrates, and of the more lofty Sophists, was making sure and silent progress.

---

[1] Cp. above, p. 241, on the question of torture, to which I may add Æschines *against Ctes.* § 224. Cope's attempt (*Introd. to Rhet.* p. 201) to make out Aristotle as disapproving torture is wholly unwarrantable. Meanwhile the reader who will compare Isocrates (p. 73 D), will see what a terrible visitation to a subject-city an Athenian man-of-war usually proved.

Let us turn from war to domestic life, and consider our great test point—the social position of women.

The ideal pictures of Euripides—Alcestis, Macaria, Polyxena, Iphigenia—these were dwelling in the minds of the people. The teaching of Aspasia, if we are to believe Xenophon (*Œcon*. p. 14) and the Socratic Æschines [1], was directed chiefly to the duties of husbands and wives, and to the bettering of the social position of Athenian ladies. There can be no doubt that the large sympathies of the great Socrates led him in the same direction. Thus the question of women's rights came up at Athens long before Plato's *Republic* was written, and before Plato had even begun to write. Our earliest hints of its existence are not only these allusions to Aspasia, which are few and obscure, but the curious play of Aristophanes called the *Ecclesiazusæ*, brought out some years after the close of the great war, and ridiculing some scheme or schemes of society strikingly similar to the theories of Plato. Of course, the picture of Aristophanes was intended to be a gross exaggeration. He contemplates the women leaving their husbands at home, and going in male attire to the agora, to make laws and reform the state. Amid all his ridicule this seems plain, that the success of the play presupposes an audience whose minds had been exercised about these social questions. The female sex, hitherto εἰθισμένον δεδοικὸς καὶ σκότεινον ζῆν—'accustomed to live cowed and in obscurity'—was distinctly

---

[1] Quoted by Cicero, *de Inventione*, i. § 31.

claiming, and giving rise to claims for, a better condition.

We see the same attitude in Xenophon's remarkable tract on *Domestic Economy*, strangely ignored by our scholars, yet containing perhaps the most complete picture we have of the duties of a model Greek gentleman, and of what might be made of a young Greek wife brought up in the ordinary way. In the dialogue Socrates represents himself as having heard all about it from a man of high position and repute named Ischomachus, who had trained his own wife, and managed his house with such success as to be pointed to at Athens for a model of a καλοκαγαθός or 'gentleman.' This very term implies a change in social views, when we compare it with the utterances of the earlier literature. It implies that combination of breeding (ἀγαθὸς) and culture (καλὸς) which we require in our own aristocracy, and which was admired, but not, I fancy, insisted upon, in earlier days. But to return to our dialogue.

'I should like to know this particularly from you,' says Socrates, 'whether you yourself educated your wife so as to make her what she ought to be, or whether you received her from her parents with a knowledge of her duties?' 'And how could I have received her so educated, Socrates, when she came to me not fifteen years old, and had lived up to that time under the strictest surveillance, that she might see as little as possible, and hear as little as possible, and enquire as little as possible. For surely you would not be content with her knowing merely how to weave wool into a garment, and how to weigh out the materials to her maids. But I must observe that in matters of cookery she came to me very well trained, a part of education which seems to me extremely important both for men and women.'

I call attention to this curious remark, showing how the society of Xenophon had already felt what our middle classes are only of late beginning to find out, namely, that a competent knowledge of cookery in the mistress of a house is necessary for comfort and culture. There are certainly more respectable houses in Ireland disgraced by their dinner table than in any other way, and I hold with the Greeks, that rudeness in this particular is a good index of general want of refinement. It was the first duty of the mythical tamers of savage men to amend them in this respect :

> 'Silvestres homines sacer interpresque deorum
> Caedibus et victu foedo deterruit Orpheus,
> Dictus ob hoc lenire tigres rabidosque leones.'

'In heaven's name, then,' says Socrates, 'tell me how you first began to teach her; there is nothing I should so much like to hear.' 'Well, then,' answers Ischomachus, 'when she had become used to my hand, and had become tame enough to carry on a conversation [1], I began to ask her some such question

---

[1] I feel quite at a loss to render in English the forcible and affecting expressions of the original, ἐπεὶ ἤδη μοι χειροήθης ἦν καὶ ἐτετιθάσσευτο, ὥστε διαλέγεσθαι. He speaks of the young creature as of a scared wild animal which only grew tame after some period of confinement and of kind treatment. This is the prose side to the fine writing of the poets about Hymenæus, and about the joys of the nuptial state.

as this : Have you ever thought, lady, what was intended by your parents and by me in making this
marriage ? Was it not that both you and I might
find the best possible partners in our house and children ? Well, then, if God grant us to have children,
we shall consult in due time about them, how we
may best educate them ; for this, too, is to us a
common good, to have them our staunchest allies
and supporters in old age. But now this house is
our common property. For I here produce all that
I have, and put it into the common stock, just as your
dowry went into the same common stock.' (There
appears to have been no allowance or reservation for
pin-money). 'And now we must not be each of us
thinking who contributed most, but rather reflect that
whichever of us makes the better use of it, has given
the most valuable share.' Then the wife said : 'How
can I help you, what power have I ? All rests with
you : but my duty, as my mother told me, is to be
chaste[1].' 'Of course,' replies Ischomachus, 'and so
also my father told me. But it is the duty of chaste
men and women to see that their property is in good
order, and that they make the greatest profit they
can from what is fair and just. Try therefore to
perform as well as possible what the gods have
suited to your nature, and what the customs of men
coincide in approving. And these duties are by no

---

[1] So Euripides :—

γυναικὶ γὰρ σιγή τε καὶ τὸ σωφρονεῖν
κάλλιστον, εἴσω θ' ἥσυχον μένειν δόμων.

Heracl. 476-7.

means trifling, any more than the duties of the queen bee (ἡγεμὼν μέλιττα) in the hive.'

He proceeds to develop with great beauty and clearness the several duties of husband and wife, derived from the difference in their physical nature and instincts, which, when contrasted, are yet so contrived as to supply one another's deficiencies, and perfect our condition[1].

He objects to artificial improvements of her person, such as high-heeled shoes, false hair, dyed hair, rouge, and pearl powder, all of which were clearly in common use among the respectable classes at Athens in his day[2]. I cannot but suspect that this implies a reaction of the ἑταίραι on Attic households, and that anxious mothers thought their daughters ought to rival the studied charms of these very serious antagonists to marriage. The Middle Comedy is full of allusions[3] to the artificial means used by these inferior ladies to enhance their attractions—and this we should have assumed without evidence; but it seems to me somewhat painful to find secluded Athenian girls so modern and advanced in their culture. On this point Ischomachus is represented as persuading his young wife easily, and she boldly lays aside all these artificial beauties.

He develops, too, as we should expect a Greek

---

[1] Διὰ δὲ τὸ τὴν φύσιν μὴ πρὸς πάντα ταῦτα ἀμφοτέρων εὖ πεφυκέναι, διὰ τοῦτο καὶ δέονται μᾶλλον ἀλλήλων, καὶ τὸ ζεῦγος ὠφελιμώτερον ἑαυτῷ γεγένηται, ἃ τὸ ἕτερον ἐκλείπεται τὸ ἕτερον δυνάμενον.

[2] Cp. also Meineke, *Frag. Com.* iv. 409.

[3] Meineke, iii. pp. 421–2, &c.

gentleman to do, the satisfaction arising from the exercise of power, from the consciousness of training and improving her household, from the dispensing of rewards and punishments according as they are deserved. He concludes his first conversation with the girl in the following noble terms. 'But the greatest pleasure of all will be this, that if you are plainly superior to me, you will become my mistress (ἐμὲ σὸν θεράποντα ποιήσῃς), and will not have to fear that with advancing years your influence in the house will wane, but will rather be assured that in old age, the better companion you are to me and the better guardian of the house to our children, the more honoured will you be at home. For you will come to be truly admired and esteemed among men, not for good looks, but for good deeds in practical life.'

Here, then, we have an advance not attained even by Pericles in the preceding generation; for he entrusted all his household affairs, not to Aspasia, but to a trusty steward, who seems to have been somewhat more frugal than a sensible manager, and withal a well-bred lady, would have been. But perhaps the most remarkable blot in Xenophon's sketch is the total absence of any intellectual requirements on the part of the woman. Socrates distinctly says at the opening of the dialogue that if the wife is bad, it is the husband's fault for not training her[1], and it is

---

[1] 'If a sheep,' says Socrates, ' is in bad condition, we generally blame the shepherd, and if a horse do mischief we generally abuse his rider; so, as to a wife, if after being well taught by her husband, she does ill, perhaps she should justly be blamed; but if he does not teach her

plain enough that at fifteen years of age there is
ample time to teach her those purely practical duties
which he exclusively contemplates. The only duty
which he presupposes to be disagreeable is the tend-
ing of sick slaves, which the wife, on the contrary,
is most willing to do, in return for the gratitude which
she will earn.

I may also observe, before passing on, that here, as
in other Greek literature, we find ladies of rank under
restraints unknown to the lower classes. Ischomachus advises his wife to take exercise by folding
up and putting by clothes, so obtaining what she
ought to have obtained by walking out[1]. This
appears to me one of the greatest hardships of Attic
city life, and again the main reason why such importance was attached to funeral ceremonies, and
other religious observances, where it was necessary to
let out ladies of the better classes. It also explains the expression of Xenophon in the same
dialogue, when praising country life : 'what is dearer

her duties, and then finds her unacquainted with them, is not the husband justly to bear the blame?' (*Œcon.* iii. § 2.) This complete post-
ponement of education till after marriage is probably the reason of
the fact which Plato notices (*Cratylus*, p. 418) that women at Athens
spoke an archaic dialect, differing from that of men. Cicero (*De
Oratore*, iii. 12) repeats the same remark about Roman ladies, but whether
he is speaking on independent grounds, or merely copying Plato, is to
me uncertain.

[1] He compares Greek women in general to those handicraftsmen,
who earn their livelihood sitting, and are thus injured in body—a thing
much despised by the Greeks. The Spartan women, on the contrary,
were carefully trained to out-of-door physical exercise. Cp. *Laced. Pol.*
cap. 1.

to the servants, or *pleasanter to the wife*, or more longed for by the children, or more agreeable to friends!'

These practical improvements in the life of married women Xenophon doubtless copied from the suggestions of Socrates, and they had been probably, as Socrates is represented to say, already advocated by Aspasia. But it was almost impossible for the advocates of women's rights to stop here, and not to recommend some change in the education of girls before marriage. In fact, it must necessarily seem absurd that men should be trained for their duties by a laborious and expensive system, while women, whose duties were, according to Xenophon, not less important, though different, should pass away their early youth in complete ignorance of anything beyond weaving wool and cooking dinners. It is therefore perfectly consistent in such a systematic and thorough theorist as Plato, that he should advance to the farther point of recommending the same education for boys and girls. Plato held the very modern theory that women had the same faculties and capacities as men, but in an inferior degree[1], and hampered by the inconveniences of child-bearing. He therefore advocated a joint education, pointing not merely to the analogy of the domestic lower animals, but to the precedent of Sparta. There, as we know, girls joined even in athletic exercises pub-

[1] That this opinion was really inherited from Socrates, appears from the corroboration of Xenophon, who puts the same sentiment into his mouth (*Symp.* ii. § 2).

licly, and ran and wrestled with one another before
the eyes of men. Many of the Greek theorists were
so shocked at this, that they were slow to allow its
expediency. Ibycus also, in his lyric poems, and
Euripides, upon the stage, reviled this shamelessness.
Aristotle says that after all it did not attain the
desired effect, for that in great dangers these un-
restrained women proved more troublesome than the
enemy. But we can hardly expect a fair judgment
from men of Ionic training. So far as I can see, the
Spartan women, to judge from the few specimens that
are known to us, were not only noble and high-
spirited, but endowed with very good sense. In
Herodotus the celebrated Gorgo seems to have been
no ordinary person, and the fact that Spartan nurses
were sought all over Greece shows not only their
physical superiority [1], which Aristophanes corroborates, but their good temper and gentleness. It is
evident that Cimon's celebrated sister, Elpinice, who
seems to have played as public a part at Athens
as Gorgo did at Sparta, rather affected this Spartan
liberty, seeing that her brother was *proxenus* of the
Lacedæmonians at Athens, and did not conceal his
admiration of Spartan life and habits as compared
with those of Athens.

It seems to me, then, that putting together the
evidence of Plato and Xenophon, as well as the

---

[1] To go out nursing was thought at Athens a very low occupation,
and only to be excused in a free woman on the ground of extreme
poverty (cf. Demosth. p. 1310). Hence it became common at the close
of the Peloponnesian war.

ridicule in Aristophanes' *Ecclesiazusæ*, we find a general stir about the position of women, a disposition to recognise their importance, to acknowledge their claims, and to keep them no longer in that state of obscurity to which they were condemned in Periclean days.

They were, indeed, far from holding their modern and Christian position; it was still common, even after the practice of selling Greek men was discredited, to sell the women of captured cities into slavery and concubinage. And what was even more significant in the matter was this, that such captives, if recovered by their relatives, and restored to their homes, were not thought the least disgraced by their misfortune. In the case of adulterers, Xenophon tells us that the laws punish them with death, because they break in upon the mutual attachment of married people, not for the more obvious reasons; 'for if such a stain happen to a woman by force of circumstances, men honour her none the less, if her affection seems to them to remain untainted [1]'—a most reasonable way of thinking, but utterly opposed to our modern notions of purity. We find, too, even in later days, such men as Demosthenes speaking about women

---

[1] ἐπεὶ ὅταν γε ἀφροδισιασθῇ κατὰ συμφοράν τινα γυνή, οὐδὲν ἧττον τούτου ἕνεκεν τιμῶσιν αὐτὰς οἱ ἄνδρες, ἐάν περ ἡ φιλία δοκῇ αὐτοῖς ἀκήρατος διαμένειν. (Xen. *Hiero*. iii. § 4.) Among the Spartans, according to the same authority (Λακεδ. πολ. c. 1) this absence of sentiment led to strange results. It was not uncommon for an elderly man to borrow a younger husband for his wife, or for a man who disliked his wife, to obtain another temporarily from a friend, with a view to fine and healthy children. The physical results were, according to the author, excellent.

in a tone to us very offensive. We must, therefore, insist upon these limitations. But there was, nevertheless, a distinct advance upon older days. This I have so far attributed to the teaching of the Socratic philosophers.

There was another cause more powerful still, because it brought out the existing want of education more practically. I allude to the rise of a class of educated and refined ἑταῖραι—a class widely different from that legalised by Solon—which comes prominently forward at Athens only with the rise of the Middle Comedy. The very history of the title is interesting and suggestive. It was used by Sappho (*fr.* 31) in the highest sense, as implying a companion of the same rank and with the same interests. There was no shade of reproach in its application to her female friends. We have, unfortunately, not much intermediate evidence, but when we come to the Middle Comedy, which reached from the days of Plato down to the Macedonian conquests, it comes to be used in contrast to wife—a most significant contrast indeed. Just in the same manner our word *mistress* was of old used in a very dignified way, and is still preserved in this sense in ordinary parlance, even as Athenæus tells us (xiii. 571 D.) that in his day girls were wont to call their female friends ἑταῖρας; yet still the word has obtained another peculiar meaning, as opposed to a lawful wife. The feeling of this double meaning in the word is apparent in the days of which we are now speaking. Antiphanes (*Hydria, fr.* 1) says : ' This man of whom I speak

fell in love with an ἑταίρα who lived in the neighbourhood, a citizen, but unprotected by guardian or relations.   She was possessed of a disposition we might
call golden in reality—a veritable *companion* (ὄντως
ἑταίρας) ; the rest traduce by their manners a name
which is really a noble one.'   It appears that if a
Greek woman of this inferior social position was indeed of gentle and refined character, her company
was regarded as far superior to that of proud ladies
of old Attic families, who were full of importance, and,
as we can see from various authors, made their rank
disagreeably felt by their husbands. Thus the country
gentleman, at the opening of Aristophanes' *Clouds*,
curses the *match-maker* (προμνήστρια) who made up
a marriage for him with a lady of the house of
Megacles[1]; for this lady brought up her son with a
thorough contempt of all his father's country occu-
pations, and taught him to look to his maternal
uncle for a model, and to squander his substance
in horse-racing.   Hence we can understand the
fragment of Amphis[2], in which the lawful wife
(γαμετή) is contrasted with the *companion*.   The latter,
he says, is far pleasanter, ' for the former with the
law on her side can afford to despise you and yet
stay in your house, whereas the other knows that

---

[1] The modern anxiety about making matches is therefore no new
thing. Thus Euripides says:—

γάμους δ' ὅσοι σπεύδουσι μὴ πεπρωμένους,
μάτην πονοῦσιν· ἡ δὲ τῷ χρεὼν πόσει
μένουσα κἀσπούδαστος ἦλθεν εἰς δόμους

[2] Meineke, iii. 301.

she must either win over a man by her manners, or go elsewhere.'

We must take care not to attach too much weight to these isolated fragments, quoted for the most part at random by Athenæus, to show his learning. They may be, like many of the abusive passages in Euripides' *Hippolytus* and other tragedies, spoken in character, and by angry or disappointed people. All that we can argue from them is, that such sentiments were suited to the audience, especially as Greek audiences, far more than we do, took to themselves lessons from the stage, and understood the maxims of the poet's characters as intended to represent his own. Still, this cannot be carried out universally, and when the characters maintain opposing views. It is quite possible that there may have been some means, now lost to us, of indicating the poet's sympathy, or of hinting in what cases he professed to speak through his actor. Thus, for example, the early critics speak in a peculiar way of Euripides' *Melanippe* (ἡ σοφή) as disclosing his philosophical views [1]. But as we cannot now always feel sure of this point, on which even the ancients made mistakes, I repeat my caution that we should not understand these fragments as giving us more than the current opinions of some sections of Greek society. Such I believe to be the numerous passages abusing

---

[1] Cp. Dindorf's ed. of the Fragments. This seems to have been believed chiefly on account of the religious scepticism of which the play seems to have been full, and which was thought the poet's real conviction.

marriage, which we find scattered all through Meineke's collection [1], and which the reader may contrast
with the *Œconomicus* of Xenophon, from which I
have already quoted at length.

'The man is actually married,' says the poet Antiphanes.   'My goodness, do you say so ; is it the
man I left alive and walking about?'   'Great Ju-
piter,' says another poet, 'may I perish if I ever
spoke against women, the most precious of all ac-
quisitions. For if Medea was an objectionable person,
surely Penelope was an excellent creature.   Does
any one abuse Clytemnestra ? I oppose the admirable Alcestis.   But perhaps some one may abuse
Phædra ; then, I say, by Jove, what a capital person
was ——.   Oh, dear ! the catalogue of good women
is already exhausted, while there remains a crowd of
bad ones that might be mentioned !'   Thus mar-
riages with heiresses are criticised as particularly
foolish and unhappy, for in those days, as now, high
connection and fortune were preferred to the more
solid qualities of a wife.   'Whosoever,' says Menander, 'desires to marry an heiress, is either suffering
under the wrath of the gods, or wishes to be called
lucky, while he is really miserable [2].'

---

[1] iii. pp. 151, 195, 261, 450, 519, &c.

[2] Cp. also Euripides, *fragg.* 504, &c. The Spartans felt so strongly
the evil of marrying for money, that they actually punished men for
doing it. At the close of his *Lysander*, Plutarch tells us, 'that the state
punished those who had been wooing Lysander's daughters, but had
retired when his poverty was disclosed after his death ; for they had
courted him while he was rich, but deserted him when proved by his
poverty to have been just and honourable. For there were in Sparta,

In spite of all these complaints, almost every play of Menander ended with the happy marriage, not, indeed, of a surly heiress, who despised her husband, but of some simple penniless girl, whose adventures during the play had excited the deep sympathy of the audience.

But satirical reflections on women are so common in almost every age of Greek literature, indeed of all literature, that they are not worth commenting upon.

it seems, penalties for not marrying, and for late marrying, and for mis-marrying, and under this last they brought more especially the case of those who sought rich connections, instead of good ones, among their own kin.'

CHAPTER X.

ATTIC CULTURE (*continued*):—CERTAIN TRADES AND PROFESSIONS.

I PREFER to turn to the literary features really peculiar to the Platonic age in contrast to Periclean days. These features are, no doubt, the decay of practical politics, and the rise of theories of state life, on the one hand, and pictures of private society, on the other. Plato is purely a philosophical speculator on education and on statecraft. Xenophon, practical soldier and keen sportsman as he is, cannot avoid the same tendency, and is, in *his* way, a speculator on politics and society. Yet both of these men clothe their teaching in the dress of social conversation, and paint pictures of private society that they may convey in them their theories. Here, then, they are in contact with the professed dramatists of the Middle Comedy, who, for the most part, ridicule speculation, and make a special butt of Plato and his notions[1], but agree with him in painting scenes from ordinary life, and representing professions and classes upon their stage. As these sketches of

[1] Allusions of this kind are found in Amphis (Mein. iii. p. 305), Ephippus (p. 332), Epicrates (pp. 370, 378, 381), and all through the fragments of Alexis.

U

particular professions are highly instructive for our purpose, I shall proceed to bring together our evidence on doctors, fishmongers, cooks, and such other classes as may be mentioned, previous to entering upon a general sketch of manners as found in the higher society of Plato's dialogues.

As to *Medical Practice*, we find, of course, that there were two schools—the old quackery of charms and incantations, and the rational observation and treatment of disease by empirical remedies[1]. In Homer the former seems prominent, and so it was even in the days of Pindar[2] and Æschylus, though the latter, in giving an account of Prometheus' gifts to mankind, mentions real surgical and medical treatment (*Prom.* vv. 476 sqq.). He also makes in the same play an allusion very characteristic of the Greek temper, and one that indicates the coming development of medicine: 'To those that are sick it is sweet to know clearly beforehand what they have yet to suffer[3].' Such an allusion points to no charms or

---

[1] The recovered medical treatises of the ancient Egyptians, and the Coptic medical papyrus show the same duality of attitude in Egyptian medicine. I have collected all the evidence, and discussed the subject fully in my *Prolegomena to Ancient History*. Herodotus lays stress on the Egyptian doctors being specialists, and only treating one disease. This was not commonly the case among the Greeks, though the scene in the *Plutus* of Aristophanes seems to imply a speciality in that temple for ophthalmia; *Ran.* 151 (Schol.) as well as *Eccles.* 363 corroborate this. But Plato (*Charmides*, 156 B) notices on the other side, that able physicians had even in his day recognised the importance of general health in special affections, and combated the latter through the former.

[2] Cp. *Pyth.* iii. 45, *Nem.* viii. 50.

[3] *Prom.* 698:   τοῖς νοσοῦσί τοι γλυκύ
τὸ λοιπὸν ἄλγος προὐξεπίστασθαι τορῶς.

wonder-making, but to the prognosis of the physician who has learned by experience what to expect from known symptoms.

This rational school had in truth been developed earlier than the age of Æschylus, and strange to say, not in relation to disease, but in relation to high physical training for athletic purposes. Plato, indeed, ascribes the origin of treatment by regimen to Herodicus of Selymbria [1], 'who being a trainer, and himself of a sickly constitution, by a happy combination of training and doctoring, found out a way of torturing, first himself, and then the rest of the world.' So then Greek medicine rather started from hygiene than from pathology. The trainer found that amulets and spells were of no use against better physical conditions. We find the most celebrated early school of medicine at Croton, which was also the home of the greatest athletes.

The tyrants, and in imitation of them the free cities, began to bid for men of this school, and give them high yearly salaries for residing among them. The case of Democedes [2] is well known. He ran away from a cruel father at Croton, and came to Ægina, where he set up in private practice ; and, 'though destitute of the needful appliances, outstripped the best physicians of the place in one year.' Ægina, being at that time the most frequented seaport and emporium in Greece proper, was able to

---

[1] Not Gorgias' brother, who was also a physician, but a native of Leontini.

[2] Herod. iii. 131.

employ him as a state physician the following year,
for a talent (£240)[1]; but the Athenian tyrants next
year bid £406 for him, and the fourth year he was
engaged, for two talents (£480), by Polycrates, the
most powerful Greek prince then living. Such a
salary seems enormous at this epoch among the
Greeks.

However, we see here the habit of having state-
physicians, to which Aristophanes, Plato, and Xenophon make many allusions in after days. There was
a technical term for such practitioners at Athens
(δημοσιεύειν), and the scholiasts on Aristophanes
(*Acharn.* 1030) say they did not take private fees.
I should infer this to have been the case in Democedes' day also, as it would account for the high
state-salary. Plato implies plainly enough that the
profession was taken up by men of culture and education, like Eryximachus, who forms one of the very
aristocratic company in his *Symposium*; and also
that they were publicly elected by the assembly, and
that they distinctly based their practice on experience[2]. It seems certain from Xenophon[3] that
they sent in applications for the post, in which they
doubtless stated their claims, and perhaps even got
testimonials as to their private practice. That their
salary was large is not only implied by Democedes'

---

[1] Plato (*Gorg.* 514 E) speaks of it as ridiculous that a man should
set up to be a state-physician till he had attained eminence in private
practice.

[2] Cp. *Rep.* 405 A, *Gorgias,* 455 B, and *Rep.* 408 E.

[3] Xen. *Mem.* iv. 2.

case, but by Aristophanes (*Plut.* 403) who states that owing to the poverty of the city there was no doctor (I suppose state-doctor), and that accordingly the craft had greatly declined. It is, on the contrary, noticed among the perfections of Spartan military arrangements, that a safe place was allotted to certain indispensable attendants on the army, and among these are mentioned *military surgeons* (*Lac. Pol.* 13), who are very seldom alluded to in Greek literature [1].

Though Xenophon (*Œcon.* xiii.) speaks of their visits to patients morning and evening, I fancy that this applies to an inferior class of private practitioners, and that the state-physicians were consulted at their official residence. They had a number of assistants, some of them slaves, who treated simple cases, and more especially the diseases of slaves, by going in and ordering the patients to take remedies; whereas with free men the practice was to persuade the patient, by full explanation of the treatment, that it would succeed. Plato is very interesting on this point. In the case of the free man, 'he [the physician] will not prescribe till he has persuaded him.' A still more remarkable case, if true, is that mentioned in the *Gorgias*, where Plato says that the physicians used to take with them Gorgias, who was the most persuasive rhetorician of the day, in order that he might convince the patients to adopt their prescriptions. These things are very curious, and show to what a pitch the Greeks had brought the

---

[1] Mr. Hager adds Xen. *Anab.* iii. 4, 30; and *Cyrop.* i. 6, 15; iii. 2, 13.

habit of inquiry and argument, in this case regardless, as it seems, of the very bad effect such discussions must have had on the nerves of many patients. But I must add, in fairness to the Greeks, that this habit of persuading the patient cannot have been universal. Plato himself speaks of enforced treatment, and Aristotle, a generation later, specially notes that the physician's duty was not to compel or to persuade, but simply to prescribe[1].

But for these saving passages, we should have been disposed to compare the state of medicine in the best days of Greece with that described by Mr. Palgrave as existing in Central Arabia at the present day, where the physician must first persuade his patient, and then bargain with him for his fee, before he can begin to treat the case. We have even a hint of such a habit being ridiculed (*Laws*, 857 E), 'For by this you may be sure,' says the Athenian speaker, 'that if one of these empirical physicians, who practise medicine without science, were to come upon the gentleman physician talking to his gentle patient, and using the language almost of philosophy—beginning at the beginning of the disease, and discoursing about the whole nature of the body—he would burst into a hearty laugh, he would say what most of those who are called doctors always have on their tongue :—" Foolish fellow," he would say, " you are not healing the sick man, but you are educating him, and he does not want to be made a doctor, but to

[1] Cp. Plato, *Rep.* 293 A, *Laws* 646, 660 A ; and Aristotle, *Pol.* iv. 2 (p. 1324).

get well."'   It appears, then, that though fashionable,
and thought philosophical, this persuasive treatment
was even in Plato's day beginning to be duly appreciated[1].   The age of Euripides was waning, that of
Menander was approaching, in which accurate discussion was no longer a duty and a delight, but a
trouble and a bore.

We know that the establishments of doctors ($\iota \alpha \tau \rho \epsilon \hat{\iota} \alpha$)
were quite different from apothecaries' shops, and
that relatively the two professions ranked as they
now do.   On the other hand, I have been unable
to find any good proof of a separation between the
medical and surgical sides of the profession.   There
is indeed, in Diogenes Laertius' account of Plato, a
separation of the science of healing into five branches,
one of which is strictly surgical.   But the term $\iota \alpha \tau \rho o \varsigma$
was used for both.   Xenophon, for example, speaks
of them (*Anab.* v. 8) as cutting and burning their
patients.   In Egypt, as I above observed, there was
probably some such separation.

But unfortunately, one solitary allusion to an hos-
pital[2], which appears to have been situated in the
Peiræus, gives us no insight into the public care of
health, beyond the appointment of state-doctors.
We hear that Peisistratus appointed part of the state-
fund to support such soldiers as were maimed in the
public service—a curious contrast to the supposed

---

[1] Cp. Jowett, i. p. 28.
[2] Παιώνιον in *Crates*, Meineke, ii. 238, and cp. Schol. ad *Aristoph. Ach.*
1211.

law about the φαρμακοί, to which I have already
alluded.

It appears that even in Platonic days, when
medicine had been long domiciled at Athens, the
traditional superiority of the Western schools, and
those of Dorian Asia Minor, still held its ground.
We may infer this from a curious point mentioned as
early as Crates, but repeated by Epicrates and
Alexis[1]. Just as our doctors must prescribe in what
is called dog-Latin, and we should look with disgust
upon the ignorance of a good English recipé, so the
doctors at Athens were despised if they did not prescribe in Doric Greek. The very remedy disdained
under its Attic name was adopted if supported by a
Doric *brogue*. Whether this fashion implies (as I
believe) that foreigners were considered the best
doctors, or that the Athenian must sojourn in a
foreign Doric school, and so learn to prescribe in its
dialect—the fact remains a very curious monument of
the modernness of Attic life.

I have been considering nothing but the social side
of medical practice in these remarks. It is, of course,
both beyond my knowledge, and beside my subject,
to criticise Greek medicine as to its principles, or to
express an opinion on such prescriptions as that of
Eryximachus, in Plato's *Symposium* (187 A). These
enquiries belong to the history of medicine, and must
be based on the Hippocratic writings—an interesting
but very difficult study. I shall content myself with

---

[1] Meineke, *Com. Frag.* ii. p. 249; iii. p. 448.

saying something on the lower side of medical practice, I mean the non-professional, or *quack* side.

This rude and ignorant practice held its place into
the best Attic times, side by side with rational
medicine[1]. It was, of course, the kind practised by
women, who were the only advisers permitted in the
case of female diseases, as appears from Euripides[2];
it was also kept up by the secret cures existing in
certain clans and families, such as that mentioned
by Dicæarchus in later times as still in his day
subsisting at Mount Pelion. There was here a
certain plant, which, according to divers preparations,
was a certain cure for gout, for mesenteric diseases,
and for ophthalmia. ' But these virtues are known
to one family in the city, said to be descended from
Chiron. The secret is transmitted from father to
son, and so preserved that no other citizen knows
it. Those who know the use of the drug have a
conscientious objection (οὐχ ὅσιον) against taking fees
from the sick, but heal them gratis.' I know of
exactly similar instances at present in Ireland ; in
one, a case of cancer was absolutely cured among
my own acquaintance, in another, a sprain, which
had baffled the best surgeons, was subdued in a few
weeks. In these cases, too, it was οὐχ ὅσιον for the
practitioner to take ostensible fees, rather however

---

[1] On Aristophanes' *Plutus* 879, the scholiast tells us in a curious note
that medicated rings were sold at Athens for a drachme each.

[2] *Hipp.* 292. There is, however (Dem. πρὸs 'Ονητ. A, p. 873), a case of a
married woman being attended by a doctor in presence of her husband.
On Dicæarchus, cp. Müller, *Fragg.* ii. 263.

from the conscientious objections of the profession than from his own[1]. I have, moreover, heard the greatest and most philosophical physicians say that there was a great deal of sound empirical knowledge in the practice of these country quacks.

But quite apart from these isolated cases, there seems to have been a systematic priestcraft attached to such temples as that of Æsculapius, where people went and lay down, hoping for a miraculous cure from the god. Doubtless the priests attached to these temples had collected a great deal of real knowledge in diseases, and applied rational cures often enough; nevertheless, the habit of asserting miracles, the occult nature of their practice, and the known conservatism of all priestly corporations, make it certain that we should count these temple-hospitals not with the licensed establishments of physicians, but with the houses of the quacks. A curious scene in one of these temples is to be found in the *Plutus* of Aristophanes (vv. 655 sqq.) where it is hard to separate the jokes from the earnest, as is usually the case in Greek comedy, but where the general *mise en scène* is of course taken from life. The various details are hardly fit for translation; but it appears that the patients were brought in, and lay down to sleep attended by their friends, being directed on no account to stir if they heard a noise during the night. The slave who tells the story then gives an amusing account how the priests stole the offerings of food

---

[1] One of these quacks told a friend of mine, who consulted him, '*that the head doctors would skiver him*, if they caught him taking a fee.'

placed near the heads of the patients, and how he
followed their example. Then he describes the god
coming in, accompanied by personages carrying his
medicine-chest and implements. The cures on this
occasion were for ophthalmia, and it may possibly be
inferred, that in the case of a well-known man, whom
the poet disliked, the appliances made him (as the
poet says) far worse ; but perhaps this is only fun, or
a wish turned into a fact.

These details, gathered from various authors, give
us a very clear notion of the social position of the
medical profession in Plato's day ; nor do I know any
better way of transporting ourselves back to old times,
than by comparing the *status* of special classes with
these same classes in our own day. For this reason
I will take up a lower profession, but doubtless a
more important one at Athens, I mean the caterers,
and this includes two great classes, the cooks, who
not only dressed, but generally provided the entertainments, and the fishmongers.

On no point is the Middle Comedy to us more
explicit, seeing that we have it filtered through
Athenæus, who excerpted largely in this direction.

There was no limit to the importance which the
cooks gave themselves, according to the Middle and
New Comedy. It was no mere trade, but a natural
gift, a special art, a school of higher philosophy.
Here is a specimen.

A. 'It is necessary for the cook to know long
beforehand for whom he is to prepare the dinner ;
for if he merely looks to this one point, how he

ought to cook the food properly, and does not foresee and consider in what manner it should be served, or when and how arranged, he is no longer a cook (μάγειρος), but a mere caterer (ὀψοποιός), which is by no means the same thing, but very far different. Thus everybody who commands a force is indeed commonly called a general, yet he who is able in a crisis to collect himself, and see his way through it, is the real general; the other is a mere general officer. So likewise in our profession, any chance fellow could prepare or cut up good material, or boil it and blow the bellows, but this is a mere caterer, a cook is quite another thing. He must consider the place, the hour, the host, and again the guest, [or the guest who has dined there before?] to know when and what fish he should buy. For you can procure all kinds at any time, but you will not find them equally grateful or agreeable. Archestratus, indeed, has written on the subject, and has the reputation among many of having said some useful things, but in most points he is ignorant, and has not made one sound remark. Don't listen to or learn all you hear; what is written for the vulgar public is as vain as if it had never been written. For you cannot lay down fixed rules about cookery, since it cannot be tied down within limits, but is completely independent, so that, however well you may apply the art, if you miss the right moment of chance (that is, if chance be against you) all your skill is worth nothing.' B. 'Sir, you are a great man!' A. 'This fellow who, you say, has just arrived with much experience in rich dinners, I shall make him forget them every one, if I merely show him a haggis, and put a dinner before him with the odour of our Attic air[1].'

This is the tone of numerous comic fragments. Like the doctors, it was grossly unfashionable for cooks to speak Attic Greek; if they did not use Homeric phrases, they were bound to speak Doric Greek[2], for there is no doubt that in Sicily the art of cooking had attained its highest development, equalled, if anywhere in Greece, at Elis only, where there was much accumulated wealth and luxurious country life, and where I suppose the Olympic festival stimulated the natives to extraordinary efforts during the great quadrennial meeting.

It was the fashion at Athens to hire both cooks and appointments for a dinner-party, and to commission the cook to undertake the marketing; the lights, tables, and other ware seem to have been supplied by a separate class of tradesmen[3]. It appears, too, strangely enough to our own notions, that the employer went into the pottery-market (τὸν κέραμον), crying out, 'Who wants to undertake the supplying of a dinner?' so that market cries, which certainly existed, as appears from Aristophanes (Meineke, iii. 68) were not confined to the sellers. A remarkable

---

[1] Meineke, iii. 547.

[2] We have our own parallel in the French *menus* set forth on fashionable dinner tables. I suppose we shall never get into the habit of good English for these purposes, in place of the mongrel, and generally misspelt, jargon dignified in these documents with the title of French.

[3] Called τραπεζοποιοί, Meineke, iii. 83, 501.

fragment in the *Painter* of Diphilus, gives the advice of an experienced caterer on this matter. I quote it here, though occurring in a later generation than Plato's, as there seems to have been no change at Athens in this respect, and it is more convenient to discuss all our evidence on these customs at once and in connection. He is addressing his colleague, the τραπεζοποιός, who was to supply the appointments [1].

'Never fear, Draco, you shall never find *me* with you in the way of business, that you will not be occupied with your contract all day, and live in the highest luxury. For I never go to a house till I scrutinise who the man is that is giving the sacrificial feast, or the occasion of the dinner, or whom he has invited ; and I have a table in which are classified under general heads the parties with whom I engage myself, as well as those of whom I keep clear. Let us look, for example, under the mercantile head. Suppose a skipper is fulfilling a vow, who has lost his mast or broken his rudder, and was obliged to heave his cargo overboard from being waterlogged, I dismiss such a fellow, he does nothing heartily, but merely to satisfy his obligation. During the very libation he is computing in his own mind what share he can put upon his ship's company and passengers, and so each man feels that he is dining at his own expense. But another has sailed in from Byzantium on the third day without accident, successful, delighted at making his ten or twelve per cent., prating

[1] Cp. Meineke, iv. p. 394.

about the passage-money, ready for any dissipation.
Such an one I take by the hands as he is disem-
barking, I remind him of Zeus Soter, I insist on
serving him. This is my habit. Again, some young
fool in love is squandering his patrimony. I go, of
course[1]. Another set having collected money for a
club dinner, come rushing into the pottery-market,
shouting, "Who wants an engagement to cook a
dinner?" I let them shout; for if you went you
would get cuffs, and have to work all night. If you
ask for your wages, you get impudence. "The len-
tils," he says, "had no vinegar." You ask again, and
he replies, "Go to the devil, king of all cooks!" and
so on. But I am now bringing you to a house of
doubtful reputation, where an ἑταίρα is celebrating
the festival of Adonis lavishly with others of her
class : you will get your fill and carry away plenty
besides.'

Having shown by these quotations the sauciness
and self-importance of these people, I will add
another curious passage on the grandeur of their
language. Like all Greeks, they excelled by their
acuteness and education the corresponding classes
in other nations. So in Epicurus' day, they at once
laid hold of his celebrated principle that pleasure

---

[1] Anaxippus (Mein. iv. 460), who makes a learned cook descant on
the various dinners suitable to various persons, mentions this class :
'a youth with his mistress is eating up his patrimony, I set before him
cuttle fish, and various shell fish, set off with rich sauces; for such a
creature is not a trencherman (δειπνητικός) but has his mind intent on
love.' The philosopher on the contrary has a large appetite, and must
be fed accordingly.

was the *summum bonum.* Of course they applied it
without the reservations of its illustrious author, and
explained it, not as he did, to be mainly mental
pleasure, but to be æsthetical pleasure, in which their
profession could claim a prominent place. His intimacy, indeed, with that prince of pleasure-seekers,
Menander, and the open support of him by the
pleasure-providing classes, produce upon us the strong
impression that the moral effect of Epicurus' teaching,
even in his own day, and from his own lips, was
not far removed from the somewhat coarse exposition
in Cicero's writings. But of these things there will
be future opportunity to speak. I return to the gran-
diloquent language of the cooks.

Strato, a poet of unknown date, but probably late
in the Middle Comedy, and about Alexander's time,
introduces an unfortunate host, saying : ' " I have taken
a male sphinx, and not a cook, into my house, for
by the gods I simply can't understand one word of
what he says. He came equipped with a new vo-
cabulary ; for no sooner was he in the house than
he asked me in portentous style, How many of the
articulately speaking ($\mu\epsilon\rho\sigma\pi\alpha s$) have you invited to
dinner ; speak?" " Is it *I* ask the articulately speaking
to dinner? You are mad. Do you think I know
such company? Not one of them is coming—a good
joke, I declare, for me to ask the articulately speaking
to dinner!" " There will not be present then any
wassailer at all?" " Not Wassailer, I think. Let me
see : Philinus is coming, Moschion, Niceratus ; this
and that other fellow, I counted them up by name ;

there was no Wassailer at all among them." "There
is no such person coming at all," said I. "What do
you say, no one at all?" and he grew very angry, as if
insulted at my not inviting some of the Wassailers—
very strange conduct.' The cook then enumerates
oxen and sheep by their Homeric names, and asks,
will they be sacrificed, so as to be available for the
feast. The host cannot understand him, and when
he deigns to explain, retorts testily: '"I neither understand you nor do I wish to do so. I am a plain
country bumpkin, so speak plainly to me." "Then
you are not versed in Homeric language?" "Let
Homer talk, O cook, just as he pleases, but by Hestia
what concern is this of ours?" "Because you and
I must transact business according to his prescription,
for I am a Homerist."' The host goes on to say
that he was obliged to take up the works of Philetas
on cookery, to find out what each thing meant [1].

This then was one of the main social grievances
which occupied the Middle Comedy, and which did
not subside till Menander's day. But with his peculiar refinement I suppose that these discussions
about the preparations for dinner parties were as
much out of taste as they would be in our better
society, and so the long lists of dishes and the
general prominence of cookery vanish from his plays,
after a long and somewhat offensive importance
of more than two centuries [2]. With regard to the

---

[1] Meineke, iv. 545.

[2] Indeed we may go back even farther. Solon, Hipponax, and
Simonides of Amorgos have left us fragments on dishes, just like the
Comic fragments; cp. Bergk, *Fragg. Lyr.* pp. 436, 762, 787.

pompous phraseology of the cooks, it should be noticed that one of the main duties of the literary critics of the day was to repress this tendency in various ranks and classes, and the cooks were not more severely dealt with than the tragic poets, who as a rule did not follow the exquisite simplicity of Euripides' diction, but aped the pomp of Æschylus without his titanic power.

The cooks however may have vanished from Menander's stage for another reason. With the Macedonian times came in the fashion, continued by the Romans, of having cooks among the slaves of their household, a custom apparently unknown to the earlier Athenians. Thus this social difficulty vanished, and the free man, with his Homeric talk, and his self-importance, made way for the expensive and well-educated, but submissive slave. The reader will here again notice the curious analogy to the history of medicine, for among the late Greeks, and among the Romans, the household physician was always a slave attached to the family.

But in the days of free Attic society, it may well be imagined that the unlucky host could not trust implicitly the marketing of the Homeric cooks; he was often obliged to go himself to market, and to encounter there a class of men hardly less manageable, the *Fishmongers*, who were decidedly the most important catering class at Athens, seeing that the Attic people ate little meat, and lived chiefly on fish and vegetables. There were indeed butchers, who exposed joints of meat for sale, but to feast on such fare is noticed as

Bœotian coarseness, while the Thebans retorted that
the Attic dinners might be elegantly served, but were
miserably stingy[1]. So again the marriage feast of
Iphicrates with the princess of Thrace was notorious
throughout Greece for its lavish expenditure, and for
the enormous joints, or even whole animals, which
were put upon the table. I think so much may be
fairly inferred despite the comic exaggeration of the
passage, which the Germans, of course, take *au pied
de la lettre*. But the maritime supremacy of Athens,
combined as it was with all manner of restrictions on
the trade of other ports, made the daily importation
of fresh fish, as well as the systematic traffic in salt
fish from the Black Sea and from Spain, one of the
most striking features in the myriad life of the
Peiræus. A few quotations on this point will not be
unacceptable. Fish being, as I have said, the staple
article of more refined Attic diet, the fishmongers
were a large and important class. It is I think very
strange, that among the various political men taunted
with having risen by the exercise of low trades, there
is not one who had practised the lucrative business of
retailing fish, and I am disposed to infer that they
were usually freedmen or metics. But however this
may be, according to the poets of the Middle Comedy,
and especially Antiphanes, their insolence and their
extortion were unbearable.

Some of the allusions are very comical. 'Both in
other respects,' says Antiphanes[2], 'they say the

---

[1] Plato, *Laws*, 849 E; Meineke, *Com. Frag.* iv. p. 433.

[2] Meineke, iii. p. 80.

Egyptians are clever fellows, and also in this, that they made the eel of equal dignity with the gods. Nay in reality it is much more precious (τιμιωτέρα) than the gods. For to them we can attain by prayers, but eels we are only allowed to smell after paying at least twelve drachmæ or more, so utterly sacred is the creature.' And again : 'I used to think the Gorgons a mere invention (of the poets), but when I go to market I believe in them, for when I look upon the fishmongers, I become petrified, so that I have to speak to them with averted countenance ; if I behold the tiny fish on which they put such a price I freeze with horror!' 'It is ten thousand times easier,' too (p. 312) to 'obtain an audience with the generals (the highest state officials) and to get a question answered by them, than by the cursed fishmongers in the market. If you ask one of *them* a question, either he takes up something lying near him, or stoops over it in silence like (the) Telephus (of Euripides). And this is fair enough, for they are every one of them homicides like him. But then as if he had not heard a word you say, muttering he shakes a polypus lying before him, and won't even utter whole words, but mutilates them into 'τάρων 'βολῶν γένοιτ' ἄν' (it might go for four obols)' and so forth ; 'this is what you must submit to when you go marketing for fish.' 'When I see the generals,' says Alexis (p. 391), 'drawing up their eyebrows (giving themselves airs), I feel vexed, but don't much wonder that those selected by the city for high honour should be more conceited than their neighbours, but when I see the ruffianly fishmongers looking down, and having their eyebrows drawn up to the crown of their heads, I choke with rage. And if you ask one of them: at what do you sell these two mullets, he says: "ten obols." "A big price, would you take eight?" "Yes, if you buy one of them." "Come friend, take the money and don't be joking." "The price is fixed, off with you." Is not this bitterer than gall itself?'

It is idle to multiply these quotations, when the idea has been fully conveyed; they show plainly what is told in hundreds of other passages, that there was a sort of trade-union spirit among the retailers at Athens, and that they had succeeded in some branches of business, at all events, in keeping up high prices. The city being four miles from the sea, it was nearly impossible to obtain fish directly from the boats, and thus the fishmongers were in a strong position. There were indeed laws enacted to prevent them from selling stale fish, for we are told that they were even forbidden to sprinkle it with water. But as they are alleged to have evaded this law by fainting at their stalls, and getting their friends to inundate them with water, so I suppose in other respects they contrived to make their profits in spite of these interferences.

It does not lie within my present scope to enter into details about trades and professions which are not prominently brought before us in the current literature. The very size and wealth of Athens, as compared to lesser Greek towns, are said by Xenophon [1]

[1] Cyropæd. viii. 2.

to have caused a great subdivision of labour, so that, for example, one man makes men's shoes, another women's, a third cuts out the leather, a fourth stitches it together [1]. It is also known that first Solon, then Themistocles, and afterwards Pericles, encouraged settlers from all parts of the Greek world, and even from among barbarians, if they were skilled artisans. The varied aspects of this motley throng afford ground for many interesting observations, but they are observations of detail, and not suited to a general sketch. This side of Greek life, or rather of Athenian life, the reader will find in Stark's edition of Hermann's *Greek Antiquities*, and in Büchsenschütz's *Besitz und Erwerb*, two excellent books, whose very excellence makes them unreadable except as works of reference.

It is far better for the student who desires to learn the subject thoroughly, to go to these authorities, than to be content with the meagre abstract which might have been added in this place. But I venture to hope that the general principles sketched out here will help him to arrange and classify the details for himself.

[1] The Greeks seem to have been very particular about the fitting of their shoes. This is shewn not only by the facts above mentioned, of comic complaints about unseasoned shoe-leather, but by a series of proverbs which express fitness by metaphors taken from shoes. Cp. the learned note on this in Donaldson's Pindar. on *Ol.* vi. 8.

CHAPTER XI.

ATTIC CULTURE.—ENTERTAINMENTS AND CONVER-
SATION. — THE EDUCATION OF BOYS. — THE
STREETS IN ATHENS.

THESE considerations, however, suggest to me to
say something more particular concerning the tone
of Greek dinner-parties, the preparation of which was
so troublesome. I shall not spend one line on discussing the peculiar dishes, and the peculiar ways of
dressing them—a minute and tedious enquiry, as any
one may see who will open Athenæus. It is not at
all so important to us to know what the Greeks ate,
as to know with what manners and conversation they
ate, and I cannot but think that most handbooks of
Greek antiquities make the mistake of confining
themselves so closely to the materials of old Greek
life, that the really important features fall into the
background.

We have, in addition to the allusions in the Middle
and New Comedy, three detailed pictures of imaginary
Greek dinner-parties, one the scene in Aristophanes'
Wasps above alluded to (p. 219), in which the gentlemanly son instructs his rude father how to behave—a
scene, by the way, which shows that I am correct in

making this particular branch of refinement a feature of the Platonic, and not the Periclean age. The two other pictures are the *Symposia* of Plato and of Xenophon, in each of which Socrates' presence at a banquet of aristocratic gentlemen is made the occasion of much philosophical and æsthetical conversation. The dialogue of Xenophon is as usual tamer and less brilliant than that of his rival, but probably more faithful to life, and a more natural specimen of Greek society than the deep and mystical composition of Plato, which, though now-a-days greatly admired, was by old critics, such as Dicæarchus [1], despised as φορτικόν.

Of course the whole tone of the entertainments was affected by the exclusion of married women, and of the children, who dined at midday [2]. As I said before, conversation took a leading place in Athenian society. 'We,' says a Spartan character [3], 'are great both at eating and working, but the Athenians at talking, and eating little, and the Thebans at eating a great deal.' Plato goes so far, in a striking passage of his *Protagoras,* as to charge with great stupidity those that introduce musicians into their feasts, as being people devoid of rational conversation, and

---

[1] Müller, *Frag. Hist.* ii. p. 243.

[2] Aristoph. *Cocalus, fr.* 2. It is not clear whether the children were sent for after dinner in these days as they were in Theophrastus' time. For the serious and philosophical conversation of the *Symposia* of Plato and Xenophon could hardly have tolerated such an interruption. It may, however, have been done at quiet family parties.

[3] Meineke. iii. p. 208.

hiring mercenary musicians to amuse their guests[1].
'The talk about the poets seems to me like a commonplace entertainment to which a vulgar company
have recourse; who, because they are not able to
converse, or amuse one another while they are drinking with the sound of their own voices and conversation, by reason of their stupidity, raise the price of
flute-girls in the market, hiring for a great sum the
voice of a flute instead of their own breath, to be the
medium of intercourse among them : but when the
company are real gentlemen and men of education,
you will see no flute-girls, or dancing-girls, or harp-
girls ; and they have no nonsense or games, but are
contented with one another's conversation, of which
their own voices are the medium, and which they
carry on by turns and in an orderly manner, even
though they are very liberal in their potations.'   This
is exactly the sort of thing we find in Plato's own
Symposium, of which there will be occasion to speak
more particularly hereafter.   The hostility to music
at dinner-parties was evidently a marked feature in
the Socratic society, for Aristophanes brings it out
in his *Clouds*, where old Strepsiades is giving an
account of how he and his son quarreled.   'As
we were sitting at table,' says he, 'first I asked
him to take up the lyre and sing some song of
Simonides, such as, *The Shearing of the Ram*.   But
he replied that playing and singing at table were
gone out of fashion (ἀρχαῖον εἶν᾽ ἔφασκε τὸ κιθαρίζειν
ᾄδειν τε πίνονθ᾽), and only fit for women grinding at

[1] Jowett, ii. p. 156 (p. 347 D).

the mill,' but ends by singing some loose lyric of Euripides[1]. I think any one who dines at those state dinners, where it is the fashion to have a band playing, will be disposed to agree with Plato that it is very injurious to conversation.

But Xenophon's *Symposium* shows that we must not take Plato's standard as the usual one, and that professional musicians, and even jugglers, were commonly employed to amuse even those Athenian gentlemen, who, like the rich Callias, affected philosophy. In that dialogue the Syracusan who has been hired with his slaves for this purpose, is much annoyed at Socrates for distracting the attention of the guests by his talking powers; and all through it is a sort of conflict between the juggler and the philosopher, whether gymnastic feats or philosophy are to have the upper hand.

But assuming that conversation was to prevail, we can easily see that this was the great reason why Attic feasts were limited to a few guests. The studied elegance and completeness of the appointments are always sacrificed if there be a crowd, and they were not so much prized by cultivated gentlemen of that day, as to make them forget that proper conversation must remain general, and never degenerate into separate *têtes-à-têtes*. In the *Symposium* of Plato, and elsewhere, Socrates is at once pulled up if he whispers, or addresses separate individuals. Even in Herodotus' day, he represents the tyrant

[1] Cp. Jowett's *Plato*, ii. p. 156 (p. 347 D) and Aristoph. *Nubes*, 1353 sqq. See also Meineke, *Com. Frag.* vol. iii. p. 119.

Cleisthenes testing his daughter's suitors τῷ λεγομένῳ
ἐς μέσον—by their powers of *general conversation.*
Thus there was in Plato's day no necessity for the
officers mentioned at a later period by the Comedians, and called γυναικονόμοι, who went round to
private houses, and punished people who had too
large a number of guests. The ostentation of these
later days, and the decay of higher culture, may
have led them back into such social absurdities as
our state dinners, which can be paralleled by the
feast which Herodotus speaks of, as given at Thebes
to the noble Persians of Mardonius' army, of whom
fifty were invited, and a Greek gentleman sat beside
each[1]. This was stately, but was not society. So
then according to the highest Attic taste the number
should not exceed the limits which render general
conversation possible.

But despite of their powers of talking, the Greeks
deprecated, as we do, any delay in serving the dinner, when the guests had arrived, especially as they
assembled in the dining-room. 'What a misfortune,'
says Alexis (*fr. incert.* 13), 'to lie down at table
before dinner is ready, for there is no chance of sleep,
nor can we attend to what any one says, for the mind
is intent upon the table.' This then is the *mauvais
quart d'heure* of the French. We may look back to
the passage in Aristophanes' *Wasps* already cited
(above p. 219) for hints as to the proper way of com-
mencing the entertainment under such circumstances.

---

[1] Cp. also the state-dinner given by Philip of Macedon, Æschines,
p. 143 (Teubner). The Athenian official dinners sometimes reached two
hundred, Æschin. παραπρεσβ. 162.

But from the fact that such remarks on the appointments are not common in Plato and Xenophon, they probably felt as we should, that praise of the banquet and the furniture before the host's face was hardly refined (ἀστεῖον). The *Flatterer* in Theophrastus is thus noted as the first to praise the appointments. He forthwith takes up some ornament on the table, and observes to the host, 'What a beautiful thing this is!'

I cannot but think that the same principles must have been applied to those stock contrivances for keeping up conversation which are so often mentioned in the Comedy, I mean the *scolia*, when one guest commenced a sentence in verse, and handed a branch to any other he chose, who was compelled to finish the verse in the cleverest way he could. Of this practice we have happily a remarkable specimen in the *Wasps*, where the only real social talent displayed by the old dicast is in rounding off the scolia with political jokes and allusions.

The other stock contrivance was the γρῖφος or riddle, which appears to have been a later fashion, and perhaps to have supplanted the scolia. The fashionable ἑταίραι were very celebrated for propounding these riddles, many of which are quoted by the grammarians. But of course, as among ourselves now-a-days riddles and acrostics and all such stuff are miserable substitutes for witty or even sensible conversation, so there seems in the philosophical dialogues of the Platonic age a silent contempt for such devices. They too, like tunes or tumbling, are

inconsistent with a really good and general conversation.

It is from the very same stand-point that Menander, whose essentially refined and social temper
belonged more properly to the Platonic than the
Hellenistic age, complains of the misery of being
invited to join a family party at dinner, whereas on
the other hand he censures as vulgar the habit of
crowding the table on such occasions with strangers[1].
Thus a marriage feast is necessarily a family party,
and to this the family alone, and old family friends,
should be invited. 'For (*fr. incert.* 16) it is labour
and sorrow to fall in among a company of relations,
where the father keeping the bottle in his hand
begins the conversation, and jokes in trite saws, then
the mother comes next, then some grandmother puts
in her talk, then a hoarse old man, her father, and
then some old woman that calls him her darling.
But he nods assent to them all.'

It appears, in spite of the constant accusations
of drunkenness brought against Greek women in
Attic Comedy, that well-bred ladies affected small
appetites, and the Milesian and Cean maidens were
even water-drinkers. Of course they were never
present except at strictly family dinners. The ladies
who frequented men's society, though they too affected the same modesty, were often led away to
greater indulgences than were consistent with the
purest Attic salt.

Drunkenness was about as common and as repre-

[1] Meineke, iv. 202.

hended, as it now is; but it is at first sight difficult to explain how the Greeks managed to get drunk on the very weak mixture they drank. Three parts of water to two of wine was the usual proportion, four to three was thought strong, equal parts 'made them mad,' as one of the comic fragments asserts [1]. Even now the wines of Greece are far too strong for Englishmen in a southern climate; and it is certain, that to them their wines were fully as strong as whiskey is to us. As to their various kinds and various value, it was as large a subject as it now is. There are in Athenæus endless discussions about them, which are now very uninteresting, as we cannot try the taste of the Greeks by any specimens. Putting snow and salt water into wine seems curious treatment. The most modern feature in Greek wine-drinking is the coming into fashion of dry wines [2], and the objections against them by the adherents of the old fashion; as in Homer, for example, sweetness was a special recommendation to wine. We hear that it was brought round in carts, like our city milk, and there are analogous complaints that it was watered before selling it (iii. 386, 405). Its *bouquet* seems to have been as important as with our wines, and there is a remarkable fragment of Hermippus (ii. 410) comparing the Mendean, the Magnesian, the Chian in this respect, giving however the palm to a wine called

[1] See on this point Meineke, iii. p. 529 and iv. p. 605. Also Bergk's *Lyric Fragments*, pp. 594 and 1027.

[2] Posidippus (Meineke, iv. 526) says: Διψηρός, ἄποτος ὁ μυρίνης ὁ τίμιος. This epithet διψηρός (dry) has greatly puzzled the Germans.

σαπρίας, literally *rotten*, but referring to a peculiar treatment of the grape, still in use [1].

These scattered details will give the reader some idea of Attic entertainments, especially if he compare them with the detailed description in Plato's *Symposium*. I think that in spite of an element of romance being admissible which is quite foreign to our notions, on the whole they were about as orderly as our gentlemen's parties, and intellectually something like an agreeable assemblage of university men, particularly among lively people, like the Irish. This is I think a juster verdict than taking Plato for an historical guide, as some Germans have done, and talking bombast about the loftiness and splendour of Attic conversation. To my taste indeed the description of his feast abounds far too much in long speeches, which are decidedly tedious, and which would certainly not be tolerated at any agreeable party in Ireland, where this is the branch of culture thoroughly understood. But of course the scene of the banquet is only a secondary point with Plato, and he has done wonders to combine deep philosophical instruction with his scenery. I am far from censuring his great genius—I only wish to point out that for our present purpose his dialogue is not a safe guide.

There are, however, some excellent points of manners in the dialogue. Even Socrates dresses himself with peculiar care, and, contrary to his usual

---

[1] The same epithet is applied by Aristophanes to a rich and luxurious peace, coming after the wants and hardships of war.

custom, wears sandals, owing to the fashionable nature of Agathon's entertainment. But nevertheless
he proposes to a friend whom he meets on the way
to come with him unbidden; and stopping in one
of his usual trances, the unbidden Aristodemus does
not hesitate to proceed by himself. 'When he
reached the house of Agathon [1] he found the doors
wide open, and a servant coming out met him,
and at once led him into the banqueting-hall [2] in
which the guests were reclining, for the banquet was
about to begin. "Welcome, Aristodemus," said Agathon, "you are just in time to sup with us; if you
come on any other errand put that off, and make one
of us, as I was looking for you yesterday, and meant
to have asked you, if I could have found you." (I
suspect this was a polite way of speaking, not meant
to be believed.) "But what have you done with
Socrates?" Aristodemus explains that he himself
had come at Socrates' invitation. "You were quite
right in coming" said Agathon, "but where is he
himself?" "He was behind me just now, and I cannot think what has become of him." Agathon
then sends out a slave, who finds Socrates in a
portico, but comes back to say that he cannot stir

[1] Jowett, ii. p. 492.

[2] Cp. on this hospitable feature the charming fragment of Apollodorus
(Meineke, iv. p. 455), a writer of the New Comedy. He says: 'When
you go to visit a friend at his house, you can perceive his friendliness
the moment you enter the door, for first the servant who opens the
door looks pleased, then the dog wags its tail and comes up to you, and
the first person you meet hands you a chair, before a word has been
said.'

him. When Agathon is assured that there is no use in farther messages, he acquiesces ; and adds : " My domestics, who on these occasions become my masters, shall entertain us as their guests. Put on the table whatever you like," he said to them, "as you do when there is no one to give you orders, which is my habit. Imagine that you are our hosts, and that I and the company are your guests, and treat us well and then we shall commend you." ' Presently Socrates makes his appearance. Agathon is himself reclining at the end of the table, which was, I suppose, the proper place for the host.

When the meal is ended, the libations are offered, and then a pæan is sung to the god, ' but as they were about to commence drinking, Pausanias reminded them that they had had a bout yesterday, from which he and most of them were still suffering, and they ought to be allowed to recover, and not go on drinking to-day.' They then agree not to drink hard, and Eryximachus next proposes, ' that the flute-girl, who had just made her appearance, be dismissed ; she may play to herself, if she have a mind, or to the women who are within !' So then it appears that the character of these flute girls did not prevent them from being received, for amusement's sake, in respectable ladies' apartments. ' But on this day let us have conversation instead.' What follows is indeed not properly conversation, but long speeches in honour of love.

These are suddenly interrupted by a great knocking at the door of the house, as of revellers, and the sound of a flute is heard. Agathon tells the attendants to go and see who were the intruders. 'If they are friends of ours,' said he, 'invite them in, but if not, say the drinking is over.' Here we again have great politeness at the expense of truth. A little while afterwards they hear the voice of Alcibiades resounding in the court; he was in a great state of intoxication, and kept shouting, 'Where is Agathon?' and at length supported by the flute-girl, and by some of his companions, he made his way to him.

I shall not follow up the very strange scene that ensued, but recommend all those desirous of seeing how far Greek ideas on some subjects differ from ours, to read Alcibiades' speech which follows. The feast is however again interrupted by another band of revellers, apparently strangers, 'who suddenly enter (p. 538) and spoil the order of the banquet. Some one who was going out having left the door open, they had found their way in, and made themselves at home; great confusion ensued, and everybody was compelled to drink large quantities of wine.' Aristodemus having at last fallen asleep, is awakened towards daybreak by the crowing of the cock, and finds that the others were either asleep or gone away; 'there remained awake only Socrates, Aristophanes, and Agathon, who were drinking out of a large goblet which they passed round, and Socrates was discoursing to them. Aristodemus did not hear the beginning of it, and he was only half awake, but the chief thing which he remembered was Socrates insisting to the other two that the genius of comedy was the same as that of tragedy, and that the writer of tragedy ought to be a writer of comedy also. To this they were compelled to assent, being sleepy, and not quite understanding his meaning.'

Such is the scene drawn by Plato of a fashionable banquet of young men of quality at Athens. It strikes us as strangely similar to one of the supper parties that most of us remember in our college days. Acute argument and philosophical discussion combined with hard drinking and perhaps some ribald talk—late in the evening an open door to any exhilarated passer by, who is attracted by the sound of revelry. In one point the Greeks had the advantage, there was none of that noisy singing, or of those stupid personal compliments in the shape of toasts, which degrade modern supper parties.

The general tone of Xenophon's *Symposium* is not dissimilar, though he admits, not drunken revellers, but professional makers of pleasure, such as the joker Philippus, and the Syracusan jugglers. The feast was given by the rich Callias at his sea-side residence in the Peiræus, and properly for a beautiful young friend Autolycus, whom he invites with his father. He meets on his way the Socratic party, five in number, and presses them to join him. 'At first,' says Xenophon, 'as was seemly, they declined the invitation with thanks (πρῶτον μὲν, ὥσπερ εἰκὸς ἦν, ἐπαινοῦντες τὴν κλῆσιν, οὐχ ὑπισχνοῦντο συνδειπνήσειν), but when they saw that he would be vexed at their refusal, they went with him.' At once however they are all so struck with the beauty of Autolycus, that they keep their eyes fixed on him, and are speechless, some of them too show signs of awkward constraint (ἐσχηματίζοντό πως). So then they dined in silence as if ordered to do so by a superior.

At this moment Philippus the joker knocks at the door, and tells the servant to announce who he is, and why he desires admission. 'It would be disgraceful,' says Callias, 'to shut the door against him, let him come in.' But the company is too serious, and will not appreciate his jokes, at which he gets very angry, and is appeased with politeness by the host. The course of this feast results in a mixture of conversation with professional entertainment, which may have made a pleasant evening, in spite of Plato's strictures on such devices. It is to be observed that Autolycus goes off to bed before the last scene (of Ariadne and Bacchus) introduced by the Syracusan—a scene which could hardly have been considered suitable before so young and innocent a guest.

It seems plain from both these dialogues, especially from the end of Xenophon's, that even when the guests became intoxicated and went out in procession through the streets, there was no other place of resort for them than the houses of their friends, especially of friends who had company on the same night ; failing these they invaded the houses of strangers. This corroborates what I said above, that we find no trace of gambling houses, and other such establishments so common in modern cities, which are only frequented at dead of night, and generally by men tired of drinking at private houses[1].

Without doubt the special feature in all these entertainments—I mean the entertainments given to their friends by men of character and position—was the absence of ladies. But this want, which is so fatal in modern society, was not felt among the Greeks. For in the first place, women of good position at Athens, and indeed elsewhere, were not sufficiently educated to stimulate and sustain bright conversation, nor had the morals of the age sunk to the level of Menander's day, when grace and *esprit* were a passport to aristocratic company in spite of moral degradation. In the next place, the feature which even apart from conversation makes ladies so necessary an ornament at a feast is the beauty and variety of their dress. Modern men have so completely resigned all hope of making themselves graceful or picturesque, that by way of modest security, they have settled upon the gloomiest and ugliest possible dress, so making a men's party a dull sameness of black and white, in which no one dreams of looking even for a variety in plainness. Now Greek men had very different notions. They wore white, and other bright colours, they wreathed their heads with fair garlands, and did not disdain the use

---

[1] There are some disreputable pothouses alluded to in the Attic orators, but they appear to have been frequented only in the day. I suppose they were either outside the walls, or closed by law at night. Cp. Lysias, pp. 122, 125, Isocrates, *Antid.* § 287 ; Isæus, p. 53 (Tauchnitz) ; Æschines *in Timarch.* § 53.

of perfumes. They sang and played in the evening as systematically as the young ladies of the present day, and, let us hope, with more soul and expression. Thus in colour and in ornament, the evening dress of Greek gentlemen was as ornamental as the dress of modern ladies ; and from an artistic point of view, decidedly superior. So far then we can see that these old classical banquets did not suffer as ours do from the exclusion of ladies.

But it will be said that I have ungallantly left to the last place the greatest attraction of modern society—the beauty of the fairer sex, and its powerful influence upon men. To this I will merely reply by pointing to the many statues still extant of Greek youths, and asking whether any modern belle has yet equalled in grace and loveliness these almost ideal models of humanity. All historians, all art critics, are agreed that in no race and at no period has there been so marvellous a development of physical perfection among men, and though I do not for one moment subscribe to such nonsense as the statement of a living German professor, that ugliness was then an actual exception, I feel justified in saying that as far as strict beauty goes, the Athenian dinner parties of young men were better furnished than almost any modern table. The modern reader will still hold that there remains a great difference, that manly beauty may indeed be very fine and admirable, but that it can never have the same effect as the gentler and softer graces of the other sex. Most men now-a-days would be almost indifferent whether the men they

met were really handsome; they are not so in the
case of ladies. It is here that we come upon a very
marked distinction between Greek and modern humanity, which I will explain as briefly as possible.

If we look at the terminology of the Greeks
generally, we find that no language is richer, or more
various in expressing its ideas. But in contrast to
this richness, we find certain words relating to
passions and desires used with a vagueness or with
a wideness of application which surprises us. Thus
Eros, even the personified Eros, is conceived by
Sophocles as not only sleeping on the maiden's
cheek, but as the Eros of wealth and of power. In
fact the love of power, and the love of riches, which
we distinguish widely from the passion of love, were
by the Greeks identified with it. For the Greeks
fixed their attention upon the subjective desire so
strongly as to consider its aim of secondary importance. It was doubtless this unity in the nature
of desire, which suggested to Plato his famous theory
of a hidden unity in the objects of desire, for he held
that all love among men, sensual, æsthetical, intellectual, were but modifications of the love of the true
and the good, and that all earthly beauties, were likewise but various imperfect imitations of Essential
Beauty. As Mr. Jowett eloquently puts it in his
masterly introduction to the Symposium (i. 485) :—

'But Diotima, the prophetess of Mantineia, whose
sacred and superhuman character raises her above
the ordinary proprieties of women, has taught Socrates far more than this about the art and mystery

of love. She has taught him that love is another
aspect of philosophy. The same want in the human
soul which is satisfied in the vulgar by the pro-
creation of children, may become the highest aspira-
tion of intellectual desire. As the Christian might
speak of hungering and thirsting after righteousness;
or of divine loves under the figure of human (cp.
Eph. v. 32 : "This is a great mystery, but I speak
concerning Christ and the church"); as the medieval
saint might speak of the "fruitio Dei," so the absorption and annihilation of all other loves and
desires in the love of knowledge is a feeling that was
at least intelligible to the Greek of the fifth century
before Christ. To most men reason and passion
appear to be antagonistic both in idea and fact. The
union of the greatest comprehension of knowledge
and the burning intensity of love is a contradiction
in nature, which may have existed in a far-off
primeval age in the mind of some Hebrew prophet or
other Eastern sage, but has now become an imagination only. Yet this "passion of the reason" is the
theme of the Symposium of Plato. And as there is
no impossibility in supposing that "one king, or son
of a king, may be a philosopher," so also there is a
probability that there may be some few—perhaps one
or two in a whole generation—in whom the light of
truth may not lack the warmth of desire. And if
there be such natures, no one will be disposed to
deny that, "from them flow most of the benefits of
individuals and states."

'Yet there is a higher region in which love is not

only felt, but satisfied, in the perfect beauty of
eternal knowledge, beginning with the beauty of
earthly things, and at last by regular steps reaching
a beauty in which all existence is seen harmonious
and one. The limited affection is enlarged, and enabled to behold the ideal beauty of all things. This
ideal beauty of the Symposium is the ideal good of
the Republic; regarded not with the eye of knowledge, but of faith and desire. The one seems to say
to us " the idea is love," the other, " the idea is truth."
In both the lover of wisdom is the " spectator of all
time and all existence." This is a sort of " mystery "
in which Plato also obscurely intimates the inter-
penetration of the moral and intellectual faculties.'

It is a corollary to this exposition that to the
Greek the love of manly beauty should not differ in
kind or in character from the love of women. ' Still
more remarkable is the fact, that the elevation of
sentiment, which is regarded by Plato as the first
step in the upward progress of the philosopher, is
aroused not by female beauty, but by the beauty of
youth, which alone seems to have been capable of
inspiring the modern feeling of romance in the Greek
mind. The passion which was unsatisfied by the
love of women, took the spurious form of an enthusiasm for the ideal of beauty—a worship as of
some godlike image of an Apollo or Antinous [1].'

Thus therefore we can see clearly how female
society was to some extent superseded by this
marvellous love of beauty in other forms, and in

[1] Jowett, i. p. 486.

consequence by the very romantic attachments which
are a leading feature in Greek history. So jealous
were these attachments, and so exclusive, that Aristotle gravely questions, in his Ethics, whether a man
can ever have more than a single friend—a belief not
less absurd than the vision of some modern romances,
that nature has produced people in pairs intended for
each other exclusively.

This peculiar feature of Greek life is not easy for
us to understand, but I need not here turn aside
to consider its varied aspects. The ordinary reader
can study the question amply in Mr. Jowett's translation of Plato's *Phaedrus* and *Symposium*, with his
admirable introduction[1].

I must not, in concluding this subject, fail to add
the effects produced on the education of boys. It
seems to me that this extraordinary attention to which
Greek boys were liable, made their moral training,
when successful, more perfect than any now aimed at,
even by the strictest parents. In fact the higher education of a Greek boy combined, with the best physical
and intellectual training then attainable, a moral supervision as strict as that which we practise in bringing

[1] I have discussed the matter as fully as was possible in my first edition,
which the student of Greek life may compare with my present remarks.
I will suggest the following additional authorities on the question:
Theognis' *Elegies* (cf. above, p. 107); Plato's *Laws* (Jowett, iv. 157,
347, 353); Xenophon's *Sympos.* (cap. viii.); Lysias' πρὸς Σίμωνα;
Aristotle in Müller's *Fragg. Hist.* (ii. pp. 132, 143, 180, 211); Æschines'
κατὰ Τιμαρχ.; Plutarch's *Agis* (cap. xi. and xiii); and Lucian's *Amores*.
These are official discussions; stray allusions, as in Aristophanes, are
endless.

up our daughters. Far from casting out their sons into
public schools, with the full knowledge that they will
there lose all their simplicity and innocence, Greek
parents of the better sort kept their sons constantly
under the eye of a slave tutor or pedagogue, a sort of
male *duenna*, who never let them out of his sight. It
is complained, indeed, both by the speakers in Plato,
and in the comedies, that these slaves were mostly old,
that they spoke with a bad accent [1], that they were
rough in their manners, and that they were chosen for
the office of pedagogue because they were useless for
any other purpose. But we should never forget that
we hear this from the very people who found them in
the way, and who were thwarted and hindered by their
presence. Thus many a most respectable and kind-
hearted duenna has been reviled, because she was
faithful to her charge, and perhaps her highest enco-
mium is this abuse from her natural enemies.

However then the pedagogues may be ridiculed, it
appears to be certain that the boys whom they had in
charge were probably the most attractive the world
has ever seen. No one can study the splendid statues
of youths in the museums of Italy, without acknow-
ledging this remarkable feature. When do we now
see among young men a proper model for a sculptor,

---

[1] If we may judge from Quintilian (i. 1. 4), the Romans were in his
day more particular about accent than the Greeks. He insists upon
the importance of a good accent in nurses, and the difficulty of correcting
bad habits of speaking, when once acquired. We know this in Ireland
but too well. He even dissuades from exclusive learning of Greek at
an early age, as it produced an effect upon the speaking of Latin.

and yet to the Greeks there was no lack of such
models, exceeding in grace and beauty even the fairest
of women? There are no sketches in all literature
more exquisite than these youths in Plato and Xenophon. They combine with the highest beauty and
intelligence a peculiar modesty and freshness, which
is worn off our boys by the soil of school life, and
which now no longer dwells among us, save in our
delicately brought up girls. All this maiden grace
and purity, this implicit obedience to parents, this do-
cility to instruction, was, I believe, the direct result of
the greater moral risks to which they were liable, and
the consequent greater chastity and reticence with
which they were brought up[1].

There was no question more agitated at Athens than
the education of boys. There was no controversy on
which party-spirit ran more hotly, or on which the old
and the new Attic life differed more profoundly. The
older fashion had been to bring up boys very much as
we bring up girls, keeping them constantly under the
eye of a special attendant or teacher, insisting above
all things on purity and modesty, teaching them the
received religion, and a little of the standard literature
and music, inculcating obedience to the gods and to
parents, but aiming at no higher intellectual standard.
If we except the gymnastic training of Greek boys in
the older Attic period, and to which the calisthenics
or deportment of modern young ladies but faintly

---

[1] Greek fathers spoke more freely with their sons on some points than
we should do. Æschines (*In Timarch.* p. 84) assumes that all the boys
will ask about this case, and have it explained to them by their parents.

corresponds, we shall, I think, see reason for the assertion that it was very like what is, and has been, the received education of girls in our own civilisation. The *locus classicus* on this question is undoubtedly the famous controversy between the *just* and the *unjust arguments* in Aristophanes' *Clouds* (vv. 934 sqq.), in which the poet, who was of the old school, puts the fairest colours on the education of his own youth. He represents all the boys of Athens going in crowds to their schools early in the morning, and not even deterred by the heaviest snow. He describes the strict supervision and discipline under which they were kept, how every gesture was watched and every transgression strictly punished. He also lauds the graceful gymnastic exercises, and the fine bodily condition which this training had produced. There seems no doubt that this description is in the main just. School training was of old a recognised public necessity among the Greeks. When the Athenians fled from Xerxes with their families, and passed over from Salamis to Trœzen, we are told that their generous hosts not only provided them with sustenance, but also with daily education for their children. So strongly did the absence of public day schools strike a later observer, Polybius, at Rome, that he could not understand how Romans were educated; and in this respect, says Cicero, he misconceived the conditions of the state which he had studied with so much accuracy[1]. I cannot here

---

[1] ' De qua Græci multa frustra laborarunt, et in qua una Polybius noster hospes nostrorum institutorum neglegentiam accusat; nullam certam aut destinatam legibus aut publice expositam aut unam omnium

discuss the details of the Greek school instruction in reading and writing, in singing and playing, generally also in drawing, and in dancing. Suffice it to say that it was essentially a liberal, as opposed to a professional education. There were no special departments in particular courses for different boys. They were taught, as our old universities ought to teach, nothing but general culture through a study of classics and science.

Whether the poet paints with equal fairness the new education may well be questioned. But the collateral evidence we possess leaves us in no doubt as to its real nature. Among the Sophists, and with Socrates, sceptical inquiry, intellectual acuteness, and rational persuasion usurped the place of the old-fashioned training in received dogmas and in popular music. Instead of playing and singing in society, their pupils were taught to discuss morals and religion, and to train themselves for politics and courts of justice rather than for the battle-field. Of course the usual results followed. Despite the great earnestness and exceeding manliness of Socrates, whose strong and healthy nature withstood the dangers and temptations of his condition, his disciples had the very opposite reputation. With a few such exceptions as Xenophon and Plato, they were daring unprincipled men, either reckless in politics, if they were ambitious ; or reckless in morals, if they were sensual.

esse voluerunt.' Cic. de Rep. iv. 3, quoted by Grasberger, *Erziehung*, &c., ii. p. 76. In fact the Romans, like ourselves, trusted to home influences, and to the care of parents. The Greeks preferred to insist upon education as a matter of state control.

This sceptical questioning fell in too well with the salient weaknesses of Greek nature to escape perversion ; and so while to the world at large, down to our own day, the gain from the teaching of Socrates has been greater than that from the teaching of any other man, to the Athens of his day the damage was, I believe, grave and remarkable. I have not the least doubt that the constantly repeated accusations of the Comic poets are mainly true, and that the idleness openly countenanced by Socrates was most injurious to his school. Of course *he* did not call it idleness ; to him a deep and earnest discussion of morals, an extracting of thought from the dormant intellect of a pupil, was the noblest and most important business of life, but as he never even hinted at a test to distinguish serious and useful conversation from idle subtilties and wordy waste of time, his school was certain to fall into this mistake. Even the greatest of them all, Plato, shows us plainly by his dialogues what a superfluity of talk was thought desirable by the school, and there is no impression stronger in modern practical minds, upon reading these—doubtless immortal but—never-ending discussions, than the feeling that the Socratic school were a school of idlers, whose time either had no other value, or if it had, was frittered away with unpardonable wastefulness[1].

---

[1] Observe the contrast of the respectable and diligent Nicias. 'Thus then guarding himself against the professional false accusers he neither dined out, nor mixed in general society or conversation, nor did he at all allow himself leisure for such amusements, but as Archon

But of course the excessive conversation of these dialogues was no general Greek type. I suppose that the Ischomachus of Xenophon's *Œconomics* would not have tolerated it. He went himself daily to look after his country farm, and took his gallop across country in order, as he says, to know how to manage his horse when he served in the cavalry in war. The very general criticism in the Comedy of the day shows what the public felt, and we may conclude that here, as usual, we have preserved to us the spokesmen of the opposite sides, and that the higher education of Athens, though deeply affected by the sceptical spirit of Socrates, nevertheless maintained the old musical and gymnastic training, nay even (as we shall see) the old orthodoxy to a considerable extent. Athenian boys were after all in most respects like our own.

If there had been any game in Attica, they would have taken to hunting, as the Spartans did ; and the theoretical educators knew quite well what most of us do not, that such field sports as this are vastly superior to pure athletics in their effects upon the mind. It were well to reflect upon this now-a-days, when boat-racing and running and jumping and

he remained at his office till night, and was the last to leave the council, having been the first to come. Nay even when he had no public duties to perform, he was hard of access and difficult to meet, for he stayed at home and in seclusion. But his friends used to receive people who came to his door, and beg of them to excuse him on the plea that even then Nicias was engaged about some public business.' Plutarch's *Nicias*, cap. v. Plutarch thinks from the tone of the comic poets, that this diligence was partly assumed. This I do not believe.

putting weights are bidding fair to take the place
of our old fox-hunting, and shooting, and fishing.
The Greeks knew very well, what we ignore, that
such sports as require excessive bodily training and
care are low and debasing in comparison to those
which demand only the ordinary strength and quickness of young men, but stimulate them to higher
mental exercise—daring and decision in danger, resource and ingenuity in difficulties[1]   Xenophon's
tract on hare-hunting shows plainly how strongly
he advocated the same views[2]. Plato argues this
point fully, and we find it again strongly put in
Plutarch's *Philopœmen.* 'As he appeared to have
natural qualifications for wrestling, and some of his
friends and tutors urged him to train, he asked
whether athletic training would at all interfere with
his condition for military purposes.' Being told that
it would, ' he not only avoided it altogether and
ridiculed it, but afterwards when commanding punished all such training with disgrace and even insult.' But he rather feared physical results. Plato
sees the mental consequences more plainly. Lastly,
Alexander of Macedon established, says Plutarch,
many poetical and musical contests, but not a single
athletic contest, which shows plainly that, like Philopœmen, he thought physical training of little use
for the serious affairs of life.

[1] Cp. Jowett's *Plato*, iv. p. 154; and Grote's *Plato*, iii. p. 174.

[2] He speaks with real enthusiasm of the wonderful delight of hunting
this sort of game, which was evidently the most prized in the Pelo-
ponnesus. His dogs were specially trained to neglect foxes, as useless
and inferior creatures.

The want of game, as I have said, in Attica, stood greatly in the way of a proper physical education, and so the high-spirited youths who could not bear to keep talking all day, were obliged to vary their gymnastics with lower amusements — dice-playing, drinking and debauchery—which are much complained of by Isocrates (ii. p. 169).

What I have said hitherto refers only to boys of some age, who were approaching the age of puberty, and had arrived at such a mental stage as was suited for philosophical discussion. As to little children we have but scanty advice, and apparently not much sympathy among the philosophers. It was in fact mainly the intellect which attracted the attention of these speculators. The only educator who seems to me to have had a really deep sympathy with the temptations of his pupils was Socrates, and he did not seem to concern himself with little children, but only with boys old enough to understand argument.

I fear Plato was an old bachelor, and estimated children accordingly. 'Of all animals,' he says in the *Laws* (iv. 322), 'the boy is the most unmanageable, he is the most insidious, sharpwitted, and insubordinate.' He notices in the sequel how peculiarly the Egyptians excelled in the education of children, thereby implying inferiority in the Greeks. He proposes indeed to have two or three stout nurses to carry about each child in his ideal State, chiefly to obviate their roaring, in which he contrasts them unfavourably with the lower animals ; but this very advice, and the reason for it, speaks plainly the unsympathetic doctrinaire.   So

Aristotle, too, when he recommends for little children toys, 'that they may not break the household furniture,' shows himself both a bad observer and a bad adviser. Toys are most injurious to the peace of mind and the good temper of children ; they will by no means save the furniture, and it is certain that intelligent children will exercise both their minds and bodies far better by inventing plays and games, as they all do, than by struggling for the possession of a new toy, which is broken and forgotten within a few hours.

I fancy, though we have little evidence, that the average Greek parents were harsher than we are. Lysis [1] says he would be beaten if he touched his mother's spinning gear. He would be called in at once if they wanted reading or writing done—an allusion which leads us to suspect that the older generation were not very perfectly educated. But in spite of the repressive system of education described in this interesting passage of Plato, we know from Plutarch's anecdote (above, p. 232) about Alcibiades, that boys even of high family played in the street, and in the cartway.

I am persuaded by other hints, that the streets of Athens were not at all more fit for respectable boys to play in than the streets of modern towns. I have mentioned people opening their doors, and shouting ἐξίστω (stand aside) to the passers by, before they threw out dirty water, as they do in the lanes of London and Dublin. We hear of no strict super-

---

[1] Plato, i. p. 49.

vision of the streets—nothing that I know of save one allusion in Aristophanes to men being arrested as intoxicated, if they went out without a walking-stick (βακτήριον), and one in Hypereides that women who misconducted themselves in the streets were fined 1000 drachmæ—an enormous fine. Nevertheless, though in theory hurried walking, or laughter, or noise of any kind was thought vulgar, the ordinary Athenian public did not live up to an ideal level. Old gentlemen often went along whistling, as Aristophanes tells us. Crowds too would gather in the streets, not only to run after a groom who was leading a splendid horse[1], as Xenophon tells us, but also to hear and join in an altercation.

A very amusing account of such a street brawl is given in one of Lysias' speeches. It was concerning the possession of a boy whom the speaker endeavoured to rescue from a drunken party attempting to carry him off by violence. They had rushed into a fuller's shop, where the boy had taken refuge and concealed himself. The boy was dragged out screaming and bawling; and many people having come up and crying out shame, the party gave them no heed, but knocked down the fuller and others who tried to

---

[1] Cp. also Lysias, p. 178, on the other side. We see how ordinary hacks were so common, that a very poor man could borrow one to ride about on business, instead of doing the more comfortable thing and driving. Isæus (p. 53) corroborates this inference, when he tells us that one could be had for three minæ (£13), apparently the lowest price. Theophrastus (p. 117, ed. Jebb) speaks of it as the mark of a boor to stand in the street and gape after a cow or an ass or a goat: ὅταν δὲ ἴδῃ βοῦν ἢ ὄνον ἢ τράγον ἑστηκὼς θεωρεῖν.

rescue the boy. The speaker then came up, and as
the boy was his special favourite, he forthwith joins
in the fight. He and the boy both take to throwing
stones, and being helped by the by-standers, there
was a general mêlée. 'In this row we all had our
heads broken[1].' He says that there were presently
two hundred people present.

The men who had been drunk and had assaulted
the speaker came afterwards and apologised, which
was the gentlemanly thing to do, as the penalties for
assault were at Athens very severe, and would be
enforced if the matter should come into court. Probably for the same reason, we are told (Lysias, p. 98)
that actions for abusive language were thought disreputable. But I must reserve the legal peculiarities
of the Athenian state for a special discussion. I have
here only sought to show that while the theories of
Plato were most advanced and philosophical on education, there was probably as great a difference between
his speculations and ordinary Athenian practice, as
there is between our theory and our practice in education. I hold it therefore uncritical to quote Plato's
Dialogues as evidences of Athenian education, except
where he alludes to the ordinary practice directly,
and often as differing from his views. Most of his
theories were peculiar to himself, or to the select
few brought up in the higher atmosphere of Socratic
teaching.

[1] ἐν τούτῳ τῷ θορύβῳ συντριβόμεθα τὰς κεφαλὰς ἅπαντες (p. 31).
There is another street brawl described in Isocrates (p. 372), which was
however quelled by the accidental appearance of a magistrate.

I think it necessary, before leaving the subject of
Attic culture, to remind the reader of its narrowness
as well as of its exclusiveness, and how it was considered by those who possessed it a special apanage
not even of all Greeks, but of the pure autochthonous
offspring of Attic soil.   Here it is that we see a very
considerable inferiority to the views of earlier civilized
Greeks, who travelled to foreign capitals, and who
respected the culture of foreign races.   Thus Herodotus evidently admires and likes both Persians and
Egyptians.   To him a Persian grandee or an Egyptian high-priest was fully as cultured a man, nay in
many respects a much more thorough gentleman than
the best of the Greeks.   The anecdotes I have above
cited (p. 158), the account he gives of Persian education
and Persian manners, especially confirm this.   In one
point only, in politics, in their free institutions, he per-
ceives that the Greeks have an inestimable advantage.

But even in that generation Thucydides and the
tragedians show the narrowing effects of Attic culture.
Thucydides thinks the quarrels of Athens and Sparta
far more important than the vast shock of East and
West in a former generation.   It was a war among
Greeks, and therefore in his mind far finer than anything in which barbarians were concerned.   And when
the Persian empire recovered sufficient strength to
profit by Greek dissensions, and to make its power
again feared, we find Greek generals and philosophers
advocating a theory called by Mr. Grote *Panhellenism*,
which means a combination of all Greeks—of all the
various Hellenic tribes who spoke the same language,
worshipped the same gods, and attended the same

festivals—for the purpose of assailing and plundering the barbarians. This theory was based on the unity of the Hellenic race, as shown by the marks just enumerated, and assumed a natural inferiority in all other races—an assumption by which Aristotle actually sought to justify slavery. He deliberately asserted that nature had made the Greeks to rule, and the barbarians—especially the Eastern barbarians—to be their servants. Aristotle was here only repeating the traditional theories of the Attic politicians, and though he stood in presence of a greater mind which sought to fuse races, and 'celebrate the marriage of Europe and Asia,' he never saw his way to that broader Hellenicism with which Alexander supplanted and absorbed the Panhellenism of the Spartans and Athenians.

The most perfect specimen of this narrower policy —a policy which was nevertheless preached as broad and philosophical in contrast to the parochial patriotism of separate cities—will be found in the works of Isocrates. This well-meaning and gentlemanly, but somewhat vapid, rhetorician set himself up as the apostle of Panhellenism, and spent his life in advocating what he thought a large and noble policy among Greeks. He was a man of culture, and worked very hard in educating the aristocratic youth of his day. So highly did he rate the advantages of the intellectual atmosphere of Athens, that he even asserts (*Panegyricus*, p. 51 A) his fellow-citizens to have caused the name of Greek to be associated rather with culture, than with race, throughout the world.

Yet I am convinced nothing could be farther from

Isocrates' mind than the views attributed to him by
E. Curtius, of advocating a new Hellenedom founded
not upon race, but upon culture. He meant no more
in this isolated passage than a bigoted Englishman
might mean if he said that an Englishman was known
among foreigners rather by his superior style and tone
than by his language and complexion. Such a man
might say this, and still hold that the style and tone
were only to be found among Englishmen. In a
similar way Isocrates declares that it is the culture
and not the breed of the Greeks which was becoming
their prominent feature. But this in no way implies
that he thought the barbarians capable of like culture.
He is not indeed very consistent with himself, and is
apt to say whatever suits him rhetorically, so that any
isolated passage has no weight in comparison with
the general tone of his thinking.

Now if we look into this larger evidence, we find no
Greek author who insists more constantly on the contrast of Hellenes and barbarians, and who is more
conceited about the inherent and indestructible superiority of the former. He had before him indeed two
remarkable examples of the extension of Hellenic
culture to these inferior races—in Cyprus and Macedonia. But though he is obliged to confess that in
both cases, a foreign or semi-foreign nationality appreciated and endeavoured to appropriate this culture, he
never contemplates for a moment any independent
development, and attributes it all to the personal
ascendency and direction of Greeks. In the case of
Cyprus it is Evagoras who conquers the island, and
by despotic rule humanizes the natives, who were (he

asserts) an old Hellenic colony under Teucer, so that they merely reverted to their pristine dignity, having been barbarized by untoward circumstances. And now it is altogether by a servile imitation of Greek manners, and by intermarrying with Greek wives, that they earn his respect. In the case of Macedonia, he lays the greatest stress on the heroic origin of Philip, whose real country is Argos, and upon his having about him large numbers of wise and enlightened Greeks. Under these circumstances, he is able, as a despot, to impose Hellenic culture on his barbarous subjects.

But had the Cyprians and Macedonians become the most refined people in the world, Isocrates would not for one moment have thought them the equals of the Spartans, whose ignorance he himself exposes in great detail. For these were at one time of his life the natural leaders of the Hellenes, and in spite of their ignorance and brutality were still the very cream of Hellenic aristocracy.

In fact the whole aim of his policy was to unite the Greeks either under the Spartans, or under Philip, in an aggressive war against the Persian barbarians. This very narrow and unjustifiable scheme might have been palliated by an open declaration that such conquest would tend to civilise the East, and open it up to commerce and to letters. But such an Alexandrian notion of Hellenic conquest was far beyond the political horizon of Isocrates. He tells us with cynical frankness the advantages gained by such conquest. It is 'that the barbarians will be turned out of their country, and taught to think less of themselves'

(p. 268 B). It is 'that all such barbarians as do not help Philip shall become slaves to the Greeks' (p. 412 D). It is in fact that the Greeks shall gain every advantage they can at the expense of the barbarians, and give them nothing instead[1]. Professor E. Curtius is indeed persuaded that this constant preaching of a war against Persia is only an obsolete theory, and that Isocrates' real creed was the spreading of a higher culture even beyond the Hellenic race. But surely there is but one isolated phrase (in the *Panegyricus*) to sustain this latter principle; whereas the aggressive war policy against Persia runs all through his works. I am therefore convinced, in spite of such high authority against me, that the passage he cites about culture is only an empty phrase, while the anti-Persian idea was his real creed. It seems to me that Ernst Curtius' theory should be exactly reversed.

It would be indeed strange to find in that very mediocre and shallow philosopher, Isocrates, a foretaste of cosmopolitanism in human culture, when such an idea was beyond the horizon of his far greater contemporaries, Plato and Aristotle. Both of these thinkers, in many respects so modern, and so beyond

---

[1] Let the reader in addition consider the *tone* of the following passages: pp. 48 A, 258 C, 278 D, 409 A, (Steph.) 61 E, 126 D (Reiske). They all breathe the same thoroughly intolerant spirit, and are directly opposed to true Hellenicism. I have elsewhere (*Academy* for April 1, 1876) already proposed to note this important distinction by the terms *Hellenism* and *Hellenicism*, with the adjectives *Hellenic* and *Hellenistic* to correspond. I still think this a convenient nomenclature, which, if adopted, will save some respectable scholars from confusion of thought on the subject.

their age, were strictly Hellenes of the Hellenes, and could not conceive the doctrine that barbarians could through culture claim equality with the Greeks.

So then the separation assumed by Isocrates between Hellene and barbarian was as deep and wide as that between Jew and Gentile under the Pharisees, as that between Turk and Frank under the Sublime Porte. It is plain then that not Isocrates, nay not even Aristotle, was the true apostle of the Hellenicism of the second century, but rather Alexander, who disregarding the advice of his tutor to treat the barbarians δεσποτικῶς, as a master, knew how to consult their interests, and to postpone the claims of the offended and astonished Greeks. Attic culture could never have widened itself to this condition, and it was therefore necessary for the progress of the world that the incomparable refinement of Athens should be rudely shocked by the Macedonians, and taught to accommodate itself to a new and subordinate position.

CHAPTER XII.

RELIGIOUS FEELING IN THE ATTIC AGE.

THE common theory as to the religion of the Greeks assumes that in Homeric days men believed faithfully in the acts and adventures of the gods, as they were collected and recited by the Epic poets. In these primitive days the personification of natural powers was universally admitted as the only reasonable explanation of the action and order of nature; and it seemed not only impious but absurd to the early Greek to regard his Helios as no longer a great god driving his chariot daily, and casting an eye of desire upon the fair things of this world, but a mere lump of whitened metal suspended in the sky, and moved at the beck of some unseen and spiritual agency. In this sense the saying of Herodotus is often quoted, that Homer and Hesiod 'made the theology of the Greeks'; in other words, these widely-spread and popular poems gave some connected view of the various scattered local beliefs concerning the gods and their relations to men.

Mr. Grote has shown with great ability and force, in his celebrated sixteenth chapter, how this simple unreasoning faith began to fade out under the light of criticism when the nation awoke into conscious reflection. The Greeks were too subtle and thoughtful a people to remain content with any received dogmas either in religion or in politics, without sifting and testing them by the light of reason ; and the Epic theology of the Greeks required no singular acuteness to disclose its inherent defects. Apart from the element of the supernatural, which must always lack *scientific* evidence, and is generally made to act without sufficient reason—apart, I say, from this element —there were open and uncensured immoralities, which must shock the moral sense of any sound human nature. To these blots in the Epic literature I have already often adverted. The constant quarrels of the gods, carried on by confessed fraud and deceit, and involving injustice in the treatment of innocent mortals, are almost the salient feature in the Iliad. In the Odyssey we have, in the same way, but little rational Providence, and in place of it, the man represented as the mere plaything of his friendly or hostile god. In addition to this, we have, in the lay of Demodocus, the first of these strange poems, called hymns to the gods, which detail adulteries and perjuries and thefts as no exceptional part of an eternal and supremely happy life.

The remarkable feature in this Epic theology is however, that it is by no means made up of immoralities. These are a frequent and prominent feature in the poems, but appear rather as the sport and recreation of the blessed gods. For there are distinct moral principles—justice, humanity, gratitude,—under-lying the levities and excesses of the gods, and it still remains to us a problem hard to solve, how these higher notions should have been combined with what was plainly disgusting and immoral, even in the serious thoughts of the poets themselves.

Of the many theories suggested in explanation I will here refute only one, because it has the merit of comparative novelty, and because it seems to me exactly to reverse the real facts of the case. For under such circumstances a refutation is a statement of the right theory. I allude to the popular views of the comparative mythologers, who hold that the im-moral stories about the Greek gods and heroes were not composed as such by the poets, but are misunder-stood and mistranslated versions of old physical aspects of nature. The old poetical view of the sun or dawn being overpowered by the dark clouds, or by the night, thus turns into the story of Helen, the wife of Menelaus, being carried away by the adul-terous Paris. The stealing of the oxen of Apollo by Hermes, as detailed in the hymn to Hermes, is the same fact, or a similar one, translated into mythical symbolism. Mythology is forsooth only a *disease in language*, a literal understanding of primitive meta-phors, a forgetting that even the ideas most remote from sense must have names of sensuous origin, and that the action most remote from voluntary action must be assimilated to it in our nomenclature. Thus, say the comparative mythologers, the Greek poets did not invent immoralities about the gods, but fell into believing them by mistake, and propagating them by tradition.

It is indeed difficult to discuss such a theory seriously, especially when we find it carried to its full results in the works of Mr. Cox[1]. In a former book I have gone into some detail upon the theory, and have shown a good many of the fundamental fallacies with which it positively teems[2]. The best and most proper answer to it is such a *reductio ad absurdum* as was performed by a brilliant and well-known writer in the fifth number of the Dublin University *Kottabos*, and which has been accepted with the highest satisfaction by competent judges all over the literary world.

But here I am concerned with only one point, the confessed immorality of so many of the Greek myths —a point which I did not touch in my former refutation. I ask, has the theory in question even attempted to explain it? For how does the misunderstanding of an old pictorial statement about natural phenomena introduce *immorality*? It may introduce volition; it may introduce motives and intentions like unto ours; but why must it give these humanised actions an immoral turn? Why must Paris be an *adulterer*? why must Helen go with him of her own accord? why must Hermes perjure himself after his theft? why must Aphrodite violate all propriety? Under their

---

[1] Especially his *Mythology of the Aryan Nations*, a book which is very useful in showing the full results of the theory.

[2] *Prolegomena to Ancient History*, pp. 42, sqq.

clouds of words, and their series of examples, the mythologers seem to have completely forgotten what they had to prove, and to have substituted assertion for argument. Given the facts in their primitive and pictorial dress, they do not suggest anything but simple acts, carried out by conscious agents, instead of mere natural forces. The old language does not suggest the motives, or paint the scenery—these must be added by the epic poet, when he is about to produce the story in a mythical form. And so if the poet were a serious and moral author, he would give these stories a serious and moral complexion, and add to the facts such motives as he thought worthy of the blessed gods ; if on the contrary he were a smooth court poet, singing to an audience of loose morals, and of doubtful honesty, he would naturally attribute to the gods motives similar to those common among his own hearers, and transfer to the immortals the foibles and the doubtful amusements of human princes and princesses.

This is what was done by the Homeric poets. The levity of the Ionic character,—which we see afterwards in the history of the Asiatic colonies, which speaks in the fragments of Mimnermus and of Anacreon,—was present in the Homeric audiences, who received with laughter and amusement these sallies about the immortal gods. We can imagine what ground for satire was given by the theory that the gods came down from Olympus, and allied themselves secretly with mortal beauties ; and we can also imagine the effect upon the morals of the day, if a breach of chastity might be ascribed to Divine persuasion, and the child of shame glorified by a supernatural origin.

The immoral elements in the Greek Epos were therefore *late additions* to the old beliefs about the gods, and invented by the rhapsodists to please the tastes of a luxurious and corrupt age. They are not nearly so prominent in what we call Homer, as they are in the *Theogony* of Hesiod and in the Homeric Hymns,—a strong argument in support of their late appearance in the Epic age. The primitive features, on the contrary, are noble and simple. The awful Zeus of Dodona, to whom the husbandman raises his hands in pure adoration, is not only older but far purer than the Zeus of Olympus, a sort of immortalised Agamemnon—the prey of moral weakness within, and of turbulent subjects without. Thus the Epic poets built upon an old and pure foundation, but deformed and defaced it with their voluptuous additions.

Far therefore from these immoralities being primitive or early features of the Greek religion, as the mythologers pretend, they were the accidental outcome of a special court poetry, and it was as such that they were so severely criticised by Xenophanes, and Socrates, and all sound Greek philosophers. These sober critics knew perfectly that they were inventions of the Epic poets, interwoven with a pure and simple basis, and could they have eliminated this feature in the Epos, they would doubtless have recommended expurgated editions, as we now have (practically) expurgated Bibles, in which we pass by, and even palliate, apparent immoralities, in order to force moral lessons out of the rude history of the old Hebrews.

This analogy is far closer than at first appears, and there is a vast deal of truth in calling Homer the Bible of the Greeks. There are indeed three or four special features so closely analogous to those of our faith in this Epic religion of the Greeks, as to be well worth a special and detailed discussion. Such considerations, if well established, should have no small effect upon the attitude we take towards our own religious documents.

The first feature to be noted is the consistent assertion of all our authorities that Homer wrote with a moral intent, and with the conscious purpose of conveying moral lessons. There is nothing to my mind farther from the truth, and yet nothing is more persistently believed by the Greeks. It is directly implied by Pindar, Aristophanes, Plato, Isocrates, and a host of other authors. It is developed in the remaining fragments of Dioscorides[1] to an extraordinary extent. In fact, just as we read the old Hebrew history to our children much more from a moral than an historical attitude, and give to all the facts a didactic turn, so the old Greeks read Homer as a

---

[1] Collected by Carl Müller, in the 2nd vol. of his *Fragmenta Historicorum Græcorum* pp. 192 sqq. Athenæus expresses the effect of all Greek literature upon him, when he says (p. 8 E): Ὅμηρος ὁρῶν τὴν σωφροσύνην οἰκειοτάτην ἀρετὴν οὖσαν τοῖς νέοις καὶ πρώτην, ἔτι δὲ ἁρμόττουσαν καὶ πάντων τῶν καλῶν χορηγὸν οὖσαν, βουλόμενος ἐμφῦσαι πᾶσιν αὐτὴν ἀπ' ἀρχῆς κ.τ.λ. εὐτελῆ κατεσκεύασε πᾶσιν τὸν βίον καὶ αὐτάρκη, because eating and drinking were prominent and dangerous appetites.

moral work, containing models of what men ought to be, exhibitions of punished vice and meanness, examples of fortitude, of temperance, of justice, and of wisdom. If we object that the Homeric poems were ill-suited to such a purpose, we shall only repeat the criticisms of Xenophanes and Plato, but not invalidate the facts.

We should do better to consider the analogy of the Old Hebrew Scriptures. I need only mention the fact that there are several chapters unsuited to modern perusal, and passed over in all family reading. This is of less importance. But what is more curious, manifest immoralities are daily read, and are glozed over by our moral attitude in such a way, that they actually fail to do the harm which might have been expected. There are cases of dishonesty in the very highest characters of the history, which somehow are passed over without making an impression on the moral reader. There are lessons in cruelty, which lose their effect by being considered Divine punishments, and special commands of the Author of our being. Thus the incidents which are in accordance with our moral sense are utilised and insisted upon, the other matters are forgotten, and so the whole annals of a race in most respects unfit for our instruction are taught as if specially written for our learning[1].

[1] I am merely speaking of these things as facts, and offering no opinion upon them. I do not know whether any better system of education will be discovered, than this moral interpretation of documents, venerable in age, and of extreme literary excellence. Certain it is that

It is not difficult to explain how the same attitude existed as regards Homer among the Greeks. The earliest known poets whom the Greeks possessed were really moral teachers. First, there was the didactic epos of Hesiod and his school, which professedly dealt in moral lessons; then came the gnomic or proverbial poetry of the early elegiac and the philosophical poets, and of the choral lyric poets. These men monopolised the moral teaching in Greece, if we except a few responses of the oracles, during the seventh and sixth centuries. It was but natural that they should represent themselves as the successors of their brilliant predecessors in more than mere poetry, and that they should ascribe to the splendid Iliad and Odyssey an aim and intent similar to their own tamer productions. Thus it came to pass that Homer, in one sense 'the idle singer of an empty day,'— because he sought no other object than the clear and deep delineation of human character and human passion—was degraded, if I may so say, into a moral teacher, and accredited with definite theories of life and of duty.

It was the same *sort* of blunder as we should make, were we to dilate upon the moral purposes of Shelley and Keats, and insist upon classing them with the school of Dr. Watts. The obsequious rhapsodist who sang before chiefs and ladies at high feasts, and depended upon their grace for his daily bread and for

all civilised men have proceeded on this plan, and no other has yet been tried with success. Still I feel bound to state the facts clearly from a purely historical point of view.

his fame, thought more of glorifying the royal ancestors of the palace where he sat, and the acts of his patron's forefathers, than of insisting upon moral saws or conveying deep lessons in voluptuous allegories. But all historical Greece thought differently. As gnomic poets were moral teachers, as the tragic poets were moral teachers, and were openly criticised as such, so Homer and his legends were accepted and taught by all respectable Greeks as inspired lessons of the highest wisdom and sanctity.

When I speak of them as *inspired* lessons, I am using no rash expression, though it may doubtless be objected that in this point lies the essential difference of the Hebrew analogy which has been suggested. We are not here concerned with the truth of this claim for the documents on which our religion is founded, nor is the present argument affected by such considerations; all that is here insisted upon is that the Greek epic poets, and indeed some of the lyric poets, *laid claim* to a closely similar inspiration. In Plato's official dialogue upon this subject, the *Ion,* he develops very fully a theory of inspiration in every respect like that claimed for the Hebrew poets. He represents the rhapsodists as asserting the great epic poems to have been written under some sort of enthusiasm akin to madness; he represents the authors as only partly responsible for what they said, and plainly asserts that the moral lessons which they claimed to teach were the inspiration of some Divine power, speaking through the bard as a mortal and imperfect instrument.

'This gift which you have of speaking excellently
about Homer is not an art, but, as I was just saying,
an inspiration; there is a divinity moving you, like
that in the stone which Euripides calls a magnet, but
which is commonly known as the stone of Heraclea.
For that stone not only attracts iron rings, but also
imparts to them a similar power of attracting other
rings; and sometimes you may see a number of
pieces of iron and rings suspended from one another
so as to form quite a long chain: and all of them
derive their power of suspension from the original
stone. Now this is like the Muse, who first gives to
men inspiration herself; and from these inspired persons a chain of other persons is suspended, who take
the inspiration from them [1]. For all good poets, epic
as well as lyric, compose their beautiful poems not as
works of art, but because they are inspired and possessed. And as the Corybantian revellers when they
dance are not in their right mind, so the lyric poets
are not in their right mind when they are composing
their beautiful strains: but when falling under the
power of music and metre they are inspired and possessed; like Bacchic maidens who draw milk and
honey from the rivers, when they are under the influence of Dionysus, but not when they are in their
right mind. And the soul of the lyric poet does the
same, as they themselves tell us; for they tell us that
they gather their strains from honied fountains out of
the gardens and dells of the Muses; thither, like the
bees, they wing their way. And this is true. For

[1] Here we have the theory of Apostolical Succession also.

the poet is a light and winged and holy thing, and there is no invention in him until he has been inspired and is out of his senses, and the mind is no longer in him : when he has not attained to this state, he is powerless and is unable to utter his oracles. Many are the noble words in which poets speak of actions like your own words about Homer ; but they do not speak of them by any rules of art : only when they make that to which the Muse impels them are their inventions inspired ; and then one of them will make dithyrambs, another hymns of praise, another choral strains, another epic or iambic verses—and he who is good at one is not good at any other kind of verse : *for not by art does the poet sing, but by power divine.* Had he learned by rules of art, he would have known how to speak not of one theme only, but of all ; and therefore God takes away the minds of poets, and uses them as his ministers, as he also uses diviners and holy prophets, in order that we who hear them may know that *they speak not of themselves who utter these priceless words in a state of unconsciousness, but that God is the speaker, and that through them he is conversing with us.* And Tynnichus, the Chalcidian, affords a striking instance of what I am saying : he wrote nothing that any one would care to remember but the famous pæan which is in every one's mouth, and is one of the finest poems ever written, and is certainly an invention of the Muses, as he himself says. For in this way the God would seem to indicate to us, and not allow us to doubt that these beautiful poems are not human, or the work of man, but

divine and the word of God ; and that the poets are
only the interpreters of the Gods by whom they are
severally possessed. Was not this the lesson which
the God intended to teach when by the mouth of the
worst of poets he sang the best of songs? Am I not
right, Ion [1] ?'

Such a theory must have afforded them a ready
defence against the moral objections above stated.
Here then we have a second and most remarkable
analogy to the religious condition of our own day.
The documents on which moral instruction was based
claimed a higher authority than mere human wisdom,
they boasted a stranger origin than human genius and
human labour, for they claimed to be in some way
dictated by the Gods, and composed under the excitement of a sudden and Divine compulsion.

Little need here be said upon the gradual development of scepticism within the Greek religion, upon the
gradual separation, and at length conflict, between
religion and philosophy ; how the higher thinkers in
politics began to despise the oracles, and the higher
teachers in morals to condemn the poets. These
things are natural to every speculative race, and this
gradual development from instinctive faith and authority to reflective faith and private judgment, and then
to absolute freedom of thought or scepticism, is one
of the most universal and ever-recurring changes to
be found in civilised races. It has been expounded
with great power and marvellous richness of illustration by Mr. Grote, indeed by all historians of Greece,

[1] Jowett, vol. i. pp. 237–8.

and my weaker pen can add nothing to what is now
historical commonplace.

I am rather here concerned with insisting upon a
point which they seem to me to have misrepresented,
either by distinct statement, or by implication. I
think they are disposed greatly to overrate the area
over which this scepticism spread, or its density within
any given area of population. It is somehow assumed,
that after the epoch of Pericles, as expounded by the
history of Thucydides, scepticism became the prevail-
ing religion of the Athenians, if not of all educated
Greeks. It is assumed that Thucydides' sneers at the
oracles, and his silence upon the interference of the
gods, are evidence of the tone of mind pervading the
general Greek public. It is assumed, contrary to all
the evidence of history, that there was no reaction
from this advanced and negative attitude, and that
the positive faith of Greece died almost as her political greatness came into full development. I know
not whether I am wronging the historians in this
matter, but such is certainly the general impression
they have left upon me, and upon many other
students whom I have consulted on this point.

But if I am in error as to their real views, I am the
more anxious to prevent others from like stumbling,
and to insist upon the true and natural attitude of
the Greeks on this all-important problem. The
general belief in the almost universal scepticism of
the Periclean age arises from our over-estimate of
Thucydides as its exponent. As I have often before
said, Herodotus is nearer the state of the public

mind than Thucydides. The latter represents a small set of advanced thinkers, such as Pericles, Anaxagoras, Damon, and probably Phidias, who led in politics, in art, and in literature, but were obliged to conceal their advanced thinking in religion, and could not lead their contemporaries here also. They were probably indifferent on this point, and thought, as many sceptics do, that faith was a good thing for the crowd. There are stories in Plutarch's *Pericles* which seem to point to some such belief in the mind of Pericles himself [1].

Thus we estimate the state of the Athenian mind in general by a few brilliant exceptions, who stood in direct opposition to it at this very time. In the very same way the great literature of the Hebrews, written by what was evidently a small though brilliant minority, blinds us to the fact perpetually breaking through the history, that the masses of the Jewish people were always idolatrous and polytheistic, though their literary monuments were composed by the cultivated monotheists; and hence these great prophets and psalmists are now generally accepted as uttering the voice of the whole nation. So in the present day, to give a more homely and practical example, because the German university men are sceptics, and the tone of German learning is scep-

---

[1] Especially the story of his being in great distress at a severe accident to a workman engaged on one of his great public buildings, and his being told in a dream of the proper remedy to apply. He came down to the Agora, and announced that the Gods had revealed to him the remedies which really proved effectual. Plut. *Pericles*, c. 13.

tical, we find it commonly believed in England that the Germans generally are an irreligious and unbelieving people—a flagrant error, which the anecdotes of the late war, and still more the politic telegrams of the German emperor, should have exploded.

But when we have gained from Thucydides this general notion that the Greek mythology was then altogether abandoned, we are so impressed with its absurdities and its immoralities that we can hardly conceive it rehabilitated, and thus we come to believe in a sort of general scepticism pervading Attic society from that day onward. This again is applying our standpoint to other men, and forgetting that only the few come to hold as absurd what they have once believed, when it has really been to them the object of deep veneration, and the source of their best and purest moral principles.

There is no more common opinion among reasonable and educated sceptics in our own day than this, that however false Christianity may be, its effects upon the moral and social history of man are such, that it must for ever be regarded with respect and high consideration. They will tell you, and with great good sense, that the scoffing scepticism of Paine and Proudhon was not only rude and out of taste, but historically absurd and ignorant, and that in a world where absolute truth is hardly to be discovered, it is a very silly proceeding to ridicule a system which, even regarded as fictitious, nevertheless impressed great moral principles upon mankind. All this applies, we may think, to our pure and venerable Christianity, but could never be asserted of those heathen systems which teemed with dishonesty and immorality.

This is the narrow modern position which I think so false. To the old-fashioned Athenian, his mythology was the source of *his* morals and of *his* highest culture. He had framed for himself ideals of bravery, of honour, of greatness from his Homer; he had seen the tragic poets draw their most splendid inspirations from these legends; he had seen the Epos inspire the painter, the sculptor, and the architect—in fact, the whole glory of Athens, literary, social, and artistic, was bound up with the Homeric theology. Supposing him, therefore, to be persuaded by the philosophers, and to abandon in secret the faith of his forefathers, we can well imagine him arguing with even more apparent force than the modern sceptic, that however false or fictitious were these ancient legends, however unproved or doubtful this ancient creed, yet at all events under it, and through it, Athens had grown in splendour, and become perfect in culture; that therefore no citizen versed in the annals of Athens, and appreciating her true greatness, could venture to speak disrespectfully of her creed, even were it proved obsolete. I must insist upon these subjective analogies, because of the common habit, which is wellnigh the essence of modern faith, of regarding one's own creed as absolute truth, and all other systems as obviously absurd and wicked.

In opposition then to all these one-sided and

partial views, it appears that the Greek public was always religious in the sense in which our own public is religious, that is to say, bound by tradition and habit to a creed, which many believe conscientiously, and which even doubters care not to disturb. There are among ourselves epochs and outbursts of scepticism, when it seems as if all the world were abandoning its faith, and as if a return to the old belief were quite impossible. Such was the outbreak in the eighteenth century; such is perhaps the present attitude of our English society in India. Such is that of the German universities, and of our own literary circles. And yet if history can be any guide, we may be perfectly certain that there will and must come a reaction into positive belief. The dogmas may vary, the articles of our faith may possibly be changed, but faith—that quality on which all our early experience, all our higher feelings, all our greatest hopes are based—faith will reassert itself.

It is a very interesting speculation, what form this faith will take, whether it will be the reassertion of some wider Christianity, or whether, as seems just now likely, it may assume the stranger form of a systematic spiritualism. When we see men who have lived and preached as sceptics all their lives coming round to believe the evidence of new miracles, to argue the possibility of a scientific system of communication with other existences, we seem to stand on the threshold of an outburst of positive belief far less rational, and therefore less enduring, than that which is now being contemptuously cast aside.

I mention these things as analogous to the Greek attitude upon religion, because they are eternal features in civilised human nature, and will repeat themselves wherever the circumstances are at all similar. In this sense our present experience may be as much a κτῆμα ἐς ἀεί applicable to older times, as Thucydides' history is applicable to our times. The important point in the analogy is this, that all through Greek history scepticism never made way among the majority even of educated people, but was merely the privilege or pain of small circles of philosophers and their followers. The Sophists indeed attempted to transfuse this mental attitude, by means of education, into the public mind, but the soberer portion of the nation vehemently and successfully resisted them.

The evidence upon this point need only be stated to convince the reader. Protagoras' books were burnt by the common hangman at Athens[1], perhaps the earliest example of this curious practice of punishing not men but things; yet less curious than when occurring in the middle ages, if we remember that there was at Athens a special court and form of trial for inanimate objects which had accidentally caused death, and which were cast beyond the border, if guilty of homicide[2]. Damon and Anaxagoras, the

[1] This must have happened after the date of Plato's *Meno*; cf. *Meno*, p. 91 E.

[2] These are the ἀψύχων δίκαι described by Pollux, and also Harpocration (sub. voc. ἐπὶ Πρυτανείῳ), but alluded to by both Æschines and Pausanias; and probably a very ancient form of trial at Athens. Cp. Hermann-Stark, *Griech. Antiqq.* i. p. 487

friends of Pericles, were prosecuted for impiety, in spite of the powerful support of the prime minister, nor did he dare to stand forward openly and defend their theological tenets. We have next the frequent and bitter complaints of Aristophanes in his comedies, the whole of the *Clouds* being directed against even Socrates' teaching, though he was confessedly no common sceptic, but a man who desired to deepen the foundations and strengthen the roots of popular faith and of popular morals. Then comes the actual prosecution of Socrates, in which the *attitude* of the prosecutors is far more important than the result— a result which depended partly upon a widespread political animosity against the aristocrats, and partly upon the contumacy of the accused. This attitude is based firmly upon the orthodoxy of the general public, and would have neither force nor meaning without such presupposition.

These are the polemical evidences on the very surface of Greek history, which need only be recalled to the reader's attention, and which need not be supported by special quotations. During all this time the youth of Greece were still being taught morals and religion through Homer and Hesiod, and the gnomic poets. The sophists talked a great deal, and made such a noise that we still hear their voices, across the gulf of centuries, above the voices of quiet and orderly people; but these latter were after all the great majority, and formed the popular mind. Take Demosthenes, or the orator Lycurgus, or Hypereides, or even any obscure contemporaries whose works have been preserved. Do they imply a public educated by the sophists? Do they preach or suggest sceptical views? Nothing of the sort. All of them address throughout an orthodox and even religious public[1]. He complains that men were wanting in energy and action, but he never attacks them for unbelief; nor, on the other hand, does he encourage it, but alludes to religion as we should do, admitting and enforcing a faith in Divine Providence, and looking to the gods for help and pardon in national dangers and transgressions.

The same was the position of Xenophon, a very good specimen of the educated Athenian in days succeeding the outburst of the sophistic scepticism. I do not so much refer to his own action in consulting the oracle at the instigation of Socrates, for in those days the oracle had been so often convicted of partiality, that the 'apostolical succession' of its priests and prophetess may have been open to general question, though the old habit of consulting it on moral difficulties still remained. But let us rather consider the tone assumed towards religion throughout his dialogues. We there find, as has been said, that a sort of average orthodoxy is professed by his speakers, and implied as the general state of belief.

Among the country folk this orthodoxy was of course stronger and clearer, and appears associated rather with a belief in some systematic ruler of the

---

[1] See for example the speech πρὸς Μακάρτατον (p. 1072), which may not be Demosthenes'. Mr. Jebb and A. Schäfer reject it, and thus strengthen my argument, but I now incline (with Dionysius) to accept it.

world, single in purpose, and not specialised in form
or character, than with a passionate capricious personage like the Zeus of Homer. Indeed I am convinced that many a good old country gentleman felt
how unworthy were the pictures of the poets, and
how much better was the rustic habit of speaking of 'God' without farther detail, and insisting
upon his general benevolence and care of human
affairs, rather than upon his amours with some
ancestress, in order to claim a divine parentage.
Many old and picturesque sayings are even now
preserved among the Greeks, which point to these
simple and reasonable beliefs ; and we can well appreciate that most poetical expression of Xenophon :
'when the late harvest time is come, do not all men
turn their eyes towards God, to see when he will
water the earth, and let them out to sow their seed[1]?'

[1] Xen. *Œcon.* c. xvii.: ἐπειδὰν γὰρ ὁ μετοπωρινὸς χρόνος ἔλθῃ, πάντες
που οἱ ἄνθρωποι πρὸς τὸν θεὸν ἀποβλέπουσιν, ὁπότε βρέξας τὴν γῆν ἀφήσει
αὐτοὺς σπείρειν. This attitude of looking to one supreme God, especially
as the ruler of the weather, fell in easily with the Christian doctrine, so
that even in the present day Greece is full of these pictorial expressions, which remind us of the old simple mythology. There are a
number of most interesting hints on this point in Bernhard Schmidt's
Volksleben der Neugriechen, especially pp. 26–35. They still say βρέχει
ὁ θεός, and even κατουράει ὁ θεός, which strangely reminds us of old
Strepsiades' remark in the *Clouds* 373. Rainwater is still called θεοτικὸ
νερό, literally Theophrastus' τὸ ἐκ τοῦ Διὸς ὕδωρ. Lightning and thunder
are still caused by the god shaking his head, which we find in the magnificent lines of Homer, A. 528, where Zeus shakes his ambrosial locks, and
as they wave upon his immortal head, all the great Olympus rocks. God
still uses the thunderbolt for his weapon as we find it in Aristophanes,
Pindar, and Æschylus. The quaint form of these expressions points to
a great antiquity, dating from long before the Periclean age, nor was the

Such people had little to say to the sophists, and cared little about the Socratic elenchus.

But even the speakers in more educated society, the gentlemen assembled at Xenophon's *Symposium*, express themselves satisfied with their faith, and desirous to practise it as a duty. It is very manifest 'that both Greeks and barbarians consider the gods to know all that is and that will be; accordingly all cities and all nations enquire of the gods through prophecy what they ought and what they ought not to do. Moreover, that we at least believe that they can do us both good and ill, this too is plain, for all pray to the gods to avert evil, and to grant prosperity. These gods, then, that are omniscient and all-powerful are so friendly to me, that through care for me they never lose me out of their sight, either by night or day, wherever I may go, or whatever I may do. But by reason of their foreknowledge how each thing will result, they give me signs, sending as their messengers (angels) voices and dreams and omens, what I should do and what I should forbear. When I obey these I never have reason to repent, but it has happened that I have been punished for want of faith in them.' Then Socrates says : ' None of these things are the least incredible ; but this I should gladly hear, how you serve them so as to make them such friends of yours.' 'So you shall,' is the reply, 'and I do it at very

habit probably ever interrupted. Thus Marcus Aurelius (**v.** 7) mentions an Athenian prayer for rain beginning ὗσον, ὗσον, ὦ φίλε Ζεῦ, which was of course very old, but used down to his days.

moderate expense. For I praise them without any cost to myself, and of what they grant me I always return them a share. I speak of them respectfully, as far as I can, and when I call them to witness, I never intentionally tell a lie.' 'Well, by Jove,' says Socrates, 'if by so doing you have the gods your friends, the gods too, it seems, are pleased with gentlemanly conduct[1].'

This then is a fair account of the ordinary Greek orthodoxy. It was not the faith of mystics, not an absorption of the mind in the contemplation of Divine perfections and Divine mysteries, but rather the religion of a shrewd and practical people, who based their worship upon their wants, and blessed their God, not like Fenelon, because he was ideally perfect, but like Bossuet, because they received from him many substantial favours. We have no reason to think that the faith of Xenophon's speakers was a decaying faith; nay rather I fancy that after the fever of the Peloponnesian war was over, when the novelty of the sophists had gone by, when the hard and selfish generation of Pericles had passed away, there may have been a reaction towards positive belief, and towards old-fashioned views. This seems to me the position of the orator Lycurgus, so far as we can judge from his remarkable extant speech. It seems also implied by the arguments of his contemporary Hypereides, whose whole speech ὑπὲρ Εὐξενίππου turns upon what we should call a state superstition, as to the special way in which individuals should announce

---

[1] *Symp.* iv. § 47, sqq.

important dreams to the state, and as to the veri-
fication of these professed dreams by sending to
Delphi [1].

Thus the Demosthenic public was probably more
orthodox than the Periclean, certainly not less so,
and the supposed destruction of the Greek religion was
like the supposed destruction of the Christian faith
in the eighteenth century—a phase in speculation,
a fashion among philosophers, but no national abdi-
cation of faith.   It was no doubt similar to the newer
outburst of scepticism under the influence of Epicurus and Menander, who embraced an atheistical
philosophy from lassitude and for pleasure's sake,
not as their ancestors had done, from hard selfishness and engrossment in the cares and ambitions of
public life.   For though even the cooks of the New
Comedy profess philosophy, and tell us that Epicurus had raised their profession to the highest in life,
yet the victory of Stoicism at the same period, and
the appearance and success of moral reformers like
S. Paul and Dio Chrysostom, show that scepticism
had taken no firm hold even then.   It was, as it has

[1] Hypereides, pp. 36 sq. (ed. Blass) : 'The people directed Euxenippus
with two others to be put to sleep in the temple, but he having slept
there says he saw a dream, which he says he will announce to the people.
If you considered this to be true, and that he announced to the people
what he (really) saw in the dream, how is he blamed for telling the
Athenians what the god directed him. But if, as you now say, you think
he belied the god, and made a false report to the people in favour of
certain (friends of his own), you should not have proposed a decree about
the dream, but as the former speaker said, (you should have proposed) to
send to Delphi, and enquire the truth of the God.' The whole argument
turns upon the treatment of this report of Euxenippus.

ever been, and probably will ever be, a transient state of the human mind, and even as such unable to retain the mass of mankind.

I have thus brought before the reader what may be regarded as important analogies between the religion professed by the Greeks and that professed in the present day—I do not mean in the dogmas themselves, but in the attitude assumed towards these venerable traditions, and towards their positive teaching of morals in old Greek days, as compared with our own. It seems to me that no branch of our enquiry has demonstrated more clearly the modernness of Attic life, and the contrast of what we call the Middle Ages to both that life and to our own. The world has not been progressing with even and steady step, but has gained from time to time great vantage ground, and has again been thrown back by the tide of circumstances. Thus we are in some respects only coming up to the level attained by the Greeks ; in some respects they were striving to attain our level, but we should class both the Greeks and ourselves as developed nations, whereas mediæval culture was rather an early and blind groping towards politics and humane society,

These reflections would however be incomplete were we not to take into account the points of contrast between Greek religion and our own. And here I still use *religion* in its subjective sense, as a state of mind, not as a collection of dogmas ; for to discuss in this latter sense the contrasts with Christianity were a mere idle enumeration of differences.

But in the other sense—of devout feeling, of reverence in the presence of awful and unseen powers, which wield weapons for the destruction and for the chastisement, as well as for the happiness of the human race—we may find likenesses and contrasts quite apart from the particular objects adored, and may compare the manner of worship, even though the matter be totally at variance.

I think the first contrast that strikes us from this point of view is the *love of mystery* in our modern religions, and its absence, or at least rare appearance, in the religion of the Greeks. On the surface indeed of the epic and gnomic poems, there is no trace of it at all. The gods assume mortal forms, and act with human feelings. They speak and argue like men, and with men. When we compare the main dogmas of our own religion, the subtleties which brought fire and blood upon the world in the Middle Ages, the secrets of the Incarnation, of the Atonement, of the Trinity, of the Intermediate State, we stand in the presence of two mental conditions totally and thoroughly opposed. The one got rid of all mystery, and made all things plain. The other adored mystery as such, regarded it as necessary to true religion, and made all things abstract and difficult. So far Greek religion is in thorough consonance with Greek art. The great reason why the Greek *chefs-d'œuvres* have been everlasting, and have spoken to all cultivated men in all ages, is that their conception was everywhere *clear* and precise. Whether in poetry, in architecture, or in painting, strict form, distinctness

of view, chastened imagination, are the eternal features of true Greek art.   And this was the spirit in
which their early poets treated religion also.   We
have inherited other traditions.   The sublime vagueness of the Egyptian priest, the conscious self-pros-
tration of the Semite shepherd, the fine-drawn subtleties of the Orientalised Hellenist, all these passed
in the ferment of Alexandrian days into our creeds,
and leavened the whole lump.

But the Greek mind was too full and diverse to
be satisfied by mere clearness and beauty.   However
hard and precise we may be in thinking, however
strict we may be in defining the outlines and bounds
of our ideas, there is still the vagueness of yearning,
the longing of unsatisfied desire, which haunts all
natures in their highest moods, and makes them feel
after the perfect, and seek an union with the Pure
and the Good,—an union closer and more passionate
than arises from the fulfilment of a moral law, or the
performance of a moral duty.   The earliest Greek form
of this deep longing and vain regret was the reflection
on the moral imperfections of the world's course, and
the seeming random distribution of good and ill.   I
have above noted (p. 93) this prominent feature in
the poets of the lyric age.   Here is such a passage,
which I quote as a fair specimen from Theognis :—

> ' Kyrnus ! believe it, Fortune, good or ill,
> No mortal effort, intellect or skill
> Determine it ; but heaven's superior will.
> We struggle onward, ignorant and blind,
> For a result unknown and undesigned ;

Avoiding seeming ills, misunderstood,
Embracing seeming evil as a good:
In our own plans unable to detect
Their final, unavoidable effect.
Tormented with unsatisfied desire,
The fortunate to farther aims aspire
Beyond the bounds of mortal happiness;
Restless and wretched in their own success!
We live like children, and the Almighty plan
Controls the froward children of weak man[1]!'

This want, which was not absent from Greek nature, they strove to satisfy by those religious Mysteries, of which we hear so often but know so little. It seems, however, nearly certain that they substituted the knowledge and belief in new revelations, in hidden dogmas, as a higher ground of action, and a more all-embracing rule of life, for the calm computation of duty or higher interest. We are told by the Germans[2] that such doctrines as the immortality of the soul and the future retribution of good and evil were among the tenets disseminated by these mysteries, and that to them such poets as Pindar owed a clear vision of these doctrines, which are foreign to Homer and Hesiod. This seems true, and is likely enough in itself, though it is hard to find any direct authority for it in Greek literature, and I now believe that we may cautiously receive it as more than an ingenious theory. The Greeks have carefully con-

[1] I transcribe this from Mr. Frere's *Theognis Restitutus*, in his *Works*, 2nd ed. iii. p 383.

[2] E. g. O. Müller, *Lit. of Anc. Greece*, vol. i. p. 76, and Hermann-Stark, *Griech. Antiqq.* part ii. p. 198, note 12, quoting from Nägelsbach and others, also Petersen in *Ersch and Gruber*, vol. lxxxiii. pp. 265-7.

cealed from us the teaching of these mysteries; they prosecuted for impiety, and punished with death or banishment any man who could be shown to have divulged them. Thus they have concealed from us one of the most interesting points in their religion, and left us to mere conjectures about the exact scope and teaching of these widely-spread and secret religious exercises. It is unnecessary to repeat these conjectures, or add to their number[1], as I am concerned with reproducing actual features in old Greek life; but it seems certain, and beyond mere hazard, that whatever was their scope, they were meant, as their very name of *mysteries* implies, to satisfy this longing after the perfect, which was inadequately provided for in the clear and human faith of the ordinary priests and their temples. At all events, with this unex-

---

[1] One remark is worth making, in opposition to the Germans and their French followers, who think the influence of the mysteries is most prominently seen in Pindar. It is Æschylus who suggests the first great change in the religious *Anschauungsweise* of the Greeks. The few additional dogmas alluded to by Pindar in the midst of his old-school morals, and his commonplace view of human life and of Divine Providence, are as nothing compared to the totally new and deep aspects which form the main burden of Æschylus' dramas. We should also remember that he (and not Pindar) was distinctly charged with having divulged some of the mysteries in his *Eumenides.* If all this be true, it points to a speculative, rather than a moral character in these religious exercises; nor is this view really contradicted by Aristotle's remark, which Synesius repeats: 'that he considers the initiated were not bound to learn anything, but rather to be placed in a peculiar emotional condition' (παθεῖν καὶ διατεθῆναι). This rather refers to the *way* of instruction in the mysteries, which were like modern religious revivals, where the new life is attained by a strong physical sympathy, and not by ordinary instruction.

plained feature in Greek religion before us, and with
the great probability that such was its principal object, we cannot assert the hard contrast between Greek
and modern piety which our other sources would
warrant. For all we know, justification by faith may
have been a standard doctrine in these mysteries, just
as atonement by human sacrifice lasted down into
historical times, and caused scenes painful and shocking (above p. 238) to such as did not embrace the
dogma, and blind their humanity by keeping the eye
of faith fixed upon its efficacy.

The remaining contrasts between Greek religious-
ness and our own are, like the former, partial contrasts only, but still contrasts, at least with the Protestantism of modern Europe ; and though Catho-
licism be in outward form not so contrasted, its whole
temper and spirit was so thoroughly anti-Greek, that
I can hardly bring myself to take it into account in
the present sketch. The first of the points alluded to
is the intimate *association of art with religion*, in the
identification of the beautiful—that is to say, the
physically beautiful—with the good ; in the offering,
as the noblest tribute to the blessed gods, the purest
and best products which human genius could attain in
art. Strangely enough it is in mediæval Christianity
that we find this feature reproduced. The magnificent cathedrals of Normandy, the divine pictures of
the Fra Angelico and of Giotto, speak a religious
temper not unlike in manifestation to that which built
the Parthenon and carved the Zeus of Olympia.
But since the days of Protestantism the analogy has

vanished, and human art has been thrust into a
worldly attitude, nay even into hostility with our stern
and gaunt devoutness. It is wellnigh incalculable
what we have lost by this disastrous dissociation, how
much on the one hand religion has suffered, by abandoning those elements which are its most essential
features, and by casting aside the beauty, in order to
proclaim the uncompromising severity, of holiness. It
is equally plain how much mankind has suffered, how
artistic and passionate natures have been repelled and
disgusted, and have preferred what were branded as
the pleasures of sin to the joyless pilgrimage through
the dry and stony waste into which the fanatic priest
would blight our beautiful world. Had the Greek
priests or the Greek oracles ever attempted such a
crusade against art, their reign would indeed have
melted like winter snow, and one generation would
have been sufficient for the abolition of their inhuman
creed.

The remaining feature is again one which we find
rather in Catholic than in Protestant Christianity, yet
even there the analogy is rather apparent than real. I
allude to the embracing of all the pleasures of human
nature within the services performed in honour of the
gods. Divine service included the whole range of
human enjoyments; there were even in the cult of
Aphrodite allowances made for the gratification of the
animal nature, and the phallic processions show plainly
how the mystery of the origin of life was not excluded
from religious services, in spite of the coarse features
which it necessarily presented. But more generally,

sport and religion were not opposed by the Greeks, but identified. 'Ye play and keep your feasts,' say the Athenians in Herodotus to the Spartans, 'and thus betray your allies and the interests of Greece.' We have it paralleled in the books of Moses : 'The people did eat and drink and rose up to play.' What the play included is plain enough[1]. This feature is really quite ancient, and opposed to any modern cult ; and the apparent jollity of Catholic feast-days, is, as I have said, no real analogy. The Catholics are in so far nearer to the Greek standpoint that they do not set their face against human enjoyment on feast-days. They permit relaxation and pleasure at the special seasons set apart for the highest religious ceremonies. But their pleasure on these days is relaxation, and not service ; it is a relief after the worship, and not the worship itself. Here is the fundamental difference. The Parisian goes to the theatre on Sunday evening, because it is a holy day, and because he is allowed relaxation and amusement after his devotions at High Mass. The old Greek went to the theatre to honour and serve his god ; his praise was offered up not before, but in, the performance. To him his pleasure, intellectual and physical, was not a concession made by the jealous Deity to his weakness, but a privilege granted by the gods who sanctioned and encouraged his enjoyment.

The psychological result of this feature in Greek religion was a certain earnestness in Greek pleasure,

[1] Cp. *Numbers* xxxi. 16, and the references there given to previous passages.

a certain seriousness in sport, which brings out a
curious analogy to the modern nation of all the most
widely diverse. The English people possess (I suppose) only two attributes which are also to be found
prominently among the Greeks—an overweening self-
conceit and contempt for all outsiders, and this remarkable mixture of seriousness and sport. But
in the latter case the result has been reached from
opposite points of view. The Greeks made their
serious pursuits, especially their religion, sportive—
real feasts, in the proper meaning of the term. The
English have made their sports serious by making
them important ends, and success in them a coveted
distinction. This was also done by the Greeks in
the case of the public games; but still the first origin,
even here, was not amusement, as with us, but religion.

It is indeed true that the Christian Church has
talked much of joy and gladness, and has affected to
have feasts, like the heathen feasts, in which religion
and present pleasure might be combined; but how is
this reasonably consistent; how is it possible for a
faith which despises the body, which hates and con-
demns bodily pleasures, which extols self-denial and
continence, to combine with these features an element
of present enjoyment and indulgence? Thus the
Christian feasts which have any real jollity about
them are those where old heathen customs have survived, and have been allowed to foist themselves
upon the creed which proscribed and persecuted them.
It is therefore rather in British sports than in religious feasts that we should look for an analogy to

the Greek combination of wild pleasure and deep
earnest.

I need not lay stress upon sundry smaller resem-
blances, which are likely to spring up anywhere from
like circumstances, such for example as hereditary
priesthoods coming to be considered comfortable
sinecures[1], or the transaction of love affairs under
the guise of attending religious worship—a thing of
every-day occurrence among strict people now-a-days,
and of course equally so at Athens, where young
women could not show themselves usually, save in
a stray peep through an open door. Human nature
will assert itself in some way, despite all restrictions, nor are religious meetings exempt from contributing opportunities for this great purpose.

I turn in preference to an isolated argument in a
speech of Demosthenes[2] which touches a very important feature in the religion both of our day and of the
Greeks. He is arguing that to deprive certain men
of immunities once granted by the State is a breach

[1] Isocrates, vol. ii. p. 118, ed. Teubner. Hermann-Stark (*Griech.
Antiqq.* i. p. 412) quote from Dionysius Halicarn, a passage implying
the public sale, and even the letting by lease of such priesthoods, which
were evidently comfortable posts, abounding in indirect perquisites, like
the post of parish priest, or incumbent of a private chapel, among us.
The prophet or seer (μάντις) was like his Hebrew parallel, not attached
to any temple, and often, as in the case of Lampon the founder of Thurii,
of great social importance. A passage in Demosthenes *concerning the
prize of trierarchy* (*Or.* 51, p. 1234) compares the jealousy of the rhetors,
who would allow no one to advise the assembly but themselves, to the
jealousy of men *holding a peculiar priesthood as a monopoly.* This
implies that it was generally a valuable monopoly.

[2] πρὸς Λεπτινήν, 495.

of public morality and not to be tolerated. 'But,' says he, 'it may be urged that these immunities from State duties include in them immunities from doing honour to the gods, by spending money upon expensive public processions and contests, and it may be urged as impious and wrong that any man should be relieved from his duties to the gods.' In fact the heaviest public burdens at Athens were expensive religious celebrations. 'Such an argument,' says the orator, 'I consider full of danger (δεινόν). For if, when they have no other way of proving it just that you should take away these privileges, they seek to do it by relying upon religious grounds (ἐπὶ τῷ τῶν θεῶν ὀνόματι), how can we acquit them of a most impious and dangerous proceeding? For in my opinion, whatever a man does, claiming the express countenance of the gods, should surely be such an action as will not appear base in the eyes of men.'

Here then we have an instance, where we should hardly have expected it, of the attempt to make religion override morals, and of defending a piece of common injustice under the plea of conferring honour upon the gods. How often this sort of argument was used in the Middle Ages, I need hardly recall to a reader of history; it has recurred whenever dogma has been made of primary importance, and where the belief in creeds has been more anxiously promoted than the doing of justice and loving of mercy. But this was not an usual fault in Greek religion, and I cannot but regard the passage as a very singular one, and not yet sufficiently considered.

I now conclude this brief chapter upon a very large subject. But the classical student will find no difficulty in illustrating for himself the general principles sketched out here in rough outline. The chief rule to be observed in this, as in all other branches of our social enquiry, is to go straight to the authorities themselves, to draw from the fountain-heads, and not be content with the speculations of learned modern thinkers. The trouble and tedium of this labour will be relieved by the consideration that where our conclusions must be formed from scattered hints and delicate inferences, no single writer can exhaust the subject, and every honest gleaner who comes after him may fairly expect to contribute materially to the result. The same text which has revealed nothing to one will suggest to others in a different frame of mind many interesting points; nay, even a reperusal discovers to the same mind many things at first overlooked or imperfectly understood. The subject of the present chapter, if fully treated by a man of English common sense, who read Greek literature through with a special attention to the allusions bearing upon it, would form the argument for a useful and instructive volume.

CHAPTER XIII.

THE BUSINESS HABITS OF THE ATTIC GREEKS.

THERE still remains an important feature of Attic civilisation, demanding a special chapter. It is well known that one of the great features in Hellenic life was its extensive commerce. From Homer's days, when the Greeks first began timidly to creep after Phœnician traders round the headlands which bounded their seas, down to Attic days, when they had long made the Mediterranean their own, and when Athens was like London, a centre for traffic extending from Pontus to Tartessus—during all this period there were few things in Greek life more important than trade. Thus the colonies were founded under solemn religious auspices, and at the advice of the Delphic oracle ; their sites were specially chosen as suitable for intercourse between the sea and the interior ; we may even fairly suppose that all the important wars which took place during the colonising epoch of Greek history were wars concerning commercial interests, and with a view to protect trade interests.

We are told, for example, that almost all Greece joined in a war between Chalcis and Eretria about

C C

the Lelantine plain—a war alluded to as contemporary by Theognis, and concerning which even Aristotle still preserved anecdotes. Historians have justly pointed out the inconceivability of all Greece being interested about some fields in Eubœa, and that the rivalry of the two towns concerning settlements at the mouth of the Euxine was the real cause, while a local dispute was the occasion, of the war [1]. The passage into the Black Sea was always of vast importance, as even in Attic days the toll levied for passing Byzantium formed a considerable item of revenue; and it appears that the Greek trading cities supported Chalcis or Eretria according as pre-existing treaties secured to them protection or immunity from either party. Thus the Lelantine war, a name unknown to our ordinary compendiums of Greek history, was a great war of traders, and in Thucydides' opinion (i. 15) the only *general* struggle throughout historical Greece previous to his own day.

These facts, as well as the innumerable speeches on commercial disputes left us by the orators, show that there was a strong trading instinct in the Greeks; and there were large portions of the community supported in this way; that it was, as now, the best avenue to wealth. No sketch, therefore, of social life among the Greeks would be complete without some notice of their business habits. Here, as elsewhere, we shall only note laws and customs as illustrative of manners and of sentiment. Innumerable books have already been written on Greek laws, on Greek notions

[1] E. g. E. Curtius, in his *History of Greece.*

of property and of inheritance, on Greek political economy and social science. We are here concerned with the subjective aspect of the facts which have been collected, and which has as usual to be gathered from stray hints and implied ideas.

Perhaps the first essential for a proper development of business habits, and for a proper confidence in the stability of trade, is a good and complete system of law, promptly and firmly administered. Without this all contracts are suspicious, and all speculations mere gambling. As we might expect, then, Attic trade could not exist without a system of Attic law, upon the general features of which the following reflections may be interesting to the reader.

If he will look into any of the Classical Dictionaries or books of antiquities on this subject, the first point which will strike him is the rich and varied terminology—the host of technical words employed, showing a well-developed and complicated system. The school-boy who knows no law is puzzled with demurrers, and bills of exception, and judgments by default, and affidavits and counter-affidavits ; every case appears to be tried in two or three forms, and no decision seems final without appeals, and motions for re-hearing. All these things indicate an advanced and systematised conception of law, and the orators justly appeal to them as a proof of culture. Not only were there a vast number of distinct courts and boards of magistrates, before each of which the procedure was distinct ; but a variety of procedure was allowed in the case of each single definite action.

'Solon,' says Demosthenes [1], 'did not grant to those who sought redress from injury some single course of procedure in each case, but many and divers.' For he knew that men would not be equal in boldness and daring, and that variety of procedure would help the simpler and gentler litigant. 'He desired then that every one should receive even-handed justice. How can this be done? By permitting many avenues for attacking wrongdoers; as, for example, in the case of theft. Is your case strong, and are you confident? arrest him; you run a risk of paying 1000 drachmæ (if the case goes against you). Are you too weak for this? lay an information before the archons; they will do it for you. Are you afraid even of this? bring an action against him. Are you a diffident person, and so poor as not to be able to pay the 1000 drachmæ? have a (preliminary) trial for theft with him before an arbitrator, and you run no risk.'

Thus, in his famous speech against Aristocrates, the same orator (p. 643) gives an exhaustive discussion of the laws concerning homicide, in which he enumerates and explains six distinct procedures, but in this case not for the same crime, but for six different shades of homicide—accidental, justifiable, in self-defence, and so forth. Similarly in the case of personal quarrels, it is noted that the Attic law allowed an action for every step in the quarrel, from the use of language 'calculated to provoke a breach of the peace,' through common and aggravated assault, up to grievous bodily harm and manslaughter. 'I

[1] *In Androtion*, p. 601.

wonder,' says a speaker [1], 'whether there is any excuse or pretence discovered among you which will
save a man from punishment if he is convicted of
assault and battery. For the laws with a very different spirit foresaw the excuses which would necessarily arise, and guarded against their being allowed
to develop; as, for example, there are actions for
using offensive language, which they say are intended
to prevent people from being betrayed by scolding
into striking one another. Again, there are actions
for insult (αἰκίας), for this purpose, that any one being
worsted in a quarrel should not defend himself with
a stone or potsherd [2], but rather await the vindication of the law. Again, there are actions for
wounding, lest from wounding manslaughter might
arise. The most trivial, I suppose, that for abusive
language, guards against the final and worst offence,
that manslaughter may not arise from a man being
gradually led on from bad language to blows, from
blows to wounds, from wounds to death; but in the
laws there is redress for each of these, that they may
not be decided by the passion or caprice of the individual.' It was indeed thought disreputable to
bring an action for abusive language [3], an offence
atoned for easily by an apology; but in theory this
is the fundamental conception of all sound law, and

---

[1] *Dem. against Conon*, p. 1263.

[2] The usual natural weapon seems to have been an ὄστρακον, and this
means, not a shell but a potsherd. Cp. Lysias, p. 37.

[3] Cp. Lysias, *Or.* x. p. 117 : ἀνελεύθερον γὰρ καὶ λίαν φιλόδικον εἶναι
νομίζω κακηγορίας δικάζεσθαι. But in this case the defendant had asserted
that the plaintiff had killed his own father.

no nation can be said to have realised it till they
have abandoned the license of the tongue as well as
the carrying of arms, and thus openly declared their
dependence on law, as opposed to force.   Thucydides
notices this carrying of arms as a sign of barbarism
in the Greece of former days, and Aristophanes introduces the same feature as a mark of troublous and
disturbed times, in his *Lysistrata*[1].   The suppression
of piracy abolished this habit, which was so completely
gone from Attic usage that there were not even laws
against it.   It may indeed have been also a provision
of the Peisistratids for their own safety, continued
afterwards on democratic grounds.

But even more marked than this abandonment of
arms was the strong feeling about ὕβρις, as they
called it, about personal violence, which they would
not allow even towards slaves.   The writer of the
tract on the Athenian polity complains indeed of the
absurd independence allowed to slaves, who dressed
like freemen, and were not afraid to meet you in the
street.   'Of course,' says Æschines[2], 'the lawgiver
was not so anxious about slaves as to make such a
law, but what he did insist upon was the repression
of the habit of personal violence, which was fostered
through violent treatment of slaves by freemen, and
of the poor by the rich.'   Hence any man, whether
concerned in the outrage or not, was allowed to
prosecute the offender.   There is a very interesting

---

[1] v. 556: ἢν παύσωμεν πρώτιστον μὲν ξὺν ὅπλοισιν ἀγοράζοντας καὶ
μαινομένους κ.τ.λ.

[2] *In Timarch.* § 16.

oration of Isocrates on the question (*Or.* 20) where
he plainly puts forward, that it is not the hurt, but
the insult, which is intolerable to a free citizen, just
as now-a-days to touch a man in anger constitutes an
assault. At the end of the speech the orator calls
upon the crowd present to stand forward and join
him in the accusation. This strong feeling was even
made the lever of raising odium against a man.
Apollodorus complains that his enemy Nicostratus
sent in a city boy from a neighbouring house to
pull up his roses, and injure his garden, in order that
if Apollodorus struck or bound him, they might bring
an action for ὕβρις against him [1].

These examples are from the criminal code of the
Athenians, which was perhaps developed at an earlier
period, and therefore may have been the most complete; but the very same variety of procedure, the
very same accuracy of subdivision, and the same sensitiveness may be found in their civil code [2]. Closely
allied to this feature, in fact another aspect of it, is
the subdivision of legal business, and the confining
of each special court to a special class of business.
Thus the Eleven, who were the chief police officers
at Athens, were occupied with burglars and thieves
and with offenders condemned to death. The chief
archon had charge of heiresses and orphans. The
king archon tried cases of impiety, and those that
arose in gymnasia. The polemarch, again, investi-
gated all cases of patrons and clients. There remain

---

[1] Demosth. *In Nicostr.* p. 1251.
[2] Cp. ib. *In Lacrit.* p. 940.

the generals, and they were concerned with the navy
and army, but not with mercantile shipping. We
have, on the other hand, in the extant fragments of
Aristotle's lost Πολιτεῖαι, a list of special boards of
magistrates supervising trade and commerce, which
is perfectly astonishing. There were ἀγορανόμοι, and
σιτοφύλακες, and ἐπιστάται, and ἐπιμεληταί over everything, even τῶν κοπρώνων, and in separate boards for
the city, and for the Peiræus[1]. There were besides
μετρονόμοι, there were ἀστυνόμοι, who controlled flute
girls and dancing girls, and scavengers ; πωληταί, who
superintended the sale of the state monopolies ; also
ἀποδέκται and λογισταί. These boards consisted of
numbers varying from five to fifteen, and all had
fixed duties. If we consider the number of these
offices, and how a great number of citizens over
sixty years of age were constantly employed as arbitrators and on juries, we must conceive the Athenian
people as very much oppressed by their self-imposed
duties. Thus, then, the Attic legal system afforded
ample means of redress, and by specialising its courts
apparently provided for a prompt and accurate treatment of disputes.

But all these courts and boards and arbitrators
were subject to an appeal to the sovereign people,
sitting in juries—the *dicasteries* of which we hear so
much. It was not thought proper to appeal to these
juries until other modes of settlement had been attempted, and many of the extant orations delivered

---

[1] See especially the fragments quoted in Müller's *Fragg. Hist. Græc.*
vol. ii. pp. 119. sqq.

before them apologise for apparent litigiousness; but still any one who could speak well, or pay a good speech-writer, seems to have been ready enough to go before them. Consequently owing to press of business, including not only city affairs, but those of their allies, owing also to the interruptions caused by critical wars or revolutions, these juries were generally far in arrear of their business, and there was great difficulty and tediousness in getting a case settled. The authorities speak of it just as our fore-fathers did of a suit in Chancery[1]. It is, I suppose, for this reason that we find suits revived after a lapse of eight or ten years, nay even of eighteen years[2]. There was indeed a statute of limitations, which laid down five years as the longest period of delay in bringing an action, but it is clear that the Attic juries were often in arrear of their work, or, like the Irish juries, did not feel themselves bound by this law, and listened to a litigant, if he spoke well, even though he was excluded from pleading by the statute book.

I have thus been passing from the strong side of Attic law to its weaknesses. Indeed it seems to me that all the inferior courts, all the preliminary en-quiries, were on the best possible footing, but that this appeal to a large and untrained body of men as jurors was thoroughly unsound, and fraught with great

---

[1] Cp. M. Strübing, *Aristophanes*, &c., p. 94, and Dem. κατὰ Στεφ. ά, p. 110.

[2] Cp. Lysias, p. 109; Dem. *In Meid.* p. 541; *Pro Phorm.* p. 950; *In Nausim.* p. 986.

mischief. But both the Greek and the English trial by jury were at one time the great political safeguard against state oppression and injustice; and, owing to this origin, free nations become so attached to it that they are blind to its defects. And just as Ireland would now benefit beyond conception by the abolition of the jury system, so the secured Athenian (or any other) democracy would have thriven better had its laws been administered by courts of skilled judges. For these large bodies of average citizens, who, by the way, were not like our jurymen, unwilling occupants of the jury-box, but who made it a paid business and an amusement, did not regard the letter of the law. They allowed actions barred by the reasonable limits of time; they allowed arguments totally beside the question, though this too was illegal[1], for there was no competent judge to draw the line; they allowed *hearsay* evidence[2], though that too was against the law; indeed the evidence produced in most of the speeches is of the loosest and poorest kind. Worse than all, there were no proper records kept of their decisions, and witnesses were called in to swear what had been the past decision of a jury sitting in the same city, and under the same procedure[3]. This is

---

[1] Cp. Lysias, πρὸς Σιμῶνα sub fin., and on its violation κατ' Ἐρατ. p. 124, Lycurgus, p. 149.

[2] Cp. Dem. πρὸς Εὐβουλ. p. 1301: οὐδὲ μαρτυρεῖν ἀκοὴν ἐῶσιν οἱ νόμοι. He quotes an exception made by the law in the case of deceased people, κατὰ Στεφ. β. p. 1131: ἀκοὴν εἶναι μαρτυρεῖν τεθνεῶτος.

[3] Cp. the witnesses called in by Demosthenes in evidence of past decisions against Meidias (p. 541).

the more remarkable, as there were state archives, in which the decrees of the popular assembly were kept under the charge of the public γραμματεύς. There is a most extraordinary speech of Lysias against a man called Nicomachus, who was appointed to transcribe the laws of Solon in four months, but who kept them in his possession for six years, and is accused of having so falsified them as to have substituted himself for Solon. Hence there can have been no recognised duplicate extant, or such a thing could not be attempted. So again, in the *Trapeziticus* of Isocrates, it is mentioned as a well-known fact, that a certain Pythodorus was convicted of tampering with state-documents, signed and sealed by the magistrates, and deposited in the Acropolis [1]. All these things meet us at every turn in the court speeches of the Attic orators. We are amazed at seeing relationships proved in will cases by a man coming in and swearing that such a man's father had told him that his brother was married to such a woman, of such a house. We find the most libellous charges brought against opponents on matters totally beside the question at issue, and even formal evidence of general *bad* character admitted. We find some speakers in consequence treating the jury with a sort of mingled deference and contempt which is amusing. ' On the former trial of this case,' they say, ' my opponent managed to tell you many well devised lies ; of course you were deceived, how could it be otherwise, and you made a false decision ;' or else, ' You were so puzzled

[1] Isocrates, p. 365.

that you got at variance with one another, you voted
at sixes and sevens, and by a small majority you came
to an absurd decision[1].' 'But I think you know well,'
says Isocrates, 'that the city has often repented so
bitterly ere this for decisions made in passion and
without evidence, as to desire after no long interval to
punish those who misled it, and to wish those who
had been calumniated were more than restored to
their former prosperity. Keeping these facts before
you, you ought not to be hasty in believing the prosecutors, nor to hear the defendants with interruption
and ill temper. For it is a shame to have the character of being the gentlest and most humane of the
Greeks in other respects, and yet to act contrary to
this reputation in the trials which take place here. It
is a shame that in other cities, when a human life is at
stake, a considerable majority of votes is required for
conviction, but that among you those in danger do
not even get an equal chance with their false accusers.
You swear indeed once each year that you will attend
to both plaintiff and defendant, but in the interval
only keep your oath so far as to accept whatever the
accusers say, but you sometimes will not let those
who are trying to refute them utter even a single
word. You think those cities uninhabitable, in which
citizens are executed without trial, and forget that
those who do not give both sides a fair hearing are
doing the very same thing[2].'

It is not desirable here to go at greater length into

---

[1] Cp. Dem. p. 1104.   [2] Περὶ ἀντιδόσ. p. 314.

a description of the jury system, especially as this has been so ably done by Mr. Grote. It is, however, worth repeating, that the inherent defects of any jury system were enhanced at Athens, not only by the absence of any judge to rule the law of the case, but by the great size of the jury. Many obvious inconveniences resulted. In a complicated will case, the speaker says[1] : 'I had intended to make out a table of the descendants of Hagnias and show it to the jury, but then I considered that those sitting far off would not be able to see it, so I must explain it in words.' Mr. Grote has also enlarged upon the psychological peculiarities of a crowd, as contrasted with single individuals, and how subject it is to sudden impulses. That these were common among Attic juries, appears from the allusions to cases where the defendant could not obtain a hearing, and when the jury decided without knowing both sides of the case. There were men condemned to death at Athens in this way[2], a melancholy and striking proof that with

[1] Dem. p. 1053.

[2] Here is a significant passage in Lysias' 19th oration (*about the property of Aristophanes*, p. 143): 'For I hear, and suppose that most of you know, that calumny is most dangerous. This is best illustrated by the case of several people being prosecuted on the same charge. For in most cases those who are last tried escape, because your anger being appeased, you listen to them, and are then willing to accept argument and evidence. Consider then that Nicophemus and Aristophanes died untried, before any one heard them convicted before him of any crime. For no one even saw them after their arrest, nor were their bodies even given back to their friends for burial, but so great a calamity fell upon them, that in addition to all the rest, they were deprived even of this.' Cp. the same orator, pp. 164-174, and Isocrates, ii. pp. 201, 208.

all the complications and refinements of their legal
system, these final decisions of large juries were a
great flaw, in fact an inherent weakness which could
not be avoided.

I do not consider the poet Aristophanes as a critic
of any historical value, and all inferences from his
broad farces must be received with the greatest
caution and suspicion ; but if he has anywhere criticised fairly and to the point, it is probably in the
Wasps, where he pulls to pieces the jury system. It
may be that the appointment of temporary magistrates, even to legal offices, made the decisions of
special boards uncertain, and that an appeal to the
people was necessary when bitter personal animosities might exist between the judge and the litigant ;
but still the principle of the Athenian sovereign
people sitting down to decide questions of law was
really absurd, and led to endless chicanery. Hence
the universal prevalence of what was called συκοφαντία,
a profession followed by men of impudence and ability
in speaking, who lived by carrying on 'speculative
actions,' as our newspapers now absurdly call them,
and who extorted money from rich and quiet people
by a sort of *chantage*, not very different from that
practised in modern Paris. All the Attic literature
is full of allusions to these villains, and it seems hopeless to deny their existence or their power. Rich
men at Athens are even described in Xenophon[1] as

---

[1] Cp. Xenophon, *Œconom.* c. ii. and xi. § 21, which show that the
Athenian people were stricter about the duties than the rights of property. This is implied in Plutarch's *Nicias*, quoted above. p. 315. See

cowering with fear before the scrutiny of these inquisitors. Of course such a state of things must have
told severely on the business habits of the age.
Honest as were the juries in their decisions, there
was nevertheless a great uncertainty in going before
them, and the timid quiet man was at a serious dis-
advantage.

As regards the literature of Greece, the effect of the
same system has been completely ruinous to Greek
legal oratory. Here the vastly inferior Romans are
on a far higher level. Take for example such a case
as that of Curius v. Coponius, argued in court by the
orators Crassus and Antonius, and often mentioned
by Cicero. The testator had left his property *after
the death of his son* to a friend, believing at the time
that he was sure to have issue. The supposition
proved false, and after the testator's death the legatee

also the curious description of the advantages of poverty in Xenophon's
Symposium, c. 4. § 29 sqq. Charmides describes his life while rich as one
of misery and constant fear, always subject to heavy state duties, and
moreover *he was not allowed to travel.* Now he is not only free, but
threatens others, travels where he likes, and the rich make way for him
in the streets (ὑπανίστανται δέ μοι ἤδη καὶ θάκων, καὶ ὁδῶν ἐξίστανται οἱ
πλούσιοι). The most barefaced attempt is that recorded by Hypereides
(p. 45, ed. Blass), where Tisis indicted Euthycrates on the ground that his
property was not private, but public, merely *because it was too large,*
amounting to sixty talents. On this occasion the accuser was disgraced ;
but there were cases where the Athenian Demos confiscated property to
obtain money, just like the worst Roman Emperors. Thus Lysias says,
p. 185 : 'knowing as I do that the Council in office, when it has sufficient
funds for its administration, does not go wrong ; but when it gets into
money difficulties, it is obliged to entertain indictments and to confis-
cate the property of citizens, and to follow the public speakers who give
the most unprincipled advice.'

claimed the property. But the next of kin argued that the conditions had not been fulfilled. The testator's son had not died, seeing that he had never been born. They therefore claimed the inheritance. It was argued on the other side, that though the letter of the will was unfulfilled, this arose merely through the incautious wording of the testator; that his clear intention was to leave the property to his friend, in default of issue by death or otherwise; that it would therefore violate the intention of the will, were its wording strictly interpreted. This remarkable case, one of the widest applications and of the greatest importance, occupied the leading counsel of Rome for days; and they spoke to competent tribunals. No such case occurs even in Isæus' court speeches. The nature of the jury degraded the eloquence of the bar at Athens. Subtle points of law, large questions of equity, were thrown away upon them. Simple and plausible statements, plenty of random evidence, and personal abuse, were the qualities desirable in their harangues. Above all, appeals *ad misericordiam* formed the staple conclusion of every speech, and it was not held undignified for the greatest aristocrats, or grotesque for the most notorious bullies, to burst out crying in court, and to bring in their children to excite the compassion of the jury by their tears. Such a course was taken even by Meidias, a sort of mock Alcibiades in Demosthenes' day, and a man of notorious profligacy and violence, though nearly fifty years of age. Such is the course expected from Conon, a member of a sort of hell-fire club at Athens, when he had knocked down a man in the street, danced upon him with his friends, and then clapped his arms and crowed in imitation of a victorious cock. It was done too by the rich Aphobus, when he begged the jury to diminish his fine [1]. 'I should not wonder,' says another speaker, pleading against two young *mauvais sujets,* ' if they try to weep and make themselves objects of compassion. But I ask you all to consider how shameful, nay rather iniquitous it is, that men, who have spent their own substance in eating and drinking with noted scoundrels, should now set up tears and lamentations in order to obtain other people's property.'

I cannot but hazard the conjecture that the Athenian juries, with their native shrewdness and intelligence, their great impulsiveness, their tendency to override strict law, and their facility of being gained over by clever speaking though beside the point, were more like the Irish juries of the present day than any other parallel which can be found. They had the same merits and the same defects, and were there not a controlling judge in the Irish Law Courts, the decisions would often be as irrelevant as those of the Athenian people [2]. There can be no doubt

[1] Cp. Dem. pp. 873, 1259, 1271.

[2] Thus in pleading a demurrer, it was generally thought necessary to prove the justice of the case on its merits apart from this formal objection to the adversary's procedure, though before a strictly legal tribunal such a digression should not be allowed. Cp. the argument to Demosthenes' speech ὑπὲρ Φορμίωνος, the freedman of Pasion. The pleading was a παραγραφή. ἅπτεται μέντοι καὶ τῆς εὐθείας ὁ ῥήτωρ . . . τοῦτο δὲ πεποίηκεν ἵνα ἡ παραγραφὴ μᾶλλον ἰσχύῃ, τῆς εὐθείας δεικνυομένης τῷ

that the eloquence of the French bar is much more like what we find in the Attic orators, than what is thought decent elsewhere in modern times. Subtle, therefore, as the Greeks were beyond all other men, there is no subtilty in their legal oratory, which is the very best field (as we should think) for displaying it. There is not a single legal principle argued by them which would be of use to modern lawyers.

No doubt the nature of the jury was one strong reason, but there was also another—the poor and shabby nature of Greek speculation, as compared with either Roman or modern civilisation. For here we come to a branch of social life in which the most advanced of the ancients were on a level with the Middle Ages rather than with ourselves. When we look into the business habits of the Attic Greeks, as shown in their trade, and their general treatment of wealth and produce, we are surprised to find them as children compared to the average German or Frenchman, not to say the average Englishman or Scotchman. The causes were many and various, but before we consider them it is well to hold fast the main facts, and they are plain enough before our eyes. In the first place the States of those days knew nothing of free trade, and were constantly passing prohibitory acts, preventing exports and insisting upon special imports. Thus it was forbidden

---

’Απολλοδώρῳ σαθρᾶς. On the question of applying torture to obtain evidence, and the universal confidence in its efficacy, I have spoken above p. 240. Demosthenes' clients constantly profess the same principle, cp. Dem. p. 875.

that any man should cut down more than two olive trees each year, because the State of Athens required much olive oil, and could produce it of the best quality. Thus there were all manner of restrictions upon the corn trade; Attic traders were not allowed to import corn elsewhere, and foreign corn ships which touched at Peiræus were required to sell two-thirds of their cargo to the Athenians.

When a scarcity arose, we have attacks upon the corn traders in Peiræus—apparently respectable foreigners settled there—like those which form so melancholy a feature in the ignorance and the tyranny of the Middle Ages; nor do I know of any document more disgraceful to Greek culture than the speech of Lysias *against the corn-factors.* All the necessary and natural causes of enhanced prices are overlooked, and, with the true spirit of the Middle Ages, the dearness is wholly attributed to a combination among the factors. The famous picture in Manzoni's *Promessi Sposi,* reproduced as it was last year in Italy—during which there have been corn riots and orders from the authorities fixing the price of bread —does not exhibit more stupidity and ignorance than the tone assumed by the orator and presupposed in his audience. 'For when the prytanes referred their case to the council they were so

[1] The *Voce Libera* of Genoa, in describing one of these disturbances at Sassari, says (impression of 24th June, 1874) 'Quel signor Sotto Prefetto ordinava indi immediatamente l'arresto di tutti i spacciatori. Il pane nascosto dai rivenditori fu venduto al pubblico al prezzo della nuova tariffa ... I signori spacciatori posti poi in libertà, colla massima tranquillità vendono il pane secondo il prezzo fissato dal municipio.'

enraged with them, that some of the public speakers declared *that they ought to be handed over untried to the Eleven that they might put them to death.* But as I considered it a very serious thing that the council should admit such a precedent, I stood up and said they should first be tried,' &c. This, indeed, seems fair in the speaker, but the whole tone of his speech appeals to the passions of the mob. It appears from the speech that these factors were not allowed to purchase more than fifty *phormi* at a time, and they were not allowed to charge more than an obol profit upon a certain measure. The accused confesses that he bought in a larger quantity, but on the advice of the archons, who partly deny the imputation, and partly equivocate about it. The orator argues that even if the archons did advise it, it was illegal, that in any case the price ran up in such a way that the ordained profit had been exceeded, and for this he demands instant death as the penalty. 'In the case of other criminals,' he concludes, 'ye have to learn their offence from the accusers, but the wickedness of these men ye all know. If then ye condemn them ye will act justly, and *make corn cheaper, but if not, dearer.*'

This harshness may be partially owing to the important fact that these factors were not citizens but aliens, and that they thought it worth while, like the Jews of the Middle Ages, to run such risks as these on account of their large profits; yet still the whole attitude of the accuser is thoroughly absurd, and the laws to which he refers intolerably mediæval. On the other hand, however, the concentration of trade, or at least of most of the trade, in the hands of foreign residents and of freedmen, produced a peculiar feature in the protective laws which we are considering. For the aristocrats, or even the body of well-to-do citizens, despised trade, and looked down upon this sort of lucre. Consequently all the prohibitory trade-laws were for the protection of the whole state, that is of the whole body of citizens, and never for the protection of some privileged class of traders, or of some trade-union powerful enough to influence the legislature. Thus the protective laws of Greece, so far as we know them, do not exhibit that odious feature so common in European history, and which forms far the worst feature in the past treatment of Ireland by England. All the other oppressions of the Irish were of no importance compared with the destruction of their trade for the benefit of English producers. The traders in Greece were a despised and politically insignificant class, who were often plundered by the State, but never protected or favoured beyond some trifling immunities. There is evidence that Pericles knew better, and sought to induce them to settle at Athens; but he was of course far in advance of his time. We may accept what we know of Athens on this point as similar to the practice of other states, but probably more generous than many of them. In some of them trade was an actual disqualification for public life.

But the limitation of profits by law points to a still more decisive feature—the ignorance that money has, like any other thing, a changeable market value, and that interest for its use is no robbery and injustice, but a most useful principle in trade. Many of the Greeks held the now exploded notion, that all taking of interest partook of the nature of usury, and except in the case of wardships and trusts, when the law insisted upon money being usefully invested, they looked upon the man who lived by investments as a bad character, and his trade as a disreputable occupation. Even Aristotle, a most advanced thinker in some respects—even Aristotle shares this national blunder, and talks the most arrant nonsense in his *Politics* about money being an essentially barren thing, which cannot produce any offspring or increase without violating nature. There is evidence that in practical life these foolish prejudices could not assert themselves. As the later Athenians began to consider trade an honourable road to riches, and aristocrats like Nicias were known as careful trade-masters, so there were instances, as in the case of wards' property, where interest was acknowledged fair ; but still we should note the persistence of the old stupid prejudice, not merely in ordinary minds, but in those of advanced thinkers.

The general absence of machinery made any large employment of hands in manufacture impossible, and the light Attic soil and limited territory made such things as the Roman *latifundia* equally so. There was considerable subdivision of labour, the various parts of a shoe, for example, being made by different classes of workmen, and so far as the population

could produce with the help of manual slave labour
there was in many parts of Greece a considerable
export trade. But still anything like our wholesale
modern manufactures they could not attain. In
another direction too, the want of mechanical development was fatal. As they had no equivalent
for our paper or token money, beyond transferable
bonds, they had no such thing as a money-market,
no such thing as state banks; in fact none of that
surprising and, to ordinary men, inconceivable sort
of trade—stock-exchange business. The objection
to interest already mentioned cooperated in this
result, but I fancy the main cause was the want of
current and universally accepted tokens. The Greeks
were like the old arithmeticians trying to solve complicated questions as compared with our modern alge-
braists. Here the discovery of the use of universal
symbols, easily handled, and so thoroughly accepted
as to make us forget the reality in the background,
has made a complete revolution in the way of handling
and solving problems, as well as in our power of
unravelling intricacies and mastering complications.
The modern stock - exchange stands to the old
methods of trade in the same relation. The symbols in a share-list are as unlike the realities as the
x and y of an equation, and I believe are often used
without any conscious reference to reality by business
men.

Here we have a modern development, not second
to any of those which separate us from former centuries; it is really a new discovery. This is indeed

fortunate in some respects for students of Greek literature. If the mysteries of such a system as our stock-exchange were argued in the Greek orations, the translation and comprehension of these documents would indeed be a most ungrateful labour. Fortunately the cases discussed in the Attic courts were of a far simpler kind. The charges of fraud, which are many, are of the vulgarest and simplest kind, depending upon violence, on false swearing, and upon evading judgment by legal devices. There is not a single case of any large or complicated swindling, such as is exhibited by the genius of modern English and American speculators. There is not even such ingenuity as was shown by Verres in his government of Sicily to be found among the clever Athenians. In this feature the Roman aristocracy seems far more advanced.

We have already discussed one reason of the poorness of Greek legal oratory—the nature of the tribunal; but it seems to me that the facts just stated must also be taken into account, as contributing to the same result. The smallness of the Greek states, so conducive to political development, was certainly unfavourable to large and safe trade. Their constant wars and disputes made all international treaties transient and uncertain, and the keen speculator, the man of large views and great capital, never had the same scope for his talents which was afforded him by the Roman Empire, or by the great modern states. The nearest approach to a large business was that established by the banker

Pasion [1], of whom I shall speak presently, who was the generally acknowledged banker for all foreign merchants, and who commanded credit all over the Hellenic world.

But there were several laws tolerated in the best Attic days, which prove in themselves that even the Athenians had no real capacity for business, or any complicated conditions of property. I allude above all to the well known ἀντίδοσις, or exchange of property, about which we hear so much in the Attic orators. In the first place their taxes were not consolidated rates, regularly payable, but occasional and varying charges, imposed in the case of war or other public necessity, and generally for the outfit of a fleet. The tax was then struck in proportion to assessed property. It was actually the law at Athens on such occasions, that any citizen who was charged for the outfit of a ship, and thought that some richer man had been passed over, could challenge this other to accept the burden, and if he refused, compel him to exchange properties for the space of a year. No law can be conceived more absurd. Any man whose property consisted in numerous investments, could not transfer it to a stranger without the chance of absolute ruin, and even in the treatment of landed property, a change of masters for one year might destroy the labour of a life, and ruin all the improvements and the outlay

---

[1] I should observe that Nicias had a thousand slaves farmed out in the mines of Laurium, but this was a business not requiring the large intelligence shown by Pasion.

of years of toil. We can imagine a man preferring to submit to the most unjust burdens in preference to such an alternative. Of course it disposed men to hide their wealth, to give false returns of it, and to resort to all manner of deceit, as we can see from the speeches of Isocrates and Demosthenes (against *Phœnippus*) on this subject. It seems simply the legislation of the Athenian mob about property which they had never possessed and did not understand, for the other alternative—that Athenian properties were small or of a simple nature, like our rentals of estates—is refuted by the many descriptions of property in the orators. It is in fact inexplicable that any intelligent people should have tolerated such a law, and it is conclusive against the business capacity of the men who tolerated it.

Similarly absurd were the arrangements for managing the ships so provided. It often occurred that two or more citizens were required to join in the expense of keeping a single ship afloat. In such cases the system obliged one of them to fit out the ship, and sail with it till his share of the time had elapsed, when the other was bound to come out, and take the ship with all its appointments off the hands of his partner in the burden. He might, however, consider these appointments too expensive, or unsound, in which case he might refuse to take them, and refit the ship for himself. Can anything more clumsy or foolish be imagined? In the case from which we know these details, that of Apollodorus against Polycles, the former had gone to great expense and done everything very handsomely. He was to be succeeded in a certain time by Polycles, but the latter, though he came out to the fleet in the Thracian waters, delayed or refused to take over the ship. He alleged that Apollodorus' ostentation had made him fit out the vessel absurdly, and that he could not take the appointments at a valuation : he did not, and perhaps could not, supply himself in Thrace ; so Apollodorus was left for months on duty beyond his time, and was sent by the generals on all manner of state missions, which inflicted upon him expense and hardship[1]. But suppose he had left the ship and gone home, what would have been the consequences? And in any case, he was a grumbling and unwilling paymaster, who only waited for his return to bring an action against Polycles, and recover from him his undue expenses.

Such a system was evidently not based on sound business principles, and shows a want of the faculty which the Romans and many modern nations have acquired. Thus, to revert to money matters, we find frequently in the orators assertions that intelligent men of business hid money in the ground. This was one of the pleas put forward by the guardians of Demosthenes[2], to show that all the property of his father had not come into their hands, and yet the elder Demosthenes was evidently a thriving man of business, keeping up two large establishments for the purpose of two distinct manufactures. Though the

[1] Demosthenes, pp. 1206, sqq.
[2] κατ' Ἀφόβου, β. p. 830.

allegation was false, the fact of its being made, and not ridiculed, shows that such stupid hiding of money was not uncommon.

But it must be added that some weight should be allowed to the bad condition of banks and banking. We know that in older days the temples were used as safe places for the deposit of treasure; we also know that loans could be effected from them, so that they may be regarded as the earliest banks in Greece. But we are in ignorance as to the terms they imposed, and indeed it may be doubted whether they lent money to individuals, and did not confine themselves to State loans. In Attic days we find no attempt made by the State either to work or to guarantee a bank, and thus this important business was left to individuals. I say to individuals, for the remarkable business invention of joint-stock companies was beyond the reach of the old Greeks, who never advanced beyond ordinary partnerships[1]. There were then a large number of private banks and bankers at Athens, on account of its great trade. They seem distinct from the money-lenders, a class of men who set up chiefly in the Peiræus, and made speculations by lending on the security of ships and their cargoes,

---

[1] There were indeed private societies called θίασοι and ὀργεῶνες, to which both women and slaves were admitted, and which were founded on some religious basis. But these private devotions are always mentioned with disfavour. On the other hand each member had a right to borrow contributions of money from the rest, if he got into sudden difficulties, such for example, as being taken prisoner in war. Ransoms were often paid in this way, and when money was so dear, these organized mutual aid societies must have been very useful. Cf. Foucart, *Les Associations réligieuses chez les Grecs.*

getting from 25 to 30 per cent. if the voyage prospered, but losing their money if the ship foundered at sea. This sort of lending was so general, that one of the speakers asserts it impossible for any ship to leave the Peiræus without having recourse to it [1], so that it must have corresponded to our maritime insurances. These money-lenders, who were looked upon with suspicion and dislike, were an inferior class to the bankers, one of whom at least, the well-known Pasion, became so important a man as to be granted the freedom of the city. Yet even among them failures were frequent [2]; there is indeed an absurd statement that when they were asked for money which had been lodged with them, they made much ado about giving it up, thinking that it had become their own. Perhaps the safest and clearest evidence as to their insecurity is the fact stated on the bankers' side, that when Pasion's son had his choice of a business worth 60 minæ, or a bank worth 100 in respective yearly income, he justly, says the orator, preferred the ownership of the business establishment, on account of the insecurity of an income made from other people's money [3]. This speaks volumes on the point, and is in itself sufficient evidence of the bad condition of banking.

But there were many difficulties in the way, among which the chief was the injustice with which aliens

---

[1] Dem. πρὸς Φορμ. sub. fin. There is a most interesting text of a συγγραφή, a bond of agreement, quoted in Dem. πρὸς Λάκριτ. p. 926. Cp. Büchsenschütz, *Besitz und Erwerb*, p. 506.

[2] ἀνασκευάζεσθαι (τὴν τραπέζαν) was the term for a bank breaking.

[3] Dem. ὑπὲρ Φορμ. 948, 9. On Pasion cp. Mr. Sandys' *Priv. Or. of Dem.* ii. *Introd*, and Schäfer's *Demosthenes u. seine Zeit*, vol. iii.

were treated even at Athens, and the disadvantages
under which they laboured in asserting their rights.
As these men had most of the trade in their hands,
and also most of the banks, it is evident that there
were insuperable obstacles in the way of any real business development.   We happen to know a good deal
about the celebrated banker, Pasion, because his son
Apollodorus very frequently retained Demosthenes
as his special speech-writer, whereas his supplanter in
the bank, and chief adversary, once, at least, secured
the same orator's services, and this in a family dispute
about Pasion's will and bequests.   From these various
speeches, which are strong evidence of the complete
impartiality of Demosthenes, who abuses the contending clients in turn according as he is paid, we can
sketch a picture of the social position of this remarkable banker, who was evidently something of a power
in Greece, and probably one of the best-known men
in the crowded Peiræus.   It is not necessary for our
purpose to detail the routine of his business, which
consisted of keeping account books and making accurate entries just as at present.

This Pasion then had been a slave, from what
country we know not, and had been the property of
bankers called Antisthenes and Archestratus. Being
found both hardworking and upright, he was promoted to places of trust and enfranchised. He then
set up on his own account, and became so important
a man as almost to monopolise the banking of the
traders to the port of Athens. He commanded credit
all over the Greek world, and having done great
service to the State, among other things by present-

ing it with 1000 shields (of which he owned a manu-
factory), he was made a citizen, and enrolled in the
respectable Acharnian deme[1], by public vote. His
wealth was sufficient to enable him to fit out and equip
five ships of war at his own cost. He kept a mistress,
whom he afterwards made his wife, but of whom
we hear a very bad character from her own son,
Apollodorus. For Pasion, doubtless perceiving that
Apollodorus was an ostentatious and idle man, with
no business habits, and that his second son, Pasicles,
was a mere child, promoted a trusty slave, Phormion,
just as he himself had been promoted, by making him
free, and finally, as he became old and anxious to
retire from business, allowing him to manage the
bank at a fixed rent of nearly £700 a year. But in
order to secure Phormion, he seems to have made himself a debtor to the bank for eleven talents (£2,680).
This Phormion certainly was a man of good business
habits, for in a great monetary crisis, when all the
other Athenian banks broke, he, in spite of his heavy
rent, sustained the public credit, and remained un-
shaken. It was probably for this that Phormion, ten
years after Pasion's death, was also made an Athenian citizen.

Pasion on his death-bed betrothed his wife with a
large dowry to this Phormion[2], and in other respects

[1] The Attic demes varied greatly in respectability, as appears from Demosthenes' speech πρὸς Εὐβουλ. p. 1316; the fact also that Pasion, whose
life was spent in the Peiræus, was enrolled in the distant Acharnian
deme, shows that the people were not tied down by local considerations,
when electing a new citizen by public vote.

[2] It was a usual proceeding for Athenians on their deathbed to betroth
their wives to some friend or relation, especially if he was appointed

treated him with great favour. He probably saw
that his business would go to ruin if left to his sons.
Hence there arose long and grievous litigation. Apollodorus charged Phormion with falsifying the will; he
openly accuses him of having seduced Pasion's wife,
Apollodorus' mother, and insinuates that the younger
son, Pasicles, who sided with Phormion, was the result of this intimacy, and not his legitimate brother.
Phormion, on the other side, accuses Apollodorus of
being an immoral spendthrift, and endeavouring to
plunder the faithful supporter of his father's house of
his honest profits. We need not go farther into the
quarrel, except to observe that Demosthenes appears
to have been first employed to argue a demurrer for
Phormion, which he easily carried, but afterwards to
have written speeches for Apollodorus in this litigation, and against other adversaries. His abuse
of his old client contrasts curiously with his former
abuse of his new client, and shows that the Athenian
speech-writers were justly contemned as plying a
venal and unprincipled trade. It is hard to make
out the real state of the case between the contradictory statements, both of them compiled with art by
Demosthenes; but this is certain, that though Pasion
was so rich and important, he bore about him the
traces of his low origin. Even his son Apollodorus
apologises in court for his own bad manners. He
attributes his common face, his quick walk, and his

executor in the will. This was not the least against Attic sentiment,
but to treat a freedman with this confidence and intimacy, was thought
strange even then. It is a melancholy proof of the low consideration in
which women were held.

loud voice to the misfortune of want of breeding[1], faults which constituted ἀναίδεια or *vulgarity*, according to Attic taste. Doubtless the son was more ostentatious than the wiser father, who was evidently a quiet, peace-loving man, even conniving at injustice to avoid incurring enmity. He lived in the Peiræus, and in later years came up seldom to Athens, though he seems to have died there.

His business was so large that he did not know all his clients. In the interesting speech *against Callippus* we have a very characteristic picture of him from his son. He is asked by this distinguished but unprincipled Athenian whether one Lycon of Heraclea had lodged money with him, and he answers (p. 1238) 'that he thinks so, but that if Callippus would like to go down to his bank in Peiræus, he could at once find out accurately.' 'Do you know why I ask, Pasion?' replied the other; 'I am consul (*proxenus*) for the Heracleots here, and as this man was killed by pirates, it is better for me to have the money than a fellow who is a metic living in Scyros, and a mere nobody.' This was Lycon's partner, entered in Pasion's books as the proper recipient of the money in case of Lycon's death. But Callippus thought that as a proxenus he could make good some claim,

---

[1] Cp. Dem. p. 1125: ἐγὼ δ' ὦ ἄνδρες Ἀθηναῖοι τῆς μὲν ὄψεως τῇ φύσει καὶ τῷ ταχέως βαδίζειν καὶ λαλεῖν μέγα οὐ τῶν εὐτυχῶς πεφυκότων ἐμαυτὸν κρίνω, and a similar passage, p. 982. The opposite character, or what we should call gentlemanliness, was σωφροσύνη, which Plato (*Charm.* p. 159 B) fully explains as the habit of doing everything in an orderly and quiet way, including walking in the streets, conversing, and every other phase of life.

if he once got possession of the money. 'Callippus,' replied Pasion, 'I desire to do what I can to please you (indeed I should be mad if I did not), yet so as not to lose my reputation or my profits. I have no objection to tell this to the two friends who were witnesses, or to his partner himself. But if they will not agree when I tell them, do you talk to them yourself.' 'Never mind, Pasion,' said the other, 'if you like you can force them.' This was Pasion's own story to his son. Of course the other people refused to have anything to say to Callippus' barefaced proposal, and then the money was given back to the proper owner. But Callippus actually prosecuted Pasion in his old age, for giving back the money without his consent as proxenus, having (as he alleged) agreed not to do so.

On the other side, the *Trapeziticus* of Isocrates gives us a very dark picture of this very Pasion's conduct when he found aliens in his power. He is openly accused of embezzlement, and even of forgery. Of course, in the absence of Pasion's defence, we cannot say how far these grave charges were well founded ; but the very fact of their being made in open court, shows that the character of this prince of bankers was not above suspicion. When combined with the previous case, my impression of Pasion is that he was a dishonest man of great shrewdness, who knew when to cheat and when to permit himself to be cheated with advantage.

But however this may be, these stories show very well the position of the richest banker at Athens, even after he had become a full citizen. We can imagine how submissively and cautiously those must have conducted themselves who were ' aliens and hence of no influence[1].' It may therefore be inferred that the utterance of Demosthenes is hardly exaggerated, when he says that honesty and ability in business were held a surprising combination.

These facts, which might doubtless be paralleled by many more through Greek literature, seem to prove conclusively the poor development of a real business spirit among the old Greeks. We do not expect these qualities now-a-days from artists and poets, and even from politicians; but among so many-sided a people, to use a very hackneyed expression, it is somewhat surprising that their wide coasting trade, and their connections all over the Mediterranean, did not generate those qualities which I believe to have existed in some degree in the Phœnicians, and still more in the Romans. The Phœnicians appear to have had a like trading genius to their brethren the Jews, and to have brought even their seamanship to a far higher level than the Greeks. At least Xenophon, in his *Œconomics*, speaks of going down to Corinth to see the big Phœnician ship, just as we should speak of visiting the ' Devastation,' and the points which he remarks are the extreme neatness and tidiness of the internal arrangements. Everything was stowed away in the smallest possible space, and ready to hand. I know

---

[1] ' Callippus,' says the speaker (Dem. p. 1243), ' was one of our citizens, and well able to do either benefit or harm, but Cephisiades was both an alien, and of no influence, so that it is not credible that my father would promote his interests against justice, rather than do justice to Callippus.'

no more certain sign of superior abilities than this very feature of cleanness and tidiness. The Romans swayed no doubt a great Empire, welded into an unity very different from the Hellenic unity, if we may use so misleading a term of the Greeks in general. But there was also something in the Roman *gravitas*, an instinct of adherence to bonds and promises, which Cicero, as I have quoted (p. 123), asserts to be foreign to the Greeks, and which is the first essential of any sound commercial prosperity.

This was in my opinion the great national blot on their character, and the principal cause of their comparative failure in this direction. I know that my judgment will be contested, that it is usual to assert the Greeks to be the greatest and most successful traders of antiquity ; but I appeal to the judicial literature in proof of the reverse, and hold that however much they may have traded, however many their ships, and various their exports and imports, all this was as nothing compared to what such a nation as the English would have accomplished in the same position. That love of overreaching, that ingrained shrewdness and intent watching of personal interests, which I have noticed all through Greek civilisation from Homer into the Attic times—these were an obstacle to all their perfection, and not least in those very branches of civilisation which are their proper field. Trade does not often fall into the hands of the aristocracy of a nation ; it is the special function of the middle classes, and hence the core of a nation must be sound, the average man must be steady and thrifty and honest, in a really mercantile people. The noblest moral principles in the leading men, the highest moral preaching among the philosophers, are not adequate, nor are they a sure sign of a solid national quality. It seems to me, upon a careful review of a very wide and conflicting body of evidence, that the Greeks had these great leaders and preachers, but that the average man was below the level of fair honesty.

It will be said in reply that the most noted trading races the world has seen have been notoriously dishonest, that the Phœnicians and Jews are striking examples of this side of the question. Even admitting this doubtful statement, and without entering into a full discussion, which would indeed require a separate volume, I shall merely observe that the Phœnicians and mediæval Jews succeeded chiefly as the Greeks succeeded, either by opening up an intercourse with savages, where mere enterprise secures great advantages, or as members of a subject race, constrained by the severest and most bloody penalties to keep within the limits of fairness. So far the Greeks succeeded in trade also. The early colonists plundered the barbarians unmercifully under the guise of barter; the subject classes at Athens, such as the cornfactors of whom I have spoken, were compelled, by fear of execution uncondemned, to keep within some limits, and under this compulsion, they may have induced people to deal with them, and so prospered under a supervision unjust as well as severe.

But when I speak of great and successful commerce, I speak of it in a free and dominant race, carried on upon large and fair principles, and without any con-

stant thought of overreaching those with whom we
deal. I speak of it, and of the business habits it
engenders, as we find it in such countries as England
and Belgium. This I do not believe ever to have
been attained by the Phœnicians, or by the Jews till
the present day, when they have taken their place as
free members of the great free nations among whom
they dwell.

The considerations hitherto adduced may be corroborated by adverting briefly to that highest and
most distinctive business of the Greeks, which is
beyond the scope of this book—I mean the pursuit
of politics. Here, if anywhere, we can find tests of
the average morality which was thought respectable,
and of the degree of dishonesty which incurred social
censure. And here too we find ample materials for
forming a judgment in the large literature of Attic
oratory, in the numerous charges and counter-charges
which have survived from the violent party conflicts
of the day. It would of course be absurd to take
these violent attacks, these systematic λοιδορίαι, as
they were called, to be sober evidence. But it is
still more absurd to reject them altogether, when
directed against some hero of modern historians, and
to believe that the Attic public would have tolerated
open and persistent charges of perjury and corruption
against a man of unsullied probity and honour, if such
there was among the politicians of the day. The
perpetual charges of treason, of corruption, and of
malversation can only have been tolerated because
the atmosphere of Attic politics made such things
easy and common, or because the ordinary acts of

public men were such as could easily be interpreted in this way.

I take up the case of the most respectable and the most eminent of the later Attic politicians. Demosthenes is a man whom all modern historians have united in lauding to the skies. We are told now that our understanding the history of the epoch actually depends on our appreciation of the purity and the spotless honour of this great man. We are told that all the attacks upon him were foul and dishonest charges by men who were themselves corrupt, and that there is no tittle of evidence to convince us that their assertions had any real foundation in fact.

I will not now dispute this verdict. I will not urge what I have often urged before, that modern philologists unconsciously transfer their admiration for the literary artist to his character, and think that because he was the greatest of orators he must also have been the noblest of men. But rather, admitting this estimate, I will ask how did it come that the Attic public tolerated all manner of scurrilous attacks upon him in the public courts? He prosecutes Æschines for corrupt malversation on an embassy, and is met by counter-charges of the grossest kind. The result of the trial is the acquittal of his adversary. In our day such an action, if met by such a defence, and not successful against it, would necessarily ruin the accuser. Later on in life, the same Demosthenes is formally returned by the Areopagus, the gravest and most solid court at Athens, for embezzling the definite sum of 20 talents, and condemned in a formal trial

by a large jury, in committee of the popular assembly,
consisting of 1500 members. We find moreover the
verdict of Greek posterity agreeing with this sentence.
Plutarch, no severe judge, and a great admirer of genius,
is convinced that Demosthenes though a great, was not
a good man. And such is the opinion of his age[1].

How are we to account for this remarkable change
of public opinion? How is it possible that the same
facts, and the same evidence (if indeed Plutarch had
not better grounds than we) can lead to such diverse
estimates? I cannot but think that we estimate
Demosthenes by the moral standard of our northern
and western Europe, where dishonesty of a vulgar
and obtrusive kind has become so dissociated from
political life, that we cannot conceive it co-existing
with true greatness. If a Prime Minister in our day
were openly charged with taking bribes, the accusation could not be overlooked for a moment. Either
the accuser or the Minister must necessarily be ruined.
But there are many nations, political nations too, in
the world, where such is not the case, and where indirect profits are allowed to politicians by public
opinion. It is no doubt our wealthy and splendid
aristocracy, whose constant attention to politics has
rendered bribery in most cases impossible, in all disgraceful. Indeed this condition of things is said not
to have existed till the present century, and perhaps
the morality of public men in our dependencies may
not have yet attained to it, for we know that the
practice of taking large presents from native princes
existed quite lately in our Indian Empire.

[1] Plutarch, *Demosth.* c. 14, and comp. *Dem. et Cic.* c. 3.

Now this is precisely the state of things which was normal at Athens, and the honesty of Demosthenes was not the honesty of a Lord Althorp, but rather of a Warren Hastings. It was not even the highest honesty at Athens, for we have in Phocion and in Lycurgus men who were never exposed to the attacks which are still extant on Demosthenes.

But I desire to insist upon this, that we must rather blame the low average of political honesty at Athens, than degrade the great orator to the position to which modern morals would condemn him. In fact the ordinary rules of political life at Athens tolerated abuses which may perhaps still exist in America, but which are happily almost extinct in England. I allude above all to the abuse of allowing indirect profits to be made by politics.

Our evidence on this point, and in the case of Demosthenes is too precise to be refuted, and shows us that he must have done many acts in his life which left him open to charges of dishonesty which he could only rebut by a general appeal to his character, but which he could never directly refute. All his accusers agree in speaking of his great wealth in mature life[1]. It is the common theory of the moderns that he made his fortune by speech-writing. But as he abandoned this profession early, and as we

---

[1] He never denies this in the *De Corona*, or appeals to his poverty as a proof of his honesty in politics. The disclaimer in the 3rd epistle, which Blass quotes (*Att. Ber.* iii. p. 45) only strengthens my conviction that the letter is spurious. At the same time I fully believe that Demosthenes applied all his wealth lavishly to public objects, and hence seems to have left no considerable fortune.

never hear of its being a very lucrative one, such an explanation is quite inadequate. How do his opponents account for it? Hypereides is peculiarly precise, and gives us exactly the information which is interesting for our present purpose. 'As I have often before said in public, judges, you allow many profits without demur to generals and politicians—not by the permission of the laws, but from your easy temper and good nature—making this one condition, that what they make must be for your sake, and not against your interests. And I suppose that Demosthenes and Demades, from the mere decrees passed in the city, and their relations with aliens, have each received more than 60 talents, apart from gifts from the Persian king[1].' We have the same thing asserted in the speech for *Euxenippus*[2] quite generally; as to Demosthenes, we have in the accusation of Deinarchus the same facts worked out in detail[3]. We are given a list of decrees which he was supposed to have carried not without gratuities for doing so, and then we are informed that he had an immense property of ready money—as much as 150 talents—the evidence of the large profits of his politics.

I can see no reason to doubt, and I am convinced no contemporary doubted, the truth of these statements as to his wealth, and his manner of acquiring it. But I repeat that it was looked upon as fair and honourable in the society of that day, provided it was obtained from friends, and not from enemies of the democracy, and provided it was spent liberally on

---

[1] Cp. Hypereides, κατὰ Δημ. fr. x. [2] Col. xxiii.

[3] §§ 41 sq., 69 sq.

public objects. In fact the ordinary formula of accusation all through these orations is not that the accused took bribes and benevolences, but that he took them καθ' ὑμῶν, against your interests, and this was the only criminal point. Accordingly in Demosthenes' replies, so far as we can judge from the *De Corona*, he never denied his wealth ; he never denied that he had received large monies on the score of politics, but he insists that he never acted or spoke except in the interests of the democracy.

It is this aspect of political life at Athens which explains to us how every speaker was permitted to attack his opponent with charges of corruption. If they all made indirect profits (with solitary exceptions like Phocion's) the distinction between harmless presents and corrupt bribes was one which could not easily be established, and every case was liable to challenge. There may have been many where the present from a foreigner or resident alien to the politician who befriended him meant no more than a lawyer's fee in the present day. But the abuse of this indirect and underhand method of payment was notorious enough, and contributed largely to the downfall of the independence of Athens.

These very important illustrations from public life will establish upon different grounds the somewhat poor estimate I have made of the business habits of the Greeks. We cannot conceive their commerce managed on higher principles than their politics. And there is reason to believe that the politics of other Greek cities stood rather lower than those of Athens in the scale of morality. The Spartan public men were notoriously venal, and whenever we hear of a defeat like that of Chæronea, from Thebes as well as Athens comes the cry 'nous sommes trahis'—the sure sign of a corrupt state of public morality[1]. Whether this cry was true or false it shews the general belief that as generals and politicians were in the habit of receiving presents, their loyalty could not be secure in the moment of danger.

The judgment on Demosthenes' public character in the foregoing pages, which was scouted as a paradox not worth refuting when it first appeared, has since been adopted by several eminent German critics, and consequently by English scholars. It was the learning and enthusiasm of Schäfer, the specialist on Demosthenes, which had led men astray. The reader will find a calm and sensible review of the controversy in a recent work, which adopts a great many of my ideas, with ample acknowledgment in many places—Adolf Holm's *Greek History*, iii. 370 sqq.

[1] Cp. Lycurgus apud Diodorum xviii; Deinarchus, κατὰ Δημ. § 74.

CHAPTER XIV.

THE SOCIAL ASPECTS OF GREEK ART.

I WILL now endeavour to fulfil my promise of completing this book with some account of the effects of art on Greek life. There is a sort of general belief, not only among scholars, but among the modern public, that, owing to a fortunate conspiracy of men and circumstances, the old Greeks were in constant contact with ideal beauty of all kinds, and that to this we owe the unparalleled influence they have since exercised upon human culture. There is also a widespread conviction that art, which is to-day the apanage of the few, and which all the efforts of modern governments have been unable to spread among the masses, was then public property, and universally appreciated. No account of Social Life in Greece can be complete which does not discuss these wide-spread convictions, and test the bold assertions which they imply.

Perhaps many of my readers will have become somewhat impatient at the detail with which I have brought before them the commonplace and even vulgar features of the old Greeks. We have heard enough, they will say, of the perpetual political squabbles of the Greeks, of their want of veracity, of their greed. We have heard too many citations from their 'comedians and their cooks.' Was not their society for all that the most brilliant and culti- vated the world has seen? How comes it that they are still our teachers, in art, of grandeur and purity both of conception and execution? Surely the splendid remains which affect us so deeply are only shattered fragments of a vast world of ideal beauty, which must either have moulded all society, or the study of art must be deemed an idle amusement, and of no prac- tical effect on the minds and morals of men.

It is necessary that these suggestions should receive some answer; but the difficulty and complexity of the problems concerned are such that I did not venture to approach them in my former editions, when I had not yet visited the country itself, and studied personally the relics of Greek art in the museums of southern Europe. And even now I must confine myself strictly to the social sides and effects of Greek art—the only aspect which I venture to discuss. The social importance of the fine arts can hardly be said to date from before the Attic period, if we except Poetry, the old national property of the Greek. The efforts of the tyrants were indeed most important, and prepared Greece for the culture of its golden age, but still the culture of a court can hardly be called national culture, and we may treat the fifth century art in Greece as a mere introduction to its truly national development.[1]

There can be no doubt that in later days Athens,

---

[1] I have given some curious specimens from Athens in my *Rambles and Studies in Greece*, pp. 61, seqq.

Delphi, Olympia, Argos, Ægina, and a host of other towns were so studded over with temples, and statues, and votive monuments, as to be almost museums or palaces of art. We know that the very commonest household furniture, lamps, pots and pans, chairs, stools, were all designed with singular grace and elegance. We seem to find a society so interpenetrated with good taste that boorishness is a crime and want of sensibility a strange disease. And yet this is the society which has been pictured in the preceding pages with no very flattering colours. It would seem at first sight either that this moral picture is too dark, or that the ordinary views of Greek art are too bright, or else that its effect on social life was less than we would fain believe. But we must not hasten to a conclusion till we have carefully considered the facts before us.

It is a commonplace at the opening of all departments of Greek history to enlarge upon the exceptional natural advantages of the Greeks for development and culture. They were surrounded, it is said, by the most various beauties in nature, and by the most unvarying beauty in man. These reacted naturally upon their minds, and gave them that æsthetic taste, that *Schönheitsinn,* which produced their incomparable art. To some extent these assertions are true, but must be received, like most of the statements of enthusiastic Greek philologists, with great caution.

I can affirm from personal observation that the physical features of Greece and of the other coasts of the Ægean are exceedingly beautiful and various,

and that not even Italy and Switzerland together
afford a greater wealth of grandeur and of pic-
turesqueness.   It is also probable that the somewhat
colder climate of classical days, together with better
cultivation, made the vegetation richer and more
lasting, and so obviated the only flaw which now mars
the perfect beauty of the country. If then a perpetual
fair prospect could stimulate art, Greek landscape
must certainly do so.   But nevertheless, as has been
long since observed, the old Greeks hardly ever speak
of scenery; they seem not to have admired it consciously, as moderns do, so that we might almost
argue the thesis, that an appreciation of landscape
beauty is the result and not the cause of a long-
developed artistic sense. Some unconscious effect
may perhaps be conceded, but surely an art either
professedly human in form, like their sculpture and
painting, or strictly artificial, like their architecture,
which never imitated inanimate objects, can hardly be
said to have been much influenced by the beauty of
surrounding nature.

When we approach human beauty as a stimulus
to art, the case is exactly reversed.   There can be
no question of its direct and clearly felt influence,
but the facts commonly alleged about its extraordinary
frequency are open to grave doubt.   As far as I can
make out, all the general descriptions of Greek beauty
come from very late authorities, who, as the nation
was then certainly not exceptionally handsome, are
evidently describing the older Greeks from the extant
statues and pictures by great masters.

Thus all the Germans quote with the highest faith and

approval a passage from Adamantius' *Physiognomica*, as conclusive in the matter.[1] The reader will naturally wonder who Adamantius was, and what opportunities he had of observing the classical Greeks. It will hardly be credited that this Adamantius is an obscure sophist of the fifth century A.D., whose Physiognomics are a tract borrowed from a similar composition by Polemo, another sophist of the third century A.D.! An examination of these tracts, which can be found in old libraries, will show how clearly Adamantius was describing, not real Greeks, but statues and pictures. He borrows a chapter on the complexion of divers races (περὶ χροιῶν καὶ τριχῶν) from Polemo, who cannot distinguish them by natural features, because, he says, they have become extremely mixed, Syrians with Italians, Macedonians with Orientals, and so forth. Here, however, Adamantius foists in a paragraph of his own. But if, he says, the Hellenic or Ionic race is anywhere to be found in its purity, its features are as follows: and then comes the description.

It is not creditable to the German savants, that such a passage as this has been copied in book after book as evidence on Greek physiognomy, and as evidence valid against the appeals to fact of Cicero and Dion Chrysostom! When will classical scholars learn to weigh evidence? For a perfectly trustworthy witness in this matter, the great phil-Hellene, Cicero, lets

---

[1] Εἰ δέ τισι τὸ Ἑλληνικὸν καὶ Ἰωνικὸν γένος ἐφυλάχθη καθαρῶς, οὗτοί εἰσιν αὐτάρκως μεγάλοι ἄνδρες, εὐρύστερνοι, ὄρθιοι, εὐπαγεῖς, λευκότεροι τὴν χροίαν, ξανθοί, σαρκὸς κρᾶσιν ἔχοντες μετρίαν, εὐπαγεστέραν, σκέλη ὀρθά, ἄκρα εὐφυῆ κ. τ. λ. ὀφθαλμοὺς ὑγρούς, χαροπούς, γοργούς, φῶς πολὺ ἔχοντας ἐν αὐτοῖς· εὐοφθαλμότατον γὰρ πάντων ἐθνῶν τὸ Ἑλληνικόν.

F f

the truth out accidentally. 'How rare,' he makes Cotta say, 'is manly beauty? When I was at Athens, you could hardly find one in each crowd of youths.'[1] Dion Chrysostom, who in his twenty-first oration (περὶ κάλλους) makes complaints like Cicero of the decay of beauty, plainly intimates that he uses sculpture as his evidence of older times. He even suspects that its excellence, and the decay of later sculpture may account for the supposed facts, but insists that this seems only partly the case, and that the natural type might have also changed. This, say the Germans, was in the decay of the nation, and the passage is indeed quoted as evidence of such decay. But I deny that we have any evidence for physical decay, and believe such a statement as Ernst Curtius', 'that among Greeks ugliness was the exception,' to be completely unwarranted.

It is quite plain to me that Adamantius is merely describing the types of statues and pictures, or in other words the ideal types of Greek art, as if they were the ordinary characteristics of the nation. More particularly what he says about the lustrous eyes is plainly copied from a feature so peculiar in the Pompeian wall-paintings, that it was probably one of the leading features in Greek pictures. The faces in the figure subjects on these walls are certainly copied from the older masters, and the eyes, which are very large and lustrous, seem consciously and manifestly exaggerated. They are exceedingly wide open, and somewhat staring. The remaining authorities cited

---

[1] *De Nat. Deor.* i. 28, 'quotus enim quisque formosus est? Athenis cuum essem, e gregibus epheborum vix singuli reperiebantur.'

in the handbooks are Lucian, Achilles Tatius, and other such very late writers.

It seems therefore that our only good evidence for the extreme beauty of the Greeks is the very chaste and noble type preserved in their sculpture, and their general reputation among the Asiatics, a reputation partly due to their intelligence, and partly to the fair complexion which is always admired by dark races. And yet the extreme fixity of type in the sculpture of the Attic age seems to me to point in a different direction, and show that as the archaic face of the stele of Aristion and other such remains is far too ugly to represent contemporary faces, so the more beautiful type of the Parthenon is far too ideal, and is probably built upon a few exceptional models, refined and exalted by the artist's genius.

It may then be possible that Greek sculpture had no higher suggestion afforded among living forms than might be found among the finer boys at Eton and Harrow, many of whom are strikingly handsome and well-formed, but yet do not belong to a nation of perfect beauty.[1] Indeed the real portrait busts of the Greek philosophers are not by any means handsomer than the busts of a similar number of intellectual Englishmen.

The result of the whole matter is this, that we must not overrate the influences of human beauty or of landscape beauty on the art of the Greeks, and must not imagine that we or any other people only require similar conditions to develop similar results. Their

[1] Of course the Greek habit of taking athletic exercise naked gave the sculptor an immense advantage for studying the play of muscle.

conditions were no doubt favourable, very favourable, but by no means so miraculous or exceptional as they are usually made out to be. In other directions, indeed, they were splendidly equipped, partly by the national genius, and partly by accident. The very flexible, rich, and graceful language which the race developed out of the primitive Aryan gave them scope and power in their poetry which has never since been attainable; it suggested to them music and rhythm; it induced harmony and grace of expression. While the subjective arts of poetry and music were provided with this perfect organ, the objective arts of architecture and sculpture found in the marble quarries of Pentelicus, of Paros, and elsewhere a material which infinitely facilitated and enhanced great effects, and even made many things possible which could not else have been imagined or attempted. But this richness of material only affects the artists and not the masses, and possibly the excellence of a man's language will not go one step towards making him a poet, if he have not the inspiration of the muse.

I have gone at some length into this question of the natural conditions of art in Greece, in order to make it plain that however national and diffused it became, this was due to careful study, and training, and legislation, and not to a sort of natural compulsion, when every man and every scene were so lovely that people who only copied them produced great works of art. As natural beauty was always the exception among Greek men, so artistic talent was also rare and special. Enthusiasm for Greek art is very laudable, but must not be allowed to misstate the facts and mislead our judgment.

There are other circumstances in the social position of Greek art which in most societies would have tended to impair its popularity and its influence. We may lay it down as a rule that all Greek artists were professionals, and that the admiration of the public did not then take the form, as it now does, of amateur attempts, or of the desire to fuse dilettantism and professional art into one another. We know, indeed, that the Seven Wise men were mostly poets as well as statesmen, and in Solon especially we have a notable example of the combination. We also know that turbulent aristocrats could be both mercenaries and poets, like Archilochus, Alcæus, and Timocreon the Rhodian, and that their personal passions and animosities were told with such power as to make them of world-wide interest. But we must remember that in those early days poetry was often studied not as an art, but as the only known means of setting forth personal history, philosophic teaching, or moral reflections. A great deal of the early elegiac poetry of the Greeks has this grave prosaic tone, and it is eminently true of the poetry of Solon. If these men did write *scolia*, or other truly lyrical pieces, they seem to have been slight and unimportant, though some of them became very popular.

But when poetry became developed into a strict art,[1] the poet became as thoroughly a professional

---

[1] It seems to me that we may fix this point at the time when the Dorian choral lyric school finally overcame in public favour the personal lyrics of the Æolians. So long as simple monostrophic outbursts of

artist as the sculptor or the painter. The appointment of the poet Sophocles to a military command appears to have excited ridicule, and I cannot remember any politician attempting to compete in his art except the tyrant Dionysius, whose tragedy appeared as much out of place as Sophocles' strategy. Indeed, the whole tone of Greek literature indicates that, although most Greek boys learned the elements of music, and some celebrated men, like Cimon, kept it up sufficiently to sing a song gracefully at an evening party, no practical proficiency was expected or indeed commended in amateurs. The case is still stronger when we consider painting and sculpture. The elements of drawing were, indeed, in the third century B.C., a part of education; but that an amateur should paint or carve anything worth speaking of, or be esteemed for so doing, seems to have entered nobody's imagination. A group, said to have been by Socrates, was set up in the Acropolis, but Socrates had begun sculpture as a profession, and his work, if it was really

feeling were popular, any cultured aristocrat might aspire to be a poet. But when the complicated antistrophic systems and epodes of Stesichorus and Arion, along with elaborate figures of choral dance, were recognised as the national form of lyric poetry, when the poet must be a chorusmaster or teacher of *orchestic*, and an accomplished composer as well, we naturally find him rapidly becoming a paid professional. The poet mercenary made way for the mercenary poet. This change seems to have been effected in the end of the sixth century. Anacreon is the last celebrated artist who cultivated that form of lyric poetry which we moderns understand and imitate. The only analogy which remains to the really Greek lyric performance, as recognised by the whole nation, is the *ballet*, which combines music and elaborate dancing; but we have abandoned the text of the story, which is only conveyed by dumb show.

there, and if it had any merit, was no example of amateur genius.

We are now living in an age full of weariness, and therefore full of distractions. Men are becoming manysided for want of clear aims, for want of honest diligence, for want of the patience to become masters of detail, for the sake of vanity, or by reason of ennui. So the fashion has come in of substituting a social intimacy with artists for a thorough appreciation and understanding of their art. Men obtain a reputation as connoisseurs, and pick up what they want for the purpose of gossiping about art in society, by interloping in studios, lounging behind scenes, and intruding at rehearsals. Every trivial detail about the non-artistic side of artists' life is eagerly repeated. Intimacy with their homes, or homeliness with their intimates, is a matter of pride, and men rave with vapid extravagance about the personal worth and the social charms of people whose art, though great, is the only contribution they have ever made to the good and the happiness of their age. Every great artist is assumed to be a social genius also, as if the history of genius in all its developments did not preach the contrary conclusion, and teach us that a man of great genius, which means a great specialist, is likely to be simple and even stupid in general matters of intelligence, as well as eccentric, if not worse, in matters of morals.

In the decay of Greek society, when politics had passed away, and men came to attend to other things, we find artists attaining some such social adoration, but of this time it is not my province to speak in the

present book. Through the Attic age on the contrary, we find that as amateur performances in art
were held of no value, so professional artists were
prized for their art alone, and did not attain through
it any exalted social position. The Greeks believed
little in sudden inspirations, in sudden flashes of
genius, in great extempore efforts. On the contrary,
they laid the greatest stress on careful training and
study, and upon the thorough completeness and
reasonableness of an artist's conception before he
attempted to carry it out. Thus while on the one
hand they discouraged amateur art, and only valued
the careful productions of a life devoted exclusively
to its object, they evidently considered the study of
art too arduous and absorbing to be a fit occupation
for a free Greek gentleman, whose first duties were
to politics and society. Hence artists were to some
extent despised among aristocratic people, and Plato
thinks it an obvious remark that no fashionable young
Athenian would choose to be even a Pheidias, with his
matchless fame as an artist, on account of his tradesman life. Again in the very interesting passage in the
Apology of Socrates, in which Plato makes him tell
how he went about seeking for wisdom, he comes,
among others, to the δημιουργοί, or professional artists,
and finds that they know their own work far better
and more thoroughly than anybody else; but they
pretend to nothing else, and are quite separate from
both politicians and poets. There appears to have
been some sort of exception in the case of architects,
if we may judge from the enormous fees paid to
them; but we do not meet any architect in Attic

society, as we do the poets, who were evidently regarded not merely as artists, but so to speak as the established clergy of the day, who looked after morals as the physicians after health.

We are therefore in presence of the remarkable fact, that in a society which more than any other honoured and understood and promoted art, the great majority of artists were not favoured, not very well paid, and rather the clients than the patrons of other men. All these considerations would seem to contradict the ordinary belief about Greek art, and prevent it from being really national, and really transfused into the masses.

But these very same causes had other effects, equally natural, which were very favourable to such a result. In the first place let us remember that by the masses in Greek towns we always mean the free population, and exclude the slaves, to whom all menial work, and all real servitude were confined. The poorest citizen was accordingly in some sense an aristocrat. He had some one to look down upon. He had something to be proud of. Above all, he had considerable leisure. Even if he condescended to trade, he could not sail in the winter, and he could not retail in the noonday heat. It is very difficult indeed to overrate the effects of this leisure, and of the advantages of having slaves, if men desire to keep a fine edge on their æsthetic faculties. It is of course a mere negative cause, but in my mind it was far more important than whatever exceptional beauty the Greeks may have had above other men.

Now all this leisure—and it was the leisure of active

and busy, not of idle and lazy, men—they spent not in trying to produce amateur works, but in criticising and comprehending the products of specially trained artists, compared with the natural models offered them by the palæstra, the festal processions, and the solemn dances, in all of which the Greeks sought to idealize human motion, as well as human rest. They did not interfere with the artist's life, they did not, so far as we know, annoy him with advice or suggestion, partly from a certain contempt and carelessness about him, partly because their energies went into politics, and they wanted to enjoy not the processes but the results of art. So then all the turbulent spirits, all the reckless and innovating minds turned to public affairs, and left the study of sculpture and painting and other arts to more sedate and sober natures, who accordingly followed the undisturbed tenor of their way, and developed the eternal laws of the ideal without hurry or agitation.

It seems to me that this is an important psychological cause of the conservatism, the chastity, the reticence of the best Greek art. Had its rewards been sufficient to entice ambitious natures, they would soon have disturbed its serenity with their personality. But here as in other great epochs, art and trade went hand in hand ; the artist was not a grandee, but a tradesman, who loves to make his work good, but makes it for an employer whom he is compelled to satisfy. Moreover, when his employer had paid him, he admitted no farther obligations of gratitude.

Thus, in Thucydides' political history, *there is not one single mention of any artist or of any work of art,* so far as I know; and even when he introduces Pericles rehearsing the glories of Athens, and speaking of the resources devised by the state for making the citizens' leisure agreeable, he speaks of contests and feasts, and elegant private appointments, but does not deign one word about the splendid artists whose genius had in that very generation given to Athens its imperishable renown.[1]

These, then, were the secular causes which tended to the stability of Greek art, and its consistency of type. A very critical public, standing apart from the artists, and regarding them strictly as a profession, accepted or rejected, but did not control, their work. Of course, almost all this work had some religious object, and this was another, and the greatest cause of its conservatism. The Greeks felt as much as we do, the sanctity of antique quaintness; and if Æschylus did not venture to compete with the Hymn of Tynnichus, we can imagine how timidly a sculptor or painter would introduce any novelty in the type of a venerated god or hero.

Let us now recall to mind the smallness of the Greek towns, and the systematic publicity of Greek citizen life; how the Agora with its colonnades, and the adjoining streets and temples formed a sort of great open-air club, with an exchange, a market,

---

[1] To any one who reads between the lines of Thucydides, and knows from Plutarch how jealous the Athenians were of Pericles' supposed intimacy with Pheidias, and how they attacked Pheidias in consequence, it will seem probable that this is the historian's silent answer to such gossip, and that he makes his hero soar above all these weaknesses. If so, the omission of all definite mention of art by Pericles is intentional, and possibly unhistorical.

and a set of law courts attached to it. In this great open-air club, in the public buildings, in the fairest suburbs, were set up all the consistent, uniform types of the great artists, along the walls were their frescoes, on the heights were their severe and symmetrical temples, in theatres and processions were their strictly conventional dramas and hymns — all these things speaking the same sort of feeling, all teaching the same sort of severe grace, all pointing to the same sort of ideal beauty. Let me add that as the citizen spent all his time in public, and only went home to eat or sleep, his house was no proper place for art, and that even family monuments, and portraits of obscure people, were set up along the most public thoroughfares[1], and therefore all the work of the artist was public and common property, not hidden in museums or private collections. The creed of the nation furthermore associated beauty, more even than goodness, with religion, and to set up a god in a form of ideal beauty was an act of greater devotion, a nearer approach to his perfection, a more lasting tribute, than to sing hymns and offer sacrifices.

Thus, the publicity of ordinary life, the publicity of art, and the publicity of religion encouraged each other, and produced an exceptionally persistent and perpetually acting influence upon the Greek citizen. But it was the exceptional genius of the artists which made this great influence the highest and the purest education towards the ideal which the world has yet seen. I am not able to explain why so many men of

[1] Cf. Pausanias, i. 2, 4, who says, 'I don't know whose the tomb is, but it was carved by Praxiteles.'

genius arose in Greece, nor do I suppose the fact will ever be explained, though it is scientifically established and has occupied philosophic historians for ages.

But I think our evidence contradicts one solution, which is that the whole nation was so exceptionally gifted, that the occurrence of the highest genius was merely the accident of a slight difference in degree among intellects all superior to those of other men. This is one of those twaddling theories about the Greeks which have been frequently opposed in the present volume. Nothing can be more false than to assert that the Greek public was made up of great intellects, and perfectly educated in the fine arts. The Greek public had its asinine qualities predominant, like every other public. As the majority of the crowd was not, I believe, beautiful, so the majority was certainly not wise. Aristophanes makes Æschylus treat it as ridiculous that an ordinary Greek public should venture to criticise poetry, and will not even submit to the Athenians as thoroughly competent. Aristophanes in his own person derides this very Athenian public, and openly rejects their decision as ignorant. The greatness of Pheidias, and the eternal monuments of his genius in the Acropolis, still new and startling in their grandeur, could not save him from odium and from persecution at the hands of these same Athenians. The painter Agatharchus, a famous man in his day, was treated with open violence as a slave by Alcibiades, and apparently without any public indignation. If Polygnotus obtained the citizenship of Athens, we may be certain that it was not his own influence, but that of his patron Cimon which obtained it for him. The tyrants of Sicily and Macedonia were more generous and appreciative patrons of tragic poetry than the Athenian Demos.

The only complete and trustworthy portrait of this Demos is to be gathered from the Comedies of Aristophanes taken together and in mutual relation. It may be left to any fair critic whether this picture is not that of a public with all the faults and vices of other publics, but endowed with a better political education, perhaps with more natural shrewdness, and placed in circumstances unusually favourable. The great artists lived and worked apart from this crowd. Most of them despised it, all of them probably feared it. For my own part, I gravely doubt whether Greek art, which certainly developed and flourished in this stormy atmosphere, would ever have attained all its greatness had not its tender beginnings been fostered and protected by the tyrants. It was, in fact, as the direct successor of the tyrants that the Athenian Demos assumed the attitude of a great art patron, if indeed it was the Athenian Demos and not special leaders— Cimon, Pericles, and Lycurgus, who led the crowd in this nobler direction. The really vital point was the public nature of the work they demanded ; it was not done to please private and peculiar taste, it was not intended for the criticism of a small clique of partial admirers, but was set up, or performed for all the city together, for the fastidious, for the vulgar, for the learned, and for the ignorant.

It seems to me that this necessity, and the consequent broad intention of the Greek artist, is the main reason why its effect upon the world has never diminished, and why its lessons are eternal. All that was special and momentary and transitory, was avoided, and the large enduring features are portrayed with calm and majestic dignity. Let it be remembered that I am now speaking of Hellenic art in its most perfect epoch, and more particularly of Attic art before the times when the city lost its imperial character, and therefore its dignity in art as well as in politics. During this great epoch, beginning in literature with Æschylus and ending with Demosthenes; in sculpture with Calamis and ending with Praxiteles, or perhaps Lysippus; in painting with Polygnotus and ending with Apelles—during this loosely-defined period, we may notice in the earlier remains a certain calmness and reticence, almost a coldness, which may have failed to satisfy the passions of the moment, which may therefore have missed its reward from the contemporary crowd.

But it is this very coldness which has secured for it the sympathy of distant ages, of strange nations, nay, even of men and women who only knew the Greeks by vague report, and understood nothing of their culture, or of the principles of their art. It is almost pathetic to see the farthest waves of the Greek Renaissance in the hideous churches and chapels of Ireland, where up to the present generation men thought they honoured their God best by setting up melancholy travesties of the great shrines of Zeus or of Athene in a foggy and Christian country. The city of London is still full of similar mongrel absurdities, more elaborate and expensive, but not less remote from their great originals. Sculpture is perpetually reverting to the Greeks, and in our own day painting shows the same tendency.

I have elsewhere explained (*Rambles and Studies in Greece*, p. 71, sq.), in connection with the Attic tombs, how the restraint of emotion was the feature which gives to Greek sculpture its eternal freshness, and attracts the ever renewed sympathy of mankind. For these works, which are full of feeling, but of repressed feeling, not only carry with them the hearts of men in their broad representations of human emotion, but even allow every spectator of every age to realize his own particular feelings under their large and comprehensive types.

I will not repeat what I have there said, but will turn in a new chapter to a more detailed consideration of the subjective arts—music and painting—which have not received their due share of appreciation in relation to Greek social life.

CHAPTER XV.

GREEK MUSIC AND PAINTING.

THE attainments of the Greeks in architecture and in sculpture are still sufficiently preserved to enable us to form a clear judgment of their merits, and to make them models for our imitation. So also their writings, both in poetry and artistic prose, have survived in sufficient quantity to teach us both the principles and the practice of Greek artists in literature. The remnants of all these products of Greek genius are, indeed, but miserable fragments of the boundless wealth of the nation. They are defaced by time, corrupted in transmission, deformed by restoration. But still the difficulty of destroying them on the one hand, and the ease of preserving and multiplying them on the other, have prevented their total loss, and have saved for us some knowledge of the greatest outcome of human genius.

The case is very different with their music and their painting. Not a single specimen of the great compositions of the Greeks in colour and in sound has survived. We have many enthusiastic descriptions of these works; we are told a great deal about their

G g

effects on those who enjoyed them ; they are not in
any way postponed by the critics to the splendid
sculpture and architecture with which they were
combined or compared. It is only by obscure and
doubtful inferences, and by the accidental preservation of four or five tunes of inferior composers, that
we can attempt to extract from the dry discussions
on musical theory what sort of thing practical Greek
music really was. In painting, the case is a little
better. We have in the wall paintings of Pompeii,
and in recent excavations on the Esquiline and Palatine at Rome, specimens of what decorative painting
had reached by Roman imitation of Greek art. These
paintings are, no doubt, as inferior to their Greek
models as all other Roman imitations are, but still
they help us to guess what attainment the world had
reached in the technicalities of painting, even of a
higher kind, such as grouping of figures, and perspective in landscape.

There is a very large number of German books
on both these lost arts of the Greeks—books full of
learning, and deeply interesting to the special student.
But their exceeding dryness and minute detail make
them quite unfit for general readers. In England
the subject of Greek painting has been entirely
neglected, and that of Greek music has not been
really sifted till in the recent work of Mr. Chappell.
But even this very learned and able writer, who has
thrown a flood of light on the musical theory of the
Greeks, has not condescended to say much on the
moral and social aspects of his subject. I will endeavour to sketch from this side the general impres-

sion produced as to Greek music and painting by
the extant tunes and pictures, the allusions of classical
writers, and the varied discussions of theorists and
art critics. I will approach music first.

As culture was much more highly prized among
the Greeks than among us, and as they did not spend
their time in acquiring languages, it seems certain
that music was a more universal and a more important feature in their education than ours. This conclusion, however, follows even more directly and
certainly from the deep moral effects which they
attached to it. The great majority of allusions to
it assume, as acknowledged, the fact that some kinds
of music stimulate to energy and manliness, while
others dispose the mind to effeminacy and luxury.
Statesmen and philosophers have this public aspect
of music constantly before them. The Spartans
punish and prohibit a musician who makes immoral
innovations in their traditional music, by adding
strings, and thus increasing the semitones and even
lesser transitions from note to note[1]. Plato and
Aristotle are most solicitous that only certain kinds
of major and minor scales shall be allowed in their
ideal State, because the others are relaxing or over-
exciting to the mind. The evidence on this point

---

[1] Here is a mediæval parallel, for no doubt Scott had good authority
on the point. In *Ivanhoe*, when the captive Prior of Jorvaulx winds
a blast for the outlaws to show his accomplishments, Robin Hood
answers: 'Sir Prior, thou blowest a merry blast, but it may not ransom
thee. Moreover, I have found thee—thou art one of those who, with
new French graces and Tra-li-ras, disturb the ancient English bugle
notes. Prior, that last flourish on the recheat hath added fifty crowns
to thy ransom, for corrupting the true old manly blasts of venerie.'

is endless, and forms one of the strongest contrasts between Greek and modern notions about music.

The first inference I will draw from this fact is not an obvious one, but one of the greatest importance. We may conclude from it that Greek music was in an elementary state. For the analogy of other nations, and the history of other arts, tell us that the moral effects of music are everywhere strongly felt, until it becomes developed and complicated. Then the pursuit of perfection, and the overcoming of technical difficulties, become ends in themselves, and while people learn deeper and more subtle sources of delight, they forget the moral side of the art. Thus the Chinese, whose music, though good and clear, has not reached a high stage, have always held opinions about its moral effects quite similar to those of the old Greeks[1]. Indeed, more generally, according as the intellectual strain increases, the emotional effect diminishes, and so we hear of our forefathers shedding tears at the singing of simple melodies, while no music would probably touch in this way the followers of Schumann and Wagner. Greek music, had, therefore, a greater national importance, because it was far ruder and less developed than ours.

But I am not the least disposed to assert more than a difference of degree between them ; and far from believing that the Greeks exaggerated the moral side, I hold that we moderns have unduly lost sight of it. An experience of many years has convinced me that the moral characters of our musicians are

[1] Cf. Dr. Plath, in the *Transact. of the Munich Academy*, vol. x, part 2, pp. 483, 515, etc.

directly influenced by the music which they cultivate. The pursuit of any kind of our music, even the severest classical quartets, seems to me inconsistent, in a real lover of them, with other intellectual work of a high order; and the constant singing, or even hearing, of the passionate love-songs of the newer Italian operas may even be directly injurious to the character. The more beautifully and perfectly the music corresponds to the words of these productions, the more mischievous they are likely to be. Thus the most perfect of love duets, that in Gounod's *Faust*, expresses so forcibly in its perpetual suspensions the hunger and longing of passion, that the mind which feeds upon it must inevitably, though perhaps unconsciously, be stimulated in that direction. When, therefore, we hear it commonly remarked that musicians are jealous and quarrelsome, or that a young man with a good tenor voice is sure to go to ruin, there may be musical reasons for these observations which did not escape the Greeks, though they are completely ignored nowadays.

It is no answer to this curious speculation to say that the moral effect belongs only to the words employed, and was transferred by mistake to the music. For among the ancients both Plato and Plutarch are vehement on the immorality of instrumental music apart from words, which indeed they condemn altogether; and in modern times little attention is paid to the words of an Italian love-song, provided the general sense is understood, which is usually clear from the character of the music. It is not even true that our purely instrumental music is all of an intellectual type, as might, perhaps, be asserted; for nothing can be more intensely passionate than violin playing, such as we hear it, not, perhaps, from Joachim but from Wilhelmj or Auer. The same might have been said of Ernst, whose well-known *Elegy* will illustrate clearly what I intend.

The Greeks, then, were agreed about the powerful moral effects of music—bad, if practised according to certain subtle and luxurious innovations; good and humanising, if practised according to the old national traditions. It seems a plain inference that they must have assumed everybody to possess the necessary taste and ear for the purpose, and this they invariably do in their discussions. There is nowhere, so far as I know, a hint that such an one sang out of tune, or had no ear. Every young gentleman was thought as capable of music as every young lady is nowadays, nor do we hear this conventional theory ridiculed then as it now is or ought to be. Polybius [1] speaks of the culture of the Arcadians as directly resulting from their diffused musical training; he even attributes the barbarous character of a particular town to the neglect of this necessary element in education.

The public festivals of the gods had always something of a choral aspect, and the preparations for the performance of a tragedy at the feast of Dionysus entailed a great deal of expense and trouble. In such celebrations it was in early times an honour to take part, but they were quite separate from the singing and playing in private society, which were cultivated a good deal at Athens, though not at all

[1] Lib. iv. sub fin.

at Sparta, where such performances were left to professional musicians. It was, indeed, universally held
among Greeks that an independent gentleman should
not spend his life in practising, or in making a slave
of himself, for any special purpose.

Professional *virtuosi*, on the other hand, rose
gradually in importance and popularity, and in the
Macedonian days we even read of whole orchestras
and regular concerts. It appears that music, having
begun, as it ought, by portraying pure emotion,
advanced to attempt the representation of external
facts—a great blunder in art, to which our *Battles of
Prague*, *Battles of Vittoria*, and other such compositions seventy years ago, afford an obvious parallel.
We hear in the days of the Ptolemies, about 250 B.C.,
of a regular symphony performed at a Delphic feast,
in which the contest of Apollo and the Python was
represented in five movements with the aid of flutes
(or rather clarinettes, αὐλοί), harps, and fifes, without
singing or libretto. The conflict itself was represented
in the third movement, in which the clarinettes had
the chief part, and in a peculiar passage called the
gnashing (ὀδοντισμός) reproduced the noise made by
the monster's teeth when struck by the arrows. The
next movement expressed the dying struggles of the
dragon by the *hissing* (σύριγγες), in which the fifes
came out. This elaborate instrumental symphony
was merely the development of the old competitions
in playing which had existed at Delphi from very
early days.

Such being the general social importance of music,
I will now say a word about the instruments used by

the Greeks, and their methods of tuning them, and also give a specimen of the extant melodies.

Our previous conclusion that the music of the Greeks was undeveloped, as compared with ours, is strengthened by a review of the instrumental aids they had invented. We may put out of account the trumpet, which was of purely military use, and in the playing of which there were indeed competitions at Olympia, but only trials of loudness. Castanets and cymbals produce rather rhythmical noise than music. We hear of a water-organ, and may suppose a wind-organ to have anticipated it, but both seem rather Roman-Greek than early Greek inventions. The double flute, also, with its bandage about the mouth, seems to have had only a single note on one of the pipes, and to have represented our bagpipes [1].

It thus appears that as the principle of bowing on strings was unknown, and as wire-strings were equally so, Greek music was confined to twanging the gut-strings of instruments made in the fashion of either the harp or the guitar, and to blowing reeds or pipes, analogous to the principle of our fife or flute, and our clarinette or hautboy. These were at first used as accompaniments to the voice, then separately, then conjointly and together with singing. The descriptions of the instruments are not very clear, but are greatly assisted by the accurate pictures we have of the corresponding ones among the Egyptians,

---

[1] I have indeed in my possession a pair of pipes, which I bought from a boy at Messina, and which he played together, putting them in his mouth without any common mouthpiece. One is tuned a good deal lower than the other, and with it he played a pretty florid accompaniment to his air on the female (or higher) flute.

whose music appears to have been adopted by the Greeks. Indeed all the musical terms for playing are very much confused, so much so that one instrument, the μάγαδις, is sometimes spoken of as a stringed, sometimes as a wind, instrument.

What sort of music did the Greeks make with these, and their voices? This is, after all, the practical question which the reader desires to see answered. Of course, there are two branches of the inquiry— that of melody and that of harmony. As to the former, we have actually two or three tunes remaining, which are not good, in spite of the enthusiasm of the Germans about them. Only one of them is alleged to be by a celebrated master ; it is the music of one of Pindar's odes, and, unfortunately, rests upon the copy, two centuries old, of the Jesuit Kircher, who alleged that he found it in a MS., which has never since been discovered. The composition, however, bears internal marks of being genuine, though it may be inaccurately copied ; and this latter is the more likely, as the comparison of MSS. of the other hymns shows considerable variation. But these are by late composers, and may, possibly, be bad specimens of Greek tunes. Most unfortunately, no accompaniments have been preserved (except one of a few bars, without its air), so that we are left to pure conjecture as to how the Greeks assisted the voice with instruments. It is also remarkable that the chorus part of Pindar's ode is written in instrumental notes, which were quite a separate set of signs from the vocal [1].

[1] We are completely informed about both these notations, which were based on the letters of the alphabet, and were applied to scales

But it seems quite certain that vocal part music was not used by the Greeks, and that any harmony they knew was confined to instruments; but, possibly, men and boys may have sung together in octaves, with a full accompaniment—a sort of music with which I was greatly struck when I heard it in the Jewish synagogue at Pesth. Another point, urged by Westphal, indicates that ancient melody was not meant to vary with varying expression in the words, like our modern tunes. The antistrophe in the Greek tragedies was certainly sung to the same music—possibly an octave up or down—as the strophe. Nevertheless, the tone of the words is often quite different[1].

I now give, for the musical reader's benefit, the notes of the best of the extant hymns. It dates from

before the intervals were properly understood. Thus, in the vocal notation Λ and B both stand for quarter tones between our G and F. Γ is F. Then Δ and E stand for minute intervals between our F and E. Z is E. In this way twenty-four signs are used within an octave, and a second octave is noted with a distorted alphabet on the same principle. The instrumental notation had sixteen letters, used in three positions, thus, E, Ш, Ǝ, for our C, C$\frac{1}{4}$, C$\frac{1}{2}$; ⊢, ⊥, ⊣, for D, D$\frac{1}{4}$, D$\frac{1}{2}$. These signs, with certain additions above and below, of later origin, make sixty-four signs in all. Cf. the elaborate discussions on these notations in Westphal's *Musik der Griechen*, and in Fortlage's article in *Ersch and Gruber*. The omission of them in Mr. Chappell's book is to be regretted.

[1] On this I must remark that Euripides, who with the greater development of music, probably felt the defect, does not usually change the subject of his choral odes until the commencement of a new strophe. The first pair of verses (so to speak) are often philosophical and general; the second approach the special subject of the act: cf. the choruses in *Alcest.* 962 sqq.; *Medea*, 824 sqq.; *Hippol.* 723 sqq., 1100 sqq.; *Heraclid.* 829 sqq. and elsewhere. This tendency increased in after years, and antistrophic odes went out of fashion.

the Roman-Greek epoch, but has good words, and
may have been thought a good composition, though
we have no evidence on the point. In fixing the
rhythm, I have been led absolutely by the metre of
the words, which is very plain and marked, and this
version differs accordingly from that of my friend
Mr. Chappell[1], who, like Brill and other German
authorities, desires to maintain the same measure all
through the melody.

HYMN TO APOLLO AND THE MUSE.

---

[1] *History of Music*, p. 169. I have also followed Westphal's reading
of the notes, which differs occasionally from Mr. Chappell's, and which
thus affords the English reader another version, and, I think, a better
one.

There is, of course, this objection to the present reading, that in two or three places long syllables come in the short note of the bar (I have indicated them, with Westphal, by *sforzando* marks) [1]. But the violence done to the metre by Mr. Chappell's version is a far more serious difficulty.

Any modern theorist, to whom this tune was brought as an exercise in melody, would point out that the opening upward progression of a fifth almost compels us to assume D minor as the key with this bass—

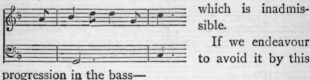 but no sooner are we well at home in this key, than we are suddenly brought up by the C natural of the seventh bar, and forced from a chord in G minor into the key of C, thus—

which is inadmissible.

If we endeavour to avoid it by this progression in the bass—

---

[1] The MSS. mark these very notes with a ∽, obviously for the same reason.

we should continue it through D to C, and this D is in discord with the tune. As almost the same phrase occurs in the next line but one, we are compelled to reconsider our first decision, and declare the tune to be meant from the beginning to move in the key of F. But, then, the opening—

is almost unbearable, and would mark the composer as inelegant, or ignorant.

The amount of modulation in the tune is also very small, and it is altogether a very thankless subject for an ingenious harmonist.

I have printed it in an easier key than Mr. Chappell, because I do not think the question of pitch determined, and we cannot tell how much the old Greek pitch differed from ours. Bellermann shows good arguments (from allusions to the ranges of voices) to prove that it was about a third higher. There can be no doubt that it was gradually raised, so that singing in the original keys became difficult, and there were some *nomes* in which transposition was not allowed. So it came that Claudius Ptolemy proposed to transpose all the scales a fourth down, and his system seems to have found favour.

The historians do not inform us concerning the history of this change of pitch, but it is very probable that it arose from the same causes which have sent our pitch up during the last century—a desire in instrumentalists to make their playing more brilliant, and in singers to show off high notes.

We are left quite in the dark as to the Greek

accompaniment, except that it usually ranged higher than the voice, and the curious reader may compare Professor Macfarren's two versions (in Mr. Chappell's book) with Westphal's (*Elemente des Musikalischen Rhythmus*, p. xviii). They are probably all equally wide of the historic truth.

But before passing on to the question of harmony, I will add what may be inferred as to melody from the extant scientific treatises. At a very early period, it had been discovered that octaves were, in some sense, the same sound, and that the progression downwards recommenced when the octave note had been reached. Hence the division of tones and semitones within the octave was analysed and determined. Three distinct ways of accomplishing this scale were in early use among the nations after whom they are called—the Dorian, the Phrygian, and the Lydian. The older seven-stringed instruments were tuned in one or other of these ways, and the earliest accompaniment being either the playing of strict unison with the voice, or in octaves with it, it follows that all songs were composed in three scales.

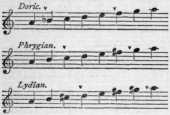

They differ merely in the position occupied by the semitone intervals, which I have noted thus ∨; but this distinctly affects the character of the scale. Thus the Lydian is what we should call major, while the remaining two are minor scales. It is possible, however, to place the two semitone intervals of a

diatonic scale in other positions than those above
specified, and thus several new scales, called hypo-
Dorian, hypo-Lydian, mixo-Lydian, etc., came gradually into use, in all of which music was composed,
and each of which was held to have as distinct a
character as the various keys which we now employ.
But the reason was different. Our major keys, for
example, of A flat and of D natural have the intervals
between the notes in the same order ; but, as the
tuning of our instruments is a system not of strict
intervals but of accommodation, these scales are not
different in pitch only, but, to an appreciable extent,
in character, owing to slight differences in the intervals
of the notes.   Theoretically, we allow only two scales,
the major and minor, though the minor down scale
varies from the up scale.   The Greeks had seven,
each of which varied in the actual progression of the
tones, which were separated by accurately determined
intervals.   Modulation during the course of a melody
was only occasional, and within strictly defined limits.
Accordingly the distinct effect produced upon Greek
ears by each of these scales seems to have been even
stronger and more marked than that of the different
keys upon modern ears, most of which cannot distinguish in what key the music is, and can only tell
major and minor distinctly.

But when instruments of two octave range came
into use, it was found that, by adhering to one fixed
tuning—that of the white notes on our pianofortes—
all the scales could be made by varying the note on
which each commenced. For example, from C to C
we have the Lydian or plain major scale ; from E to

E we have the Dorian; from A to A the hypo-Dorian. This fact has led to the serious mistake of saying that the Greek scales were mere differences of pitch—a statement very likely to mislead the modern reader. It was only owing to a fixed system of tuning that the various scales became attached to fixed keynotes; and, even then, the scales differed not only in pitch, which was unessential, but in the arrangement or progression of the notes, which was the essential feature [1].

The Greeks were not confined to these diatonic scales; they knew chromatic, and even enharmonic scales, in which they used intervals of quarter tones which are unknown in our notation, though often played on strings, and sung by voices, in *legato* transitions from one note to another. These subtleties were, however, much studied by the Greeks, whose melodies evidently attained an extraordinary elabora-

---

[1] Sir Robert Stewart has pointed out to me a very interesting parallel in the Irish harp music of the last century. These harps, which included about four octaves, were always tuned to the scale of G, with no sharp except the necessary F sharp. Nevertheless, with this fixed scale, the harpers composed and played tunes in four distinct keys—in that of G (such as the *Coolin*) of course, in that of E minor (*Remember the Glories of Brian*), of D major, and of A minor. Specimens may be found in Bunting's work, but later versions must not be consulted, as singers often modified the tunes by introducing additional sharps suggested by the ear. On the old harps this variety of key was attained by dwelling on the keynote—perpetually returning to it, as Aristotle says the Greeks did, and also by avoiding the phrases which required the additional sharps. The familiar flat seventh in Irish music arose naturally from playing tunes in D major on instruments tuned in G. Thus an ignorant harper might tell us that these old harp tunes only differed in pitch, which distorts the facts of the case, for the pitch is only changed in order to obtain a different key and character.

tion, and would be often quite unintelligible to modern ears[1]. It is remarkable that these very small intervals, which can only have been used for passing notes, were, nevertheless, played on stringed instruments, without bowing, and therefore without sliding from one to the other. Yet the effect of rapid execution was such as to bring down storms of applause from great audiences, when this sort of playing was well done, without any accompaniment.

The joyous or sombre character of a scale appeared in them in no way associated with the character which we call major or minor. Thus, their only purely major scale, the Lydian, is always regarded as soft, plaintive, and effeminate ; though the hypo-Dorian, which nearly approaches a major scale, was thought manly and vigorous. On the contrary, the Dorian, which is distinctly minor, was considered martial and inspiring ; whereas the Phrygian, also minor, was orgiastic and passionate. Bellermann has observed, that in the extant fragments the Lydian greatly predominates, and it seems very natural that it should be so ; but this was evidently owing to practical musicians being guided by ear, and not from a scientific appreciation of major scales.

On the whole, it is likely that even were several good Greek melodies accurately handed down to us,

[1] Fortlage thinks that Greek melody was somewhat analogous to modern harmony. We are not now improving in melody, or making any advances in it, but have of late times been altogether bent on perfecting harmony. The Greeks, in contrast, never thought of making new discoveries in harmony, but were always devising novelties to improve their melodies. This difference of attitude shows the difficulty of appreciating what the Greeks have written on the subject.

we are not in a position to understand or appreciate them, for several reasons : first, because of the different tuning of their instruments, to which I will presently revert. This difference is not merely important in itself, but educated the ear of the nation, and so made them enjoy and dislike with a different taste from ours. I will not assert that the laws of harmony are conventional—the physiological reasons of consonance and dissonance are scientifically established, and must always have guided the human ear ; but still, within large limits, melody is a matter of taste, as Wagner and Brahms have proved clearly enough, and by training even one generation, men can come to admire tunes which they once thought hideous. How much more may this be the case with the national training of centuries ! While, therefore, I confidently assert that such a phrase as this (from the opening of the Hymn to the Muse)

is very disagreeable, I will not take upon myself to say that Greek melody was positively bad : I will only say that it differed so widely from the music of modern Europe, that its beauties are completely lost upon us.

This argument is greatly strengthened by another reason—the wide differences between the Greek notions and ours, concerning harmony. This is, to my thinking, the most difficult problem of all those with which Greek music abounds for us. For it seems as if one essential element in modern harmony, an element without which it cannot exist—the use of thirds

—was absent from concerted music. The ancients tell us a great deal of consonances and dissonances, and are unanimous that octaves, fourths, and fifths are harmonious; but they seem equally agreed that thirds, both major and minor, are discordant, and may not be used. Mr. Chappell has even explained scientifically how this resulted from their tuning, which found the next full tone to any note by going down to the fourth below, and then going up a full fifth. This process, when twice repeated, gives the *ditone* of the Greeks—a greater third, so sharp as to be unbearable. Accordingly, there is no trace of any statement that Greek harmony consisted of three simultaneous notes, nor are there any rules given for it by any of the theorists. Hence, many authors have been led to assert that there was no harmony in Greek music save that of octaves, with fourths and fifths, which, when used consecutively, are very offensive to every good ear. If Greek music was of this kind, it could only be fitly compared to the present music of another very civilised race—the Japanese, who seem to have no concords but these[1]. This may have been the condition of Greek harmony in early days.

Fortunately, however, we are in possession of some hints which make us pause before we dismiss the question. It is known that practical musicians (ἀρ-μονικοί) did not bind themselves by scientific canons —that they followed their ear in preference, and made many modifications not admitted by the theorists (κανονικοί). Thus, they flattened some strings in the tuning; they objected to consecutive fifths; they

[1] Cf. the passage in Mr. Chappell's *History of Music*, i. p. 304.

even spoke of thirds as παράφωνα, or something between concords and discords — nay, they mention
passing discords as permitted in harmony. Plato,
too, in a celebrated passage, speaks of the accompaniment as an elaborate thing, and independent of the
air, running counter in motion, and using various intervals, even as we accompany our modern songs, in
contrast with the old humdrum accompaniments of
former generations.

These, and other stray hints which Mr. Chappell
and Westphal have gathered with great care, and
quite independently, have persuaded them that the
Greeks and Romans did know and use harmony in
our sense. Every Hellenist will be anxious to agree
with them, and to vindicate for the Greeks a high
position in this art also. I may add to their arguments that the enharmonic and chromatic tetrachords
of Didymus and Ptolemy are based upon the intervals
$4:5$, and $5:6$, which are the greater and lesser third,
and thus show an attempt to recognise these as
natural intervals in music. It is likewise known [1]
that in the Middle Ages thirds, though used, were
not admitted to be a perfect consonance, and that it
required the genius of Descartes to break through
this prejudice also, and first declare the truth in his
' Treatise on Music.'

On the other hand, it must be confessed that all
the authorities whom Mr. Chappell has quoted are
comparatively modern — the pseudo-Aristotle, Gau-
dentius, and the Latins—and that the clearest evi-

[1] Cf., on both points, Fortlage in *Ersch and Gruber's Encyclop.*, art.
Greece, vol. ii. pp. 198, 207.

dences are certainly those derived from Cicero and Seneca. In fact, all the earlier hints, including the very old Egyptian pictures, are reconcilable with a concord of two notes only. The silence of our authorities as to any rules on the subject is equally striking and inexplicable ; nor do I think the extant tunes are in any respect like the tunes we might expect from a nation trained in real harmony. The setting of them in their proper scales, even with modern resources, is awkward and clumsy, as may be seen from the version of such a harmonist as Sir George Macfarren.

I feel therefore obliged to conclude, upon the evidence before us, that in the great days of Terpander, Alcæus, Sappho, and Pindar, there was little that we could call harmony, and that music was practically in a rude state. It appears that in course of time actual performers may have accommodated their instruments to real harmony, and composed real accompaniments ; but the theory of music, which had been so advanced in Pythagoras' day, did not keep pace with these practical improvements, and fell into great arrear, compared with the art. While players and singers were delighting vast audiences, and inventing various combinations of scales and of instruments, the theorists wasted their time on useless subtleties, and did not even amend their instrumental notation, which was framed before the distinction of a full tone and a semitone was properly understood.

We may, therefore, console ourselves for the loss of the elaborate music with which Pindar, Æschylus, Sophocles, and all the other poets, accompanied their splendid odes. I do not believe that it would improve these poems in our ears. It would, no doubt, explain to us many difficulties about rhythms and metres—it would, above all, bring us one step nearer to a full understanding of Greek life ; but it would probably not add to our æsthetic pleasure, though it might give us some new elements to work into the music of the future.

With these remarks I leave a subject of which the details are drier and more uninteresting than those of any other phase of Greek art.

When we turn to the history of painting, we find many analogies to music. It arose among the Greeks as the handmaid to architecture—so music was to poetry—and found the same difficulty in freeing itself, and rising to the condition of an independent art. Painting among the Greeks has accordingly the history of an auxiliary art, beginning obscurely, developing late, and rising to dignity and splendour when the greater arts have decayed. The first application of colours, in the painting of stone temples, of wooden statues, of clay vases, was not entrusted to any special artist ; nor, indeed, do we often hear of great statues being handed over to the painter, so that the colouring must have been thoroughly conventional, and easily applied. This strikes us as evident in the archaic vases, which show but few colours, and apply them without regard to nature. It is true that vase-painting was afterwards looked on with contempt by greater artists ; but there can be little doubt that these humbler productions, which ultimately sank into the position of mere tradesman's work, were originally of equal standing and merit with other painting. They have, in fact, preserved to us the archaic features of the nascent art, and from this point of view are of great historical interest. There is one class of them, the Attic λήκυθοι or oil-flasks, which have many-coloured figures on a white ground, and which are thought by most competent archæologists to be of peculiar value for the solution of this question.

If we compare these indications of archaic painting with older sculpture, we find that the Greeks did not by any means obtain from the use of colour a nearer approach to realism. The eyes of profile faces are always painted full, and in early vases are even conventionally varied, to mark the distinction of sex; those of women being of oblong form, white with red pupils, those of men scratched on the vase—a circle, with two strokes attached to it. The flesh of women is painted white, that of men is black or red. But, on the other hand, the early painters used their advantage in portraying violent action, which sculpture could not dare to attempt before the genius of Myron realised the impossible. Thus the old vases often show us rushing figures, and drapery tossed with the wind—features which the poetic instinct of Keats seized as of peculiar interest—

> What men and gods are these? What maidens loath?
> What mad pursuit? What struggle to escape?
> What pipes and timbrels? What wild ecstasy?[1]

---

[1] From the *Ode on a Grecian Urn*. The fact of this urn being of marble does not in the least affect the statement that the old vases had a character which struck Keats when he saw a specimen—though it may have been in marble, and of very different execution from the painting on pottery.

But of realism in the sense of anatomical drawing, of perspective—in short, of anything like illusion—old Greek painting was quite ignorant. And, of course, in the absence of perspective, any attempt at landscape was not to be expected, nor did any artist desire to essay it, till new and peculiar circumstances, as we shall presently see, forced it into notice.

Thus Polygnotus, the first painter of really national importance, and all his immediate school, were altogether figure painters, and used the least possible accessories of landscape, if an occasional rock or house can be called such. This great man, a native of Thasos, but settled at Athens, and even promoted to its citizenship, might be called the Phidias of Cimon, on account of his intimate relations with that statesman. His frescoes on the Acropolis were, unfortunately, so decayed that when Pausanias saw them he was only able to describe a few figures—a thing much to be regretted, as he has left us a very full and interesting account of a wall painting by the same artist, in the λέσχη, or assembly-room of the Delphians, built as a votive offering by the Cnidians.

The two main walls were covered with two great subjects—the Fall of Troy, and the Visit of Ulysses to the regions of the Dead. These were each painted in two long panels, one over the other, and I fancy, from the way in which Pausanias passes from the lower to the upper panel, and then back again, that they must have been broken by vertical lines in the decoration of the wall. The figures seem not so much grouped as put into a sort of irregular series,

with their names—as on the vases—written over
them.

Polygnotus and his immediate successors only used
or combined four colours—blue-black, yellow, red,
and white. He knew nothing of light and shade, or
of foreshortening. Nevertheless Pausanias speaks of
various striking effects in his paintings. There were
leopard and bear skins represented in them—there
was a strand with pebbles, and the sea. There was
the river Acheron, with reeds, and sedge, and fishes
in the water, which looked shadows; there was the
vampire Eurynomus, painted the colour of a blue-
bottle fly, apparently because he devoured human
flesh ; above all, there were various mental states—
grief, indifference, anger—conveyed by these frescoes.
But let us always remember that a violent 'pre-
Raphaelite,' like Pausanias, will discover pathos and
expression in such old work where there is really
none. It is said that Polygnotus was the first to
depart from the conventional way of painting the
human face; yet in his long description, Pausanias
does not say one word about the beauty or sentiment of the faces, merely noting that some have
beards, while the majority have none. It seems that
all the expression was to be inferred from the atti-
tudes.

The glory of Polygnotus and the honour in which
he was held show that the public were thoroughly
satisfied with his art; and had Cimon, who was his
patron, held sway at Athens, instead of Pericles, it
is more than probable that painting, instead of the
sculpture of Phidias and his pupils, would have been

the chief ornament of the Parthenon. But, among other contrasts with Cimon, Pericles was far-seeing enough to know that Greek sculpture was ever to be the greatest of arts, and the frieze of the cella proclaims its victory over the picture-gallery of the Propylæa, which, even in Pausanias' day, was fading out beyond recognition.

The next step in Greek painting was made, not by a great artist, but apparently by a practical man, working hurriedly, and seeking to meet a growing want—that of adequate stage-scenery for the now popular tragedy. This remarkable man, Agatharchus, employed by Sophocles, and by Æschylus in his later days, first attacked the question of perspective, which he perceived to depend upon the painting of light and shade. He wrote a tract on the subject, which stimulated the philosophers Anaxagoras and Demo- critus to study the matter further, and so led the way to the adoption of his principles by Apollodorus (400 B.C.), who is called the first *shade painter* by the Greeks. But it is very significant that the term *scene painter* was used as synonymous. Pliny's remark, that Apollodorus' paintings are the earliest worth looking at, is probably based on a sound appreciation of the requirements of the art, and confirms our suspicion that Polygnotus was (ethically, perhaps, but) not æsthetically to be admired. From the days of Apollodorus, however, *figure painting* also made rapid progress. Wall decoration became subordinate to the painting of pictures proper; and a long series of great artists, such as Zeuxis, Parrhasius, Pamphilus, Timan- thes, and many others, led up to Apelles, the contemporary of Alexander, who brought this species of painting to an unapproachable perfection.

With the splendid works of the sculptors to rival them, these figure painters had no easy task in maintaining their position; and the fact that the public, accustomed to the bronze and marble of Phidias, Polycletus, Euphranor, and Lysippus, not only tolerated, but delighted in their pictures, shows that they must have had real merit. This is further proved by the technical details preserved to us. They studied light and shade, and perspective, increased the number of their colours, and used varnish to soften and preserve their colouring. The figure subjects still extant at Pompeii are in accordance with these evidences. Though they are only the wall decorations of a second-rate mongrel Greek town, there are both grace and power in many of the figures. The colouring is bright and lifelike, and the faces full of expression. It is, in fact, a thoroughly realistic development of art, and bears comparison with the beautiful bronzes of the place, though none of the pictures equals the *Narcissus* or the *fishing Hermes*.

It thus appears that this side of painting attained a splendour and an independence far superior to that of music. It freed itself from all relation to architecture; and great masters, such as Zeuxis and Apelles, enjoyed a social position never accorded to musicians who were mere performers, as distinguished from poets who composed airs for their own odes. But any one who chooses to follow up subtle analogies might well occupy himself with the advance from four colours, without light and shade, to all the appliances of

Apelles on the one hand; and the similar advance from a three-stringed lyre, or Pandean pipes, to the varied scales and subdivisions of tone in the days of Aristoxenus. If, however, my estimate of the comparatively backward condition of Greek music be just, it will be easy to find in Greek painting a much closer parallel, as regards social position and general importance—I mean the parallel of *landscape painting*.

I have already explained how figure painting made a new start, as soon as Agatharchus was led by scene painting to study the optical illusions produced by drawing and colour. But surely, we should have thought that these ideas would have been infinitely more useful in the development of landscape painting. It is true that the scenic requirements of the extant plays are not very great. In most cases an architectural background—some royal palace, or temple—is the main feature, and changes of the whole scene were not practicable, as a fixed wooden (and canvas?) structure, of great height, so as to shut out the natural background, occupied the whole rear of the shallow stage. Two triangular prisms (περιακταί), with varied sides, supplied the part of our shifting side-scenes, and were turned on pivots when any modification was required. Still this kind of landscape should have been accurately studied, not merely in reproducing well-known scenes, such as the groves of Colonus, the Acropolis, or the outlines of Mount Parnes—which would be ridiculous if very unlike the originals—but fancy pictures also, foreign palaces, and cities of strange men. And even beyond this there are, though rarely, really picturesque scenes presupposed—tented camps on the sea-shore, lonely and desert islands, rocky homes of ancient worship. All these subjects should have been suggested, and their imitation developed, by the scene-painting for the great Athenian theatre ; and yet nothing is more certain than that landscape painting, as such, did not arise for generations to come. Among all the roll of great painters down to Apelles, there is not one celebrated for depicting scenery, nor is there aught beyond the slightest allusion to the scenery of their figure painting. In fact, the Greeks felt no want of landscape painting, and did not perceive this dark spot in the field of their artistic vision.

This apparent defect in Greek taste has much exercised the critics. It is called a want of feeling for the picturesque ; and some have even inferred that the pleasure in beautiful scenery is of modern growth —a late compensation for the unceasing toil and weariness of mankind. But the general sensitiveness of the Greeks, together with the innumerable proofs in their poetry that they appreciated the *sounds* of nature as we do, show that the matter cannot be so easily settled. It was not from want of perceiving the beauty of external nature, but from a different way of perceiving it, that the Greeks did not turn their genius to portray, either in colour or in poetry, the outlines, the hues, and contrasts of all the fair valleys, and bold cliffs, and golden noons, and rosy dawns, which their beautiful country affords in lavish abundance.

Primitive people never, so far as I know, enjoy what is called the picturesque in nature. Wild forests, beetling cliffs, reaches of alpine snow, are with them great hindrances to human intercourse, and difficulties in the way of agriculture. They are furthermore the homes of the enemies of mankind, of the eagle, the wolf, or the bear, and are most dangerous, in times of earthquake or tempest. Hence the grand and striking features of nature are at first looked upon with fear and dislike, so that even nowadays, simple peasants, who regard the earth merely as a source of subsistence, feel much wonder at the admiring tourist, and are only taught to understand his taste for the picturesque by the direct benefit it confers upon their pockets.

I do not suppose the early Greeks differed in this respect from other people, except that the frequent occurrence of mountains and forests made agriculture peculiarly difficult, and intercourse scanty, thus increasing their dislike for the apparently reckless waste in nature. We have even in Homer a similar feeling as regards the sea—the sea that proved the source of all their wealth, and the condition of most of their greatness. Before they had learned all this, they called it 'the unvintageable brine,' and looked upon its shore as merely so much waste land. We can, therefore, easily understand how, in the first beginnings of Greek art, the representation of wild landscape would find no place, whereas fruitful fields did not suggest themselves as more than the ordinary background. Art in those days was struggling with material nature, to which it felt a certain antagonism.

There was nothing in the social circumstances of the Greeks to produce any revolution in this attitude during their greatest days. The Greek republics were small towns, where the pressure and fatigue of city life was not felt. The Greeks themselves were essentially townsmen, who never desired to see more of the country than its olives and its grapes, and would not accept even the large plenty of a farming life, with its want of refinement and of discussion.

But as soon as the days of the Greek republics were over, and men began to congregate for imperial purposes into Antioch, or Alexandria, or, lastly, into Rome, then we see the effect of noise, and dust, and smoke, and turmoil, breaking out into the natural longing for rural rest and retirement, so that after Alexander's day, and beginning with the Alexandrian Theocritus, we find not only bucolic poetry starting into new favour, but all kinds of authors—epic poets, lyrists, novelists, and preachers, agreeing in the praise of nature, its rich colours, and its varied sounds. Hence it was that landscape painting, as such, did not become an independent art till this period, and even then suffered from the lateness of its origin, and the decay of Greece in genius; for with rare exceptions, architectural subjects and figures predominate, in spite of this desire to escape from them. We are justified in making this assertion from the many specimens preserved on the walls of Pompeii, from the more important pictures exhumed on the Palatine and Esquiline at Rome, and from detailed notices, such as the εἰκόνες of Philostratus, and the criticisms of the elder Pliny.

Thus lasting natural causes seem to have counteracted the impulse given to landscape painting by the scene painting of Agatharchus, whose discoveries concerning perspective, as well as his portraiture of familiar views, ought to have stimulated a school of imitators. We should have expected the many-sided Athenians to have taken up this branch ; and, as they had a school of *rhopographers*, or painters of homely life (like the Dutch), they should have had a school of pure landscape painters. The fact that they had not is certain, and perhaps the natural causes I have assigned may seem hardly sufficient to account for it.

Indeed, the knowledge of perspective attained by Democritus and Anaxagoras was either in itself defective, or little propagated, for the architectural landscapes of Pompeii, in spite of considerable merits in other respects, display most absurd ignorance in their perspective. But this is not the real want in ancient landscape painting. It is rather the absence of a deep feeling for nature as such, for its curious symmetry amid countless variety—for its natural contrasts of texture and colour—for its matchless response—now to the vehemence and trouble, now to the peacefulness and repose, of the human breast. How is it possible that the sensitive, poetical Greeks should have missed this infallible comfort, and lived without this most unfailing and perpetual delight ? It is an answer, but a very partial one, to say that beauty of landscape is so constant in Greece that it might fairly be taken for granted, without special allusion. The nations of southern Europe, who live in the fairest clime and the clearest atmosphere, have always left landscape painting to northern artists, where fog, and mist, and dulness of outline give a strange zest to exceptional beauty. How few of the Italian painters have thought of landscape! How few Italians and

Spaniards travel to see it! Hence it may fairly be said that we should not expect to find Attic, Ionic, and Theban poets insisting upon things which everybody saw and felt every day. But yet how keen is their enjoyment of the *sounds* of nature! How they loved the swallow and the nightingale, the humming bee and the shrill cicada, the whispering leaves and the murmuring water! The rose, too, and the violet, the white narcissus and the deep clustering ivy were to them no less fair in colour, or delicious in odour, than they are to modern men. Among all the pathetic passages in the tragic poets, there are none so affecting as those in which a dying hero or heroine addresses the fair light of the sun, the woods and fields, the cliffs and mountains. These appeals are, moreover, common to them all, and not merely one of the special features in Euripides. Surely such men could not but feel the beauty of large grouping of mountain, and wood, and water.

They did indeed feel it, but as Greeks, and not as moderns. They did not oppose themselves to nature, and study their own consciousness as contrasted with the spontaneous or instinctive life of nature. To them mountains, and rivers, and forests were full of conscious being—the home, nay, the impersonation of gods, who thought and felt like men. For their religion, a sort of anthropomorphic pantheism, taught them that all the life of trees and rivers was not unconscious, but the manifestation of a hidden god; and that solitude, as we call it, was peopled with oreads, hamadryads, fauns, and satyrs. They believed that in the wild mountains forest gods held their court, and

demanded awe and worship from those who entered
the bounds of their domain.   Thus the old Greek who
spoke of a river or a mountain named the god whose
dwelling-place it was, and remembered the myths and
legends of the poets, which, perhaps, made this god
his ancestor, or at least identified him with the history
and fortunes of the country.

The enjoyment of mere landscape was thus excluded and anticipated by a deeper sympathy—that
humanising instinct which saw conscious life, and life
of a human type, through all the kingdom of nature.
And so it came that to the Greek the most adequate
representation of a landscape was a representation of
the gods who were identified with its rivers and mountains.   *The sculptor accordingly took the place, and
performed the work, of the landscape painter.*

In earlier days, the mere human figure was thought
sufficient likeness for a god, and no special care was
taken to suit his outward form to the peculiar nature
of his attributes, or his special kingdom.   Thus, in
the famous pediments of the Parthenon, so many
personified features of Attica were introduced, that a
great art critic—Brunn—has even declared these
groups to have been simply plastic landscapes, intended to symbolise all the natural beauties of Attica.
The Ilissus, the Cephissus, Mount Parnes, Mount
Pentelicus, the fountain Callirrhoe—all these were
figured as divine men and women in the coloured
marble.

But the fragments which remain do not show any
desire to express by peculiar features each peculiar
character.   The glory of solving this subtle problem

was left for those successors of Phidias who, as they could not equal him in grave majesty, sought to excel him in expression. In the scanty fragments and weak copies of their work, we can still feel distinctly the peculiar genius of two of them in imitating, or rather *suggesting, landscape by sculpture.* To Scopas was due the fixing of the general type for the great company of gods and nymphs which inhabited seas and rivers—matted locks of dripping hair, and a longing melancholy of expression, in which the restless moaning of the troubled sea finds its plastic utterance. To Praxiteles was due the analogous type for the forest gods—the fauns and satyrs, which, with their gnarled and knotty joints, and roughness of skin, image even more clearly the sylvan forms which the superstitious traveller saw with terror in the fantastic stems of aged trees. Nay, even in his ideal *Faun*—a creature of perfect beauty—the listening attitude, the Pandean pipe, the indefinable suggestion of wantonness, and of mystery, speak a deeper feeling for the beauty of forest life than could be conveyed by any ordinary landscape painting.

So true is it, that the sculptors were the landscape artists of the Greeks. Accordingly, in later days, when men had advanced to the notion of painting mountains and rivers, as they appeared in nature, the artist hardly ever omits to paint a figure of the god sitting on his mountain, or by his river, thus showing that the actual coloured sketch of the place did not satisfy the spectator without the figure of the being who gave it life, and instinct, and poetry—nay, who alone gave it a distinctive name.

The history of Greek painting is, therefore, in every direction controlled and limited by that of sculpture, which rivalled and outdid it in the idealising of figures, and which actually invaded its peculiar province in the representation of landscape.

A comparative review of the arts in Greece shows that the most independent and self-contained—Architecture and Poetry—began with the dawn of history, and reached their climax with the political climax of the nation. After the year 400 B.C. there was little more than imitation or repetition attempted in either, till actual debasement set in. Sculpture started later, reached its acme at the same time, but sustained itself with a noble and continuous development, till far into the decay of the nation, as the *Laocoon,* the *Apollo Belvedere,* and the *Dying Gaul,* testify. Music and painting may have begun with sculpture, but were far longer in reaching perfection, so that the highest outcome of both is to be sought in the days when the other arts had passed their prime. They are, in fact, the arts of private life, as contrasted with the political arts of antiquity, and did not take the lead till the society of Menander had said farewell to public affairs, and turned to individual culture as the chief end of life.

It may be well, after these chapters of detail, to close with a few general reflections upon the aspects of Greek social life. So great a subject can never be treated adequately or finally; all that this book can pretend to do, is to support clear and sober views upon a subject much obscured by vagueness and pedantry, and generally handled by men in little contact with real life.

We can quite imagine that had the mere master-pieces of Italian art and literature survived to us from the middle ages, had we lost the endless chronicles, and acts, and letters, which admit us to the secrets of the age, and disclose in all their nakedness the burning passions and the dark vices of artists, and kings, and bishops, we might have formed a very different and a very false idea of the brilliant Italian republics, which supply the only real analogy to the Greek states of classical days. We can imagine the admirers of their noble pictures and churches, of their splendid costumes and pageants, of their great patriotism and valour, of their refined chivalry, to have scouted any stray suspicions as to their darker features. The Madonnas and other saints would be taken as the ordinary type of their women, the apostles and martyrs of their men, and they would be reported a people of such universal beauty, that ugliness was quite an exception. The diffusion of their art through so many cities would prove that they were all trained in the fine arts, and skilful judges of artistic excellence. Their piety would be a national feature, their poetic and chivalrous love would be national also—in fact we might have a picture very like the ordinary notions about the Greeks, with the addition of some splendid features resulting from a higher and purer faith. And these would probably compensate for the undeniable inferiority of their art to that of the Greeks.

Yet all this picture would be, as we know, historically false. The Italian republics were torn with wild and savage passions ; their citizens were violent and lawless, grossly immoral in their lives, and reckless in their actions. Their despots were cruel and inhuman beyond all decent description, and the Christian faith which they professed had no more influence on their lives than the moral lessons of the old philosophers and poets upon the Greeks—nay rather, the possibility of deathbed absolution may have acted as a release from all moral obligation during active life.

Nevertheless, these peoples' art *was* splendid ; their æsthetic sense was not dimmed by their crimes, and even the most abandoned of them have about them something truly and justly fascinating. And again their pure and saintly men stand out in strange and splendid relief. We thus come to see how great intellectual and artistic excellence is compatible with great moral faults, with vice, and with meanness. We come to see that ideal conception and perfect execution imply lofty genius and patient diligence, but do not imply in the appreciative spectator either of these qualities, and in the artist no moral counterparts. But we may also learn how the artist, or the school and succession of artists, may always be the few, the exceptional, and the isolated among the crowd, and how their great works may vaguely educate the judgment of the masses, without affecting their principles.

I am not sure whether our extant evidence is sufficient to lead us to a similar decision concerning the social aspects of Greek art. So far as we can see, the private life of the Greeks was better than that of the mediæval Italians—at least better on the average, for if there were fewer miscreants, there were also fewer saints. But these yawning gulfs in the morals of any society are always injurious, and so probably the Greeks benefited by the absence of both extremes. The art of the Greeks was also far purer and more lasting than that of the Renaissance, so that the comparison may still hold good. It is therefore not impossible that the somewhat homely features which I have found in the old Greek were combined with intellectual and artistic powers quite apart from them, and as it were a separate life in the nation. The Greeks may have been somewhat mean, overreaching, untruthful, and not very courageous, and yet have been highly gifted, and keenly alive to the noble and the true in art and literature. It is the ignorance that such combination is possible in human nature, both singly and collectively, which has made some zealous Grecians in England very adverse to such a theory. But mankind is a more complex thing than they imagine, and will not simplify itself for the convenience of even the most accomplished scholar.

Yet on the whole, I am more inclined to adopt the other suggestion already made, and hold that the great Greek writers and artists stood as far intellectually from the masses as such men now do, and owed their stronger influence to their greater relative number, and to the greater publicity of every-day life. Why they were so frequent is the point which cannot be explained. But why they more easily reached the public is evident from the habits of southern climates, and from the smallness of the Greek states.

It has been long ago shown by historians that a quantity of neighbouring contesting states of small dimensions are infinitely more stimulating to human culture than the great centralised empires of modern Europe. Now everybody and everything goes asleep in the provinces; then there were no provinces for men to sleep in. Capitals abounded, centres of art and of politics abounded, and life attained an intensity in all directions, which we moderns in vain attempt to realise. The Italian republics satisfied this condition. The smaller German states might have done so, with the increase of democracy in Europe, had they not been swallowed up by the retrograde despotism of Prussia. And even their local tyrants, like the Greek tyrants, did a great deal for art and literature; for local tyrants, with their rivalries and competitions, are never so benumbing to culture as the great central despots, who are absorbed in military projects, and kill every higher ambition for the sake of conquest.

Thus it must be confessed, that if these political conditions produced Greek culture, or enabled it to be produced, modern Europe is travelling in the opposite direction, and yearly attaining a condition less and less favourable for a diffused intensity of life. Railways and steamers have so immensely aided centralization in great capitals, that it is now hopeless to attempt the opposite policy, nor does it survive except among the Home Rulers in Ireland, or among those wretched nationalities in the East of Europe, concerning whose state we may remark (with Tacitus) that it is harder to say what ought to be done than to say that what is being done is the worst possible. Perhaps modern civilization has in it other elements which may counteract this injury, and it may yet be the privilege of great states, like North America, to combine intensity of life with a vast unity of empire. But it is plain that such a development must be widely different from that of the Greeks. Their culture stands before us as a great complex growth, of which the very conditions have passed away, and which can never be reproduced in its old perfection.

INDEX.

A.

Printed in Great Britain by R. & R. CLARK, LIMITED, *Edinburgh.*